Sin, Sex & Subversion

Also by David Rosen
Sex Scandal America: Politics & the Ritual of Public Shaming
Off-Hollywood: The Making & Marketing of Independent Films

Sin, Sex & Subversion

How What Was Taboo in 1950s New York
Became America's New Normal

DAVID ROSEN

CARREL BOOKS

Carrel Books books may be purchased in bulk at special discounts for sales promotion, corporate gifts, fund-raising, or educational purposes. Special editions can also be created to specifications. For details, contact the Special Sales Department, Carrel Books, 307 West 36th Street, 11th Floor, New York, NY 10018 or info@skyhorsepublishing.com.

Carrel® and Carrel Books® is a registered trademark of Skyhorse Publishing, Inc.®, a Delaware corporation.

Visit our website at www.skyhorsepublishing.com.

10 9 8 7 6 5 4 3 2 1

Library of Congress Cataloging-in-Publication Data is available on file.

Cover design by Rain Saukas

ISBN: 978-1-63144-044-1
Ebook ISBN: 978-1-63144-045-8

Printed in the United States of America

He who transgresses not only breaks a rule.
He goes somewhere that the others are not;
and he knows something the others don't know.
—Susan Sontag

For Dara, Jessie, Madeline & Irma—
and in memory of Bill—a love supreme.

CONTENTS

PREFACE

We live in the shadow of the 1950s, of the turbulent post-World War II era of 1945–1960. It saw America remade; marked by reconversion, the United States underwent a transition from a national war economy to an international consumer society. It was the period of Elvis and the Cold War; of white flight to suburban prosperity and growing inner-city decline; of the mass adoption of television and commie witch hunts, including the execution of two New Yorkers. It saw old-fashioned moralists contesting nonconformists, *outsiders*, over sin, sex, and subversion. The '50s was a tumultuous era.

Sin, Sex & Subversion: How What Was Taboo in 1950s New York Became America's New Normal is an unorthodox historical tale. The book has two theses: first, that during the '50s, sin and sex were as threatening to the moral order as Communism; and second, that Gotham was the epicenter of two "wars"—a "cold war" waged against subversion and a "hot war" against sin and sex. These struggles, *wars*, were two sides of the same historical experience.

In this book, sin, sex, and subversion are broadly conceived categories, suggesting more moral concerns than religious, academic, or legal definitions. Broadly speaking, sin is considered as an illicit or unacceptable belief or value; sex is conceived as the erotic sensibility, one's physical pleasures, outside conventional heterosexuality and marriage; and subversion is understood as critical social engagement, one's politics, whether expressed in word or deed, that questions established authority. Today, much of what used to be considered sin (e.g., homosexuality or pornography) has been normalized, integrated into the market economy. In terms of sex, anything goes whether noncommercial (e.g., fetishists) or commercial (i.e., prostitution) as long as it's "consensual" and among age-appropriate participants. In terms of subversion, 9/11 redefined loyalty to include support for any actual or possible "national security threat."

This book consists of three "threads"—sin, sex, and subversion—and each includes a series of separate "strands," in-depth analyses of major Cold War–era confrontations involving moral, personal, and political concerns. Each chapter is anchored in the experience of a '50s "outsider," someone who challenged a social convention and made an important contribution to America's changing moral order.

What we take for granted today, especially in terms of sin, sex, and subversion, are issues that were bitterly fought over a half century or so ago. And most of the people who fought the battles over the nation's moral order, who sought to push the boundaries of the acceptable, were defeated. Some were arrested and imprisoned, many were fired and blacklisted, others denounced and shamed, and two were executed. With few exceptions, the outsiders profiled in this book did not personally know one another.

While most '50s outsiders lost their respective battles, they were ultimately victorious. America's moral order changed! Pornographers were shut down; comic book publishes censored, their books burned; prostitutes busted; homosexuals shamed and fired; entertainers blacklisted; birth control materials seized; suspect teachers fired; commies jailed . . . and two put to death. But remarkably, the conservative campaign to contain the nation's changing moral order failed. Postwar prosperity demanded a new value system, one fostering the pleasures of consumerism, "legitimate" free expression, dissent, and the Pill. Important Supreme Court decisions defined the shift in values, legitimizing the social revolutions that accompanied those decisions. Today, the once forbidden has become the new normal.

Outsiders of the 1950s prefigured and fashioned the emerging twenty-first-century moral order. Among the issues and individuals considered are:

- Gender—Christine Jorgensen;
- Comic books—Bill Gaines;
- Obscene images—Irving Klaw;
- Prurient words—Samuel Roth;
- Live performances—Club 82 female impersonators;
- Prostitution—Polly Adler;
- Homosexuality—Liberace;
- Identity—Milton Berle;
- Sex panic—Wilhelm Reich;
- Birth control—Margaret Sanger;
- Loyalty—Julius and Ethel Rosenberg;
- Race—Paul Robeson;
- Subversion—Howard Fast;
- Crime—Frank Costello.

Susan Sontag best described the outsider when she said, "He who transgresses not only breaks a rule. He goes somewhere that the others are not; and he knows something the others don't know." These people—and the issues they confronted—truly went places others did not. They helped shape today's moral order.

Sin, Sex & Subversion need not be read in sequential order. The introduction frames the discussion, situating New York and some of the moral issues of the 1950s; the conclusion brings the threads of sin, sex, and subversion forward to the twenty-first century, illuminating how the postmodern moral order was fashioned. Each of the other chapters focuses on a critical issue and stands on its own; the issue may reemerge in another chapter. Like real life, history often overlaps on itself and can be reconceived in different contexts.

As history shows, everything is more than it appears. The book draws upon a diverse range of sources to tell its fascinating story. They include Congressional testimony; court decisions; unpublished manuscripts, oral histories, memories, and autobiographies; popular literature, newspapers, and magazines of the period; police and other public records; and secondary sources such as biographies, popular histories, and scholarly studies. Where available, the book includes links to YouTube and other archival media sources. The magic of multimedia is transforming the old-fashioned printed book into a postmodern media-rich experience; the audio, video, and text references included fill out some of the complex drama the book seeks to suggest.

I wish to especially thank my agent, Christopher Rhodes, of the James Fitzgerald Agency, for believing in the book and finding a supportive publisher. And special thanks to my editor, Maxim Brown, for his critical reading and careful editing of my book—he made it a better book. Finally, a special recognition to two dear comrades, Peter Hamilton and Donald Nicholson Smith, who long, long stuck with me.

INTRODUCTION

OUTSIDERS

CHRISTINE JORGENSEN, 1926–1989

New Normal

During the 1950s, sex was as threatening to the nation's moral order as Communism. New York City was the epicenter of two "wars": a "cold war" waged against subversion and a "hot war" against sin. These wars were fought on multiple fronts, including music, theatre, movies, fashion, and literature as well as birth control, homosexuality, teen sex, pornography, Communism, unions, and race relations. With the major exception of abortion, those wars are effectively over.

The United States is in the midst of a fourth sexual revolution, this one pushing further the revolutions of the 1840s, 1920s, and 1960s. Over the last century, but especially the last quarter-century, the boundaries of the "forbidden" have eroded. Among age-appropriate youths and adults, anything goes, including commercial sex, as long as it's consensual. Sex has shifted from a moral issue—"sin"—to a legal concern—"consent"—whether public or private. Today's only true sex crime is the violation of consent or the equality of all participants, whether involving rape, pedophilia, child porn, sex trafficking, or lust murder.

An illustration of this shift in values can be found in the transformation of homosexuality. From a once-hanging offense or pathology, it is now conceived as part of the human condition, with gay marriage accepted by a landmark June 2015 US Supreme Court decision.* Still other formerly unacceptable sexual "perversions"—like porn, sex toys, transvestism, sadomasochism (S&M), bondage & domination (B&D), water sports, and fetish outfits—are, today, enjoyed as normal expressions of sexual wellness by a growing number of adults, especially women.

Today's sexual revolution pushes the previous revolutions one step further. It introduces a sexual value system based on the belief that, essentially, anything goes as long as there is mutual consent among the participants. This postmodern sexuality assumes that each participant is an adult, eighteen years or older, and capable of making rational decisions. Those who violate mutual consent are considered immoral, pathological, or criminal. More and more Americans are engaging in a host of sex practices previously identified as deviant, and doing so with little of the sense of personal shame, social stigma, police harassment, or incarceration common throughout the nation's past.

Nothing signifies the mainstreaming of sin better than the *Fifty Shades of Grey* phenomenon. Based on E. L. James's original erotic novel, it developed from a self-published e-book into a global literary and movie blockbuster. More than one hundred million copies of the book have sold (and it's been translated into fifty-plus languages) and the movie has generated over $410 million in worldwide ticket sales, with only $130 million in the United States. As a cultural phenomenon, it's similar to Stephanie Meyer's Twilight series and Stieg Larsson's Millennium trilogy. However, while those others refer to sex, James made it the central issue. And while most early mass-market pornography of a half century ago, like *Playboy* and a host of fetish publications, targeted men, the principal audience for 50 Shades is women.

---

* See "Lavender Peril."

The adult consensual sex market is booming. CNBC estimates that porn "generated roughly $14 billion in revenue per year in 2012," including print, TV/cable, in-room, DVD, and online programming and services. The sex paraphernalia market—now rebranded as "sexual wellness"—is estimated to be a $15-billion business, with Amazon the nation's largest purveyor. Gentlemen's clubs are no longer limited to Las Vegas; the Ultimate Strip Club List, a website of strip clubs, includes about three thousand operating throughout the country. In the twenty-first century, the 1970s swinging scene is back; NASCA International, a swingers association, identifies 168 swingers clubs across the country. Explicit adult "safe sex" clubs for gays and straights operate throughout the country; specialized fetish clubs catering to B&D, S&M, and other once-perverse tastes can be found in many cities, often hosted by a professional dominatrix. Prostitution is legal only in parts of Nevada, yet illegal commercial sex is estimated to be an $18-billion business and is easily arranged through escort services, massage parlors, or "freelance" out-calls. Illicit noncommercial hookups can be arranged through Internet sites, wireless "apps," or phone calls. And gay bathhouses, bars, public rest stops, and other private settings remain notorious venues for sexual liaisons. Consensual adult sex is everywhere one looks.[2]

Nature Undone

In 2012, Donald Trump, owner of the Miss Universe and Miss USA pageants, changed the organization's official rules so that a twenty-three-year-old contestant, Jenna Talackova, could compete in the Miss Universe Canada contest. Talackova, who had lived as a female since the age of four and had undergone sex reassignment four years earlier, was initially disqualified from the contest because she was born a male. Following Trump's intervention, she competed.

Sixty years earlier, in 1952, George Jorgensen, a twenty-six-year-old former private in the US Army, traveled to Denmark to undergo a gender reassignment procedure, what was then known as a "sex change" operation. Returning to New York as Christine Jorgensen, her daring gained a famous *Daily News* headline: EX-GI BECOMES BEAUTY.[3]

Gender reassignment is but one of a series of significant technological breakthroughs that, over the last half century, have revolutionized human sexuality and social relations, and contributed to remaking the moral order. In 1960, the Federal Drug Administration (FDA) approved "the Pill," a safe oral contraceptive that represses ovulation in women, initially developed by Gregory Pincus and John Rock in 1954.* Other advances in birth control involved artificial insemination (e.g., in vitro fertilization [IVF] for "test tube babies") and the "morning after" pill (e.g., levonorgestrel, Plan B, and ulipristal, Ella). Drugs ostensibly designed to address male erectile dysfunction (ED)—like Viagra and Levitra—have become multi billion-dollar commercial successes. War has long been thought of as a masculine ritual and rite of passage. Soldiers can be emasculated, however, by damage to their genitals. Sexual prosthetics, particularly genital reconstruction, represent one of the marvels of the twenty-first-century military-industrial complex.[4]

Jorgensen retuned from WWII an Army veteran with his genitals intact. In popular before-and-after photos from the period, it appears that a male was not merely transformed into a female, but a butterfly was liberated from its caterpillar self. A reportedly meek, retiring guy left New York; a glamorous, sexy gal returned. The new Jorgensen appears with high cheekbones, long eyelashes, and full, painted lips, wearing a stylish hat and often wrapped in a full-length fur coat.[5]

Jorgensen was born on May 30, 1926, and—along with his sister, Dorothy—grew up in the Bronx, children of working-class parents. Like many transsexuals, he was not a homosexual but long felt he was a female living in a male's body. He researched scientific literature about people suffering similar conditions, including Paul De Kruf's 1945 study, *The Male Hormone*. Jorgensen wanted to be a documentary filmmaker and went to Europe ostensibly to make a

---

* See "The Pill."

vacation film. While in Denmark, he sought out medical assistance from Dr. Christian Hamburger; over a three-year period, he received hormone therapy from Dr. Harry Benjamin as part of the gender reassignment procedure.* (Jorgensen underwent further vaginal surgery procedures during the 1970s and 1980s.)

Returning to the Big Apple, Jorgensen initially lived with her parents and received considerable media attention—not all of it favorable. The media was divided over the efficacy of sex reassignment. A handful of publications accepted Jorgensen's new femininity, including *Pose, People Today*, and *American Weekly* (the latter paid her $20,000 for an exclusive profile); they often focused on her relations with the men she was dating. However, most publications, especially the popular tabloid magazines like *Uncensored, Whisper*, and *Confidential*, were contemptuous of her sex change, drawing pitiful attention to the apparent differences between her feminine legs and arms from her supposed masculine ankles and hands. *Quick,* a '50s pinup magazine, insisted she was not a "real woman" but a "mentally ill transvestite." But no publication was more critical than *Time*, which, in its April 20, 1953, issue called her an "altered male" and a "male castrate," claiming she was exploiting her transition to make money. Nevertheless, Jorgensen took full advantage of her newfound celebrity, becoming a popular nightclub performer. She entertained her audiences with dancing, humorous commentary, and chanteuse, singing "I Enjoy Being a Girl."[6]

Technology revolutionizes the personal life, eroticizes the flesh, and changes what is understood as normal—thus, refashioning the forbidden. Jorgensen's sex change procedure was one of twentieth-century medical technology's greatest achievements: the transformation of a male into a female. It was a truly forbidden accomplishment, an act that reconfigured the most basic element of the human condition: gender identity. And if nature was not fixed, immutable, what else about sexuality—and modern life in general—was open to change?

---

* Benjamin is author of the pioneering study, *The Transsexual Phenomenon* (1966).

Capital of the Twentieth Century

"New York is not a state capital or a national capital," E. B. White famously wrote in 1949, "but it is by way of becoming the capital of the world."[7] While London, Paris, Berlin, and Tokyo recovered from a devastating war, the Big Apple was all powerful. In 1950, the city's population topped 7.5 million people; Washington, DC, was about one-tenth its size, with 800,000 residents.

The city was the center of global capitalism. It was home to 135 of the nation's largest industrial companies, including General Electric, Standard Oil, Union Carbide, and US Steel. The city had the world's biggest port, accounting for more than 40 percent of the nation's shipping. It was the world's leading manufacturing hub, with 40,000 factories and over a million factory workers. It was also the nation's largest wholesaling center, accounting for a fifth of all US wholesale transactions.[8] New York was the media capital, home to the leading newspapers, magazines, book publishers, record companies, TV networks, and ad agencies. Wall Street was the world's financial center.

The end of WWII brought more than peace to New York and the nation. In the decade following the war, the United States was remade. It was transformed from an agricultural to an industrial economy; from a local to a continental territory; from a rural to an urban and, increasingly, a suburban nation; from a white to a mixed-race society; and from a nation state to a global power. And so too, the nation's sexual and political cultures were transformed. The Big Apple was at the epicenter of this transformation.

Mid-century Gotham was awash with sin, sex, and subversion. Priests, politicians, cops, judges, psychiatrists, pundits, and moralists of every stripe railed against the twin evils of Communism and vice. Prostitution was decried, homosexuality denounced, fetishists mocked, premarital sex shamed, sex education rejected, birth control restricted, and pornography censored. Yet, temptation was everywhere, including gambling and illegal drugs. At the same time, the greatest threat was questioning the established order—asking why? Those who did—whether teachers, civil servants, writers, entertainers, radio personalities, media makers, union members, or ordinary citizens—were denounced as subversives, Communists, or "red" sympathizers and threats to national security.

In the '50s, New York City was jumping. The drinking age was eighteen and bars stayed open until 4:00 a.m. Celebrated nightspots like the Stork Club, El Morocco, and the St. Regis Roof welcomed big-spenders, while the Village Vanguard, Birdland, and Jimmy Ryan's hosted a hot time for everyone else. During WWII, Harry Belafonte, a US Navy laborer, was denied entry into the Copacabana ("Copa"), one of the city's most exclusive clubs; in the '50s, he broke the color line and appeared as a headliner. The Village scene was but another front in the postwar culture war, welcoming beat poets, jazz musicians, and folksingers as well as interracial mixing and gay men and lesbians.

On August 1, 1954, Alan Freed, a Cleveland radio DJ brought his traveling music revue—the Moondog Jubilee of Stars Under the Stars—to New York.* It was held at Brooklyn's Ebbets Field, still home to the Dodgers, and featured performers included Fats Domino, Muddy Waters, Count Basie's Orchestra, the Dominoes, the Clovers, and the Orioles. Most significant, it drew a large, racially mixed audience. A month later, Freed signed a lucrative contract with radio station WINS, launching his daily "Rock 'n' Roll Party." Together with Murray Kaufman, of the Murray the K's Swingin' Soiree, and Douglas Henderson, of the *JOCKO, the Ace from Outer Space* show, a new era of Gotham's popular entertainment was born.

In 1955, Freed pushed further the subversive appeal of rhythm-and-blues (R&B) and rock & roll by hosting two popular and racially mixed concerts, one in Hell's Kitchen, the other in Brooklyn. In January, he held two dance concerts at the St. Nicholas Arena on West 66th Street, a popular boxing auditorium. The concert of all-black entertainers—including Fats Domino and Joe Turner—drew an estimated twelve thousand paying attendees. In September, he hosted an

---

* Freed was forced to stop calling himself "Moondog" after being sued by the blind street musician, "Moondog," a.k.a. Louis Hardin, the composer of the "Moondog Symphony"; he famously stood silently in Viking attire on Sixth Avenue between 53rd and 54th Streets.

eight-day stage show at the Brooklyn Paramount dubbed the "First Anniversary Rock 'n' Roll Party." Among the performers were Chuck Berry (singing "Maybellene"), Al Hibbler, The Harptones, and Red Prysock and his band. It was so popular, ticket sales hit $178,000, topping the $147,000 gross of the recently staged Dean Martin–Jerry Lewis comedy show held at the New York Paramount.[9]

Not all parts of the city were booming, however. The Depression and WWII took their toll on Gotham, especially Harlem. The nation's financial collapse cut back on consumer spending, especially by white people looking for a good time. Harlem's unemployment rate hit 50 percent. The repeal of Prohibition in 1933 eroded the uptown scene; the '35 Harlem race riot was the nail in the coffin. Some nightspots—most notably Minton's Playhouse, at 210 West 118th Street—hung on through the war, buoyed by the one million African Americans who loyally served and the city's increased war-related manufacturing. But most of the jazz clubs that made Harlem world famous during the Roaring '20s either went under or relocated to midtown, many clustered along West 52nd Street.

The postwar recession of 1948–1950 was the first bump, foreshadowing troubles yet to come; the city went through a second downturn in '53–'54 following the Korean War. The decade ended with the deeper, worldwide recession of '57–'58 that some argue was the most severe economic crisis of the postwar era.[10] In 1957, the New York Giants and the Brooklyn Dodgers packed up and relocated to San Francisco and Los Angeles, respectively. While Robert Moses was restructuring the metropolis, white flight to the suburbs took its toll, most acutely reflected in the eclipse of Times Square. In the '50s, city officials focused development efforts on East 42nd Street and the centerpiece of this campaign was the United Nations complex, a seventeen-acre plot donated by the Rockefeller family and developed by the real estate magnate William Zeckendorf.

The west side, especially the legendary Great White Way, "the Crossroads of the World," became a dead zone. The city took a hands-off approach to the growing underground economy that flourished in the Times Square honky-tonk. The number of shops offering under-the-counter porn magazines and other sex paraphernalia increased, as did 24/7 grind house theaters screening provocative movies, jazz clubs showcasing strip acts, massage parlors serving men's other needs, and bars facilitating female—and male—prostitution. The decline of midtown's appeal created a vacuum that organized crime filled.

During the 1950s, a dark shadow hovered over New York. Political radicals had long been a feature of city life, whether antislavery advocates during the antebellum era, anti-interventionists during the Great War, organizers during the Depression, or supporters of the Soviet Union during WWII. During the '30s and '40s, the Communist Party (CP) had strong popular support, leading the fight for unionization, against evictions, and for racial justice. During WWII, the interests of the United States and the Soviet Union aligned and the party saw its membership grow. The popularity of its major cultural institution in the city, the Jefferson School of Social Science, increased and CP or pro-CP "fellow travelers" were elected to the city council and the US Congress.

In the postwar era, the Red Scare decimated the party and the broader left. In 1949, the US government brought charges against eleven CP members for refusing to sign the 1940 Alien Registration Act; the Smith trials dragged on until '58 before all were convicted. The trials of Julius and Ethel Rosenberg—along with Morton Sobell—commenced on March 6, 1951; the couple were electrocuted on June 19, 1953, the first civilians in American history to be executed for espionage. Three months after the Rosenbergs were killed, in September 1953, Senator Joseph McCarthy (R-WI) held hearings in the city, grilling subversive writers, most notably Howard Fast, as to their role promoting the Communist threat. Numerous other federal and state anticommunist hearings were held at which teachers, entertainers, and ordinary citizens were hounded about their beliefs. The choice was stark: name names or to go to jail. Innumerable people's lives were destroyed.

American Dream

General Dwight Eisenhower took office as the thirty-fourth president on January 20, 1953, formally ending two decades of Democratic rule, thus also ending the New Deal and the Fair Deal. He replaced them with a new era of postwar prosperity and peace that transformed American life. During the period from 1945 to 1960, the nation's population increased by 28 percent, to 181 million from 140 million, but the gross national product (GNP) more than doubled, to $503 billion from $212 billion. This was a new America.

The United States was successfully undergoing a process known as "reconversion," in which American society—its major industries and nine million demobilized military personnel—shifted from a war back to a civilian economy. Many conservatives feared that the US would face an enormous spike in unemployment, unable to absorb the millions of men returning home. They worried that the drop in federal spending as a proportion of GDP—from 41.8 percent (1945) to 17.9 percent (1946)—would only compound the problem. There were a couple of hiccups during the late '40s through the mid-'50s, but a spike in unemployment did not occur. Maintaining a broad Keynesian outlook, much of the continued economic growth during the '50s was spurred by federal spending, especially the construction of the interstate highway system, the use of veterans' benefits to underwrite higher education and housing, and the establishment of what Ike would sorrowfully come to call in his famous Farewell Address, "the military-industrial complex."

Ordinary Americans—mostly white—benefited from the economic growth. The anchor purchase was the new home, especially by first-time buyers. The highway system facilitated the great population relocation from the east to the west and from the city to the suburbs; the GI Bill helped underwrite the mortgages that financed the suburban dream house. Between 1945 and 1960, twelve million houses were constructed across the country. William J. Levitt, the creator of "Levittown," sold houses for as little as $7,000, and a more up-market ranch-style house sold for about $10,000; down payments were low and financing was only 2 to 3 percent.* The Levittown development on eastern Long Island, New York, consisted of 17,400 houses, some

---

* $7,000 in 1950 is the equivalent of $69,220 in 2015 dollars;
  http://www.usinflationcalculator.com

sporting three bedrooms, a fully equipped kitchen and bathroom, and a living room with a panorama window. The development was home to more than 80,000—all white—residents.[11] Racism was as alive in the North as in the South.

And if one had a new home in the suburbs, one needed not only a car to get to work or shop or drop the kids at school, but also all the households amenities—modern, high-tech devices—required to run it. Between 1945 and 1949, Americans purchased more than twenty million cars—as well as twenty million refrigerators, 5.5 million stoves and five million television sets a year. This does not include the untold number of washing machines, vacuum cleaners, and toasters, essential conveniences of modern life. The consumer revolution was launched and drags on to today.

The postwar era witnessed a second reconversion, this one involving domestic life. With nine million military personnel (mostly men) demobilizing, domestic life changed. Many women who had served in the war effort, whether in the military as nurses or in civilian jobs in factories, were displaced and forced to return to traditional domestic life. By the '50s, a new trend was emerging. Couples were marrying younger, women at 20.5 years and men at 22.5 years, and they were having more children (3.2 on the average). But something was not right in America. In its June 26, 1950, issue, *Time* ran a disturbing article entitled, "Medicine: The Cold Women," and noted: "Some doctors suspect that about three in every four U.S. women are frigid, i.e., get no sexual satisfaction."

This message never made its way onto America's new communications medium, television. Some programs offered serious dramas, with shows like *Playhouse 90* and *Kraft Television Theater* showcasing top writers and actors. Some played on mounting Cold War fears, most notably *I Led 3 Lives*, which ran for three years (1953–1956) and was based on the life of Herbert Philbrick who served for nine years as an FBI spy on Communists. But the most popular shows—*Ozzie and Harriet* (1952–1966), *Father Knows Best* (1954–1960), and *Leave It to Beaver* (1957–1963)—invoked the neutered world of cultural conformity, the "togetherness" of the all-American, middle-class, white suburban family. They inhabited a clean, morally ordered yet funny world; everything was manageable. No one got angry; mothers never worked; money issues were never considered. And women's sexuality was never discussed. The real world—outside this fictional suburban bubble—didn't exist. In this sculpted world order, everyone was white; no one drank, cursed, or cheated on their spouse.

Nevertheless, for all their bravado, the '50s were a fearful time. For all the prosperity and promise, many worried that the end was at hand. The world was divided; the Soviet Union threatened the United States for global power; Communism contested democratic capitalism for ideological hegemony. The world was at a standoff between belligerent nuclear powers. People built bomb shelters in their homes and New York school kids practiced periodic duck-and-cover exercise, as if a cheap classroom desk would protect them from an atomic—or hydrogen—bomb. Americans waited in wonder.

Moral Order

In the 1950s, obscene materials included printed books that ranged from literary works, poetry, and pulp fiction to advice and scientific studies; still images appeared as artistic paintings and prints as well as pinups, post-cards, and photos. In addition, a variety of black-and-white pictorial works sought to meet the specialized erotic fantasies of especially masculine men; these included pictorial works promoting nudism, female "cheesecakes," male "beefcakes," and specialty "fetish" publications exploring S&M, leather, and bondage. An estimated ninety million comics were sold each month during the mid-'50s. Finally, movies came in a growing number of formats, including 16mm, 8mm, and super-8mm film; they were shown in private "smokers," grind house theaters, and peepshow booths. If one knew where to look, one could get what one wanted.

However, for nearly a century, from the post–Civil War era to the post-WWII period, the policies conceived by Anthony Comstock, the father of modern censorship, defined America's moral order. He believed in employing the power of the state to restrict adults from acquiring and consuming allegedly "obscene" or "pornographic" materials, be they erotic or medical, no matter whether image, text, or device. His major accomplishment was the passage of the 1873 federal censorship legislation barring obscene materials of every kind from the US mail.* The law covered nearly every form of communications and exchange then known or anticipated:

> No obscene, lewd, or lascivious book, pamphlet, picture, paper, print, or other publication of an indecent character, or any article or thing designed or intended for the prevention of conception or procuring of abortion, nor any article or thing intended or adapted for any indecent or immoral use or nature, nor any written or printed card, circular, book, pamphlet, advertisement or notice or any kind giving information, directly or indirectly, where, or how, or of whom, or by what means either of the thing before mentioned may be obtained or made, nor any letter upon the envelope of which, or post-card upon which indecent or scurrilous epithets may be written or printed, shall be carried in the mail.

Comstock was appointed a special officer of the US postal system and given the power to seize what he labeled as obscene materials as well as arrest those he identified as pornographers.[12]

The law was so effective that within the first six months of passage, Comstock boasted that it led to the seizure of 194,000 pictures and photographs, 14,200 stereopticon plates, and 134,000 pounds of books and other media. In the 1910s, near the end of his life, Comstock claimed that he had destroyed 3,984,063 photographs and 160 tons of "obscene" literature.[13]

The Comstock Law began to erode in the mid-1930s, when it was partially reversed by the Supreme Court with regard to medical and scientific materials; most notably *United States v. One Package of Japanese Pessaries* (1936). The landmark 1934 ruling involving the importation of James Joyce's *Ulysses* further extended free-speech rights to literature. In the '50s, a series of court decisions expanded

---

* It is formally titled: "Suppression of Trade in, and Circulation of, Obscene Literature and Articles of Immoral Use."

free speech expression, including what was previously identified as obscene; including *Burstyn v. Wilson* (1952) and *Roth v. United States* (1957). These new freedoms extended free-speech protections to movies, literature, and poetry, but not to comic books.[14]

Decency

Six months after taking office, on June 13, 1953, President Eisenhower gave a seminal address on free speech and censorship, second in importance to his legendary 1960 Farewell Address warning about the growing influence of the military-industrial complex. In his '53 Dartmouth commencement talk, Ike tried to square the circle. "Don't join the book-burners," he championed. "Don't think you are going to conceal faults by concealing evidence that they ever existed. Don't be afraid to go in your library and read every book," he encouraged the graduates, "as long as any document does not offend our own ideas of decency. That should be the only censorship." He concluded his lecture by drawing a telling parallel concerning the meaning of free expression. "How will we defeat Communism unless we know what it is," he asks, "and what it teaches, and why does it have such an appeal for men, why are so many people swearing allegiance to it?" He noted, "it [Communism] is almost a religion, albeit one of the nether regions."[15]

For Eisenhower and other Cold War warriors, "free speech" was an essential weapon in the anticommunist crusade. It distinguished the United States from the Soviet Union. The United States had a free press; the government may influence but did not control it. However, free speech had its limits and—like the Soviet Union—the government could enforce them. Formally, Congress and the courts set the limits; practically, the executive branch implemented them. But appropriate suggestions to "loyal" publishers was often more effective.

The key word in Eisenhower's cautionary address was "decency"— it, as Ike stated, "should be the only censorship." Unfortunately, the president did not define the term. The concept of decency has all but disappeared from the twenty-first-century popular lexicon. But in the '50s, decency mattered. It divided the hopes of the consumer revolution from the fears of the Cold War. It was the knowledge that distinguished traditional values from the new—and, for many, unacceptable and corrupting—forms of expressions spreading through the organs of popular culture. Decency bespoke the moral order or accepted standards of discourse, of what was *good, wholesome, American.*

Nevertheless, decency was under attack. Beat poets, novelists, spoken-word artists, singers, scholars, indie filmmakers, pornographers, and comic book publishers promoted new voices and visions. And this said nothing about what was being promoted by fashion, cosmetics, sports, and advertising. More troubling to those so offended, the nation's consumer society seemed to be propelled by the seductive, eroticized spectacle of the purchase; people felt empowered and fulfilled when buying. Still others challenged the growing conservative political order, whether regarding foreign policy, labor unrest, or civil rights. Boundaries were being pushed; resistance to established notions of moral order was spreading through the nation.

In the '50s, the meaning of decency split society. Did it uphold traditional values or suggest a different, more humane standard? It defined the culture war.

The Catholic Church's Legion of Decency was the era's leading private organization championing traditional moral rectitude. Inspired by Anthony Comstock's New York Society for the Suppression of Vice (NYSSV)—which had been backed by the Young Men's Christian Association (YMCA)—of the 1870s, the Legion was founded in 1934 to combat immoral, unacceptable expressions in word or image, especially in movies. In '58, the Catholic Church took up a campaign against pornography, establishing the Citizens for Decent Literature (later renamed Citizens for Decency through Law), targeting illicit materials at local newsstands. It was headed by Charles Keating and, at its height, claimed to have three hundred chapters and one hundred thousand members.* Its efforts were part of a larger "purity campaign" that defined the Christian Right's moralist agenda.

---

* In 1992, Keating was busted and went to jail for his part in the savings-and-loan debacle; see John D'Emilio and Estelle B. Freedman. *Intimate Matters*, pp. 283–84.

A very different notion of decency was famously expressed by Joseph Welch, council to the US Army, in his legendary 1954 encounter with Senator Joseph McCarthy over subversion in the military. Rebuffing McCarthy's claim that one young attorney on his staff had Communist sympathies, Welch simply asked: "Have you no sense of decency, sir, at long last?" This exchange was a major media event, broadcast nationally in real time over the new mass medium of television. The confrontation galvanized the nation's attention, much like the Cuban Missile Crisis and Kennedy assassination a decade later. And it broke McCarthy; he was stripped of his committee chairmanship and died in '57, a drunk, defeated man.

Post-WWII American life was conditioned by what George Orwell labeled in 1945, "the cold war." He knew the world had changed with the dropping of the atomic bombs and the emergence of two superpowers; it was a world divided. A year later, Winston Churchill gave the concept greater resonance in a speech in Fulton, Missouri, dividing the world by an "iron curtain." For the United States, the era's new ethos was reflected in the all-mighty dollar. According to the Treasury Department, the motto "In God We Trust" was originally placed on US coins in 1861 due to increased religious sentiment at the start of the Civil War. A century later, on July 30, 1956, President Eisenhower approved a Joint Resolution of the 84th Congress making the slogan "In God We Trust" the national motto; he added it to US paper money. The Treasury's website does not mention the role of the Cold War in Congress's action.[16]

In the '50s, the US Congress, both the Senate and House, led the nation's battle against sin, sex, and subversion. In the House, the principal vehicle of this campaign was the Un-American Activities Committee (HUAC), established in 1938 to investigate disloyalty; it was formally terminated in 1975. In the postwar era, HUAC's principal target was Communists in every form, whether Hollywood stars or Puerto Rican nationalists. It welcomed former CP members like an old-fashioned revival meeting would embrace lost sinners. Those who testified in, for example, hearings about the CP in New York were engaging in an act of contrition for a moral failing. Genuflecting before the public tribunal, they received redemption.

HUAC singled out prominent entertainers (e.g., screenwriters), public employees (e.g., teachers), and organizations (e.g., labor unions) suspected of having Communist ties. In 1947, it launched its first attack on Hollywood, calling ten witnesses to testify in open session, including Dalton Trumbo, Ring Lardner Jr., John Howard Lawson, and Albert Maltz. In '48, Representative Richard Nixon (R-CA) famously grilled Alger Hiss, a former State Department official, as to his Communist affiliation. In '51–'52, HUAC returned to Hollywood, this time subpoenaing Larry Parks, Zero Mostel, and Sam Jaffe; Budd Schulberg and Elia Kazan were "friendly" witnesses, naming names. In '55, among those subpoenaed were folksinger Pete Seeger, David Alman (of the Rosenberg support committee), and the actress Lucille Ball; bandleader Artie Shaw, director Robert Rossen, actor Lee J. Cobb, and choreographer Jerome Robbins appeared as "friendly" witnesses. And in '56, Arthur Miller and Paul Robeson were subpoenaed.

Simultaneously, the House conducted a parallel campaign against obscenity. In '52, it established the Select Committee on Current Pornographic Materials, chaired by Representative Ezekiel Gathings (D-AR). It looked into pocket-book pulp fiction, including crime, horror, and lesbian works. Lesbian pulp fiction was a postwar literary genre that rankled the morals of upstanding citizens, especially old-fashioned males. The great irony was that while many of these works were sexually suggestive and decried as obscene, they were targeted to male readers and often written by male authors. As one observer noted, "lesbian women were never the primary market." The committee urged the restriction of such material from the US mail and encouraged the publishing industry to adopt a policy of self-censorship. In '55, Representative Kathryn Granahan (D-PA), chair of the House Subcommittee on Postal Operations, chastised US postal officials for permitting obscene materials to reach innocent youths, thus contributing to the rise in juvenile delinquency.[17]

In the '50s, three agencies—the Federal Bureau of Investigation (FBI), US Postal Service, and US Customs Service—oversaw federal efforts to suppress pornography. Under the 1873 Comstock law, the Postal Service was empowered to prohibit obscene material from the mail; such material included erotica, birth control information, and sexual implements. The FBI was founded in 1908 and, in 1910, began collecting and analyzing obscene materials. In 1942, it established the Obscene File and, during WWII, focused on pornography and other moral issues like homosexuals in the US military and government. The Customs Service sought to restrict such material from entering the country.

Two opportunist Senators, McCarthy and Estes Kefauver (D-TN), took full advantage of their elected positions to conduct a series of official hearings into the moral state of the nation. McCarthy led the Senate's anticommunist campaign to cleanse and purify the nation's political ethos. In 1950, he announced that he had a list of 205 State Department employees who were CP members. That same year, he served on the Subcommittee on Investigations of the Committee on Expenditures in the Executive Departments that directly linked subversion and sexuality. It held hearings investigating "homosexuals and other sex perverts" working for the government. It found that the mental health of federal employees affected national security:

> In the opinion of this subcommittee homosexuals and other sex perverts are not proper persons to be employed in Government for two reasons: first, they are generally unsuitable, and second, they constitute a security risk. [emphasis in original]

In the wake of this and other Congressional hearings, a series of Washington, DC, witch hunts purged thousands of so-called perverts from government jobs. For McCarthy, Communism and homosexuality were but two sides of the same corruption undermining the nation's moral order.

McCarthy leveraged his anticommunist and anti-homosexual crusades into the chairmanship of the Senate's Investigations Committee between 1953 and '55. In '53, he held hearings at New York's federal courthouse grilling subversive writers—most notably the novelist Howard Fast, the newspaper columnist Drew Pearson, and Louis Budenz, the former editor of *the Daily Worker*, as to their respective roles promoting the Communist threat. In '54, the nation witnessed live TV coverage of McCarthy's legendary encounter with Welch over subversion in the army.

In 1950, Kefauver, an ambitious senator from Tennessee, began planning his bid for the '52 Democratic presidential nomination. He used the Senate committee investigation process to gain national name recognition. His 1950 hearings targeted a different menace threatening the nation's moral order: organized crime. He took his roadshow to fourteen cities across the country, calling some six hundred witnesses to testify, including reputed Mafia bosses. He became a national celebrity when his New York hearings of Mafia figures were carried live over nationwide TV coverage. Never missing a chance at self-promotion, he appeared on the popular TV game show *What's My Line?* Failing to get the '52 presidential nod, he again took advantage of a Senate investigation, this one in 1954 and '55 on juvenile delinquency and obscenity, to secure a successful bid as Adlai Stevenson's running mate in the '56 election. The Republican Eisenhower-Nixon ticket won decisively.

Outsider

On November 10, 1956, Billie Holiday gave two sold-out concerts at Carnegie Hall, singing some of her favorite songs, including "Lady Sings the Blues," "Ain't Nobody's Business If I Do," and "My Man." On stage, she was warmly celebrated by some of the generation's jazz giants, including Kenny Burrell, Roy Eldridge, and Coleman Hawkins. Also appearing on stage was Gilbert Millstein, the *New York Times* jazz critic, who read excerpts from Holiday's recently published autobiography, *Lady Sings the Blues.* The concert marked her triumphant New York comeback and is memorialized in a celebrated album, *The Essential Billie Holiday: Carnegie Hall Concert Recorded Live.*[18]

Yet, for all its festivity, the concert could not conceal a deeper foreboding. Millstein warns in the album's liner notes, it "was evident,

---

* It was written with William Duffy.

even then, that Miss Holiday was ill." He goes on to paint a grim picture: "I was shocked at her physical weakness. Her rehearsal had been desultory; her voice sounded tinny and trailed off; her body sagged tiredly. But I will not forget the metamorphosis that night. She was erect and beautiful; poised and smiling. And when the first section of narration was ended, she sang—with strength undiminished—with all of the art that was hers." (Holiday's declining but resolute spirit was eloquently captured in Audra McDonald's 2014 Tony Award–winning one-woman show, *Lady Day at Emerson's Bar & Grill.*) Lady Day died of liver failure on July 17, 1959.

The 1956 concerts marked Holiday's return to the Big Apple, following nearly a decade in which she was barred from performing in city commercial clubs. It represented the capstone of her work with Norman Granz, a remarkable jazz entrepreneur who became her manager in '52. In early '54, Holiday undertook an acclaimed tour of Europe, playing sold-out shows in Amsterdam, Basel, Brussels, Copenhagen, Frankfurt, Dusseldorf, the Hague, Hamburg, Manchester, Oslo, Paris, Stockholm, and London's Royal Albert Hall. Lady Day was the queen of American music.

A decade earlier, Holiday was just as hot. She went to the Crescent City to act as a singing maid in the 1947 film *New Orleans,* directed by Arthur Lubin; her idol, Louis Armstrong, also performed in the movie. Back in the Big Apple in May '47, she was busted for heroin possession; she claimed it was her boyfriend's stash. She pleaded guilty and was sentenced to one year and a day at a federal rehabilitation facility in Alderston, West Virginia. On March 27, 1948, ten days after her release from prison, she performed her first Carnegie Hall concert, singing some thirty songs to a packed house. Because of her felony conviction, her license—her "cabaret card"—to perform in city nightclubs selling liquor was revoked. Nevertheless, in the late '40s, Holiday regularly performed at the Ebony Club, located on Broadway between 52nd and 53rd Street, partially owned by John Levy, her manager and lover during the period.[19]

Holiday is an iconic New York outsider, celebrated for the white gardenia she wore in her hair and her unforgettable rendition of

"Strange Fruit," a lamentation on the horrors of lynching. Based on a poem, "Bitter Fruit," it opens:

> *Southern trees bear a strange fruit,*
> *Blood on the leaves and blood at the root,*
> *Black body swinging in the Southern breeze,*
> *Strange fruit hanging from the poplar trees.*
>
> *Pastoral scene of the gallant South,*
> *The bulging eyes and the twisted mouth,*
> *Scent of magnolia sweet and fresh,*
> *Then the sudden smell of burning flesh!*
>
> *Here is a fruit for the crows to pluck,*
> *For the rain to gather, for the wind to suck,*
> *For the sun to rot, for a tree to drop,*
> *Here is a strange and bitter crop.*

In 1999, *Time* magazine named "Strange Fruit" the "song of the century." The Library of Congress put it in the National Recording Registry. Its full power can only be truly appreciated by listening to—and seeing—Holiday's performance.[20]

A half century earlier, "Strange Fruit" confronted a very different moral order. According to legend, a man approached Holiday at a jazz club and handed her a poem, "Bitter Fruit." Working with pianist Sonny White, Holiday adapted the poem into a song that was released in July 1939 and reached number 16 on the music chart. Among those that denounced the song was *Time*, calling it a "prime piece of musical propaganda."[21]

The man who approached Holiday in the jazz club was Abel Meeropol, a Dewitt Clinton (Bronx) high school English teacher and member of the Communist Party. He wrote the poem in '37 after seeing a photograph of two lynched men, Thomas Shipp and Abram Smith; he published it under the pseudonym Lewis Allan. In 1940, Meeropol was called to testify before the state's Rapp-Coudert Committee investigating Communism in city public schools. One of the issues it pressed him on was if he was paid by the party to write the song. He vehemently denied the suggestion. This was the era of the Alien Registration Act (Smith Act) that made it a crime to "knowingly or willfully advocate . . . overthrowing the Government of the United States or of any State by force or violence." In 1953, following the execution of Ethel and Julius Rosenberg, the Meeropols—Abel and Anne—adopted the Rosenbergs' children, Robert and Michael, aged six and ten.[22]

In the '50s, the New York outsiders who most eloquently articulated the new postwar aesthetic sensibility were the Beats—poets, writers, painters, dancers, and other cool cats that gave voice to an era. They got their name from Herbert Huncke, a petty thief and male prostitute, who went public in an influential 1952 *New York Times* profile by John Clellon Holmes. "The origins of the word 'beat' are obscure," Holmes wrote, "but the meaning is only too clear to most Americans. More than mere weariness, it implies the feeling of having been used, of being raw. It involves a sort of nakedness of mind, and, ultimately, of soul; a feeling of being reduced to the bedrock of consciousness." And he added, "A man is beat whenever he goes for broke and wagers the sum of his resources on a single number; and the young generation has done that continually from early youth."[23] It was a beat generation.

Nothing more eloquently expressed the beat ethos than Allen Ginsburg's poem, "Howl." The poem opens with the immortal lines:

> *I saw the best minds of my generation*
> *destroyed by madness, starving hysterical naked dragging*
> *themselves through the negro streets at*
> *dawn looking for an angry fix,*

Often forgotten, Ginsberg's book of poetry, *Howl & Other Poems*, was first released in New York in 1956 and approved by the local Customs Service. Its seizure in San Francisco in '57 culminated in one of the most celebrated First Amendment cases of the postwar era.

Since its founding, New York has had a legacy of grand outsiders, men and women who made a difference, helped redefine the

city's—and nation's—moral order. In the '50s, outsiders lived different lives. Some were successful, with a long and enduring influence;
some were shooting stars, aglow for the blink of the eye yet unforgettable. Some went to jail, their lives destroyed by the forces of moral
order; and two were executed as subversives. Outsiders flourished in
every dimension of social life, especially domains involving sin, sex,
and subversion. They pushed the boundaries of what was acceptable,
marking the different phases of the city's social evolution. Each is an
illuminating example that reveals how the boundaries of acceptable
moral order was contested and changed.

The '50s culture war could not sustain itself. It could not maintain
traditional values; too much in American society was changing. Perhaps most consequential, the Cold War was being normalized by the
mid-'50s and accepted as a standoff between two nuclear superpowers. The freezing—or standoff—of geopolitical tensions between the
United States and the Soviet Union, with periodic skirmishes in far-
off, underdeveloped places (e.g., Cuba, the Congo, Vietnam), had significant consequences, including defusing domestic anticommunist
hysteria. This was most evidently expressed in 1954 when McCarthy
burned out in his showdown with Welch during the army hearings.

Without a "cold war" aimed at a military showdown between good
and evil or between capitalism and Communism, the social and cultural "hot war" against sin, sex, and subversion lost much of its rage.
The vibrant consumer revolution, one based on a vast majority of citizens having money in their pockets and desire in their eyes, defused
the war against alleged immorality, whether involving comic books,
Bettie Page, or homosexuals. And while HUAC remained opera-
tional until 1975 (subpoenaing Yippie leaders Abbie Hoffman and
Jerry Rubin in '67), it lost its moral bite as the anticommunist hysteria
peaked with Senator McCarthy's eclipse. A new spirit of possibility
was percolating through society, represented by important Supreme
Court decisions including the *Miracle* decision in 1952, *Brown* in '54,
Roth in '57, and that Communists got their passports back in '58.* The

---

* *Burstyn v. Wilson* (1952); *Brown v. Board of Education of Topeka* (1954); *Roth v.
U.S.* (1957); and *Kent v. Dulles* (1958).

decisions reflected—and propelled forward—the emerging civil-rights movement, changes in popular culture, and a new, new Left.

Nevertheless, the culture war persisted. In 1952, the American Psychiatric Association (APA) introduced the first "bible" of mental health, *The Diagnostic and Statistical Manual of Mental Disorders* (*DSM*). Psychiatry was then in thrall to the psychoanalytic model, especially when it came to the notion of perversion. As Paul Friedman states in the 1959 *American Handbook of Psychiatry*, "Broadly speaking, we designate as sexual deviation or perversions any patterns of sexual behavior which differ from normal coitus and serve as major sources of sexual gratification rather than as foreplay to coital activity." The key phrase—"sexual gratification rather than as foreplay"—locates perversion as a sexual experience desired as an end in itself, a threat. Among the "special" psychopathological conditions Friedman identified were coprophilia, exhibitionism, fetishism, overt homosexuality, necrophilia, pedophilia, sadomasochism, transvestitism, voyeurism, and zoophilia.[24] In 1973, the same year as the Supreme Court's *Roe* decision, the APA removed homosexuality from its list of psychiatric disorders.

Making a Life

Christine Jorgensen was not the first American, male or female, to undergo sexual reassignment. Researcher Emylia Terry found that in 1937 the *Los Angeles Times* reported that a "Montana Girl Becomes Man by Sex Change and Weds" and, in 1941 reported on Barbara Anne Richards, "who believed herself to be a male until recently," so she could marry. In 1952, the *Las Vegas Review-Journal* announced in a bold headline, "Christine in Reverse Is Now a Happy Father," a woman transitioned in New Orleans.[25]

But Jorgensen was the first transsexual person to create a successful career as an entertainer, and she hit her stride in the mid-'50s. She worked closely, if often with difficulty, with a series of agents and managers that included Charlie Yates, Betty Walton, and her mother, Florence Jorgensen, and she crafted an inviting stage presence that endeared her to audiences throughout the United States, big venues and small, and throughout the world. In the mid-1960s, she began her acting career in Long Island, New York, and Columbus, Ohio, summer stock productions of *Old Dad, Poor Dad* and *Mary, Mary*, under the director Bill Hunt. However, she still confronted significant prejudice. In 1960, she was almost busted in Long Beach, California, for violating a city ordinance prohibiting "employees" from performing in drag; police identified her as a "contractor." As her biographer Richard Docker points out, after securing a contract to perform at a US military base in Germany, "the Army higher ups in the Third Armored Division nixed the deal, supposedly to protect the morals and health of the tank corps."[26]

In 1959, Jorgensen again got front-page headlines when the city refused to issue her a marriage license. She was engaged to Howard Knox, a Washington, DC, typist who was the only man she apparently had sex with. However, he lost his job when the engagement to Jorgensen became known. The city blocked the marriage on the basis that Knox could not prove he was legally divorced and Jorgensen's birth certificate listed her as a male; a New York court refused to reassign her birth certificate identity. Jorgensen never married.[27]

Jorgensen relocated to Southern California in the early1960s and continued as an entertainer. She released her autobiography in 1967, a gossipy tale focusing on her showbiz career, name-dropping every chance she gets. The memoir led to a movie deal and *The Christine Jorgensen Story* was released in 1970 to poor reception; Docker called it "a dismal flop."[28] She was diagnosed with cancer in the late 1980s and died in April 1989.

The world has changed since Jorgensen returned from Demark in 1952. In 1965, Johns Hopkins University established the nation's first gender-identity clinic under the direction of John Money, PhD. A half century later, the Williams Institute, a research organization specializing in sexual orientation and gender identity issues, estimated that there were 700,000 transgender people in the United States.[29] "Trans" people continue to experience discrimination and social stigma with regard to employment, housing, health care, the judicial system (especially in prison), and simply using a public restroom. Nevertheless, the world has changed.

In 1973, the APA removed homosexuality from its classification as a mental disorder. The diagnosis had been established in the first 1952 edition of the *DSM*. Four decades later, the APA's latest edition, the *DSM-5*, reclassified "gender identity disorder" into "gender dysphoria," emphasizing a person's distress instead of disorder with regard to their gender identity. Perhaps more significant, changes in federal policy transformed the status of trans people. In July 2014, President Obama issued an executive order adding "gender identity" protections to federal contracting guidelines, covering some 200,000 contractors. Medicare now covers sex-reassignment surgery and insurance companies are covering transition procedures as medically necessary rather than merely a cosmetic option. The trans issue gained visibility when Bradley Manning, the army whistleblower who released an enormous number of classified government documents to WikiLeaks and is now serving a thirty-five-year prison sentence, made a very public decision to shift from a he to a she, now renamed Chelsea Manning.

Most recently, transition has become a mainstream gossip event when Bruce became Caitlyn Jenner. Jenner, an Olympic gold medalist and part of the Kardashian orbit, has apparently come to terms with a deep-seated need to be another gender, but also has turned a personal experience into a media spectacle.[30]

On June 22, 2014, thousands of New Yorkers and out-of-towners strolled along West 27th Street between Tenth and Eleventh Avenues in their wildest erotic finery. Men and women, gay and straight, black and white, young adults and aging hunks mingled, embraced, kissed, and tenderly fondled one another. Clad in leather harnesses and chaps, smoking cigars and other herbs, and proudly displaying their most outrageous tattoos, the strollers gathered to celebrate sexual deviance. Started in 1997, the Gotham event is a modest copy of San Francisco's legendary fetishist jamboree, the Folsom Street Fair.

On September 21, 2014, an estimated 400,000 sexual outsiders, their admirers, and voyeurs attended the San Francisco fair celebrating its thirty-first anniversary. The last Sunday in September is reserved for the world's largest assembly of erotic fetishists. The Folsom Street conclave is the capstone of San Francisco Leather Week, a smorgasbord of lectures, fetish demonstrations, dances, and sex parties. It's all adult-only, consensual, and legal. What began in a side-street alley as AIDS was about to ravage the city has evolved into a spectacle that spans some thirteen blocks in the now oh-so-hip SoMa (South of Market) area. It hosted some two hundred booths, many specialty vendors selling the latest sex toys and other erotic pleasures. The fair's become so much a part of city life that, in 2013, the Marriott Hotel, a Mormon family–owned enterprise, was one of the fair's corporate sponsors.

HONKY-TONK

TIMES SQUARE

Crossroads of the World

The Times Square New Year's Eve festivity has become one of the world's biggest media events, drawing an estimated one million people to the square and a billion-plus TV and online viewers worldwide. Revelers have been gathering in the square since 1904 when 1 Times Square began hosting a rooftop gala to bring in the New Year. The first ball-lowering celebration took place in 1907 and, over the century, it has become an all-American—and, eventually, a global—event.

Times Square is still fondly known as the Crossroads of the World. Today it is Disneyland North, a perfect urban tourist "destination," with plenty of theaters, restaurants, and shops appealing to every taste. It's one of the city's most visited tourist attractions, welcoming an estimated thirty-nine million visitors annually; an estimated 330,000 people pass through it daily. It's clean, safe, and has few street-level illicit temptations. This was not always the case.

Over two nights in July 1954, between 9:30 p.m. and 2:30 a.m., the *New York Times* reported, "nearly sixty detectives, plainclothes men, patrolmen and Narcotics Squad specialist swooped down on the amusement area [Times Square], bounded by Fortieth and

Fifty-eighth Streets and Avenue of the Americas and Eighth Avenue." The paper ran front-page coverage of the raids, reporting that during the first roundup, 125 people were arrested, and, during the follow-up raid, twenty-three additional people were busted. Those pinched during the first night were mostly males, aged seventeen to thirty-five, including "juvenile delinquents, hoodlums, prostitutes, sex perverts and other undesirables."[31]

Those arrested were charged with a variety of offenses, including "vagrancy, disorderly conduct, loitering, using loud and boisterous language, annoying passers-by and blocking sidewalks." According to Police Commissioner Francis Adams, the city received "hundreds" of complaints from local merchants and citizen's groups about deviant activities taking place in what was known as the Broadway "midway." The raids were part of a campaign to clean up Times Square, ostensibly targeting "narcotic peddlers, known criminals and draft dodgers," though few of them seem to have been arrested. Not to lose an opportunity for self-promotion, the police staged the raids to coincide with the American Legion's New York State chapter's annual conclave.

In the '50s, Times Square was the epicenter of city's seedy social life. In the wake of the Great Depression and WWII, midtown west came to rival Coney Island as the locus for popular, working-class, and low-life amusement. It welcomed people of all ages but especially young adults out for a night on the town, offering popular entertainment at an affordable price. It also welcomed hucksters, con artists, hookers, taxi dancers, male hustlers, panhandlers, street preachers, nightclub patrons, the "raincoat crowd" seeking pornography, moviegoers at grind house theaters, and undesirables of every persuasion.

Times Square was formerly known as Long Acre Square, renamed in 1904 when the *New York Times* relocated to its new West 43rd Street headquarters. In the '50s, it was a perfectly situated midtown zone for social engagement. It had easy proximity to the Lincoln Tunnel, the metropolitan region's principal bus terminal, and a major subway junction. It offered affordable counter restaurants, bars, hotels, burlesque houses, jazz joints, and round-the-clock grind houses. Bookstores met the needs of the endless stream of passersby, whether looking for "how-to" and civil-service "prep" manuals, joke and comic books, horoscope pamphlets, scandal or gossip rags, and pulp fictions of every variety (e.g., romance, crime, adventure, war stories, Westerns, and lesbian). An under-the-counter market in erotica thrived. On Times Square streets, especially at night, female and male prostitutes plied their trade, often inviting well-healed patrons to an East Side apartment to enjoy a "sex circus."*

The July '54 police raids came amid a growing effort by local property owners and businessmen to rezone the Broadway midway for economic revitalization (i.e., gentrification). They sought to ban the cheap amusement attractions they considered immoral and which they thought threatened their property values. The Broadway Association, representing midtown real estate interests, had, in '52, appealed to the City Planning Commission to rezone the Times Square area. That year, the *Times* undertook an unofficial census of the area and found it reflected a distinct urban culture. It was marked by a half-dozen "penny arcades"; eight dance clubs, "some with canned music blaring into the streets over raucous loudspeakers"; eight record shops with "loudspeaker nuisances"; several auction houses that "pipe their blare to the streets"; a host of shooting galleries and bazaars; gift shops "of a junky nature, 'last day' sales, 'riot' sales"; live turtle emporiums; shops for "passport shots, jokes, magic tricks, monogrammed cowboy hats"; and "lurid, sexy and sadistic movie advertising." Still other attractions included wax museums, flea circuses, freak shows, and skeeball centers. The *Times* observed: "Added to all these and kindred pleasures for the pedestrian is the eye-filling whirlwind swirl of dust and paper with the city's Sanitation Department hasn't caught up."[32] At the time of the July '54 raids, little had changed.

One of the iconic 42nd Street dives that drew scorn from those with better taste was Hubert's Museum located at 228–232 West 42nd Street. Founded by Hubert Miller as a Coney Island midway spot, it

---

* Sex circuses were a unique after-hours indulgence of the Roaring '20s; see "Flesh Trade."

appears to have opened on 42nd Street in 1925. In the mid-'50s it was managed by a husband-and-wife team, R. C. "Charlie" Lucas, a former Ringling Brothers fire-eater popularly known as "Woo-Foo," and Mary Wigfall (a.k.a. Mary Sahloo, "Princess Sahloo," and "Princess Wago") who performed as the "Voodoo Jungle Snake Dancer." Lucas performed "Jump on a Bed of Nails" and the museum featured a crime exhibit highlighting John Dillinger, Baby Face Nelson, and Bonnie Parker. Among others performing at Hubert's during the mid-'50s were a sharpshooter, a sword swallower, a contortionist, a magician, a strongman, and a midget appearing as Patoachess, advertised by "Comedy, Songs, Dancer."[33]

The Times Square honky-tonk became a serious political issue in the 1953 mayoral election. In January, the Planning Commission held a hearing at City Hall to consider the district's rezoning. The Broadway Association, along with thirty other civic, real estate, business, and welfare organizations, backed a rezoning plan prepared by a private consulting firm, and a good-government group, Citizens Housing and Planning Council, supported it. However, the Council's Ira Robbins warned that Manhattan was fast becoming a two-tier city with "luxury apartments on the one hand and public housing on the other." He hoped the plan would check this trend. The private Real Estate Board raised opposition to the plan, calling for a new study with greater input from more groups. Nothing was resolved.[34]

A special mayoral-candidates debate over the rezoning of Times Square took place on October 19, 1953, just two weeks before the election. Organized by the Drama Desk of theater critics and reporters, the event was held at Rosoff's Restaurant at 43rd Street, east of Broadway. Three candidates participated and offered different positions. Republican Harold Riegelman advocated a "get-tough policy." "The age of the honky-tonk has gone a lot further than it should," he insisted. Yet, he offered a cautious proposal: "As leases expire, it should be possible to gradually to cut down on the midway type of establishment." The Democratic candidate, Robert Wagner, and the Liberal, Rudolph Halley, took more nuanced positions. Neither was a moralist. Halley said he was "not quite so worried about honky-tonks" and argued: "The fellow who wants to find amusement in a penny arcade is as much entitled to do so as any who wants to find his amusement in the drama." Wagner took a different tact, contending it was "rather dangerous to a have a zoning law affect one particular area." Getting to the heart of the matter, he reminded his audience, "I think the poor people have a right to entertainment, too."[35] Wagner won the election and a new, modified midtown-west rezoning plan was introduced.

Wagner was in office from 1954 to 1965 and focused city development with two landmark efforts. The first took place during the early days of his mayoralty and involved the far-east 42nd Street area, along the East River. The centerpiece of this campaign was the United Nations complex, the anchor point in an increasingly international order, which symbolized Gotham's position as the capital of the world. With the end to WWII, the international community of nations superseded the nation-state as two superpowers fought over their relative spheres-of-influence. Viewed from a Google Maps image, the UN is a seventeen-acre plot that runs from 42nd to 46th Streets along the East River.[36] The Rockefeller family donated the land and it was developed by real estate magnet William Zeckendorf. It was only a step or two on 42nd Street that brought one to Grand Central Terminal (which survives thanks to the efforts of Jackie Kennedy Onassis) and then to the Public Library (underwritten by nineteenth-century aristocrats) and Bryant Park (originally a potter's field, then a reservoir). There development stopped.

Mayor Wagner and other city power brokers saw Times Square as a dead zone, corrupting city renewal. For them, it was, in author Marc Eliot's words, "a moral leper colony."[37] The city had limited resources and, for the time being, could do little about the fate of midtown-west. At best, the city used the '54 zoning plan to shut down numerous bars that allegedly facilitated prostitution. Underdevelopment sustained an underground culture and, with it, underworld operations. During the '50s, Times Square stagnated.

In the '60s, Wagner took up the Times Square challenge, but made the centerpiece of the campaign the Lincoln Center complex in the West 60s. Again, the Rockefeller fortune stepped in to underwrite urban renewal. Today, Times Square is back. It's been redeveloped, cleaned up, once again the Crossroads of the World. It's clean, safe, and with few of the street-level deviant temptations that marked its past for so long.

The Midway

"Suddenly I found myself on Times Square," writes Jack Kerouac in his 1957 classic, *On the Road*. "I had traveled eight thousand miles around the American continent and I was back on Times Square; and right in the middle of a rush hour, too, seeing with my innocent road-eyes the absolute madness and fantastic hoorair of New York with its millions and millions hustling forever for a buck among themselves, the mad dream—grabbing, taking, giving, sighing, dying, just so they could be buried in those awful cemetery cities beyond Long Island City."[38] Kerouac knew New York.

Times Square runs from West 40th to 47th Streets on Broadway and Seventh Avenue; the avenues intersect at 45th Street, the Crossroads of the World. "The Deuce" was the few blocks on West 42nd Street between Sixth and Eighth Avenues, known as the Crossroads of the Girls, the locus of Gotham's illicit sin scene.[39] Today, Times Square has been cleaned up and the Deuce is the name of a luxury condo, designed by Brian Boyle, at 534 West 42nd Street; consisting only of seven units, prices start at $1.7 million and run to $4.5 million for the penthouse duplex.[40]

During the postwar decade, the Beat poets were regular habitués of Times Square and the Deuce. Kerouac, Ginsburg, William Burroughs, and Huncke, the self-proclaimed "Junkie King of Times Square," called it a second home. They visited the Angle Bar at 42nd Street and Eighth Avenue that was, in Huncke's words, "where pimps and drug dealers and small-time crooks hung out." Kerouac liked the Playland arcade at 246 West 42nd Street, especially its Pokerino pinball game.[41] Much of their time was spent at Bickford's Cafeteria at 225 West 42nd Street. "Not only did they have very good food, excellent food and very cheap, but also they were all meeting places, drug meeting places," Burroughs recalled. "The 42nd Street Bickford's was a notorious hang-out for thieves and pimps and whores and fags and dope pushers and buyers and everything."[42] In '56, Ginsberg, who once worked as a dishwasher and floor sweeper at the eatery, immortalized it in *Howl*:

> *who sank all night in submarine light of Bickford's floated out and sat through the stale beer afternoon in desolate Fugazzi's, listening to the crack of doom on the hydrogen jukebox . . .*[*43]

Prohibition turned midtown west into the wet zone, home to many of the city's most popular and fashionable speakeasies. Clustered from 45th to 56th Streets and from Madison Avenue west through Broadway to Eighth Avenue, speaks welcomed anyone with money in his/her pocket, a yen to imbibe, and a willingness to break the law. In this urban bazaar, one could stroll into almost any building and purchase liquor, but for a good time one went to a quality speak.

Wet-zone clubs included popular cabarets run by the legendary Texas Guinan and other celebrities as well as dance clubs like Roseland, featuring Louis Armstrong, and the Kentucky Club, where Duke Ellington got his start. The wet zone was also home to drinking clubs like the Pen and Pencil and Artists and Writers. Still other popular speaks that dotted the area included, on 49th Street, the Chesterfield Inn and Tony Soma's; on 52nd Street, the Biarritz, Furnace Club, and the Onyx; on 53rd Street, the Don Juan and the Park View Club; on 54th Street and Broadway, the Hotsy Totsy Club; on 55th Street, The Tree Club; and on 56th Street, the Long Cabin, Back Stage Club, Merry-Go-Round and Hi Hat. In the wake of the stock market crash and the Depression, many of these speaks closed.

In the '40s, the nation was at war and New York welcomed freewheeling servicemen with money in their pockets and a desire in their pants. Times Square was the locus of their attention, attracting an enormous number of single men, many just passing through on

---

* Fugazzi's was a bar located at 305 Sixth Avenue in the Village.

their way overseas to an uncertain fate. It was a general entertainment area where mingled servicemen, visitors, young people on dates, gamblers, con men, street preachers, taxi dancers, barflies, hookers, panhandlers, grind house moviegoers, and whoever else.

After the war, the Times Square scene deteriorated, dragging down the legendary West 52nd jazz scene, which had migrated to that area in the wake of the '29 crash, the deepening Depression, and the '35 Harlem race riot. Numerous celebrated 52nd Street clubs closed. The Spotlight, at 56 West, home to Charlie "Bird" Parker, Jay McShann and J. J. Johnson, shuttered its doors in '46. Dixon's, at 131 West, initially hopping with Joe Mooney's Quartet, had been, by the fall of '47, replaced by Club Troubadour. Even the legendary Downbeat, at 66 West, which had hosted John Birks "Dizzy" Gillespie, Coleman Hawkins, and Billie Holiday, went under in '48. Other short-lived joints included the Keyboard and La Zambra at 127 West.

Arthur ("Artie") Jarwood was a leading 52nd Street jazz promoter. He had a financial interest in or ran a number of the most popular clubs on the Street, including the Onyx, the Three Deuces, and the Famous Door at 56 West (1947–1950); he also was involved in lesser-known venues like the Pick-A-Rib and the Riobama. Looking back on Times Square's in the '50s, Jarwood lamented, "You know here was once the Gay White Way. That was when Broadway was the big attraction in New York City." Gong further, he reminds people, "but in this period, Broadway didn't mean a thing. It was 52nd Street that was known throughout the world." He observed, "So the Street combined music, burlesque, and good, raucous entertainment."[45] One club, Jimmy Ryan's, celebrated jazz for more than five decades, from 1934 to '62, at 53 West 52nd Street; then from '62 to '83 at 154 West 54th Street.

On December 31, 1945, La Guardia, the "little flower," ended his twelve-year tenure as mayor. He was followed by a series of forgettable mayors: William O'Dwyer (1946–1950), Vincent Impellitteri (1950–1953) and the aforementioned Robert Wagner (1954–1965). While east-side development was promoted, midtown west rotted. Local business interests complained, but the city essentially allowed the Times Square area to become a postwar "red-light" district.* No serious effort was undertaken to reverse the economic stagnation that marked the area. In this void, a new generation of burlesque and strip joints took root.

Not unlike the Village and uptown near Columbia, midtown was one of the few areas in the city that welcomed a diverse range of people, especially during the afterhours. According to Jarwood, 52nd Street drew "*aficionados* [who] were knowledgeable, sophisticated, generally well-fixed people who came for the music." Equally important, it "was the only street in the world where you could walk alone and never be lonely." Jarwood reflected, "it was like one big party. Where else could black and whites get to know each other, work together, and form lifelong friendships. There was no other place at the time."[46]

Glory Days

The modern, twentieth-century era of popular entertainment began on March 3, 1915, when D. W. Griffin's movie *Birth of a Nation* premiered in Times Square. It opened at the Liberty Theater located at 236 West 42nd Street, between Seventh and Eighth Avenues. The *New York Times* reported, "Eight months were taken in making the picture, which is said to be of the most elaborate ever produced. There are 18,000 people and 3,000 horses in its many scenes."[47] The movie's producers took advantage of all the tricks in the promotional arsenal to build audience acceptance—and it worked. Their campaign featured larger-than-life Klan nightriders pictured on Times Square billboards and horsemen dressed in Klan regalia riding

---

* During the late nineteenth century, cities throughout the country attempted to regulate commercial sex, restricting it to designated "red-light districts." Between 1898 and 1917, New Orleans's Storyville was a regulated zone of legal prostitution, drinking, and gambling. In Denver, it was Market Street; in Baltimore, it was the Block; in Chicago, the Levee; and in New York the red-light districts were in the Bowery, Five Points, and Tenderloin; see Ruth Rosen, *Lost Sisterhood*, p. 70.

through midtown streets. They even chartered special trains from New Jersey and Connecticut to bring white movie patrons to the city. Not mentioned by the *Times*, the NAACP held daily picket lines in front of the theater.[48]

During the '20s, Broadway was a locus of controversy, sometimes ending in police raids, forced closings, and the arrest of performers. Issues ranging from abstinence and sex to race relations were addressed in dramatic plays and song-and-dance shows. These live performances provoked intense civic debate over what were American values. Theater joined literature, music, and the movies in an all-out artistic—if subversive—questioning of America's dominant moral standards. Collectively, they successfully challenged the nation's moral order. The Broadway stage was an important venue in which abstinence was fiercely debated, often making drinking fashionable. Theatre historian Larry Clark reports that, between 1920 and 1933, fifty-eight plays and musicals were performed on Broadway that dealt with illegal alcohol consumption, bootleggers, or speakeasies. The 1926 musical *Oh, Kay!*, with music by George Gershwin, lyrics by Ira Gershwin, and a book by Guy Bolton and P. G. Wodehouse, set the era's tone with its telling comic punch line: "The difference between a bootlegger and a Federal Inspector is that one of them wears a badge."

Eugene O'Neill's play, *All God's Chillun' Got Wings*, is an uncompromising critique of the "miscegenation" taboo—sex across the color line.* It opened at the Village's Provincetown Playhouse on May 24, 1924, and is one of the most controversial plays of the first

---

* The term "miscegenation" was coined in 1863—at the height of the Civil War—by David Cole and George Wakeman, two New York "copperheads," Northern supporters of the South. It is derived from the Latin "miscere," to mix, and "genus," race, and was intended to be a scientific-sounding term to demonize race mixing and replace the notion of "amalgamation." Amalgamation had long been used in America and came from European usage, referring to the mixing or blending of two or more distinct ethnic or racial groups through intermarriage or nonsexual cultural exchange; see Leslie M. Harris, "From Abolitionist Amalgamators to 'Rulers of Five Points,'" p. 191.

† For more on Robeson, see "Warrior."

half of the twentieth century. It explores the consequences of slavery and the reconfiguration of Northern urban life that accompanied the vast black migration to the North. It presents a white woman who not only loves and marries a black man, but has sex with him to their mutual happiness and pleasure. Most stunning for the era, on a live stage, the wife kisses her husband's hand. Paul Robeson and Mary Blair were the lead actors.† O'Neill received death threats from the Ku Klux Klan and Mayor John Hylan ordered an investigation into the play's morality and refused to allow children to perform in it. Other plays of the era that dealt with controversial, highly politicized issues included Pierre Frondaie and George Hazelton's *Aphrodite* (1919–1920), O'Neill's *Desire Under the Elms* (1924), and Edouard Bourdet's *The Captive* (1924–1926) that dealt with, respectively, infanticide, interracial sex, and lesbianism.

"The Depression forced the American theatre into a decline, and the 42nd Street theatres suffered particularly," writes Ken Bloom in his invaluable resource, *Broadway: An Encyclopedic Guide to the History, People and Place of Times Square*.[49] The 1929–30 season saw 233 productions open; the 1930–31 season had only 187 productions; by 1939, productions had shrunk to only 139. According to one estimate, 25,000 theater hands lost their jobs. Ticket prices were squeezed, with some musicals dropping prices to twenty-five cents, with a top price of $1.00.[50] Theater managers had a choice: close down and leave the theater dark or come up with a low-cost entertainment alternative and keep the lights on. Investment dollars dried up; ticket sales dropped; producers offered noncontroversial works. The Palace Theatre (1564 Broadway) was Broadway's last vaudeville stage, closing in 1932. In its last years, it showcased popular works like the Gershwin's *Strike Up the Band* (1930), a political satire that ran for 191 performances, and *Girl Crazy* (1930), a love story about a New York playboy and a Wild-West cowgirl; it ran for 272 performances.

Sometimes adversity engenders innovation. Amid the Depression, some of the most original works of the American stage were premiered. For example, in January '33, Elmer Rice's *We the People* opened and ran for fifty performances; in April '33, *The Threepenny*

Opera by Bertolt Brecht and Kurt Weill premiered and ran for only twelve performances; and in '34, *Four Saints in Three Acts*, an opera by Gertrude Stein and Virgil Thomson, opened and ran for eighteen performances.[51] However, in October '35, with the Depression at its nadir, George and Ira Gershwin introduced *Porgy and Bess*, a uniquely American opera at the Alvin (250 West 52nd Street); today, it's the Neil Simon Theatre. The Gershwins, working with black writer DuBose Heyward, combined classical, popular, and gospel musical styles to tell the love story of a poor black couple living in Charleston's dockside tenements. It ran for 124 performances and remains America's finest opera.[52]

During the Depression, Gotham, like cities around the country, sprouted "Hoovervilles," homeless encampments. A dozen or so operated throughout the city. Central Park hosted "Hoover Valley," "Shanty Town," "Squatters Village," "Forgotten Men's Gulch," and "Rockside Inn." Other Manhattan encampments included "Camp Thomas Paine" in Riverside Park and the West 70s and "Hardlucksville," the city's largest squatter zone, at 10th Street at the East River. Bryant Park, only a few blocks east of Times Square, was its own Hooverville.

The Big Apple was the nucleus of the war effort, with an endless stream of war materiel and more than three million (mostly male) military personnel passing through its harbor. An estimated one million New Yorkers took war-related jobs and the city served as the center of news and public affairs media. The upturn in the city's financial wellbeing, particularly all those passing through town with money in their pocket, fueled a rejuvenated nightlife. The increased popularity of nightclubs, movie, and legitimate theaters, dance halls, and restaurants served a high-turnover crowd. As Gotham's legendary mistress, Polly Adler, observed, "the streets swarmed with 'V-Girls,'" and she wondered, rhetorically, "whether the V stood for victory or venereal?"[53]

The erosion of Broadway legitimate theater scene continued through the war-weary '40s and dragged on into the '50s. Two remarkable plays premiered during the '50s that captured the period's changing ethos, Michael Todd's *Peep Show* and Lorraine

Hansberry's *A Raisin in the Sun*. *Peep Show* opened on June 28, 1950, at the Winter Garden Theatre (1634 Broadway at 50th Street) and ran for 278 performances, with a cast of now all-but-forgotten song-and-dance actors; *Raisin* opened on March 11, 1959, at the Ethel Barrymore Theatre (243 West 47th Street), starring Sidney Poitier and Ruby Dee; it ran for 530 performances. *Times* theatre critic Brooks Atkinson took a dim view of *Peep Show*. "Mr. Todd, never noticeable for reticence, throws sex at the customers like a schoolboy who has run away from home and just discovered sin in the big city," he groused. He disparaged the work, calling it "an old-fashioned girlie-girlie carnival" and "pure corn." More pointedly, he lamented, "Mr. Todd has exuberantly thrown in all old hokum—the grinds, bumps and strip-tease which to use to put the license commissioner on his mettle." Criticizing Todd's stagecraft, Atkinson concluded his review: "But the formula is an old one and gets stupefying before it is worked out. Maybe sex has blown out."[54] *Raisin* appeared on Broadway five years after the Supreme Court's landmark *Brown v. Board of Education* (1954) decision. The *Times'* Atkinson found it "a Negro *The Cherry Orchard*" and praised Sidney Poitier's performance.

On May 14, 1960, the *New York Times* ran an in-depth investigative report on the crisis enveloping West 42nd Street, "Life on W. 42nd Street: A Study in Decay," by Milton Bracker. It detailed the causes for the "deterioration of the midway of Manhattan" and opined on the "unease" people felt visiting the area, especially the "hundreds of thousands of tourists" passing through the Crossroads of the World. It warned, "this uneasiness tends to grow as plans for the 1964 World's Fair progress."[55]

The *Times* story identified five factors contributing to 42nd Street's erosion—"grind joints," homosexuals, loiterers, cheap shops, and prostitutes. The reporter is remarkably insightful, giving voice to the appeal that the street's "decay" had for likely non-*Times* readers, the city's youth, low-life undesirables, and visitors passing through. While often sympathetic to those drawn to the Honky-Tonk area for its affordable good times, the reporter nevertheless blamed the victims for causing the troubles besetting the Square.

Bracker argued "the general atmosphere of the theatres breed crime." He noted that the ten grind houses in midtown had 10,104 seats and were open from 8:00 a.m. to 4:00 a.m. Most troubling, these theaters showed movies that "emphasize sex and violence" and "attract undesirables," and unescorted women did not feel safe. Grind houses were theaters mainly showing exploitation movies, including suggestive erotica, war sagas, and exciting sci-fi. They emerged in the 1920s, getting their name from former burlesque theaters featuring provocative "bump and grind" shows and were easily adapted to the new film medium. In the '50s, grind houses could be found across the nation, from Times Square to Seattle's First Avenue and New Orleans' Canal Street, and offered nonstop screening of "B" flicks, often featuring continuous double- or triple-feature programs running back to back.*

"Homosexuality is an obvious problem on Forty-second Street," observed Bracker. The reporter pointed out the while local clergy, merchants, business organizations, and the police warned that there had been a spike in homosexual activity over the preceding few years in the area, "police report no increase in arrests for homosexual offences for the same period." Arrests were made under what was known as the "D.C. 8" of the Penal Law (Section 722, sub-section 8) for one who "frequents or loiters about any public place soliciting men for the purpose of committing a crime against nature or other lewdness." The *Times'* reporter recognized "that even neighborhood 'experts' are not of one mind as to who is a homosexual." Going further, he points out, "In the beatnik era—and an era with relaxed standards of dress at many levels of the population—it is impossible to equate the way a man dresses with a behavior pattern that is against the law." He noted that while the number of homosexuals in the Times Square areas appeared to have increased, the number of "'flagrant' deviants—those who wear make-up, a feminine hair-do, and walk with a 'swish'—has decreased." He identified two "flagrant" males—"a Negro who wore fluffed hair and heavy black make-up on his brows and lashes" and "a white youth with thick blond hair and

---

* See "Obscene Image."

handsome features who wore make-up on his eyebrows . . . [and] spoke effeminately and shifted his hips and legs as he spoke." He observed that their respective friends, youths both black and white, male and female, accepted them for who they were.*

Loiterers posed a different problem. Bracker was particularly troubled: "Often these loiterers are noisy. Their eyes are not reassuring. They are apt to have bad complexions and matted heads of hair. They may mutter at passing women and occasionally they may walk a few steps alongside them." "But," he insisted, "their behavior can hardly be compared to an overt criminal act." Many youths hung out in what was known as "the hole," the below-ground arcades clustered in the 42nd Street subway stations at Seventh and Eighth Avenues. Youth from all backgrounds—white, black, Puerto Rican, and gay, mostly males but some females—seemed to have no problem easily mingling with one another. One twenty-two-year-old white youth admitted, "As long as nobody bodders me, I don't bodder them." The reporter noted that their aimlessness occasionally turned into violent outbreaks, but quickly dissolved. Showing genuine sympathy, he compared these "rootless young men" to the hero of Paddy Chayefsky's 1953 TV-drama, *Marty*, not to crime-prone gangsters. He added, most poignantly, "a terrible, corrosive loneliness characterizes hundreds of the drifters of Times Square."

"And then there is 'Fascination,'" Bracker declared, a shooting-gallery game "that fifty-four persons can play at one time. . . . It is like a constant barrage of anti-aircraft fire, faint and incessant." It was but one of the multitude of low-cost attractions welcoming visitors to the street. Other draws included pizza joints and shops selling everything from fruit drinks, to radios and sportswear, and to "stiletto-like cutlery." Books and semi-nude art could be easily acquired and some shops offered under-the-counter "obscene" materials that the police regularly confiscated. A stroller could even play chess and checkers. Merchants complained that the "honky tonk reputation of the street tends to attract more sightseers than customers."

---

* See "Lavender Peril."

Bracker revealed that street prostitutes were "usually over 35, repeaters who are well known to the police." "This ancient vice, in midtown surroundings," he reported, "traditionally depends on the cooperation of cheap hotels that ask no questions, save one usually whispered by the clerk to the woman while the client checks in 'Is he all right?'" The "Murphy Game" was an area specialty that regularly duped young servicemen. A street conman offered to escort an inexperienced "rube" to a prostitute located not far off 42nd Street. Along the way, he tells the serviceman to leave him the money before entering the hooker's building, so no one can get busted for solicitation. Bracker observed, "escort and cash vanish—and nobody comes to the door."

Bracker concluded his portrait of midtown's decay on a somber note. "The paradox of West Forty-second Street and the midtown half-mile of Eighth Avenue," he pointed out, "is that places that attract deviants and persons looking for trouble are interspersed with places of high standards of food, drink and service." "Yet," he lamented, "to a certain extent, the best Eighth Avenue bars suffer from the ugly repute of the worst." Going further, he argued: "The street is unsightly, raucous, offensive and, at times, dangerous." He warned, "Some sources feel that the process of deterioration, now in its third decade, has been arrested. But no one seems to know any way to reverse it."

Two weeks after the exposé appeared, on May 27, 1960, the city—in partnership with the New York World's Fair 1964–1965 Corporation—entered into a lease for Flushing Meadow Park, Queens, for the purpose of holding the fair. Four years later, on April 22, 1964, the fair opened and an estimated fifty million people attended. It celebrated American modernity, a break with the past. It looked forward and visitors were seduced by the world of tomorrow, a world driven by space-age technology symbolized by the computer. The fair's major underwriters were companies like Bell Telephone, Westinghouse, and International Business Machines, soon to become IBM. Little noticed, the '64 Fair took place against mounting social battles over the Vietnam War, civil rights, and counterculture values.[56]

On May 14, 1959, President Eisenhower headlined the ground-breaking ceremony that inaugurated the redevelopment of the west side, future site of Lincoln Center for the Performing Arts. The event drew an estimated 12,000 people and was broadcast nationally on radio and television. "Here will occur a true interchange of the fruits of national cultures," the president opined. "Here will develop a mighty influence for peace and understanding throughout the world. And the attainment through universal understanding of peace with justice is today, as always, the noblest and most shining ideal toward which man can strive and climb." Joining Ike at the dais were the center's chairman of the board, John D. Rockefeller III; New York State lieutenant governor Malcolm Wilson; Mayor Wagner; and Robert Moses, the tsar of the city's infrastructure modernization. After Ike's brief speech, Leonard Bernstein, the New York Philharmonic's conductor, led a choir from the Juilliard Music School and musicians from the Philharmonic in Handel's "Hallelujah Chorus." The *New York Times* dubbed it "an historic moment."[57]

Planning for Lincoln Center began in 1955 with the establishment of the Lincoln Square Urban Renewal Area Project. In May 1956, the city's Board of Estimate officially designated the Lincoln Square site as an urban renewal area. The plan covered a seventeen-block, fifty-three-acre area between 60th and 70th Streets and between Broadway and West End Avenue. In the 1950s, it was a poor and working-class neighborhood, popularly known as "Hell's Kitchen" for the Irish or "San Juan Hill" for the Puerto Rican; residents were nearly three-fourths (73 percent) white; 13 percent Puerto Ricans, and 4 percent African Americans. Its building stock included numerous small stores and warehouses as well as a variety of private residences, including tenements, rooming houses, row-houses, and middle-class apartment buildings. It was the locale for Bernstein's 1957 musical, *West Side Story*.

During the '50s and '60s, the postwar "white flight" to suburbia took its toll on Times Square. Samuel R. Delany's ode to midtown west, *Times Square Red, Times Square Blue*, acknowledged the role played by such areas in facilitating sexual deviance. "If every sexual encounter involves bringing someone back to your house, the general sexual activity in a city becomes anxiety-filled, class-bound, and choosy," he reflected. "This is precisely why public rest rooms, peep shows, sex movies, bars with grope rooms, and parks with enough greenery are necessary for a relaxed and friendly sexual atmosphere in a democratic metropolis."[58]

Over the following two decades, Times Square continued to flounder amid the city's changing fortunes and administrations. John Lindsey, mayor from 1965–1973, established the Office of Midtown Planning and Development to clean up the midtown west area, and targeted massage parlors, spas, single room occupancy hotels (SRO), peep shows, live burlesque shows, and adult book and video stores. Ed—"How'm I doin'?"—Koch was mayor from 1978 to 1989 and picked up the baton promoting the area's revitalization. In 1981, he proposed a redevelopment plan which, in 1984, the Board of Estimate approved. However, William Stern reports that during the mid-'80s, while he headed the Urban Development Corporation, "I would walk through Times Square at night, a state trooper by my side, and feel revulsion." He passed "prostitute-filled single-room-occupancy hotels and massage parlors, greasy spoons and pornographic bookstores; past X-rated movie houses and peep shows and a pathetic assortment of junkies and pushers and johns and hookers and pimps—the whole panorama of big-city low life."[59]

During the tenures of David Dinkins (1990–1993) and Rudolph Giuliani (1994–2001), Times Square began to turn around. In 1990, Viacom, Nickelodeon, and MTV moved into 1515 Broadway and, in 1992, Bertelsmann AG bought 1540 Broadway. In '93, Morgan Stanley acquired 1585 Broadway and the Walt Disney Company took over the New Amsterdam Theater. In 1995, a number of additional entertainment companies relocated to the Square, including AMC and Madame Tussaud's Wax Museum; Tishman announced its plan to open a major hotel; and the Durst Organization committed to a 1.5 million-square-foot office building.

According to Stern, Times Square's turn around was due to three interrelated factors—the adoption of a tough anti-crime campaign; rezoning to remove the flesh trade; and generous tax giveaways to "big businesses willing to locate in the area." First, the city's new get-tough policy led to 12 percent drop in the crime rate between 1984 and 1991. Second, the city took advantage of the Supreme Court's 1976 ruling, *Young v. American Mini Theatres*, which permitted cities to set zoning ordinance to regulated porn theaters (and other businesses); Giuliani pushed sweeping regulations restricting sex-oriented video stores, X-rated theaters, and topless bars in Times Square. Third, generous tax incentives worked. Tax abatements to George Klein's Park Tower Realty ($240 million), Morgan Stanley ($40 million), Disney ($25 million), and Ernst & Young ($20 million) paid off. According to Stern (and chastising his free-market critics), "The results show the power of supply-side tax cuts: more than $2.5 billion in private-sector investment," he noted.

Times Square is once again cleaned up, the riffraff removed and temptation integrated into the market economy. It's once again the Crossroads of the World. And all the vices that once so threatened moral order? The city has been eclipsed in terms of erotic excesses by San Francisco and Las Vegas, let alone Amsterdam, Berlin, London, and Rio de Janeiro. Where have all the New York outsiders gone?

SIN

COMIC BOOK CORRUPTION

BILL GAINES, 1922–1992

Batman Lives

On October 9, 2014, the US Postal Service dedicated the limited-edition forever Batman stamp. The USPS timed the stamp's introduction to coincide with the opening of New York Comic Con 2014, the US's biggest pop entertainment event. It was held at the Javits Convention Center and, according to ReedPop, the company that organized the event, 151,000 people bought tickets.[60] NYCC attendance outsells the Super Bowl.

Comics have been around for more than a century, starting off innocently enough as newspaper comic strips before spinning out as printed booklets—and now expressed in all analog and digital media formats. Comic Con started on March 21, 1970, as a one-day "mini-con," originally called San Diego's Golden State Comic-Minicon and held at the Grant Hotel in downtown San Diego. It drew about one hundred attendees. Like a contemporary crowdfunding campaign, the one-day event generated both interest among enthusiasts and enough underwriting to host a follow-up event five months later, on August 1–3, 1970. The three-day gathering, dubbed San Diego's

Golden State Comic Con, welcomed noted guests Ray Bradbury, Jack Kirby, and A. E. van Vogt.* Some three hundred people showed up, enjoying panels, film screenings, and a dealers' room.[61] That year, Archie was the most popular comic book in the United States, selling nearly a half-million copies a month. Simultaneously, an underground comics culture thrived.

Over the last four decades, Comic Con has quietly become the world's largest pop culture gathering and a global phenomenon. This year's San Diego Comic Con drew 130,000 attendees, hitting the convention center's maximum limit. In addition to New York and San Diego, Comic Con gatherings take place in Atlanta, Baltimore, Denver, Detroit, Phoenix, Salt Lake City, and other US cities. Comic Con has a strong international following, with gatherings in Stockholm, London, Paris, Moscow, and Bucharest. Comic Con is a testament to the globalization of the comic book phenomenon.[62]

Comic Con is a unique feature of the multibillion dollar industry of comic representations that range across all media formats, whether print, games, TV, online, mobile, movies, or fashion. Comichron and ICV2.com estimate, based on data from Diamond Comic Distributors, the 2013 comics market—trade paperbacks and magazines—was $870 million. Five out of the top ten grossing movies of 2013 were based on comic characters and together brought in $1.5 billion in box office sales.[63] And video games—many based on comic characters—generated an estimated $20.5 billion in revenue in 2013. Comic Com offers a social experience, one in which fantasy and reality play out simultaneously. In an age when everyone is, potentially, an independent contractor or an entrepreneur, creativity is coveted. No one knows where the next original idea—app, product, brand, or category—will come from. At Comic Con, one sometimes wonders whether the person next to you dressed as Batman could be the next Stan Lee or Steve Jobs.

A half century ago, this was not the case. In 1954, the Book-of-the-Month Club assailed *Batman*: "It is like a wish dream of two

---

* Ray Bradbury, author, *Fahrenheit 451*; Jack Kirby, comic book artist; A. E. van Vogt, author, *The World of Null-A*.

homosexuals living together." The media decried Superman, some wondering if he was not a fascist; Wonder Woman was condemned as "a morbid ideal . . . Her followers are the gay girls." And Catwoman was attacked because she was "vicious and uses a whip." Popular comics like *The Crypt of Terror* and *The Vault of Horror* were denounced as "sex horror serials" and "pulp paper nightmares" that created "ethical confusion."[64]

Congress acknowledged the crisis. In late 1953, the Senate established a special subcommittee to investigate juvenile delinquency. As part of its efforts, it held public and private hearings in Washington, DC, Boston, Denver, and Philadelphia that culminated in New York in April of 1954. Senator Estee Kefauver (D-TN), an ambitious politician, was a member of the subcommittee. In 1950, he gained national attention heading an influential Senate investigation of organized crime;[*] three years later he turned his attention to juvenile delinquency. He believed that "obscene" media came in all forms and contributed to the rise of youth crime. However, he singled out comic books, especially those labeled crime and horror, as promoters of violence.

"Marijuana of the Nursery"

In 1947, twenty-five-year-old William (Bill) Gaines took over the management of Educational Comics (EC), a small downtown publishing company. His appointment came following the death of his father, Max (M. C.) Gaines, in a boating accident on Lake Placid. It took place during a family vacation and the younger Gaines forever felt guilty about his father's death; he long believed that, had he gone on the family vacation that weekend, he would have been at the boat's helm and prevented the accident. EC's six-room office was located in Little Italy, at the end of a long hallway on the seventh floor of an old, ten-story Greek Revival building at 225 Lafayette Street, off Spring Street.

---

[*] See "Underworld."

The younger Gaines was little prepared for his new challenge. He had served three years in the Army Air Corp during the war and, as he recalled in a 1983 interview, "I was finishing up my work at NYU and I had planned to be a chemistry teacher and I had a year to go when this happened." Comics were his father's life, and he ran the company with a business manager, Sol Cohen. Younger Gaines wanted to make his own life. "I really had no interest in the business at all and didn't feel I could run it because I didn't feel I had any talent for business. . . . I wanted to close it up and be done with it." He discovered that the business was $100,000 in debt. "As I said to my mother, 'If he was losing money, what do you expect me to do?'"[65]

In photos of him at the time, Bill Gaines looks like a character out of an early episode of *Mad Men*, someone very much of the '50s, with short-cropped hair, horn-rimmed accountant's glasses, a serviceable gray suit, and a standard-issue white shirt and tie. He lived in Brooklyn, on Fort Hamilton Parkway, in a three-bedroom apartment with his mother. He was not a beat writer, a jazz musician, a transvestite, a porn star, or a mobster; he seems to have spent little free time among the postwar avant-garde. Nevertheless, he was a New York outsider; his sensibility helped fashion a distinct form of postmodern expression. The comics he published during a thirty-five-year career at EC, like *Crime SuspenStories* and *Mad*, helped remake America's cultural vocabulary. His creativity gave voice to a generation of mostly young people contesting accepted verities shared by government officials (i.e., local, state, and federal), moralists (e.g., preachers, pundits), teachers, and parents alike.[66] His early publications, along with those of other comic book pioneers, were subversive in word and image, in their narrative stories and graphic fantasy. Gaines's publications articulated a new American pornographic imagination.*

In 1889, Joseph Pulitzer, publisher of the *New York World*, introduced *The World's Funny Side*, a single-page, black-and-white humorous comic section in the paper's Sunday edition. The first strip was *Hogan's Alley*, developed by Richard F. Outcault, chronicling life in the city's slums; it featured the "Yellow Kid," the first comic

---

* See Susan Sontag's article, "The Pornographic Imagination."

character. Five years later, Pulitzer bought a color printing press and transformed mass media by introducing a color version of the comic strip. This innovation is comparable to the introduction of color to movies and to television, innovations that define twentieth-century media. It helped open up an older communication medium to a newer mass audience. In 1896, William Randolph Hearst joined the first comic wars, publishing the *American Humorist,* an eight-page color comic supplement in the Sunday *New York Journal.* His most popular strip was *The Katzenjammer Kids,* introduced in 1897, the creation of Rudolph Dirks.[67]

M. C. Gaines is credited with inventing, in 1933, the first four-color, saddle-stitched newsprint comic pamphlet. Working with his business associate Harry Wildenberg at a printing company, his earliest comic books were *Famous Funnies,* comic-strip compilations given away as free promotional offerings for products like Wheatena and Canada Dry.[68] Gaines took advantage of the new publishing format, establishing EC and introducing a series of comic book lines, including *Carnival of Comics* and *Picture Stories from the Bible,* his biggest seller.

The younger Gaines brought a different sensibility to the business, one with little experience but willing to take risks. Inheriting a company deeply in debt and a declining value of his library, he had a simple choice—innovate or die. Working closely with a young (and fellow Brooklyn) comic artist, Al Feldstein, they pushed the envelope. "I grew up on the horror pulps and the science-fiction pulps and *The Witch's Tale* on the radio and things like that and at that point they had things on television like *Suspense, Lights Out, Inner Sanctum,*" he recalled. They sought to leverage the creative cutting edge of popular media to an old medium, comics. They introduced *Tales from the Crypt* and *The Vault of Horror;* the original title, *The Crypt of Terror,* was changed to *Tales from the Crypt* because wholesalers objected to the word "terror." In January 1950, they rebranded their new effort "New Directions," introducing five titles; they maintained the horror line until 1954, finally succumbing to censorship.

Looking back in 1983, Gaines rememberd, "In the '50s I was an extreme liberal." He admitted, "I'm not against abortion, I'm not against pornography, I'm not against living together without getting married because I've been doing it with my dear young lady here for ten years, and the last thing in the world I would do is get married because I'm convinced that will wreck it." Gaines was a classic Brooklyn liberal who had backed President Roosevelt and fought in the war. He approached his masterwork, *Mad*, with a fine-tuned subversive sensibility. Introduced in October 1952, "We like to say that *Mad* has no politics and that we take no point of view, which is basically true." However, everything in American society—from the president and Senator Joe McCarthy to its latest fad, fashion, and celebrity—was fair game for critical exposure and mockery. *Mad* thrived as America unraveled; it was a 1950s version of Jon Stewart's *The Daily Show*.

It was a different story in 1947 when Gaines took over EC. He confronted not only a company in trouble, but a business assailed by moral reformers and politicians throughout the country. His father had launched the new publishing medium in '34 with *Famous Funnies* and the medium gradually grew. The next year, Malcolm Wheeler-Nicholson published *New Fun*, a sixty-four-page, four-color book with original comics. Many early comics featured classical literary characters like Robin Hood, Robinson Crusoe, and King Arthur. The Depression, however, Americanized comics, introducing an assortment of futuristic superheroes like Batman (1938), Superman (1939), Captain America (1941), and Wonder Woman (1941) to address the nation's ills.* During the war, comic characters took up arms in the nation's defense (even Wonder Woman served as a nurse and in the intelligence corp) and many comic books featured appeals for war bonds and stamps.

When the war ended, comics were a mass-market phenomenon. In 1945, the Market Research Company of America estimated that seventy million Americans (about half the nation's population) read

---

* Bill Finger and Bob Cane created Batman; Jerry Siegel and Joe Shuster created Superman; Joe Simon and Jack Kirby created Captain America; William Moulton Marston, a psychologist who invented an early lie detector, created Wonder Woman; see Hajdu, p. 30; Jill Lepore, "The Last Amazon," pp. 64–73.

comic books. The greatest percentage of these readers was young people between six and eleven years old; it reported that 95 percent of boys and 91 percent of girls read them. It also found that adults between eighteen to thirty were avid comic consumers; 41 percent of men and 28 percent of women reported regularly reading comics.[69] One study estimated that in 1946 nearly 540 million comics were published and, by the mid-'50s, monthly sales had skyrocketed to an estimated ninety million.

No one knew what would find an audience, so innovation was encouraged—and knockoffs were an accepted feature of the business. People from all ethnic backgrounds and walks of life, including precocious youths, African Americans, and even women, got their start working in comics, including such popular authors as Patricia Highsmith, Stanley Kauffmann, and Mickey Spillane.[70] The media "establishment"—consisting of "serious" writers, artists, and critics—looked down on comics, dismissing them as an unsophisticated kid's medium. Comics were part of an insurgent youth-oriented culture, a consumerism complemented by movies, music, fashion, and cigarette smoking. It was a subversive culture rooted in rebellion, challenging parental authority and sexual standards. It was a culture that threatened established order; juvenile delinquency represented stepping over the line. The battle over delinquency would remake the nation's moral order.

With success came scrutiny. Many Christians complained that newspaper comic strips were published in Sunday supplements, thus defiling the Lord's Day. In the '40s, critics characterized comics as immoral, corrupting America's youth. Sterling North was one of comics' earliest critics. In a May 1940 *Chicago Daily News* editorial, he complained that comics were "a poisonous growth" consisting of "graphic insanity" and "sadistic drivel." Eight years later, radio broadcaster John Mason Brown denounced comics as "marijuana of the nursery; the bane of the bassinet; the horror of the house; the curse of kids, and a threat to the future."[71]

The gravest voice raised against the alleged threat posed by comic books came from a prominent New York psychiatrist, Fredric Wertham. He was European educated and considered a progressive.

Earlier in his career he worked with Clarence Darrow as a pro bono psychiatric witness to defend African Americans in court cases. In '32, he was appointed senior psychiatrist to the city's Department of Hospitals for the Court of General Sessions. In 1936, he became director of Belleview Hospital's Mental Hygiene Clinic, and, in 1940, he moved to Queens Hospital Center as director of psychiatric services. Wertham was a sought-after expert on comics and juvenile delinquency who published extensively about the evils of comic books. Between the late '40s and the mid-'50s, he wrote for *Collier's, Saturday Review of Literature, This Week, National Parent Teacher Magazine, Ladies' Home Journal* and *Reader's Digest*, and other magazines. The capstone of his career came in '54 with the publication of *Seduction of the Innocent: The Influence of Comic Books on Today's Youth*. The National Education Association named it "the most important book of 1954" and it's journal proclaimed, "This book, if read by the great body of American citizens, would help to build the understanding essential to the growth and survival of our free democratic society."

Showdown

The Senate's hearings on juvenile delinquency and comics were held in New York on April 21, 1954, and continued the next day; they concluded concluded on June 4. The hearing on the twenty-first began at 10 a.m. in room 110 at the federal court house in Foley Square in lower Manhattan. Senator Robert C. Hendrickson (R-NJ) chaired the committee and, in his opening comments, wrapped himself in the flag. He declared: "We are not a subcommittee of blue nosed censors. We have no preconceived notions as to the possible need for new legislation." He spelled out the committee's mission: "We are examining the reason why more and more of our youngsters steal automobiles, turn to vandalism, commit holdups, or become narcotic addicts."[72]

Senator Kefauver made a short introductory comment, adding the FBI's authority to Hendrickson's remarks: "I think it is also important to point out that Mr. J. Edgar Hoover's report of yesterday shows that whereas the increase in population last year was 5 percent, crime had gone up 20 percent and the particularly large increase was in connection with burglary and stealing of automobiles." He concluded, "The interesting point is that a large part of the burglaries was committed by juveniles. Also juveniles, according to the FBI report, comprise 53.6 percent of those arrested for stealing automobiles."

The committee noted that crime and horror comics are "printed in gaudy colors an often grim and lurid scene contrived to intrigue prospoective [sic] purchasers into buying them." Its interim report estimated that in the spring of 1954 "over 30 million copies of crime and horror comic books were being pronted [sic] each month." It went on to argue: "If only 50 perscent [sic] of that number were sold by the retailers, the annual gross from crime and horror comic books had reached $18 million." These genres made up only about one-fifth of the comic book industry.

A number of exhibits were presented, but the one that drew Kefauver's great ire was entitled "Are You a Red Dupe?" a provocative comic flyer equating the censorship of comics with Soviet tyranny. He questioned who was its author and was informed it was Gaines, publisher of the EC Group. The flyer's opening sentence was especially provocative: "Here in America, we can still publish comic magazines, newspapers, slicks, books, and the Bible. We don't have to send them to a censor first. Not yet." It concluded, "The group most anxious to destroy comics are the Communists." Before the hearings opened, Gaines had provocatively sent a copy of the "Red Dupe" flyer to Hendrickson, serving only to antagonize the committee.[73]

The afternoon session drew the greatest fire. Wertham testified first and drew the committee's attention to three often-overlooked aspects of comics' narrative and visuals elements. First, comic book advertisements promoted unhealthy products, including rifles, knives, daggers, and even whips. Second, comics perpetuated racial stereotypes; heroes were nearly always white, while the villains were often portrayed as ethnic minorities whether foreign born, Asian, Italian, or of dark-skinned races. Third, he argued, "all comic books have a very bad effect on teaching the youngest children the proper reading technique, to learn to read from left to right." He asserted that this was due to the "balloon print pattern" used in comics. The most memorable point of Wertham's testimony came in an exchange with the committee chairman:

KEFAUVER:	Would you liken this situation you talk about, showing the same thing over and over again until they finally believed it, to what we heard about during the last war of Hitler's theory the story over and over again?
HENDRICKSON:	The "big lie" technique?
WERTHAM:	Well, I hate to say that, Senator, but I think Hitler was a beginner compared to the comic-book industry. They get the children much younger. They teach them race hatred at the age of 4 before they can read.

Yes, he insisted: "I think Hitler was a beginner compared to the comic-book industry." Following Wertham's testimony, the committee broke for lunch.

At 2:00 p.m., Gaines took the witness seat. He was alone among comic book publishers of horror and crime works to voluntarily appear before the committee. He began his testimony recalling his family's long involvement in the industry. "Two decades ago my late father [W. C. Gaines] was instrumental in starting the comic magazine industry. He edited the first few issues of the first modern comic magazine, *Famous Funnies*." He added, "My father was proud of the industry he helped found. He was bringing enjoyment to millions of people."

Gaines then took the proverbial bull by the horns: "I was the first publisher in these United States to publish horror comics. I am responsible, I started them." He then directly attacked Wertham. "It would be just as difficult to explain the harmless thrill of a horror story to a Dr. Wertham as it would be to explain the sublimity of love to a frigid old maid." He insisted, "Pleasure is what we sell, entertainment, reading enjoyment. Entertaining reading has never harmed anyone." He invoked Judge John M. Woolsey's 1934 decision lifting the ban on James Joyce's *Ulysses* to legitimize horror as a form of free speech.*

Following his opening remarks, committee members took up the battle with Gaines over horror comics. The chief counsel, Herbert Beaser, questioned Gaines, then Kefauver jumped in:

KEFAUVER: Here is your May issue. This seems to be a man with a bloody ax holding a woman's head up which has been severed from her body. Do you think that's in good taste?

GAINES: Yes sir, I do—for the cover of a horror comic. A cover in bad taste, for example, might be defined as holding her head a little higher so that blood could be seen dripping from it and moving the body a little further over so that the neck of the body could be seen to be bloody.

KEFAUVER: You've got blood coming out of her mouth.

GAINES: A little.

The afternoon's sessions ended with brief appearances by three creative industry representatives: Walt Kelly, creator of "Pogo"; Milton Caniff, creator of "Steve Canyon"; and Joseph Musial, educational director for the King Features Syndicate and educational director for the Cartoonist Society.[74]

It its final report, the subcommittee warned: "This country cannot afford the calculated risk involved in feeding its children, through comic books, a concentrated diet of crime, horror and violence. . . . Rather, the aim should be to eliminate all materials that potentially exert detrimental effects. To achieve this end, it will require continuing vigilance on the part of parents, publishers and citizens' groups."[75]

"I'll tell you the truth, I was so nervous when I was up there that I barely knew what I was doing," Gaines later admitted. "First of all, I'd been up all night writing my introductory speech, which I wrote with Lyle Stuart [EC's business manager]." He had been up every

---

* *U.S. v. One Book Entitled Ulysses by James Joyce* (1934).

night during the preceding week, dropping Dexedrine tablets and drinking coffee nonstop to keep going. "And when I got into the Senate Subcommittee hearings my Dexedrine wore off," he lamented. "A wet sponge, that's how I felt. And I didn't know what I was doing. I just wanted to get the hell out of there." The committee faced him like a "prosecuting attorney" and he felt shamed, guilty. "It was rough answering all these questions. Everybody looking at you like you're a freak and a criminal and so on and so forth."

In the wake of the hearings, Gaines saw the handwriting on the wall and quickly attempted to protect himself and his business. In September, he moved to establish the Comics Magazine Association of America (CMAA), an industry self-regulatory body. That same month, Gaines announced that EC would discontinue its horror and suspense comic lines. In October, the association released a new code of conduct that was far more restrictive than the earlier 1948 code and what Gaines wanted. The new code prohibited comics from discussing crime, sex, and violence as well as prohibiting the use of such words as "horror" and "terror" in titles. Even traditional romance stories had to adhere to a new moral sensibility by "emphasiz[ing] the value of the home and the sanctity of marriage." Gaines refused to go along with the association and rejected the code. One consequence was that the number of new comic titles released fell by nearly two-thirds in two years, to 250 in 1956 from 650 in '54.[76]

Book Burning

Some Americans have long been frightened of words and images, whether considered blasphemous (i.e., sacrilegious), pornographic (i.e., sexually suggestive) or subversive (i.e., a threat to government). On October 17, 1650, the General Court of the Massachusetts Bay Colony condemned a 158-page theological book, *Meritorious Price of Our Redemption*, by William Pynchon, a merchant and founder of Springfield, Massachusetts, because it questioned the Puritan doctrine of atonement. The book was banned from the colonies and all copies publicly burned in the Boston marketplace.[77]

Three centuries later, two issues galvanized the call for censorship of horror and crime comics—the popularity of comic books and the rise of juvenile delinquency. Concern about youth crime began to surface during the war in light of an apparent decline in parental supervision as men went to war and women went to work. In June 1943, FBI director Hoover warned in a *Los Angeles Times* editorial of "Youth . . . Running Wild," and that "a creeping rot of disintegration is eating into our nation. . . . The arrest of 'teen-age' boys and girls, all over the country are staggering."[78] Later that year, Senator Claude Pepper (D-FL) chaired a hearing on the war's impact on civilian life spotlighting the role of comics.

Hoover's lamentation came in the wake of the long-simmering "zoot suit" wars. Cab Calloway, the legendary bandleader, defined the outfit as, "The ultimate in clothes. The only totally and truly American civilian suit." It was a distinct look: a narrow, knee-length dress-coat cut with wide shoulders; billowing, navel-high pants pegged at the ankle and held up by suspenders; a short tie accompanying a button up shirt; flashy shoes; and often either a fedora or a *tando* hat sporting a feather. And it was hot.

In Los Angeles, cultural differences between ethnic groups fueled mounting tension. In '41, clashes between Mexican American zoot suiters and white servicemen, many from the South, broke out in movie theaters, dance halls, and other venues. In the summer of 1942, the federal War Production Board effectively banned the zoot suit, claiming it used too much material. However, minority youth and workers ignored the ban, many proudly sporting their zoot. Things came to a boil in June '43 when the "zoot suit riot" erupted. Over five days, white soldiers and sailors attacked zoot-suit-wearing Mexican Americans—called *pachucos*—and more than 110 civilians and servicemen were injured. *Time* reported that, "The police practice was to accompany the caravans of soldiers and sailors in police cars, watch the beatings and jail the victims." Suppressed in Los Angeles, riots spread to other towns in California and Arizona.[79]

Concern over youth crime mounted during the postwar decade. Warnings came from traditional organizations like the Fraternal Order of Police, the American Bar Association, and the Daughters of the American Revolution as well as from a growing number of academics. Psychologists Eleanor and Sheldon Glueck were among the most influential, arguing in their highly regarded studies, *Unraveling Juvenile Delinquency* (1950) and *Delinquents in the Making* (1952), that family structure significantly determined delinquency. For all their analysis, the Gluecks offered Americans a simple answer to a complex problem: troubled families breed psychologically maladjusted kids and foster juvenile delinquency. "[T]he delinquents, as a group," they warned, "were excessively the victims not only of unstable households but out and out broken homes . . . the lawbreakers, far more than the nondelinquents, grew up in a family atmosphere not conducive to the development of emotionally well-integrated, happy youngsters, conditioned to obey legitimate authority."[80]

Between 1941 and 1957, the FBI found in its 1959 Uniform Crime Reports that juvenile court cases increased 220 percent. The Senate also found that juvenile delinquency was on the increase throughout the country. While predominately an urban phenomenon, it reported that in 1957 youth crime saw a 7 percent increase in the suburbs and a 15 percent increase in rural areas. Hoover joined the chorus of those exhorting their fellow Americans to "stop mollycoddling juvenile criminals. It is against the instincts of most Americans to get tough with children." He added, "But the time has come when we must impose sterner penalties and restrictions on young lawbreakers for the protection of the law abiding."[81]

Words can lead to action. In the late '40s thru mid-'50s, comics were subject to repeated waves of censorship campaigns that took place at both the city and state level. Just in the period of 1947 to '49, more than one hundred cities across the country, big and small, passed laws or ordinances to ban the display or sale of comic books. These campaigns took place in Chicago, Detroit, and Los Angeles, and in Baltimore, Cleveland, Hartford, Indianapolis, Milwaukee, New Orleans, and Sacramento as well as Ann Arbor, Michigan, Coral Gables, Florida, Falls Church, Virginia, Hillsdale, Michigan, Mt. Prospect, Illinois, and Nashua, New Hampshire.[82] The anti-comics climate heated up in '54 and '55 with more than a dozen states either considering or enacting legislature to regulate or suppress comic books. Among those states were California, Connecticut, Illinois, Maryland, Montana, Nevada, New Jersey, North Carolina, Ohio, Oklahoma, Oregon, Texas, Virginia, and Washington.[83]

Efforts to censor comics were probably the most contentious in New York State because a good number of the publishers operated out of Gotham. In 1948, the US Supreme Court, in *Winters v. New York*, struck down as unconstitutional a state law prohibiting the publication and/or distribution of material "principally made up of criminal news, police reports, or accounts of criminal deeds, or pictures, or stories of deeds of bloodshed, lust or crime."[84] However, in '49, state assemblyman James Fitzpatrick organized the Joint Legislative Committee to Study the Publication of Comics to fashion legislature to circumvent the court's ruling. Part of his effort involved surveying state judges and district attorneys. In '54, the state legislature held hearings on juvenile delinquency, with Wertham as the star witness. The state assembly and Senate passed a number of bills to restrict comics but Governor Thomas Dewey vetoed them on constitutional grounds. However, in '55, the new governor, Averill Harriman, approved what was dubbed the "Fitzpatrick Act," restricting comics.[85]

The call to censor comics during the late '40s and '50s was fueled by isolated—but recurring—incidents of juvenile delinquency involving either retail theft, car robberies, murder, or suicide. Wertham, among others, repeatedly linked comics to crime. One incident galvanized New Yorkers. In August 1954, four white, Jewish Brooklyn youths—Jerome Lieberman, Melvin Mittman, Jack Koslow, and Robert Trachtenberg—were arrested for murdering Willard Mentor, a thirty-four-year-old black man who worked at a local burlap bag factory. At trial, it was alleged that the foursome had earlier killed another man. Equally titillating, the youths were accused of attacking neighborhood girls walking in local parks, whipping them with a bullwhip that was ordered from a comic book classified ad. Koslow admitted that he was a regular comic book reader, inspired by the series *Nights of Horror*.

Wertham, although asked to serve as an expert witness to determine the youths' sanity, never testified. The media branded the teens the "Brooklyn Thrill Killers" and they became the poster boys of juvenile delinquency.[86*]

Ray Bradbury published his sci-fi classic *Fahrenheit 451* in 1953. The title signifies the temperature at which book paper burns. It's a dystopian novel about futuristic "firemen" who censor threatening texts by burning them and the small, isolated communities of people committed to keeping the written word—as a memorized, spoken text—alive. Bradbury wrote his classic tale during a period in which a dozen or so communities around the country burned comic books. In 1945, students of Saints Peter and Paul School, in Wisconsin Rapids, Wisconsin, a town of 11,000 located about a hundred miles north of Madison, participated in a school-sponsored comic book collection drive. They piled up more than 1,500 comic books and set them ablaze. In '48, book burnings took place in West Virginia, Illinois, and New York. In October, students at the Spencer Graded School, in the small town of Spencer, West Virginia, encouraged by parents, teachers and religious leaders, collected a six-foot pile of comic books and set them on fire in the school yard. With an irony lost on no one, a Superman comic was first ignited and then used to set the pile afire. In December, students at St. Patrick's Parochial School in Binghamton, New York, collected and burned some two thousand comic books and pictorial magazines. The bonfire was staged in the school's courtyard and most students attended. Students also lead a boycott targeting local merchants who would not pledge to withdraw "objectionable and indecent literature, comic books and the like" from their newsstands. Also in '48, comic book bonfires were staged at the St. Peter and Paul Parochial School in Auburn, New York, and at St. Cyril's Parish School in Chicago.[87]

In '49, comic book burnings took place in Rumson, New Jersey, and Cape Girardeau, Missouri. In Rumson, cub scouts conducted a two-day drive to collect objectionable comic books and burned them in the city's Victory Park; scouts who gathered the most books won the right to start the fire. At the last minute, school officials decided not to burn the books but rather dispose of them in the

---

* See "Sex Panic."

trash. In Cape Girardeau, Girl Scouts led the charge. They collected comics and brought them to St. Mary's, a local Catholic high school, where students held a mock trial as to whether comics were "leading young people astray and building up false conceptions in the minds of youth." The jury found the comics guilty and the students burned them.

Last Laugh

One can well imagine Bill Gaines roaring in his grave, gleeful over how he ultimately got his sweet revenge. The moralists who so persecuted him, most notably Kefauver and Wertham, have long been relegated to the dustbin of history. And the comic business that he spent more than three decades nurturing is today a multibillion-dollar international industry symbolized by Comic Con.

But in the wake of the '54 Senate hearing, Gaines's life was a mess. His decision to drop EC's crime and horror lines cut significantly into the company's revenues. He knew that the dictates of the new trade association, the CMAA, would prohibit him from pushing comic book aesthetics, its critical sensibility. In the wake of these challenges, he reinvented himself and the comic book medium.

The anchor of this reinvention was *Mad* magazine. Introduced in '52, it was billed as "Tales calculated to drive you MAD? Humor in a Jugular Vein." It initially adhered to the thirty-two-page comic book convention, offering four stories that parodied other EC comics and sold for ten cents. In '55 Gaines renamed it *Mad Magazine*, reconfigured it into a conventional black-and-white publication and offered it bimonthly at twenty-five cents. And, like EC comics, it did not depend on advertising.

Mad was radical not in an ideological or conventional leftist sense, but subversive in that nothing was above critical exposure and mockery. As Nathan Abrams noted, the magazine's "consistent inconsistency ran counter to the dynamics that formed the New York intellectual community, which were clearly aligned on ideological and political grounds." He argues, "Neither did Mad offer any affirmations or alternatives to the American way of life that it held in such contempt. Thus, in its failure to affirm or support anything, Mad possibly deserved the title of 'dissent' more than *Dissent* magazine itself." He found *Mad* more radical than contemporary "progressive" publications like *Commentary, Partisan Review*, and *The New Leader*.

Nothing escaped *Mad's* critical eye. Comic book characters were the easiest to ridicule. Disney's loveable Mickey Mouse was recast as a rat-faced vermin called "Mickey Rodent"; Superman became "Superduper Man?" a loser (National Periodicals, the owners of Superman, threatened a lawsuit); and the oh-so-innocent Archie and Jughead became, in "Starchie," chain-smoking juvenile delinquents. In '53, the Cincinnati Committee on the Evaluation of Comic Books found *Mad* objectionable and gave it a "C" rating. It also poked fun at political figures, most notably Senator McCarthy. In a 1954 piece entitled, "What's My Shine!" the comic linked the popular game show *What's My Line* to the Army-McCarthy hearings, punning one of McCarthy's closest aides, David Schine. The critic Dwight Macdonald understood the magazine's appeal: "Mad expresses the teenagers' cynicism about the world of mass media that their elders have created so full of hypocrisy and pretense governed by formulas." He went on, "But Mad itself has a formula. It speaks the same language, aesthetically and morally, as the media it satirizes; it is as tasteless as they are, and even more violent."[88] And it was popular.

In 1982, Gaines sold *Mad* to Time-Warner for—according to Al Fredman—$5 million and continued to have editorial control. Gaines was a tough boss, requiring graphic artists and writers to surrender their intellectual property rights to get published. This became EC policy in 1948 and, while newspaper comic strips adhered to the policy, EC was alone among major comic book publishers employing this business model. Gaines controlled all the rights. Perhaps Gaines's biggest laugh is knowledge that the director John Landis, of *The Blues Brothers, Trading Places*, and other popular movies, is developing a biopic based on him and the EC story, called *Ghoulishly Yours, William M Gaines*.[89] Gaines died in 1992.

OBSCENE IMAGE

IRVING KLAW, 1910–1966

Porn Goes Mainstream

Do you remember Anthony Weiner? He is the former Congress-man (D-NY) and 2013 New York City mayoral candidate who became sexting's first celebrity causality. On May 27, 2011, Weiner released a Twitter message to a twenty-one-year-old female college student with a link to a photo of his erect penis in revealing boxer shorts; within weeks he was forced to resign his Congressional seat. Undaunted, two years later, on July 23, 2013, Weiner, while running for mayor, was outed again, this time as "Carlos Danger," for send-ing sexting messages to other young women; he refused to quit the campaign and suffered a humiliating drubbing.[90] Today, Weiner has disappeared from the political stage.

It was only a few years ago when sexting was a national concern. Congressmen Weiner and Chris Lee (R-NY) were forced from office for exposing themselves in revealing sexts; states across the coun-try passed laws making it a crime; hundreds of kids were busted for doing it; and talking heads, along with religious leaders and other social worthies, bemoaned the fate of American youth. Sexting was scary, a threat to moral order.

Today, sexting has all but faded from public discourse. Sure, occasional teens are busted, but they capture far less media attention than just a few years ago. Why? What's happened to make the hottest media story all but disappear from the public spotlight? With rare exception, the popular media are driven by the crisis du jour, the latest body count report, terrorist attack, natural disaster, or political sex scandal. So, yesterday's news is *so* yesterday.

But sexting is more than yesterday's media story. It is the first original form of pornography to emerge in the twenty-first century, an original form of do-it-yourself (DIY) or user-generated-content (UGC) media—amateur porn. It began as a subversive art, with young people taking, sending, and receiving explicit nude, semi-nude, and provocative still images, video clips, and/or text messages of themselves and others via a smartphone or another mobile communication device. Estimates vary as to the number of teens engaging in sexting, with some studies putting the level at between 10 to 20 percent of American young people. Sexting may have disappeared from the media attention, but it has not disappeared from public life.[91]

Sexting is not child porn, nor sexual bullying; for the most part, sexting is not a form of sexual exploitation or violation. Rather, it is a postmodern aesthetic with roots reaching back to pre-modern forms of female erotic representation, from the original seventeeth-century "posture girl."* The teens engaging in sexting are but the tip of an increasingly popular social phenomenon.

Sexting has gone mainstream. Like adult pornography, it is being accepted as just one more of the "50 shades" of sexual titillation. The most revealing testimony to this development is a 2014 *Washington Post* piece, "A guide to safe sexting: How to send nude photos without ruining your life, career and reputation." Its warning is simple: "Repeat after me: If you can't prevent people from spreading your nudes, the next-best thing you can do is prevent them from ever

---

* Posture girls were celebrated erotic performance artists in England during the eighteenth and early nineteenth centuries; the most famous was Emily Lyon, later Lady Emma Hamilton; born Amy Lyon, she lived from 1765 to 1815; see Iwan Block, *The Sexual Extremities of the World*, p. 327; Randolph Trumbach, *Sex and the Gender Revolution*, pp. 107, 157–59.

knowing said nudes belong to you." The *Post* instructed readers to follow two essential rules for online posts. First: "Never include your face in the photo. Make the background nondescript. Cover or omit distinguishing features, like birthmarks and tattoos." Second: "Anonymize the photo file itself. All photos, even ones taken on a smartphone or tablet, are embedded with information about how, when and where the photo was taken. This is called EXIF data, and you want to strip it from any photos you may need to deny ownership of in the future."[92] One can only wonder how many inside-the-Beltway players saved the article. Sexting has become an all-American form of sexual self-expression.

Moral Order

May 31, 1955, was a mild day in New York with the temperature reaching a balmy 72 degrees. However, the temperature in the cavernous US courthouse in Lower Manhattan's Foley Square was much hotter. Senator Estes Kefauver (D-TN), an ambitious presidential candidate, was overseeing his latest Congressional hearings on the moral crisis of American youth. For this round of hearings, he subpoenaed a dozen publishers to testify on pornography's influence on the apparent rise in juvenile delinquency. He claimed that the interstate traffic in "lewd literature, cartoons, photographs, films, records, and other pornography" had an estimated value of $350 million. The hearings got front-page coverage in the nation's press and on radio programs and TV news shows; they were even telecast live at Times Square theaters. The *New York Times* proclaimed, "Smut Held Cause of Delinquency."[93]

The Senator was considered a liberal who would, in 1956, refuse to sign the "Southern Manifesto" opposing racial integration. Along with many likeminded citizens, he believed that obscene publications—including pinup photos, girlie magazines, pulp novels, comic books, and porn movies—represented a threat to America's moral order. He was especially concerned about the role of comic books in seducing America's virtuous youth, the nation's very future. In May

1954, he held hearings in New York on the threat posed by comic books, warning that they provided prepubescent male youths with a "short course in . . . rape, cannibalism, carnage, necrophilia, sex, sadism, masochism, and virtually every other form of crime, degeneracy, bestiality, and horror."*[94]

At this hearing, Kefauver singled out for special rebuke the photo and film producer and publisher Irving Klaw. Klaw ran one of the city's most successful movie-star photo shops, but the Senator believed that Klaw's customer list included the names of underage girls, thus possibly exposing them to pornography even though they likely sought movie-star photos. Wearing his customary white shirt, tie, and shabby suit, Klaw, replying to a subpoenae, "took the Fifth," refusing to provide income tax returns and financial records. When the hearing ended, he was not a happy man, worried what would happen to him, his family, and his business when the day's events were finally over. The hearings ruined Klaw.

Klaw originally opened a small, basement-level retail sales and mail-order fulfillment business in 1938 on East 14th Street. It sold secondhand books, movie-star photos, and erotic paraphernalia. It grew in popularity and, by the '50s, was offering a host of suggestive, cheesecake photographs, "3D color stereo slides" and short, semi-professional 8mm and 16mm movies or "loops," dubbed "stag" film. A 4"x5" black-and-white shot sold for forty cents each, or eight for $2.00.[95] One scholar described him as "perhaps the most prolific supplier of girlie photographs to both underground and legitimate magazines."[96]

Klaw's greatest discovery was the celebrated Bettie Page, often referred to as the "Queen of Bondage." Forgotten for decades, Mary Harron's 2005 biopic, *The Notorious Bettie Page,* put her back in the spotlight. Page reigned as one of America's foremost pinup girls of the mid-'50s, second only to Marilyn Monroe. Her images adorned tabloid magazines, record albums, and matchbooks; her likeness served as the model for innumerable figure-drawing books, automobile ads, and covers of pulp magazines. She was featured in seven *Playboy* centerfold spreads, including *Playboy*'s Playmate of the

---

* See "Comic Book Corruption."

Month—with a cover shot—for January 1955. It was Klaw's bondage, sadomasochism (S&M), spanking, and fetish photos of Page and other women that incited the underlying desires—perversions—that so offended Kefauver.

During the '50s, two criteria distinguished an obscene female representation—the display of full frontal nudity or pubic hair. Ever fearful of police harassment, seizure of his inventory, and costly legal battles, Klaw vigorously avoided shooting nudes. Burlesque star Tempest Storm revealed that Klaw required models to wear two pairs of panties lest any pubic hair peek through.[97] Klaw considered himself a businessman, not a pornographer; he saw the sexual images of women he shot as products meeting a market need. He was a family man, happily married to his wife, Natalie, and the father of two sons, Arthur and Jeffrey. He was also a lifelong business partner with his sister, Paula; her husband, Jack Kramer, ran the company's Jersey City, New Jersey, warehouse; in time, their son, Ira, worked for the family business and eventually took it over. There are no reports of Klaw "getting off"—engaging in sex with or being sexual aroused by—any of his numerous models.[98]

Richard Foster, author of *The Real Bettie Page*, argues that Klaw's initiation into fetish photography, many featuring Page, was driven by a desire to pose models "to meet specific customer demands." His images "ranged from girls dressed in bikinis to photos of girls with bare feet, or girls wrestling, getting spanked, and tying each other up." His photographs featured women—and occasionally transvestites—decked out in provocative outfits, including high-heel shoes, thigh-high boots, satin lingerie, leather costumes, and even ropes, chains, and whips. "For Irving Klaw," Foster insists, "no fetish was too weird as long as it didn't involve nudity, sexual acts, or physical harm to one of his models."[99]

Mechanical Pornography

Paintings, drawings, lithographs, sculpture, cards, and books long offered erotic representations. Walter Benjamin noted that engraving and lithography were the first mechanical means of image capture and display. However, they were techniques applied to natural substances like leather, wood, and stone. Benjamin recognized that the photography engendered the aesthetic sensibility of the modern age, extending image reproduction from the natural to "man-made" or manufactured substances, specifically chemical-based processes.[100] Photography introduced a new way of capturing and rendering an image as well as a new way of seeing, and thus a new category of art, and artist, the photographer. It fashioned the modern aesthetic sensibility that has shaped visual culture over the last two centuries.

Steven Lubar, former curator of engineering and industry at the Smithsonian Institution, speculates that "the first person to take a photograph was Joseph-Nicephore Niepce, in 1824." In 1832, Louis Daguerre announced his innovative process to the French Academy of Science and, in 1837 (after forming a partnership with Niepce), introduced an improved process using a copper plate coated with silver iodide.[101] This launched the age of analog media. Joseph Slade found that the first pornographic photograph was introduced in 1846, "depicting a rather solemn man inserting his penis into the vagina of an equally solemn middle-aged woman."[102]

Since its introduction, photography was subject to repeated waves of industrialization. Innovative formats were introduced, camera production was rationalized, costs rapidly declined, and a new visual sensibility was fashioned. In the early 1850s, new techniques sped up the photographic production process from several minutes to twenty seconds. The market for photographic images significantly expanded and the cost of a commercially produced daguerreotype photograph rapidly dropped from fifty to twelve and a half cents. Linda Williams found "[the] mid- to late-nineteenth century was a period in which a new porno-erotics of corporealized observation began."[103]

George Eastman introduced the relatively inexpensive Kodak camera in the 1888, taking advantage of the then breakthrough technology, nitro-cellulose roll film. Eastman significantly lowered the cost of the medium and fostered a new school of artists and amateurs with greater control over image production. The Kodak system democratized media communications and expanded the production of pornography. Williams reported, "it seems quite likely that a wider range of classes of both sexes had an opportunity to observe such [pornographic] images."[104]

Projected film emerged in the late nineteenth century and the first storefront movie theaters opened at the turn of the new century. One of the earliest picture shows at a Chicago penny arcade was *How Girls Undress*; it was displayed on a "mutascope" system and attracted many young boys.[105] Movie theaters at that time were one of the few acceptable social spaces in which white men and women, often unchaperoned strangers, could share an intimate proximity and an exciting visual experience; African Americans were barred from early New York movie houses. Other than the saloon, the dance hall, or church-sanctioned gathering, young men and women (excluding prostitutes) had few public venues in which to socialize let alone flirt, touch, or kiss. "The very darkness of the room," warned the social reformer Jane Addams in 1909, "is an added attraction to many young people, for whom the space is filled with the glamour of love making."[106]

The "vitascope" was a late-nineteenth-century advanced technology, one of the earliest moving-image projection systems. William Heise's classic vitascope film *The Kiss*, which runs sixteen to fifty-one seconds (depending on version), depicts a close-up of John Rice and May Irwin passionately kissing.[107] It was first shown, projected onto a large screen, at the Koster & Bials Music Hall in New York in 1896 and the performance excited many. The display of a larger-than-life sexual intimacy must have been thrilling, even overwhelming. Early movies must have felt like a cascade of images reinforcing the complexity, confusion, and rawness of modern urban life. A newspaper critic of the day exclaimed: "Magnified to gargantuan proportions, it is absolutely disgusting. . . . Such things call for police intervention."[108]

In 1923, Kodak targeted a new market for its moving-image equipment: the amateur filmmaker. They introduced comparatively lower cost 16mm film equipment. Early porn film producers adopted the new technology and used it to circumvent Comstock laws prohibiting "obscene" materials from the US mail. Amateur and semi-commercial pornographers screened stag films in non-commercial, semiprivate venues operating throughout the country, including as part of evening "smokers" or, as Williams calls them, "primitive genital shows."[109] Often smuggled into small towns by travelling salesmen, stags were shown at a variety of private venues where groups of men gathered, including Elk's clubs, college fraternities, bachelor parties, and military events.

Stags stimulated sexual anticipation by titillating hetero-erotic fantasy; women, who frequently attended, added to the fantasy foreplay. As Williams points out, the appeal of stags was based on a particular form of male bonding and sexual fantasy. "The stag film does not seem to want to 'satisfy,'" she argues. "Its role seems rather to arouse and then precisely not to satisfy a spectator," she adds, "who must subsequently seek satisfaction outside the purely visual terms of the film—whether in masturbation, in actual sexual relations, or by channeling sexual arousal into communal wisecracking or verbal ejaculation of the homosocial variety."[110] Stag films depicted a range of sexual performance that reinforced gender-based social conventions and power relations. Some of these flicks, as Slade notes, "depicted hard-core sex, usually intercourse, but also masturbation, penetration with objects and other activities involving genitals."[111] They drew upon fantasy and fetish role-play, including nudity and violence, sometimes enough to make actual sex unnecessary.

King of Pinups

Irving Klaw was born in Brooklyn on November 9, 1910, the son of subway conductor on the old Brooklyn BMT line. His parents were both divorcees and their combined family included six children, three boys and three girls. The Klaws lived a hardscrabble life and his father died when Irving was in high school. Remarkably, Klaw developed a special—and mutually shared—affection with his youngest, non-biological sibling, Paula. During the Depression, between 1933 and 1937, he worked as an apprentice in the fur trade and, in 1938, he opened a used bookstore in a basement-level store at 209 East 14th Street. Klaw gambled everything and both won and lost.

The Klaws, brother and sister, formed a life-long business partnership, an unlikely-looking couple of pornographers. In photos, Irving comes off as a short, balding, portly man who regularly dressed in a white shirt and tie. In '47, the *New York Times* described him as "a short, jovial, roly-poly man [who] looks like King Cole."[112] Paula was taller, thinner with lush, long brown hair often worn in a pompadour style; Foster describes her as a "slightly homely girl."[113]

The Klaws sold books, magazines, and entertainment memorabilia. Ever entrepreneurial, Klaw established Nutrix (i.e., new tricks), a company that sold magic tricks and novelties through the mail. According to legend, Klaw noticed a young girl ripping out a picture of Clark Gable from a photo magazine and decided to sell still pictures of movie stars. He soon added pinups of movie stars and erotic photographs, also offering them through a biannual mail-order catalog, *Cartoon and Model Parade*. As his business took off, he relocated to the street-level storefront, keeping the store open from 10:00 a.m. to 11:00 p.m. With further success, he moved to a large storefront across the street, at 212 East 14th Street. He initially renamed the business "Irving Klaw's Pin-Up Photos," but soon changed it to "Movie Star News"; he stopped selling used books. The store's window had a sign reading: "Pin-up photos of your favorite movie stars, latest movie scenes, bathing beauties, popular cowboy stars and vocalists, bandleaders."

Klaw was repeatedly profiled in the New York press as the pinup king. In 1944, the *New York Herald Tribune* ran a glowing report calling him "the world's busiest salesman of movie stills," with a library of two million stills and serving an estimated quarter-million customers. His biggest sellers were shots of Rudolph Valentino and Jean Harlow and his "best customers [were] GIs." In '47, the *Times* declared, "Klaw's establishment has magnetic hold on movie enthusiasts." It noted that his clientele ranged across dress designers, hair stylists, magazine illustrators, scholars, and "a number of top-bracketed, dignified business customers," including Wall Street bankers.[114]

According to Paula Klaw and John Coutts (a.k.a. John Willie, a noted '50s pornographer and publisher of *Bizarre*, a leading S&M and fetishist magazine) and acknowledged by Rick Klaw, Klaw's grandson, sometime around 1947 he "was approached by a prominent lawyer with some 'special needs.'" The lawyer, fondly named "Little John," was a wealthy man into S&M who offered Klaw a deal he couldn't refuse. The terms were simple: Klaw agreed to produce original bondage pictures while the unnamed lawyer would pay all associated costs, receive a copy, and Klaw would retain the rights. "The man who started us in this business," Paula Klaw later recalled, "ironically, died that very way because he himself got tied up by some model who used a cigarette on him and he died of burns." Klaw also worked with other special interest customers, including men looking for photos of models posing in black rubber outfits and in white underwear. They followed Little John's deal, paying for the model's time and film stock and giving Klaw the rights.[115]

Klaw's first "special needs" bondage star was Lili Dawn (a.k.a. Lili De Mar) who posed for Klaw and other freelance photographers in midtown studios. Dawn starred in *Violated*, a 1953 film produced by the porn distributor Eddie Mishkin.[116] By the late '40s, Klaw's S&M photo business was quite successful and, as it grew, he changed his business model. He opened his own porn production studio, Beautiful Productions, in a third-floor room above his East 14th Street shop and worked with freelance photographers like Jack Bradley.

Klaw worked with Page from 1952 to 1957.[117] Born in Nashville, Tennessee, in 1923, Page, a college graduate, moved first to Hollywood in the late '40s to pursue an acting career. She took a screen test at Twentieth Century Fox, but refused to acquiesce to the pay-to-play sex demanded of most actresses. She moved to New York and, in 1949, took classes at the HB Studio, cofounded by Herbert Berghof and Uta Hagen. To make money, a city cop recruited her to pose for amateur camera clubs. Her first recognition came at the Concord Camera Circle, located at 218 West 47th Street, and run by Cass Carr, a Jamaican-born former bandleader. Her presentation got favorable reviews by the Associated Photographers' Club, making her a popular model. She also posed before groups of male photographers at studios on Cedar Street, on West 47th Street, and at the Harlem YMCA on West 132nd Street. Sometimes she even posed for outdoor shoots in Westchester County.[118]

At these clubs, Page posed as a modern posture girl. A group of twelve to fifteen male photographers paid the club manager $4 or $5 for a photo session and Page made $10 per hour for indoor and $25 per hour for outdoor shoots. Other models included Cocoa Brown and June King, but Page was the most popular, explains her biographer, "because of her cheerful willingness to work nude and to strike almost any pose with a down-home smile." The photographers included a city policeman, businessmen, and students as well as the legendary urban chronicler Weegee, or Arthur Fellig. Weegee had an ongoing personal friendship with Page and they both lived in the Tenderloin; she on West 46th Street, he on West 47th Street. According to one story, Page was taking a bath while he was visiting when, in order to get just the right shot, the photographer, fully clothed, jumped into the bathtub; she kicked him out of her apartment.[119] Page worked with other girlie magazine publishers, including Robert Harrison who profiled her in *Beauty Parade*, *Wink*, and *Titter*. Bradley and other photographers produced the nude shots of Page, not Klaw.[120]

To take advantage of the growing popularity of his new art form, Klaw transformed his Nutrix magic tricks company into a S&M and bondage/disciple (B&D) publishing house. The *Nutrix* magazine, sometimes called *Mutrix* and even *Nutrix/Mutrix*, was notorious for displaying provocative, suggestively mid-twentieth-century "hardcore" scenes, featuring shots of women in elaborate leather and latex outfits. Klaw, however, drew the line on full nudity. He operated in the underground economy on a word-of-mouth basis. Female—or female-looking—performers were recruited through personal contacts; media production and reproduction took place under the radar; sales were discreet, a cash exchange, no questions asked. He welcomed strippers, burlesque performers, and models to pose, including Blaze Starr, Tempest Storm, and Baby Lake as well as Rose Erna, Lynn Lykles, Vickie L. Hayes, Francis Adams, and Joan Rydell, photographer Bradley's wife.[121] Klaw maintained a good working relationship with his models. "He was nice to them, but it was all business," reports Bradley. "After a shoot on a Saturday afternoon . . . he would take everybody who wanted to go up to a nice restaurant for dinner like the Press Box . . . and pick up the tab, but he never made any moves on anybody. He was all business."[122]

Baroness, a professional dominatrix, and Tana Louise, an S&M fetishist and wife of Leonard Burtman, the publisher of *Exotique*, a leading porn publication, were regular visitors to the Klaws' studio. Models often dressed in dominatrix gear emphasizing high heels, protruding braziers, garters, and black nylons. Many of Klaw's photos mimicked damsel-in-distress scenarios, featuring women in bondage scenes and dressed in revealing lingerie.

The Klaws—Irving and Paula—had a very close relationship, both personally and professionally. At the office, Irving did the production and marketing; Paula ran the business but did, at times, shoot both still and filmed works. Perhaps most important, she played a consoling role with many of the female models, thus ensuring their loyalty to her brother. Mary Harron, director of *The Notorious Bettie Page*, found that "when Paula talked about [the business], you always felt like they were selling Girl Scout cookies." Paula developed close relations with Page and other female models and even, on occasion, photographed them. Years later, she admitted in a *High Society* interview that she sometimes posed in a costume, filling in "here and there when a girl didn't show. I'd put on a little mask."[123]

Klaw had a not uncommon movie-making technique. "Irving Klaw had this loft and he was acquainted with an awful lot of strippers," recalled Lili St. Cyr, a popular performer. "His mode of operation was that he would take these separate segments—one with me, and one with Betty [Bettie] Page, and all these other girls—then he would splice these together until he had enough time, fifty minutes or whatever, and make what he would call a full picture." Klaw would then put together "a bunch of segments of ten or twelve different girls doing their various acts," she reported. "He'd piece them together in several different movies."

In a pathetic attempt to recall the grandeur of burlesque of the past, Klaw shot a number of movies of striptease performances

accompanied by comic sketches. Page was featured in the 1953 burlesque film *Striporama*, starring St. Cyr.[124] Two of Klaw's "classic"
stag movies—*Varietease* (1954) and *Teaserama* (1955)—also featured Page; St. Cyr appeared in *Varietease* and Tempest Storm in
Teaserama. Often overlooked, these two works of ostensible heterosexual imagery include as a featured performer Vicki Lynn, a
celebrated drag queen. In *Varietease*, Lynn appears in a red wig
and dress and performs a provocative dance. After the dance, he
pulls off his wig and, ever masculine, lights a cigar. Lynn raises the
stakes in *Teaserama*. He first appears in full drag only to perform a
provocative striptease that ended with him removing his wig and
the top of his costume revealing his flat chest. "The sight of a man in
a dress in the burlesque films is not, as one might expect given the
period, demeaning, nor is it comic in the same way as Milton Berle's
cross-dressing," notes historian Eric Schaefer.[125]*

Paying the Price

The federal government had long kept a watchful eye on Klaw as
a promoter of alleged obscene materials. During the early '40s, the
US Postal Service investigated him after receiving three complaints
about Movie Star News catalogs. It found the pinups he sold, including provocative shots of movie stars like Betty Grable and Rita Hayworth, "though questionable if not definitely obscene." However, in
1950 federal obscenity policies tightened. Reviewing his catalog,
Cartoon and Model Parade, it argued that Klaw "is too smart to deal
with or handle strictly obscene material . . . [the images] are performed by females and . . . Klaw has kept males out of the pictures so
as to cunningly avoid what many possibly appear to be obscene." The
head of the FBI's New York office issued an internal memorandum
to Hoover: "Irving Klaw Interstate Transport of Obscene Matter." It
stated, "Individuals who handle such material, however, are also frequently found to handle material of a definitely obscene nature."[126]

---

* On Berle, see "Identity Crisis."

The '55 hearings on juvenile delinquency and pornography were staged against the recent bondage death of Kenneth Grimm, a seventeen-year-old Coral Gables, Florida, Boy Scout. It received sensational media coverage, adding purpose to Kefauver's mission. A Kefauver associate quizzed Grimm's father, Clarence, who offered a heart-wrenching saga of suffering at the evils of pornography. Another witness, Dr. George Henry, a Cornell professor of clinical psychiatry, argued that there was a link between Klaw's sexually provocative depictions and the boy's death. Kefauver's associate noted, the boy "was found hanging in an inverted position from a stick or board suspended between the forks of two trees, and trussed up in a fashion whereby his legs and arms are tied behind him, and a rope is thrown around his neck so that he strangles himself. He strangles himself by the position in which he has been forced."

Offering no proof that the youth had ever seen a Klaw photo or movie, a commission associate referred specifically to two of Klaw's loops, *Chris Strips for Bed* and *Lounging Around in Lingerie*. The tenor of the hearing is captured in the questions posed by a committee staffer to Dr. Henry: "Doctor, I ask you is it your opinion, from perusing this article, from looking at the picture, would you say that this is the end result of a sex crime? Does this impress you as the type of thing that can happen as the result of bondage—this fetish we have been discussing this morning?" The good doctor answered in the affirmative. Sadly, no one asked whether the death could have been the result of autoerotic strangulation or asphyxiation.[127]

As vividly depicted in Harron's biopic, Page was subpoenaed but did not testify. All except Samuel Roth invoked their Fifth Amendment protection against self-incrimination. Failing to provide his financial records or answer direct questions, Klaw—along with William (Eddie) Miskin and Abraham Rubin—was held in contempt of Congress. His lawyer, Coleman Gangel, feared that the more he revealed about his business, the more charges Klaw would likely face. Committee aids claimed that his "smut" business netted between $550,000 and $1.5 million annually. Klaw was now dubbed the nation's "Smut King."

Ironically, because of Klaw's strict adherence to a non-nude photographic policy, the FBI found none of his photos obscene. Kefauver, however, invoked a higher moral standard and found Klaw's publications perverse. He charged that the works fell into "a twilight zone of obscene material . . . and deals particularly in fetishes, masochism, sadism, and other forms of perversion." Going further, he insisted that Klaw dealt "exclusively in fetish, bondage, whipping, torture, and related pornographic material."[128]

The outcome of the Kefauver hearings could almost be predicted given '50s sexual politics. It had a devastating impact on both Page and Klaw. Fearful that she might face prosecution, and tired of posing for girlie magazines, Page moved to Florida in 1957, where she modeled fashion for a few years, often working with the acclaimed photographer Bunny Yeager. In the late '50s, Page became a devout Christian and worked as a fifth-grade teacher.[129]

Sadly, as John Heidenry reports, "the [investigation] process broke Klaw." He adds: "withdrawing from the [porn] business, [he] died years later, a bitter man." Klaw was hounded by US government agencies during the next five years, making his life miserable. The firm that long reproduced his photos—and also had Disney as a client—dropped him, apparently under FBI pressure. He shuttered his 14th Street operation and had his sister open a new business in Jersey City. In '56, Abe McGregor Goff, the Post Office's solicitor, denied Klaw use of the US mail, insisting he was "one of the nation's largest dealers in pornographic material." Adding insult to injury, some claim his phones were bugged and mail intercepted. In '56, Klaw's forty-seven-year-old sister, Mrs. Fanny Cronin, was busted for operating a $2 million New Jersey "pornographic films and photos mill." In 1963, three years before his death, Klaw and his brother-in-law, Jack Kramer, were indicted—and convicted—for conspiracy to send pornographic materials through the US mail. Robert F. Kennedy, the liberal, Catholic attorney general, soon-to-be Democratic Party presidential candidate and an assassinated martyr, led the campaign against Klaw. The Supreme Court overturned the conviction.[130]

According to Rick Klaw, in order to avoid a $5,000 fine and a five-year prison sentence, Klaw agreed to destroy some five thousand photographs (including many original glass negatives) and movie negatives. Rick Klaw, reflecting philosophically, noted, "My grandfather never really understood what he had done wrong. He had never knowingly broken any laws. He always paid his taxes." He added: "He was just a businessman. For the remainder of his life, Irving Klaw would collect bondage images from wherever he could find them, hoping to redeem his reputation by demonstrating that others were producing similar images without legal problems." Years later, Paula Klaw revealed that she had hidden a cache of Klaw's bondage negatives. "Paula, unbeknownst to her brother, preserved his legacy—and her financial future—by hiding thousands of the images," notes Rick Klaw. "Without Paula's foresight, Irving Klaw might have been just an odd, barely remembered footnote in the annals of pin-up history and Fifties puritanism."

During the Labor Day weekend of September 1966, Klaw suffered an appendicitis attack yet went to work; during the day, his health condition deteriorated due to peritonitis and he unexpectedly died. He was a defeated man. A half century later, in July 2012, after nearly seventy-five years in business, the Klaw family enterprise finally closed. Ira Kramer, Paula and Jack's son, had taken over Movie Star News, still located on 14th Street, in 1996 following his mother's death. He sold the Klaw archive of some three million photos, ten thousand movies, and 250,000 negatives for a reported seven-figure sum. "It's one of the most important photo archives in Hollywood history," said Stuart Scheinman, co-owner of the Las Vegas-based Entertainment Collectibles, who purchased the collection.[131]

Aesthetic Spectacle

Between the late '40s and the early '60s, the United States faced its second great culture war. The first war took shape during the late nineteenth century and was expressed in Comstock-obscenity regulation, the anti–birth control movement, and the call for abstinence; it culminated in the adoption of the Eighteenth (Prohibition) and Nineteenth (Suffrage) Amendments. A half century later, the United States faced a third culture war, one that took shape in the wake of the Supreme Court's 1973 *Roe v. Wade* decision and lingers on to this day. The '50s culture war took numerous forms, but was distinguished by changes in America's visual erotic sensibility. This change was most acutely manifested in still and filmed pornography, popular Hollywood movies, and a series of state and Federal court decisions. Each culture war expresses a critical aspect of the nation's social transformation: the first, from a rural to an industrial nation; the second, from a national to an international power; and the third, from an international player to the dominant global power. The mainstreaming of pornography and the remaking of America's moral order accompanied each phase of this transformation.

Klaw's still images and loop movies represented one form of the overall transformation of the nation's visual—especially film-based—pornographic expression. His productions were part of the stag film genre that were not normally shown in legitimate theatres. A separate form or genre of porn consisted of "adult" movies that were shown in select movie houses. In addition, the porn market included a growing assortment of DIY amateur or home-movie porn. However, the most consequential development in the transformation of what Susan Sontag called the pornographic imagination involved Hollywood movies, movies that challenged the 1930 Production Code. Together, these genres of sexual visual representation cultivated America's modern erotic aesthetic.

Stag movies date from the earliest days of filmed entertainment with the release of the 1915 shorts, *A Free Ride* and *Inspiration*.[133] In the 1950s, stags became "beaver" movies, often depicting women in various forms of erotic presentation. One of the most renowned '50s stags is *Smart Alec* (a.k.a. *Smart Aleck*), a short black-and-white film—ten to twenty minutes long depending on the version—starring the sixteen-year-old Candy Barr (a.k.a. Juanita Slusher), soon to be a leading stripper. The basic beaver showed a woman stripping to display full frontal nudity; the "split beaver" displayed a woman spreading her legs and/or her vulva; and the "action beaver" depicted soft-core lesbian scenes. Stags and beavers reinforced the formal structure of how the (subservient) female was expected to serve the (dominant) male.[134]

By the late '50s, stags were being shown in peep show booths, an innovative form of media technology popular in Times Square entertainment arcades. These booths were originally adapted from Thomas Edison's earliest peepshows and were mounted in wooden booths and outfitted with 16mm and 8mm film—and, later, analog videotape—image-projection systems. After the viewer placed a coin in the money slot, a "loop"—a projected pornographic movie sequence—was shown. Peep booths were often located in a darkened commercial venue that permitted, in addition to the viewing of porn shorts, customers to engage in other sexual activities, including masturbation and fellatio. There's much controversy over who "invented" the peep booth. Some claim it was Reuben Sturman, a Cleveland porn entrepreneur; others insist that it was Martin Hodus, of New York, whose initial loops consisted of two-minute movies featuring topless women.[135]

A second pornographic genre involved a network of "adult" filmmakers who came to prominence during the mid-'50s through mid-'70s. Their works were shown in legitimate movie theaters that pushed the boundaries or aesthetics of what was considered pornography. This sensibility was most notably articulated with the 1956 release of Roger Vadim's *And God Created Woman*, starring his wife Brigitte Bardot; the opening shot displays Bardot's eroticized *derrière*. Two of the foremost American proponents of this new generation of filmmaking were New York's Doris Wishman and Russ Meyer from Los Angeles. It reached its zenith with the opening of *Deep Throat* in June 1972 at the New World Theater in Times Square. It was a porn flick that one reviewer characterized as having "a plot . . . and a coherent one to boot, with the actions of characters more or less plausibly motivated."[136] According to one scrupulous critic, *Deep Throat* displayed "fifteen nonsimulated sexual acts, including seven of fellatio, four of cunnilingus . . . and others requiring more imagination."[137]

John Waters, among others, consider Wishman the "mother" of modern filmed pornography. She was a self-taught independent filmmaker who wrote, produced (and found the money!), directed, cast, edited, and acted in nearly all of her thirty films. Her films ranged from "nudie cuties"—including *Hideout in the Sun* (1960), *Nude on the Moon* (1961), and *Blaze Starr Goes Nudist* (1962)—to "roughies" to "chesties" and, finally, to "slashers," reflecting the changing underground cult porn scene of the late '50 through '70s. A film critic once opined, "Doris Wishman is not merely the Grand Dame of bargain basement sexploitation films, she is the Godard of low-budget genre films." She kept making films until her dying days and repeatedly quipped while still quite alive, "After I die I will be making movies in Hell!"[138]

Russ Meyer, dubbed "King of the Skin Flicks," represented the new West Coast porn aesthetic characterized by sexually desiring women, often with very big breasts; one of the "stars" he discovered, Lorna Maitland, is reported to have measured 42D-24-36. During WWII, Meyer served as a photographer in the army signal corp. After the war, he shot pinup girls for the growing men's magazine trade and got his start in film working on "industrials," corporate training and promotional shorts. His porn career spans two decades, from 1959 to '79, and, like Wishman, he played many roles—director, producer, screenwriter, photographer, cinematographer, film editor, and even actor. His breakthrough was the '59 classic, *The Immoral Mr. Teas*; in 1970, he direct *Beyond the Valley of the Dolls*, which Roger Ebert co-wrote. Ebert fondly recalls their collaboration: "He stages his films like military operations, casting himself as the tough sarge who blows the bugle at dawn." A biopic about this collaboration, *Russ and Roger Go Beyond*, starring Will Ferrell, is reportedly in development.[139]

Erotic Sensibility

In 1930, the Hollywood studios established a self-censorship system, the Production Code (or Hays Code), to forestall government regulation of the industry. While never fully effective to calm moralists' concerns that movies corrupted American morals, the code served as a useful fig leaf during the Depression and WWII eras. However, in the postwar period, movies began to break out of the code's false restrictions. Two movies by Otto Preminger, *The Moon is Blue* (1953), starring William Holden and David Niven, and *Man with a Golden Arm* (1955), starring Frank Sinatra and Kim Novak, were released to popular success without code approval. They were followed by other movies that further undercut the code, including *Baby Doll* (1956), based on a Tennessee Williams play and starring Carroll Baker and Eli Wallach. These movies were part of a larger phenomenon that recast movie aesthetics and involved both sexual representation and youthful rebellion.

Marilyn Monroe introduced the era's iconic female image, the unthreatening, eroticized, dumb blonde, in two 1950 movies, John Huston's *The Asphalt Jungle* and Joseph Mankiewicz's *All About Eve*. Her on-screen celebrity led to being pictorially profiled in *Playboy*'s legendary 1953 first issue. Other '50s female movie sex symbols included Bardot, Jayne Mansfield, in *The Girl Can't Help It* (1956), and Jean Simmons, in *Guys and Dolls* (1955). A new generation of male sex symbols included Marlon Brando in *On the Waterfront* (1954); Paul Newman in *The Silver Chalice* (1954); James Dean in *Rebel without a Cause* (1955); and Elvis Presley in *Jailhouse Rock* (1957). They reconceived masculine identity.

A series of youth-oriented Hollywood movies drew moralists' scorn, but were wildly popular, especially among younger audiences. These movies included *The Wild One* (1953), directed by László Benedek and starring Brando; *Rebel without a Cause* (1955), directed by Nicholas Ray and starring Dean; *Rock, Rock, Rock* (1956), directed by Will Price, starring Sal Mineo and featuring Frankie Lymon singing "I'm No Juvenile Delinquent"; and *Teenage Rebel* (1956), directed by Edmund Goulding and starring Ginger Rogers. Equally important, numerous "B" movies—like *Teen Crime Wave* (1956), directed by Fred Sears, and *The Delinquents* (1957), directed by Robert Altman—further pushed the boundaries of sexual expression. But the movie that drew the most controversy was *Blackboard Jungle*.

Metro-Goldwyn-Mayer released *Blackboard Jungle* in 1955. Based on a novel by Evan Hunter, the film was written and directed by Richard Brooks and nominated for an Academy Award for Best Screenplay; it features Glenn Ford, Vic Morrow, Anne Francis, and Sydney Poitier. The movie is set in a racially integrated New York vocational high school and explores the problem of juvenile delinquency. It features students sporting leather jackets (made popular in *The Wild One*), pompadour hairdos, and a soundtrack that includes Bill Haley & His Comets' hit song, "Rock Around the Clock." Numerous cities banned the movie because of the dance sequences deemed inappropriate for school-aged youths and for depicting black and white students leering at white women. The National Council of Parents and Teachers, the Girl Scouts, and the Daughters of the American Revolution denounced it. Clare Booth Luce, then ambassador to Italy, pulled the movie from the '55 Venice Film Festival for fear of it being used in Communist propaganda to present an unflattering portrait of American youth.

In June 1955, Senator Kefauver held yet another round of Congressional hearings on juvenile delinquency, this one in Los Angeles. The hearings targeted Hollywood "smut mills" and, among other things, Marilyn Monroe's "undraped torso" on playing cards and calendars. Among the executives who appeared were Jack Warner (Warner Bros), Frank Freeman (Paramount), and Dore Schary (MGM). The committee's ire was particularly focused on *Blackboard Jungle*, warning, "many of the type of delinquents portrayed in this picture will derive satisfaction, support, and sanction from having society sit up and take notice of them." The committee worried that seeing the film could stimulate a youth's "attitudes of brutality and violence may be given a further push in that direction." MGM's Schary strongly objected, insisting, "There's no fire in the picture. They can't pin that on us."[140]

Against the background of the Kefauver hearings and changing aesthetics of both "porn" and Hollywood movies, a series of state and Supreme Court decisions fundamentally reshaped the visual erotic landscape. In 1954, Walter Bibo released *Garden of Eden*, the first nudist movie. It screened in thirty-six cities across the country, but was found obscene by New York's SUNY Regents, which then had authority over such matters. At the time of the movie's release, pressure from an activist nudist movement championing naked-ness as part of a healthy lifestyle was gaining traction. Bibo fought back and, in July 1957, Judge Charles Desmond of the state court of appeals ruled: "There is nothing sexy or suggestive about it . . . nud-ists are shown as wholesome, happy people in family groups prac-ticing their sincere but misguided theory that clothing . . . is delete-rious to mental health."[141] According to one estimate, between 1957 and 1963 "dozens of nudist camp movies played across America."[142] In these movies, "viewers were treated to endless scenes of nudists playing volleyball, nudists practicing archery, nudists performing on the accordion and nudists doing pretty much everything except what you want to see nudists doing—having sex."[143]

Four pivotal '50s-era Supreme Court decisions transformed the movie industry and redefined obscenity. The landmark 1948 Para-mount decree formally broke up the Hollywood studios' monopoly on movie distribution.[144] Second, its 1952 decision *Burstyn v. Wilson*, which involved the screening of Roberto Rossellini's film *The Mira-cle*, overturned the 1915 *Mutual Film Corporation* ruling, formally granting movies First Amendment protection. According to the legal scholar Richard Randall, "The *Miracle* decision did not outlaw government censor boards per se, but it did provide a constitutional basis for challenging their rulings."[145] Third, in *Roth v. U.S.* (1957), it established the principles of community standards and considering the work as a whole as judgment factors in determining whether a work was obscene.* And fourth, in *Jacobellis v. Ohio* (1964), the court found a provocative French film, *Les Amants* (The Lovers), shown at a Cleveland Heights, Ohio, movie theater, not obscene; Justice Potter Stewart, trying to distinguish between "soft-" and "hard-" core por-nography, famously exclaimed, "I know it when I see it."

The court has since, however, affirmed the ability to regulate obscene material in three critical ways. In 1978, it limited seven

---

* See "Prurient Word."

words deemed unsuitable for broadcast on radio and television airways in a legendary Supreme Court case, *FCC v. Pacifica*. In *Ferber v. New York* (1982), it permitted states to criminalize the depiction and distribution of pornographic materials involving children sixteen years or younger. In *Renton v. Playtimes Theatre* (1986), it permitted cities to use zoning ordinances to restrict porn exhibition to one thousand feet from a residential zone, single- or multiple-family dwelling, church, park, or school. But, outside these restrictions, anything goes.

Amateur Pornography

"Amateur" artists, be they painters or writers, sculptures or musicians, have long created UGC or DIY media. During the postwar era, the amateur arts expanded to include photography, filmmaking, photocopying, and home video. Together, technology and the emergence of a more "liberated" sexual consumer, transformed the pornographic imagination. In 1948, Edward Land revolutionized photography with the introduction of the Polaroid self-developing instant camera. It brought mechanical reproduction to UGC, empowering amateur photography. It enabled users to take a photograph and have it automatically duplicated in about a minute. Polaroid named one of its first low-cost cameras "The Swinger," in keeping with the new sexuality pioneered by Hugh Hefner's *Playboy* magazine and the '60s sexual revolution. In 1972, amateur photography underwent a second revolution with the introduction of the self-focusing camera.[146]

Forgotten by many, the Xerox photo-duplication process introduced in the 1960s helped rationalize the mass reproduction of erotic images, if only in black and white. Xerox copies of pictures from X-rated photos, magazines, books and calendars proliferated. Often overlooked, the office photocopier contributed a unique form of user-generated imagery as innumerable employees captured their most private representations, often on company time. Whether they exposed their butts, breasts, or penises, if not couples coupling, employees duplicated their most private parts for posterity.

What Polaroid did for the still image, Panasonic's VHS home video did for the moving image. Until the introduction of home video, unless one was exceptionally competent technically, the ordinary amateur could not reproduce 16mm or 8mm film—or a photograph for that matter. He (or she) needed a commercial vendor to process moving or still images. As often happened, unfortunately, if a customer's image alarmed the vendor, the police were called and the image-maker arrested.

Cable expanded porn to many more than those who visited a XXX-retail outlet. One night in November 1979, the posture girl became the performance artist. Tara Alexander, a lanky, long-haired amateur porn star, had sex with eighty-six men. The event was backed by two of the city's leading sex-*preneurs*, Al Goldstein, publisher of *Screw*, and Larry Levenson, proprietor of Plato's Retreat, the city's hottest hetero sex club. They billed it as the Spermathon. It was videotaped and soon thereafter shown on the city's new X-rated cable show, *Midnight Blue*.[147]

Complementing such semi-commericial efforts, UGC helped foster a new type of erotic fantasy that did not rely on the foreign otherness of commercial porn represented by the professional star. UGC conceived video as a mirror, depicting the maker as both the subject and object of fantasy representation. What it lacked in professional quality, UGC porn made up in viewer identification, a sense that one was watching the real thing, oneself. It found a welcoming audience for, by the late '80s, DIY video porn accounted for 30 percent of new video releases.[148]

The new technologies of the '80s and '90s further extended the boundaries of the pornographic imagination. The opening of telephone voice services (i.e., 900 numbers) to commercial porn added an often-unappreciated dimension to pornography—live and prerecorded voice. In 1988, the Information Industry Bulletin estimated annual revenues for the dial-a-porn industry at $54 million. That same year, the Associated Press (AP) reported that the Federal Communications Commission (FCC) imposed a $50,000 fine on a Mill Valley, California, firm for permitting underage children to use its porn service.[149] The adoption of digital technologies in the '90s transformed porn production and distribution. The digital camera and the computer-based editing and graphics programs (e.g., Apple's Final Cut) remade video production; the compact disc, the Internet, and wireless communications revolutionized distribution. A new media culture was born and, with it, a new generation of pornography.

The early adoption of a non-graphic Internet led to the establishment of numerous online discussion groups, including Usenet and innumerable "alternative" groups, the most notorious was alt.sex. Usenet also hosted a wide variety of sex-related groups, including alt.sex.pictures, alt.sex.movies, alt.sex.voyeurism, and alt.sex.masturbation. In the late '80s, the graphic artist Mike Saenz introduced "Virtual Valerie," an interactive erotic computer game on a floppy disk and then a CD-ROM; it allowed the (male) user to repeatedly insert a dildo into Valerie's vagina. In 1995, Danni Ashe, a former stripper and nude model, started "Danni's Hard Drive," one of the earliest online porn sites; CNN reported it had revenues of $6.5 million in 2000.[150] Online and stored commercial porn as well as amateur sites like YouPorn and PornoTube expanded the porn market. Sites like SuicideGirls and eroticBPM helped turn soft-core porn into a feature of goth and punk aesthetics, further integrating porn into popular culture.

More than a century after the introduction of the beaver shot, full genital exposure and intercourse—penile and vaginal or penile and anal—became the iconic pornographic representation of postmodern sexuality. It defines the aesthetics of much of today's commercial female and male hetero- and homoerotic porn. Moving-image media augmented the postmodern beaver shot with the "cum" or "money" shot, male ejaculation onto a woman's body, face, or into her mouth. The beaver and the cum shots speak to the continuing aesthetic tyranny of male erotic fantasies. The apparent popularity of "gonzo" porn pushes further hard-core or anti-female representations.[151] Surprisingly, few teen sexting messages currently seem to involve gonzo porn.

America's pornographic imagination has come a long way since Irving Klaw took his scandalous shots of Bettie Page in the 1950s.

Porn production has relocated from New York to San Fernando, California, and now is shifting to Nevada and Florida as well as Brazil, Eastern Europe, and other parts of the world.[152] Porn is a big business in America with estimated revenues of $10 billion-plus. According to Kassia Wosick, a New Mexico State University sociologist, the globall porn market is estimated at $97 billion, with the United States accounting for between $10 and $12 billion of it.[153] According to one estimate, there are nearly twenty-five million porn sites worldwide making up 12 percent of all websites. Sebastian Anthony, writing for *ExtremeTech*, reports that Xvideos is the biggest porn site on the web, receiving 4.4 billion page views (pvs) and 350 million unique visits per month. He claims porn accounts for 30 percent of all web traffic. Based on Google data, the other four of the top five porn sites—and their monthly page views—are: PornHub (2.5 billion pvs); YouPorn (2.1 billion pvs); Tube8 (970 million pvs); and LiveJasmin (710 million pvs). In comparison, Wikipedia gets about 8 billion pvs.

Sexting

Teen sexuality has been a moral battleground since the nation's founding. It was under attack during the two George Bush administrations, but Christian conservatives exercised considerable influence, particularly during Bush II, promoting sexual abstinence, a policy that saw adolescent sexuality as a threat to childhood "innocence."[154] They sought to end government programs that provided sex health information, HIV-AIDS safe sex prevention, and birth-control assistance. However well-intentioned—if mean spirited—these efforts were, they did little to address the commercial culture that kept pushing the boundaries of teen sexuality. Bush II policies intensified the teen sexuality crisis.

The Obama administration has accepted the sexualized teen as a social and marketplace reality. The Guttmacher Institute found that, as of February 2012, 13 percent of fifteen-year-old girls had had intercourse and 70 percent of nineteen-year-olds of both sexes had had intercourse. Surprising to many, as Lydia Shrier of the

Harvard Medical School, found sexually active young people fifteen to twenty-one years old report more positive feelings on the days they had sex than on the days they didn't. Nevertheless, close to one million young women under the age of twenty-one become pregnant each year and one seventh (13 percent) of all annual births are by teenagers.[155]

Sexting has become an original form of self-expression for this new, twenty-first-century youth generation. It represents a technological advance over earlier forms of UGC. It involves the instantaneous capture of a very personal, if not illicit, forms of self-expression and its instantaneous transmission to another device user. Thought is minimized; impulse dominates. The transmission can go through two different forms of communications. The first is a one-to-one exchange, facilitated through a wireless network; a teen takes a photo and sends it to a recipient with a device capable of receiving the transmission (e.g., a smartphone). The second involves a one-to-many exchange mediated through a wired or wireless network and often facilitated through the Internet. A surprise to many young people, a private sexting titillation can go viral almost instantaneously. The person's image of sexual display can quickly become available to not only the intended recipient but also a community of "friends" that can range from the person next door to someone one does not know located across the globe.

Sexting, like all other forms of mechanically reproduced, distributed, and displayed erotic imagery, suffers from its technological limitations. Most screens on smartphones have a very small display or aspect ratio. This places significant limitations on the viewing experience. At the 2008 Academy Awards ceremony, Jon Stewart famously mocked watching David Lean's epic, 70mm film *Lawrence of Arabia* on a tiny iPhone. According to Pew Research, as of April 2015, two-thirds (64 percent) of American adults had a smartphone, up from one-third (35 percent) in 2011. Lean's film is available through Apple's iTunes. Mobile devices are uniquely suited to reinforce the twin tendencies of postmodern visual culture: ever-faster editing cuts and ever-tighter close-up shots.[156] Sexual representation adapts to the limitations of the image display medium, whether a nineteenth-century photograph or a twenty-first-century smartphone. The wide-scale adoption of mobile tablet computing devices (e.g., iPad) will likely, yet again, reframe the pornographic imagination.

Teens and young adults around the United States are being arrested in growing numbers for engaging in sexting. In 2011, researchers at the University of New Hampshire's Crimes Against Children Research Center surveyed some 2,700 US law enforcement agencies. In a series of reports in *Pediatrics*, the authors found that between 2008 and 2009 law-enforcement officials handled an estimated 3,477 cases of "youth-produced sexual images." According to law-enforcement officials, these images "constituted child pornography under relevant statutes." They also found that a majority of these cases (66 percent) involved an "aggravating" circumstance beyond the conventional definition of sexting, including a minor engaged in abusive behavior (31 percent) or an inappropriate adult was involved (36 percent).[157] As of yearend 2011, according to the National Conference of State Legislatures, at least twenty-one states and Guam introduced bills or resolutions aimed at suppressing sexting; bills were enacted in five states: Florida, North Dakota, Nevada, Rhode Island, and Texas, as well as Guam.[158]

In the United States, child pornography is a crime. The Supreme Court adhered to a belief that there is a constitutional difference between art, "soft core," which titillates, and obscenity, "hard core," which excites. This difference between art and obscenity was ineloquently drawn by Justice Potter Steward's legendary obfuscation, "I know it when I see it." Nevertheless, it is a difference with significant consequence. First Amendment protections do not apply to obscene or pornographic works. The Reagan-era "war on crime" first promoted child sex abuse as a prominent issue. In 1982, the Supreme Court ruled, in *New York v. Ferber*, that child pornography was an exception to First Amendment free-speech protection. It insisted, "a child has been physically or psychologically harmed in the production of the work." In this way, it was similar to a handful of other forms of expression, including libel, profanity, and sedition.[159] Today, sexting has become an all-American sport, for teens and adults alike. Anyone with a smart device—whether phone, tablet, laptop, or desktop computer—can access more porn than either Senator Kefauver or Irving Klaw could ever have imaged.

PRURIENT WORD

SAMUEL ROTH, 1893–1974

Dirty Words

Since the founding of the United States, sex has been a terrain of social and personal conflict. It was once considered the devil's vice. Nevertheless, an ever-growing number of Americans fought to expand the meaning—and scope—of the sexual experience. Today, sexuality is accepted as part of the human condition, a uniquely natural experience, one both social shared yet deeply personal, psychological, and physiological. Since Puritans settled New England, moralists have decried the sin of pleasure in all its forms of representation, especially involving the "obscene" written word.

The post-WWII consumer revolution transformed sexuality. The body was secularized and scientifically commercialized; no part, function, or possibility was left unexploited as medical science extended and enhanced modern physical life, especially the sexual experience, most notably with the contraceptive and erectile-dysfunction pills.* Simultaneously, the body became a terrain of plunder, proving that nothing human could not be turned into a commodity.

---

* See "The Pill."

During the twentieth century, the prurient word was superseded by the obscene media representation, whether still, moving, or enhanced by recorded audio. Initially, analog media included radio, records, movies, television, home video, video games, and telephone voice services. Over the century, analog media gave way to digital technologies. Analog media established the modern era's erotic aesthetic sensibility; digital technologies have extended and intensified the experience.

Today, no one really cares what one says—except with regard to the Federal Communications Commission (FCC)–regulated "public" media outlets of broadcast TV and radio or what is directed to underage children and youths. All else is unregulated, whether print, cable, or online. Almost anything can be said. E. L. James's erotic Fifty Shades trilogy, has been translated into more than fifty languages and has sold one hundred million copies worldwide; a Hollywood movie version generated more than $100 million in ticket sales. Fifty Shades suggests how far popular culture has come over the last half century. A half century ago, Samuel Roth was the leading porn publisher who—federal prosecutors estimated—had an income of about $1 million. In his now famous case, *Roth v. U.S.*, the Supreme Court rejected his First Amendment claim and he was sentenced to a five-year prison term for sending obscene materials through the US mail.[160]

The most recent major battle fought over obscenity took place a decade ago. On February 1, 2004, when Janet Jackson and Justin Timberlake took the stage at the Super Bowl XXXVIII halftime show at Houston's Reliant Stadium and—for about 9/16 of a second—a CBS TV audience of nearly 150 million viewers was exposed to a "costume malfunction" revealing Jackson's bare breast and nipple shield. The FCC received 540,000 complaints about the incident, many call-ins orchestrated by conservative morality groups. FCC chairman Michael Powell called Jackson's exposure, "a classless, crass, and deplorable stunt," and promised a tough response. In March 2004, the FCC imposed a $550,000 fine against CBS for its display of a "fleeting instance" of indecency in line with its 1972 "seven dirty words" standard. CBS appealed the decision and, in June 2012 and, following an earlier ruling by the US Third Circuit Court of Appeals in Philadelphia against the FCC, the Supreme Court refused to reinstate the fine.[161]

A quarter-century earlier, a major battle was fought over prurient expression when the Supreme Court ruled in 1978 against Pacific Radio for broadcasting George Carlin's "seven dirty words." The words are: shit, piss, fuck, cunt, cocksucker, motherfucker, and tits; one can write them but can't say them on broadcast radio or television. Carlin famously uttered them in a 1972 comedy skit that was broadcast in '73 by New York's WBAI radio, a community station. His standup performance knowingly challenged the US government—regulators, enforcers, and judiciary—over what words could be uttered on the public airways. Pacifica—and Carlin's seven words—lost and the court's decision remains the law of the land.[162] The FCC's obscenity standards were designed for an analog era, one defined by limited mass-market media. That world has been superseded. The analog "public" has been privatized, individualized, and enormously expanded by the digital "online" media.

Porn Gladiator

"I have never offered books to juveniles, and refused to serve them whenever they were so identified in my mails," Samuel Roth insisted before a special 1955 Congressional subcommittee hearing on juvenile delinquency. The hearings, chaired by Senator Estes Kefauver (D-TN), were held at the US courthouse—since renamed the Thurgood Marshall Courthouse—at Foley Square in Lower Manhattan.* He was subpoenaed along with a half-dozen other publishers and distributors of what the Senators considered obscene materials. Roth was identified as the nation's foremost porn publisher—and, although claiming his right against self-incrimination—was the only witness to critically engage the subcommittee on the meaning of obscenity. This debate defined the limits of '50s free expression.

---

* For more on the Kefauver hearings, see "Comic Book Corruption" and "Obscene Image."

Roth and David Alberts, soon-to-be defendants in the landmark 1957 Supreme Court decision *Roth v. U.S.*, were two of the dozen or so subpoenaed to testify. Others forced to appear were the now all-but-forgotten small-time publishers William (Eddie) Mishkin, Abe Rotto, Abraham Rubin (a.k.a. Al Stone), Louis Shomer, Arthur Herman Sobel, Eugene Maletta, Aaron Moses Shapiro, and Irving Klaw.* Shortly after the hearings, Roth and Alberts (who lived in Los Angeles) were busted for sending obscene materials through the US mail.

Roth may have thought that he could outsmart Kefauver, but he was playing a losing hand. Postwar optimism had given way to a great fear of social subversion. The Cold War was in full swing; a few years later, President Dwight Eisenhower would identify its principal driving force, the military-industrial complex." The war against Communism abroad was mirrored in an equally forceful campaign against subversion and immorality at home. In addition to Kefauver, champions of moral rectitude included FBI director J. Edgar Hoover, columnist Walter Winchell, and the Catholic Church's New York cardinal Spellman. They claimed pornography, juvenile delinquency, and Communism were intimately linked, together eroding the soul of the nation.

A month before the Kefauver hearing, on April 13, New York police forcefully entered and searched—ransacked—Roth's home at 11 West 81st Street, and his offices at 110 Lafayette Street. The district attorney, Frank Hogan, initiated the raid; it was a case of harassment as the charges were ultimately dismissed. A month after the Senate hearing, federal authorities served Roth with a twenty-three-count indictment for sending obscene materials through the mail. In '57, the Supreme Court handed down the *Roth* decision with two curious results. The key principles of the court's decision would lead to the mainstreaming of pornography, yet landed Roth five years in a federal penitentiary.†

---

* On Klaw, see "Obscene Image."

† Roth was at the Lewisburg, Pennsylvania, federal penitentiary during the same period as Wilhelm Reich, David Greenglass (Ethel Rosenberg's brother), and Harry Gold, a principal witness in the Rosenberg case.

Roth, like other mid-twentieth-century publishers of "obscene" material, appears as genuinely committed to expanding the scope of free expression as to furthering his right to make a buck. Postwar sex-*preneurs* asserted the right of all (male) adults to enjoy risqué materials as a consensual exchange, a private contract between the maker (and, if photograph or film, the female and/or male "talent"), the distributor, the seller, and the consumer. Federal and state restrictions were seen as violations of an adult American's rights to free speech and to a free market.

Between the 1920s and the '50s, Roth was the nation's leading pornography publisher, pushing the limits of free expression more than any other American publisher. He was born in 1893 in a small village in Galicia, an Austrian province that lies on the northern slopes of the Carpathian Mountains. At four years old, his family immigrated to New York, settling in Manhattan's Lower East Side. As a poor Jewish youth, he worked as an egg candler (someone who used a candle to determine if the egg was fertilized), newsboy, baker, and, at sixteen, a reporter for the New York *Globe*. He received a scholarship to Columbia College where he edited *The Lyric*, a poetry magazine.

During the '20s, Roth launched a number of literary magazines, including *Beau* (similar to *Esquire*) and *Two Worlds* that serialized— without permission—excerpts from James Joyce's *Ulysses*. The Joyce selections caught the attention of New York Society for the Suppression of Vice, an organization originally founded by Anthony Comstock in 1873. In 1928, Roth was busted for selling pornography, convicted and served a seventy-five-day prison sentence.[163]

As his biographer, Jay Gertzman, notes, "Roth was the most often incarcerated, the most feckless, and quite likely the most resourceful booklegger of his time, challenging moral and legal authorities with quixotic bravado."[164] In addition to Joyce's *Ulysses*, he was the first to release a pirated edition of D. H. Lawrence's *Lady Chatterley's Lover*. Gotham's publishing and literary communities assailed him for releasing these works, expurgated and without permission. He also published avant-garde writers and critics of the period like George Sylvester Viereck, Clement Wood, Milton

Hindus, and Gershon Legman, as well as a series of parodies with titles like *Lady Chatterley's Friends*, *Lady Chatterley's Husbands*, *The Great Lindbergh Hullabaloo*, *The Intimate Journal of Rudolph Valentino, Loose Shoulder Straps*, and *Self Amusement*. Two political exposés, Gaston Means's *The Strange Death of President Harding* (1930) and John Hamill's *The Strange Career of Mr. Hoover Under Two Flags* (1931), drew much critical attention. In 1933, he published one of the first gay transvestite novels, *A Scarlet Pans*, and, the following year, Roth released his most controversial book, *The Jews Must Live*; its subtitle raised deep concern among many: "An Account of the Persecution of the World by Israel on All the Frontiers of Civilization." In the late '30s, he published *Inside Hitler*, written by David Plotkin, and *I Was Hitler's Doctor*, written by a psychiatrist, Eric Krueger and with a foreword by Upton Sinclair. He was a publisher who pushed the edge.[165]

Roth loved words. He wrote for *The Nation*, *Harper's Weekly*, *Poetry*, *Menorah Journal*, and other magazines. He also ran a variety of bookstores, including the Poetry Book Shop in Greenwich Village and another specializing in erotica. He operated under innumerable pseudonyms, including Francis Page and David Zorn.[166] For his efforts, he was busted innumerable times and served two terms in the Lewisburg federal penitentiary, between 1936–39 and 1957–61.

It was, however, Roth's 1956 federal indictment for sending allegedly obscene materials through the US postal system that brought him immortality. In its indictment, the US government accused him of publishing porn through a variety of media. In terms of print publications, it exhibited issues of his magazines, *Good Times* and *American Aphrodite*. Other media materials included stereoscopic pictures of moving women's lips, thighs, and breasts and "strips sets," images of women undressing that simulated a filmstrip. Most provocative, the indictment includes reference to what was identified as "Wallet Nudes," perhaps old-fashioned pinups?

The *Roth* decision—which was combined with the *Alberts* case—established the postwar era's framework defining obscenity.[167] Following the lead of Justice William Brennan, the five-member court majority defined obscenity in terms of two criteria. First, that "to the average person, applying contemporary community standards, the dominate theme of the material taken as a whole appeals to prurient interests"; and, second, that the work is "utterly without redeeming social importance." Most significant, the court insisted, "We hold that obscenity is not within the area of constitutionally protected speech or press."[168] So was delineated "soft" and "hard" porn.

Postwar publishers of obscene written works—like nearly all other American small businessmen—were motivated by self-interest and the opportunities offered by an expanding consumer market. Some, like Roth, were also compelled by more high-minded concerns. Hugh Hefner, a Chicago publisher, is the most celebrated example of this type of businessman specializing in erotica. He promoted a distinct type of soft-core pornography uniquely suited for the emerging post-WWII generation of educated, middle-class, white, consumer-oriented males. He launched *Playboy* in 1953—amid the Korean War—with nude photographs of Marilyn Monroe, followed by shots of Bettie Page and other female strippers.

Hefner and other more mainstream publishers helped create a new language of pornography, one socially aligned to postwar notions of acceptable sexual representation and pleasure.[169] Roth represented a different, more radical sexuality. For nearly half a century he pushed the limits of acceptable erotic discourse. He was one of a small but critical community of publishers promoting unacceptable written—and pictorial—material. By the mid-'50s, the boundaries of unacceptable expression ranged from major literary works, like Allen Ginsberg's *Howl*, to underground gay and lesbian fiction, and to enormously popular comic books. The battle over the word, of the boundaries of what was prurient, defined the '50s.

This new intellectual current, one both critical and erotic, gave voice to what became the '60s counterculture. It provided the theoretical and analytic basis to begin to formulate a new, utopian vision of sexuality, a sexual revolution in which mind and body were integrated and engaged in by free, consenting adults. It fostered a new type of critical discourse about sexuality and social life.

Obscene Literature

In 1957, the San Francisco publishing company City Lights released Ginsburg's poetry collection, *Howl & Other Poems*. Local customs officials confiscated it as obscene, leading to one of the twentieth century's most important free-speech cases. The poem opens with the immortal lines:

I saw the best minds of my generation
  destroyed by madness, starving hysterical naked dragging
    themselves through the negro
  streets at dawn looking for an angry fix

However, the lines that engendered the most controversy included:

who distributed Supercommunist pamphlets in Union Square weeping
  and undressing while the sirens of Los Alamos wailed them down,
  and wailed down Wall, and the Staten Island ferry also wailed,
who broke down crying in white gymnasiums naked and trembling
  before the machinery of other skeletons,
who bit detectives in the neck and shrieked with delight in policecars
  for committing no crime but their own wild cooking pederasty and
  intoxication,
who howled on their knees in the subway and were dragged off the
  roof waving genitals and manuscripts,
who let themselves be fucked in the ass by saintly motorcyclists,
  and screamed with joy,
who blew and were blown by those human seraphim, the sailors,
  caresses of Atlantic and Caribbean love,
who balled in the morning in the evenings in rosegardens and the
  grass of public parks and cemeteries scattering their semen freely
  to whomever come who may[170]

Often forgotten, *Howl* was first released in New York in 1956, approved by the city's Customs Service.

Howl was part of a growing body of mid-'50s literature that pushed the boundaries of acceptable erotic discourse. A new sexual vocabulary was being formulated and literature, including poetry, was one form of expression. It was articulated in the up-market fiction of novelists like Norman Mailer, John O'Hara, and Ray Bradbury; it was expressed in the pulp fiction works reflecting on male homosexuality and lesbian life; and it was graphically reflected in comic books, which were selling an estimated ninety million copies each month. This new sexual discourse also included scientific studies, particularly the works of Alfred Kinsey and Wilhelm Reich, as well as pictorial magazines, including black-and-white female "cheesecake" and male "beefcake" porn, and specialty "fetish" publications (e.g., S&M, leather, bondage).[171]

One of the unintended consequences of WWII was the formation of a male homo-social culture. It was forged during four long years of battle and involved the most intimate human experiences, including trauma, killings, and death. During the postwar era, this war-tested intimacy found expression in implicitly homoerotic literary works like Gore Vidal's *The City and the Pillar* (1948) and John Burns's *Lucifer with a Book* (1949), as well as Tennessee Williams's 1947 play, *A Streetcar Named Desire*.

Lesbian pulp fiction was a postwar literary genre that rankled the morals of upstanding citizens, especially old-fashioned males. In 1952, Representative Ezekiel Gathings (D-AR) held Congressional hearings on the growing threat—popularity?—of lesbian porn. The great irony was that while many of these works were sexually suggestive and decried as obscene, they were targeted to male readers and often written by male authors. As one observer noted, "lesbian women were never the primary market." Among these works are: Simon Eisner's (a.k.a. C. M. Kornbluth) *Naked Storm* (1952); Fletcher Flora's *Strange Sisters* (1954); Alan Marshall's *Sally* (1959); and Sheldon Lord's (a.k.a. Lawrence Block) *Candy* (1960) and *Of Shame and Joy* (1960).[172]

Tereska Torrès and Vin Packer were two female pulp fiction authors who drew much attention. Their works framed the debate over the lesbian element of lesbian pulp. Torrès served in the Free

French forces during WWII and wrote one of the most celebrated works of the genre, *Women's Barracks* (1950), reflecting the experiences of women in combat. Born Tereska Szwarc, she was married to Meyer Levin, author of the popular 1956 work *Compulsion*, based on the Leopold and Loeb case. Her book includes suggestive lesbian content and is reported to have sold four million copies. In a 2012 obituary, the *New York Times* noted the original congressional committee "found the book's offending passages too lurid to quote in its official proceedings."[173]

Vin Packer—a.k.a. Marijane Meaker—released her classic *Spring Fire*, a more explicit lesbian tale, in 1952. It is the story of an ill-fated romantic relationship between two women and reportedly sold over a million copies. In a 2012 interview, Meaker admitted, "I came to New York after graduating from the University of Missouri in 1949. I could not get an agent. . . . I decided to just have stationery printed and be my own agent." The book was inspired by her experience attending an all-female Southern boarding school, but the publisher, Gold Medal Books, insisted she not discuss the students' sexual experience because they were underage, thus risking censorship. She had no qualms editing her work: "All I could think of was that I'd be published—that the Meaker agency's client would have a sale."[174]

Gold Medal Books, launched by Fawcett Publications in 1950, was the leading publisher of lesbian and other pulp genres. Among its leading lesbian titles were Fay Adams's *Appointment in Paris* (1952), Ann Bannon's *Odd Girl Out* (1957), and Valerie Taylor's *The Girls in 3B* (1959). It also published westerns, crime, and PI works by such legendary authors as John D. MacDonald and Jim Thompson. It promoted two types of publications, republished hardcovers and paperback originals. Bigger media conglomerates eventually gobbled it up.

Roth on Trial

During the postwar era, New York and federal authorities busted Roth a half-dozen times. He was the perfect target, an unabashed free-speech advocate who championed unconventional voices and visions. The cycle of his busts illuminates how sexual mores—combined with the increasingly authoritative enforcement powers of local, state, and federal law enforcement agencies—evolved during the postwar era.

In November '47, Roth was busted for "mailing salacious advertisements for obscene books," including *Self Defense for Women* and *Waggish Tales of the Czechs*. In October '50, he was busted for "fraudulent mailings of salacious advertisements for books not in themselves deemed obscene," including Raymond Radiquet's *The Devil in the Flesh*. The following year, he was arrested for "mailing [an] obscene book," *Beautiful Sinners of New York*, with a preface by "Louis Berg, MD" In April '54, he was arrested yet again, this time for the possession of some fifty thousand obscene books, magazines, and pamphlets as well as a list of three hundred thousand mail order customers. During this period, Roth repeatedly escaped jail time, but his luck was running out. In July 1955, he faced a federal indictment for "mailing obscene advertisements and obscene books." This arrest and conviction culminated in the legendary '57 Supreme Court decision that sent Roth to five years in a federal penitentiary.[175]

In response to a federal subpoena, Roth appeared on May 31, 1955, before the Senate committee investigating juvenile delinquency. The encounter between Roth and the committee's chairman, Senator Kefauver, set the stage for one of the most revealing public debates about sexuality and free speech to take place in US history. Rarely do truly different points of view clash in an open public engagement. The most celebrated such debate was the legendary Lincoln-Douglas debates of the pre–Civil War era that confronted the issue of slavery; today's presidential debates have been sanitized into clever beauty contests.

Kefauver's hearings on juvenile delinquency were a corollary to the legendary Army-McCarthy hearings that took place two years earlier, in April and June 1953. The Kefauver hearings focused not on loyalty but morality. While the army hearing felled McCarthy, Kefauver proved victorious in the porn wars. Roth first briefly appeared before the committee on comic books in April '54, invoked his Fifth Amendment protection, and was excused because of a pending New York court case. At his second appearance, in May '55, he did not invoke his Constitutional protections and engaged in a spirited give-and-take with Kefauver and other committee staff. Nicholas Atlas represented him, but had little to say.

Roth immediately challenged his presence at the hearing. "If this committee is limited to an inquiry into the causes of juvenile delinquency in our midst, it is going far off its course in questioning me," he insisted. "With the single exception of a book of instruction for children, entitled *Tina and Jimmy Learn How They Were Born*, written by my daughter for the instruction of her own children. I have never published or advertised a book an adolescent would bother to read. I have never offered books to juveniles, and refused to serve them whenever they were so identified in my mails."

Minority counsel Peter Chumbris sidestepped Roth's assertions and sought to paint him as a publisher of obscene works. He entered into evidence numerous complaints sent from parents from around the country reporting their children received promotional materials from Roth's company, Gargoyle Books. For each accusation, Roth parried back that announcement had been sent accidentally in a mass mailing. More importantly (if dubiously), he argued that his publications did not appeal to youths. "They [juveniles] would disregard them because the language which my circulars are written in may mean something to a Senator, may mean something to a mature adult," he insisted, "but cannot mean anything to a boy or a girl." His exchange with Kefauver got testy:

ROTH:	When you put these pictures against the battery of females that any child sees on any morning in a ride through the subway, in a walk through a street, this is ridiculous as an argument against my business. These are . . .
KEFAUVER:	Mr. Roth, just a minute.
ROTH:	Forgive me. I shouldn't have said that at all. I am sorry.

The debate continued, going to the heart of the matter:

ROTH: Because children's minds are different. They are probably better than the minds of mature people in that respect. A child you have got to tell, to give a real image, or the child just disregards it . . .

KEFAUVER: Whatever they are, you think men are more susceptible to being affected by them than children are?

ROTH: I think that is a matter of course. . . . [M]y real point is that if they reached minors they couldn't possibly have any bad influence on them, and they would disregard them. They would disregard them because the language which my circulars are written in may mean something to a Senator, may mean something to a mature adult, but cannot mean anything to a boy or a girl.

When pressed as to why he included suggestive images in his work, Roth admitted, "I said that I do hope to excite the men into buying these good books." Kefauver seemed dumbfounded: "You think men, then, are more susceptible to harm from pornography, or lewd pictures, than children?" Taking the bull by the horn, Roth insisted, "I don't consider these lewd pictures by any means."

The cat-and-mouse exchange persisted to the bitter end. In his concluding remarks, the Senator gave no quarter: "I think I must say that I know of no one that we have been in touch with who doesn't feel that the kind of slime that you have been sending through the mails is highly deleterious to our young people, and damaging to their morals, and part of the whole picture that we have today of the breakdown among a percentage of our children." Roth was not shamed: "I believe the people who have criticized me are wrong. I believe you are a great deal more wrong than they are, because you are sitting in judgment on me, and I believe that I will someday within the very near future convince you that you are wrong."

The hearings upended Roth's life. In July '55, the postal system indicted him on twenty-six criminal charges. In September, his appeal for dismissal was declined and he was ordered to stand trial. In January '56, he was tried, convicted, and fined $5,000. Most revealing, during the federal appeal process, this sixty-four-year-old businessman was denied bail. Roth's initial appeal to the regional court was denied; however, in January '57, he was granted a Supreme Court certiorari appeal. In June '57, the Court ruled against him.[176] He died in 1974.

Show It All

Pornographic representations—whether in word, sound, image, video, interactive, or live performance—have been part of the US underground sex scene since the nation's founding. Each US war since the Civil War has been accompanied by a significant increase in the availability of pornographic material. During WWII, the underground went above ground to meet the needs of an enormous all-male military. While veterans returned home—to wife, family, home, job, and debt—their sexual needs could not be completely repressed. A host of media promoted very diverse forms of sexual representations.

"Girlie" magazines were introduced during the postwar period. "Most of these publications ran articles and photos that focused on strippers and show gals," notes A. W. Stencell in his wonderfully entertaining tour of the carnival-like world of the bump-and-grind, *Girl Show*. As he reminds readers, "Most men couldn't name their local senator, but they all knew Sally Rand and Georgia Sothern," two popular strippers. Girlie magazines grew out of a combination of the decades-old tradition of burlesque shows, carnival sideshows, and pinups. During WWII, pinups, postcards, and photos became especially popular among servicemen. While such material traditionally would have been considered obscene and the maker and consumer arrested, the war needs of millions of men—including their sexual ones—came first. New York's Irving Klaw, who famously posed Betty Paige, was considered the nation's leading promoter of such material; he received a special commendation for his help in the war effort for supplying girlie pinups. However, when the war ended, America's second twentieth-century culture war took over.

A variety of erotic publications targeted to the male reader flourished during the mid-'50s. *Playboy* was the leading soft-core porn magazine, appealing to the more mainstream, white-collar, professional, "cultured" male consumer. Hefner got his start in the porn trade as promotion director for George von Rosen's Publisher's Development Corporation. It released titles like *Modern Sunbathing & Hygiene*, featuring nudists, and *Modern Man*, an adventure magazine for men filled with lots of pinup girls. Numerous sexually provocative magazines briefly appeared and—all too often—quickly disappeared. Cheesecake and beefcake extended the pinup to the photo-magazine format, offering a wide assortment of nearly all-white women and men posed in all manner of dress—or undress. Robert Harrison's *Titter*, *Wink*, *Flirt*, *Eyeful*, and *Whisper* publications resembled older style pinup magazines. Bob Mizer's *Physique Pictorial*, a beefcake magazine, appealed to yet another subculture, the (homosexual) bodybuilder.[177] Costumes ranged from swimwear and lingerie to athletic, western, stage, and burlesque costumes. Harrison's publications introduced a new feature to the genre, "photostories." Writing in the preface to *The Best of American Girlie Magazines*, Harald Hellmannzsh said, "two- to four-page humorous photostories was something new and proved a gold mine." He added: "In fact even the most banal of them sufficed to have scantily clad girls capering through the comic slapstick situation."[178]

In contrast to the clean-cut depictions in cheesecake and beefcake magazines, more sexually radical, hard-core, publications were the S&M-oriented magazines *Bizarre* and *Exotique* and the *Caprice Catalog*. *Bizarre* is wonderfully bizarre. Its twenty-six issues were published between 1946 and 1959 by an Englishman, John Alexander Scott Coutts, who dubbed himself John Willie—"willie" is English slang for "prick." The magazine is devoted to portraying women adorned in (very) high-heeled shoes, boots, and other fetish footwear; corsets, garters, and high gloves; assorted leather, rubber, and plastic attire; and equipped with a wide assortment of whips, riding crops, and other devices. *Bizarre* provides a unique portrait of what must surely have been a fascinating sliver of 1950s hetero-sexual deviant community. As Eric Kroll notes in his preface to the *Bizarre* collection, "I don't think [Willie] was into extreme cruelty. He believed in consensual bondage."[179]

Sharing a similar spirit as *Bizarre*, *Exotique* is wonderfully exotic. Founded and edited by Leonard Burtman, it was, as Kim Christy, the editor of the reissued series, dubs it a "digest format photo-magazine." In the first issue, released in 1951, *Exotique* featured shots of Bettie Page, decked out in high-heels, leather boots, and all manner of S&M attire. The magazine's real star was Tana Louise, a former burlesque stripper and Burtman's wife. According to Christy, she "stirred the darker side of many a man's sexual fantasies. Her savage look was allegedly derived from her Native American heritage."[180] The sexual arousal Louise engendered in males was only exaggerated and made more threatening—and, thus, more pleasurable—when she was decorated in S&M, leather, and other fetish ware.

While following a format of stories and photos not dissimilar to that pioneered in *Bizarre*, one *Exotique* editorial from 1957 is worth particular attention. In part it states:

> In recent decisions, the Supreme Court of the United States [i.e., *U.S. v. Roth*] has upheld Federal and state laws outlawing the sale and distribution of obscene and pornographic material. These decisions place heavy responsibility on local officials to exercise discrimination and common sense in enforcing such laws. For better or for worse, the responsibility is theirs. . . .
>
> Of course, parents have a responsibility for watching over what their children read. But they have other responsibilities as well.
>
> As citizens in a democracy, they are obligated to protect the expression of ideas no matter how contrary they may be to their own personal views. And if they wish to continue to enjoy the works of "free people" they must safeguard the freedom of the press.[181]

Burtman broke with the convention of the day. Instead of treating the reader as an anonymously voyeur, he speaks directly to him, challenging him to consider pornography as subject of political engagement. Giving the editorial its full value, it must be noted that it appears juxtaposed to a shot of Tana Louise, in full leather S&M attire and with her hips thrust in an explicitly provocative pose.

Also in the '50s, Herman Womack published a series of male physique magazines, *MANual*, *Trim*, and *Grecian Guild Pictorial*, that included photographs of attractive men. Many men were depicted in a seminude posture, often their legs spread, buttocks exposed, pubic hair showing, and an erect penis outlined under a tight-fitting outfit. The males occasionally appeared in pairs, sometimes provocatively in leather fetish wear and even swords and other long, pointed objects that Yale Law School profession, William Eskridge found, "emphasize homoerotic possibilities." In May 1960, the Alexandria, Virginia, postmaster seized 405 copies of Womack publications for violating the 1873 Comstock Act.[182]

Censorship

Based on information gathered during the Kefauver and other Congressional hearings, local police in Houston, Minneapolis, and other cities undertook raids against those who sold obscene magazines, books, and other media. In '58, the US Customs Service seized William Talsman's *The Gaudy Image*, a gay novel set in New Orleans and originally published in Paris by the Olympia Press.[183] In Los Angeles, Alberts and his wife, Violet Evelyn Stanard Alberts, were proprietors of what Richard Kuh, a former New York City assistant district attorney, called "an unadorned, non-literate West Coast mail-order business in filth." Kuh claimed that the business "consisted of bondage and torture pictures (showing young women, partially clad, sometimes in leather garments and with uncomfortable high spike heels, sometimes chained or bound, whipping or otherwise maltreating each other), books of sadistic and masochistic tales (containing descriptions of similar activities), and pictures of nude and partially clad girls, some of unusually gifted development."[184] The Alberts were busted, their business closed and their case finally reached the Supreme Court as part of the 1957 *Roth* decision.

In New York, the police engaged in a militant campaign to confiscate pornographic works and arrest their suppliers. In one of the most famous efforts, they attempted to shut down Mishkin's porn business. Kuh described him as "probably America's leading pornographer of the offbeat." Among Mishkin's publications seized were *Violated, Cult of the Spankers, Bound in Leather,* and *Dance with the Dominant Whip.* He argues that in "Mishkin volumes one finds no imaginable literary merit and little story line." Going further, Kuh vividly describes Mishkin's works: "In some there are male-female sexual encounters (conventional, oral-genital, and sado-masochistic) sensually described in detail. In others, there are interminably varied combinations of whipping, paddling, spanking, stretching, gagging, straight-jacketing, manacling, racking, and in other fashions generally abusing the female body, torments inflicted by imperious women upon servile female acolytes."[185]

In still another campaign, the city secured an injunction to ban fifty-four magazines with, as Kuh notes, "titles ranging from *Adam* through *Venus,* and including along the way: *Bare, Black Garter, Boudoir, Consort, Fling Festival, Follies, Gala, Kuties, Minx, Ogle, Scamp, Sizzle,* and *Torrid."* In a follow-up raid, the police seized an additional thirty-nine "girlie magazines" with titles such as *Bachelor, Black Lace, Brunette, Demoiselle, Flame, French Frills, Les Girls, Satin and Silk,* and *Tempest.*[186] These censorship efforts were not limited to photo magazines. In 1955, city anti-vice agents were able to secure an injunction against a paperback fiction series, *Nights of Horror.*

With equal vigor, the legal system went after pictorial and literary works that appealed to gay men. In 1960, the Post Office barred three Womack magazines—*MANual, Trim,* and *Grecian Guild Pictorial*—because of their alleged obscenity. In a US government brief, the images in these publications were described as follows: "Many of the photographs were of nude models, usually posed with some object in front of their genitals . . . a number were of nude or partially nude males with emphasis on their bare buttocks." It noted, "Although none of the pictures directly exposed the model's genitals, some showed his pubic hair and others suggested what appeared to be a semi-erect penis." The magazines appealed to other, more prurient tastes. They "combined photographs of virtually nude models wearing only shoes, boots, helmets or leather jackets. . . . There were also pictures of models posed with chains or of one model beating another while a third held his face in his hands as if weeping."[187*]

Among next-generation porn magazine publishers, three in particular had significant influence. William Hamling published *Rogue*, a Chicago-based men's magazine between 1955 and '67. In June 1963, almost a decade after the Kefauver hearings, Ralph Ginsburg went on trial in the Philadelphia federal court for sending through the US mail the artistic, up-market, and hardbound quarterly *Eros*. In his defense, he argued, "Even the US State Department bought copies to exhibit at USIA libraries overseas as exemplars of American periodical publishing." He was convicted and, in March 1966, the Supreme Court upheld the conviction, including a $42,000 fine and five-year prison sentence. The appearance of *Screw* magazine, edited by Al Goldstein and Jim Buckley, in 1968 signaled the end of Comstock-era censorship.[188]

Shortly after the '57 *Howl* verdict was announced, New York's *Evergreen Review*, a literary magazine founded by Barney Rosset, republished the poem to popular acclaim. A WWII veteran, Rosset produced the critically received film *Strange Victory* in '48 and, in '51, acquired the Village-based Grove Press, running it for three decades. At Grove, he championed the beats and the off-beats, the European *avant-garde* and modernist innovators. In '59, he released D. H. Lawrence's *Lady Chatterley's Lover*, which Rosset subsequently admitted, "I didn't really like. It affronted me in certain odd ways. It was written from a very class-conscious point of view, which didn't particularly appeal to me."

---

* In 1962, the Supreme Court ruled in *Manual v. Day* that the Post Office could not refuse mail services for male physique magazines. In his ruling, Justice John Marshall Harlan distinguished between a "prurient" appeal and an obscene image and wrote that the images in *MANual* were not "patently offensive" based on community standards.; see Erkstein/ft 619, 620.

In 1959, Rosset launched a well-planned campaign against federal censorship regulations by mailing copies of an unexpurgated version of *Lady Chatterley's Lover*. "We prepared very carefully," he recalled. "We decided the best thing to do was send the book through the mail so it would be seized by the post office. . . . The post office is a federal government agency, and if they arrest you, you go to the federal court." His legal team argued that it was a work of literature and had the support of such literary luminaries as Malcolm Cowley and Alfred Kazin. He lost the court case, but won on appeal. Strengthened by the verdict, he went on to publish Henry Miller's *Tropic of Cancer* and such major literary and political figures as Samuel Beckett, William S. Burroughs, Marguerite Duras, Jean Genet, Jack Kerouac, Harold Pinter, and Tom Stoppard as well as Frantz Fanon and Malcolm X. Equally critical, in '68 he began distributing the Swedish film *I Am Curious (yellow)*. Because it depicted male frontal nudity, it was found obscene, a ruling the Supreme Court upheld.[189]

ILLICIT PERFORMANCE

CLUB 82, 1953–1978

Strip

Strip clubs are no longer limited to Las Vegas. TUSCL, a website of strip clubs, lists nearly three thousand operating throughout the country; another estimate puts the number of clubs at four thousand. Estimates of the number of employees—dancers and support staff—range from 400,000 to 500,000 people serving some 1.2 million customers a day. Various estimates claim that the industry's annual revenues are between $3.1 and $7.5 billion. These clubs "sell a higher percentage of high-end liquor and champagne than other clubs." In addition, some thirty club-chain operators control over three hundred adult clubs across the country and one chain, Rick's Cabaret, is publicly traded on NASDAQ.[190]

A strip club is legally identified as a SOB, a "sexually oriented business," a commercial enterprise where the primary business involves goods and services that are (as stipulated in Texas and other states) "intended to provide sexual stimulation or sexual gratification to the customer." Other SOBs include adult bookstores, porn theaters, and sex paraphernalia shops.[191]

According to Amy Baker, writing about Las Vegas but appropriate throughout the country, a strip club is a unique homo-social male entertainment venue. Women, other than as entertainers, rarely attend on their own; if they do attend, they either come with a male or group of women. A club is distinguished by a bar, sound system, and erotic performance space. The entertainment offered includes females performing a striptease, a pole dance, a lap dance, and still other, more illicit, encounters. Some high-end clubs offer specialty or "VIP" services, often taking place in a more intimate space, "the champagne room."[192]

Performers are referred to as "strippers" or "exotic dancers" and perform either in suggestive outfits, topless, or fully nude. They are not employees but—in the great twenty-first-century new-speak euphemism—"independent contractors." Like most urban taxi drivers who license the cab for the day, dancers pay a fee as well as a portion of the tips they earn in private engagements to perform at the club. Strippers get tips while performing; lap dancers normally get tips on a per-song basis. Other services are paid for on an as-performed basis.

Like many specialized trades, stripping and the strip club have their own nomenclature. Among the common terms are "Air Dance"—a lap dance with no contact; "Blue Light Shoppers"—guys who attend for the two-for-one dance specials and nurse their drinks all night; "CIM"—cum-in-mouth; "DATY"—dine at the Y, cunnilingus; "Extras"—involves commercial sex services and includes "HJ" (hand jobs), "BJ" (blow jobs), and "FS" (full service); "Nipple Feels"—tipping a dancer between her breasts so that the customer can cop a feel of her nipple when she grabs for the money; and "Pervert Row"—the seats around the stage when poor tippers sit and try to get close-up views of dancers leaving the stage. Stripping is its own subculture.[193]

Local laws govern SOBs and are often referred to as zoning regulations or "public nuisance" ordinances. They are ostensibly designed to maintain public health and morals; they are directed at preventing prostitution, sex trafficking, and sexual assaults as well as the sale of drugs and illegal weapons. SOB rules also apply to such issues as age of performers and customers (e.g., liquor consumption); the kind of contact dancers and patrons can have with each other (e.g., lap dances); how dancers perform (e.g., nude or semi-naked, with breasts or gentiles covered); and distance separating the SOB from a church or school. Enforcement seems arbitrary.

Drag

For two decades, Club 82 was the nation's premier showcase for female—and some male—impersonators. It opened in 1953 at 82 East 4th Street following the closure of the 181, a gay bar located at 181 Second Avenue; the 181 lost its liquor license following exposure in the tabloid, *USA Confidential*. The 82 had the same management, personnel, and scene as the 181. One accessed the 82 by climbing down a long, steep stairway and entering a large space featuring a central bar with tables and booths and decked out with lots of fake palm trees and other decorations. As could happen only in New York, the nation's leading transvestite performance club was located across the street from the Hell's Angel's headquarters.

The club's drag shows took place on Friday, Saturday, and Sunday nights and welcomed a mixed clientele, both gay and straight. The club had 350 seats, but often welcomed between eight hundred and one thousand customers. Shows ran between one and one-and-a-half hours and featured "strippers, dancers, comediennes, show girls and singers." According to one estimate, management spent $40,000 a year on costumes. It was popular with celebrities, welcoming Judy Garland, Montgomery Cliff, Kirk Douglas, Elizabeth Taylor, Milton Berle, and, as one reporter notes, "a flock of members of the Kennedy clan." Errol Flynn, a regular, was rumored to have played the piano with his penis.[194]

The 82 was a Mafia-run joint, operated by the Genovese crime family. The ostensible owner was reported to be Mathew Jacobson. The original manager was Steve Franse who was also supposed to manage Vito Genovese's second wife, Anna Heck Genovese, while the mob boss was hiding out in Italy avoiding an arrest for murder. When Heck divorced Genovese, she squealed to the liquor authorities about the mob's operations in numerous city gay clubs, the mobster allegedly had Franse killed.*[195]

The club was run as a professional entertainment spot. No entrance fee was charged, but customers had a $5 drink minimum.† The musicians, all straight men, were member of Local 802. Featured performers got $180 per week, but the American Guild for Variety Artists refused to represent them because they were drag performers. Waitresses were women dressed as men and described as "bull dikish." The club was popular with suburban women's groups and groups of non-gay men; drunk men were turned away. The bouncer was a man, but not in drag.[196]

Kitt Russell was the celebrated director of the "Club 82 Revue," a world-renowned troupe. Walter Winchell dubbed Russell "America's top femme mimic." While dozens of drag queens performed at the 82 over the years, the main attraction was Ty Bennett. He was described as a "Sophie Tucker look-alike" and was a larger-than-life—in size and impact—performer who started at the club in '58 and appeared at other clubs and on TV shows. Mr. August was another featured performer. He grew up in the Midwest and started performing in drag at fifteen impersonating Betty Grable. He became a celebrity while performing in San Francisco nightclubs as Lena Horne, Bette Davis, and Judy Garland. In addition, Vicki Lynn, who posed and stripped in the porn films produced by Irving Klaw and other '50s pornographers, also performed at the club.

K. Stormé DeLarverie, originally from New Orleans, came to the 82 after a long run as the only male impersonator performer with the Jewel Box Revue, a popular drag performance group that toured the country and inspired the '80s musical La Cage aux Folles. (DeLarverie was an early and longtime member of the Stonewall Veterans' Association.) International Chrysis was a Bronx-born drag star and the subject of a 1993 documentary Split: Portrait of a Drag Queen. Stephen Holden, the New York Times film critic, described him as "sporting long red hair, a ferociously engaging smile and oversized

---

* See "Underworld."
† This is $45 in 2015 dollars.

breasts that she liked to show off in New York City nightspots like La Vie en Rose and Club 82." Holden snidely added, "Although friends compared her to Rita Hayworth, she more closely resembled a plump Raquel Welch." Still other impersonators included Nesto (a Cuban dancer), Tony Lee (Chinese toe dancer), Brandy Alexander (exotic dancer), and Trish Sandburg (a singer and "real girl") as well as Kim August and Dale Roberts.[197]

During intermissions, performers mingled with customers, often being offered tips and free drinks. Some of the male performers were reported to be married and have children. According to Raoul Mac-Farlane, "The fact that they are professional transvestites . . . is not proof that they are homosexuals." In the age of Christine Jorgensen, much discussion among the male performers concerned sex change. So popular was Club 82 performers that they appeared in movies, including *The Tiger Makes Out* (1967), starring Eli Wallach and Ann Jackson, and *No Way to Treat a Lady* (1968), starring Rod Steiger and Lee Remick. Following the Stonewall riot and the rise of gay rights movement, transvestite identity shifted as drag shows moved into more mainstream settings, including Las Vegas. In the '70s, Club 82 declined into a "glam" rock hangout—famously showcasing the New York Dolls—and closed in 1978.

One of the club's regulars—and its greatest chronicler—was the acclaimed photographer Diane Arbus. She first showed up in 1958 and started taking pictures from the audience's perspective. In time, she went backstage and, in '59, visited the dressing rooms and shot frontal poses of the performers. Art critic Maria Mitropoulos recognized the social tension at the heart of Arbus's photos: "The hand of one of the young men rests tenderly on his companion. His friend holds his hands in a classically 'sissy' gesture. Both are wearing makeup." Analytically stepping back, she noted, "The challenge is of course to the preconceptions of masculinity that dominated the Cold War. These young men are obviously different. For some indeed they would be 'freaks' or 'sissies.'" According to Laureen Trainer, "Arbus was concerned with how bodily decoration, like make-up, dress, and jewelry, were used by the men to produce an image that was congruous with the culturally-determined idea of how a woman should look."[198]

Drag shows had long been part of the city's live, illicit-performance scene. Richard Bruce Nugent, a noted Harlem Renaissance writer, made the rounds of popular drag shows during the 1920s and '30s. The Ubangi Club, at 131st Street and Seventh Avenue, had a "chorus of singing, dancing, be-ribboned and be-rouged 'pansies.'" It featured Gladys Bentley who famously dressed in a white tuxedo and top hat, sang and accompanied herself on the piano. Jackie ("Moms") Mabley was another Harlem favorite, often appearing in men's street attire. As Nugent recalls, Walter Winston's performance as "'Sepia Gloria Swanson'—with her loud, friendly expansiveness, her 'boy friends,' furs and evening gowns, her ever-ready wit and lace-draped apartment—easily became and remained queen of them all."

Nugent also visited midtown clubs and reports that Jean Malin, a popular drag entertainer, was the toast of Jack "Legs" Diamond's Club Abbey. The Abbey was located in the Hotel Hardin at 203 West 54th Street and featured Malin with a chorus line of "pansy" showgirls. The Pansy Club, located a couple blocks south, at 48th Street and Broadway, next door to Niles Granlund's famous Hollywood Restaurant, in the heart of the Theatre District, was another drag club. Karyl Norman, popularly known as the Creole Fashion Plate, was the club's mistress of ceremonies. Born George Peduzzi in Baltimore, Norman performed widely on the drag circuits in the United States, Europe, and Australia. Remarkably, he performed both in and out of drag. Moving to Los Angeles, he appeared in the 1933 movie, *Arizona to Broadway*, but died the same year in a car crash.

Posture Girl

The modern presentation of the erotized performance female dates from the celebrated "posture girl" of English court life of the late-eighteenth and early-nineteenth centuries. None of these was more famous than Lady Emma Hamilton. Born Emily Lyons (1765–1815), she was an unwed mother at sixteen who later gained renown throughout Europe as the wife to an ambassador and who had an out-of-wedlock child with Britain's Admiral Horatio Nelson. She was celebrated for her "body poetry," "plastic poses," and "living statues." No less an authority of beauty than Johann Wolfgang von Goethe, author of *Dr. Faust*, was captivated by her very licentious performance. "Then she loosened her hair, took a few shawls and arranged a series of attitudes, poses, gestures, so that one finally thought that one was dreaming," he wistfully recalled. "Standing, kneeling, sitting, lying, earnest, sad, droll, debauched, repentant, enticing, threatening, terrifying, etc. . . . She knew well how to choose and change the folds of her veil for each expression."[203]

The posing of sexually provocative females in live public performances emerged slowly in New York and the nation. In 1827, a scandal greeted Madame Francisque Huntin, a celebrated European dancer and the first solo ballerina to perform in Gotham. She debuted at the prestigious Park Theatre on Park Row and her costume overshadowed her performance. A contemporary observer noted that she wore loose trousers and, over it, "a light silk frock which, when she makes her 'pirouettes' . . . becomes . . . inflated with wind and flies up like a parachute, displaying her person to the waist." This was a shocking display before respectable society, for only prostitutes and "waiter girls" (quasi-prostitutes working in concert saloons) showed their ankles.[204]

By the late 1840s, female performers began to appear in tights and to act out "living statuary" shows in all-male saloons and theatres. These performers took well-known poses, postures suggesting a character from a classical tale or sculpture like "The Greek Slave" or "Venus Rising from the Sea." In the post–Civil War period, female performers regularly appeared in tights or "union suits" (i.e., one piece, head-to-foot undergarments), increasing erotic exposure. In 1866, Niblo's Garden, on Broadway near Prince Street, hosted Gotham's first musical comedy, "The Black Crook." A pious minister, Reverend Charles B. Smythe, who presided over the First United Presbyterian Church, on East 116th Street, denounced the play: "The first thing that strikes the eye is the immodest dress of the girls with short skirts and undergarments of thin, gauze-like material, allowing the form of the figure to be discernible."[205]

In its heyday, burlesque was like no other popular form of commercial entertainment. The first American performance of this new form of theatrical art occurred on the evening of September 28, 1868, when British star Lydia Thompson and her troupe, the British Blonds, took the stage of the George Wood's Museum Theatre, on Broadway and 31st Street, and performed the *Ixion*. The eight-hundred-seat house was sold out and the audience was delighted, according to a *New York Times* report, by a star "of the purest type, saucy, blue-eyed, golden-haired and of elegant figure." The performers wore provocative outfits, including flesh-colored tights and "skirts cut above the knee, their legs clad in pink tights." Most scandalous, they all dyed their hair blond. The production included the dancing of the cancan, only recently introduced in Paris, and "jigs, hornpipes, and parodies of minstrel show numbers." In no time, Thompson became a national sensation and, almost singlehandedly, instituted a new, popular art form that competed with traditional legitimate theatre.[206]

Two factors distinguished burlesque from other forms of popular, nineteenth-century (male) entertainment. First, it drew inspiration from and found a loyal, enthusiastic audience among working-class men. It represented a different aesthetic or theatrical sensibility than more middle- and upper-class live performances, whether vaudeville or legitimate theater. Second, the early woman burlesque performer represented the most radical expression of female identity, of what would come to be known a half century later as the "new woman." Burlesque's new woman combined what theatre historian Robert Allen calls "sexual allure and inversive feminine insubordination." "Either half alone could be controlled and made to please without seriously undermining the position of the male spectator," he points out. "Fused together in a single performer, however, this combination was much more threatening."[207]

The original burlesque star directly engaged her (mostly) male audience, challenging the established masculine prerogative about direct sexual expression. She undermined the male's exclusive control over the expression of erotic desire. Thompson and other early burlesque performers foreshadowed the modern female pop star, whether Mae West, Marilyn Monroe, Madonna, or Lady Gaga. The early burlesque star's performance was in stark contrast to the more legitimate vaudeville theatre of the early twentieth century typified by the Ziegfeld Girl who pranced to please, an object of conquest. The burlesque performer engaged the male audience, directly and actively, through her revealing display and provocative stage performance.

On a particularly hot evening in 1917, Mae (sometimes spelled May) Dix promenaded before an enthusiastic, nearly all-male audience at the Minsky's National Winter Garden Theater. Dix was, recalls Morton Minsky in his tell-all memoir, *Minsky's Burlesque*, "a red haired beauty with a gorgeous figure and a great way of putting over a comedy song." Amid the night's revelry, she "accidentally" stripped off her showgirl's costume, a short black dress with detachable white collar and cuffs. "At the end of her song one hot summer night," Minsky recalls, "she removed her collar as she walked offstage, trying to forestall the next laundry bill." Her "accident" changed popular entertainment.

The National Winter Garden Theater was located on Second Avenue and Houston Street, an epicenter of Gotham's early twentieth-century downtown entertainment scene. It was on the sixth floor of a nondescript building accessed either by trudging up five long flights of stairs or taking the rickety freight elevator. And, in an era before air conditioning and no-smoking laws, the theater was likely insufferably hot, suffocating with bodily aromas and cigarette smoke. Nevertheless, Dix's show was a hit.

Inspired by the loud applause and catcalls from the audience of mostly working-class, ethnic men, the starlet returned for an encore. Dix casually removed her costume's detachable wrist cuffs and, as Minsky recounts, "between the heat and the applause, May lost her head, went back for a short chorus, and unbuttoned her bodice as she left the stage again." Her display broke a long-held legal and social convention that barred women from fully exposing themselves in entertainment venues while performing. Dix's performance announced a new aesthetic, the female nude as an erotic spectacle.

By World War I, the striptease had become the principal attraction on the burlesque circuit. For a half century, burlesque, a distinct theatrical art form, had cultivated generations of famous comics, singers, and performers. Yet, by 1917, it had been reduced to a rigid form of erotic representation, the striptease. An erotically suggestive nude female pranced the bump-and-grind or another act on a stage before the gaze of a predominately male audience. How this came about is the story of how modern, urban America was fashioned.

In 1919 and 1920, Reverend John Roach Straton went underground to assess the immortality of Gotham's urban vice. He followed in the well-trod footsteps of earlier moralists Anthony Comstock and Reverend Charles Parkhurst who had uncovered the sins of the city. Straton, who presided over Calvary Baptist Church on West 57th Street, boldly ventured into illicit dance halls, boxing matches, speakeasies, and Broadway theaters. He found vice everywhere, including card games, jazz music, modern art, romance novels, movies, women in low-cut dresses, and the Museum of Natural History.

Writing in a 1920 tract, "The Menace of Immorality in Church and State," Straton admitted being shocked attending a 1919 performance of "Grove of Aphrodite" at the Century Theater, at Central Park West and 62nd Street. "I visited one of the most famous midnight shows on Broadway the other evening. The place simply reeked with the commingled odors of cheap perfume and expensive food," he lamented. Going further, he found "one suggestive song followed another. The dances of the performers were exactly the same as those performed for men only in 'resorts' in former years. Not content with singing these songs on the platform, the singers formed in line, the girls sandwiched between the men, and marched around between the tables, swaying in the most suggestive manner possible." What he found most galling was that "not a single person sitting at the tables protested. In fact they all smiled their approval."

"This show is a challenge, not merely to religious convictions but to elemental decency," Straton advised. "It was a nightmare of nude men and women, with bare-legged negro men, in addition to the white men, squirming in and out and rubbing against the practically naked white girls." He found "it was an orgy of sensuality and shame, with men and women, in a condition of almost complete undress, hugging each other, and slobbering over each other, and lolling on couches with each other, and dancing in feigned drunken revelry together." Stanley Walker, author of the celebrated Depression-era classic *The Night Club Era* (1933), and who was then the editor of the *New York Herald Tribune*, called "Aphrodite" "a production which, for those days, was regarded as pretty far south." Straton concurred, insisting, "it is an affront to the intelligence, as well as to the moral ideals, of our citizenship. It is not 'art'; it is abomination. It is not 'love'; it is lust. It is the apotheosis of everything that is vile and degrading." His rant led to the firing of the African American performers.[208]

In the years following Dix's performance, the striptease began to move in two directions depending on the performance and the venue. Performance involved how the female stripper removed her costume—was it the strip or the tease? The strip involved the practice of disrobing, the shedding of one's performance skin; the tease involved salacious seduction, the art of disrobing. The venue involved the physical space—and the paying customer—where the performance took place. In simplest terms, strips taking place at theaters catering to downtown working-class males and uptown sophisticated swells were different. The striptease's popular appeal precipitated a major anti-vice campaign led by Mayor LaGuardia. In 1938, at the height of the Depression, he shut down all of Big Apple's burlesque houses. During WWII, with the enormous increase in single men passing through the city to face an unknowable fate, the city relaxed its anti-vice standards.

In 1951, Harold Minsky, Abe's son, moved the family's burlesque business to downtown Newark, New Jersey. A number of burlesque houses operated in Jersey, including Union City's Hudson and Newark's Empire Theaters, often drawing New Yorkers—like H. L. Mencken—out for some old-time fun. Minsky renovated the Adams Theater , claiming his theater was the "Radio City Music Hall of Burlesque." "We try to give them not dirt-sex, but fun sex," he opined. Always looking for a promotional angle, he showcased Christine Jorgensen after her sex change operation. According to historian Rachel Shteil, "Jorgensen's association with burlesque revealed how in this era strip tease was linked to deviance."[209]

In 1957, the year the Supreme Court handed down the landmark *Roth* decision, it ruled, in *Adams Theatre v. Keenan*, to uphold a 1953 New Jersey decision that applied a higher obscenity standard to live public performances than to books, magazines, photos, and films. The Newark ordinance targeted a burlesque house and prohibited "the performance of any dance, episode, or musical entertainment, the purpose of which is to direct the attention of the spectator to the breasts, buttocks, or genital organs of the performer."[210]

Rubbing Bodies

According to legend, taxi-dance halls emerged in San Francisco in the late nineteenth century and, by the 1920s, were a nationwide phenomenon. These heterosexual venues permitted what was then referred to as "erotic" or "sensual" dancing. They encouraged the "girl" to engage in suggestive body rubbing, touching, the use of provocative language, and even masturbation to bring the male customer to orgasm. Taxi-dance halls did not permit intercourse. Nevertheless, as one female performer warned an investigator, she could "starch your underwear."

Taxi-dance halls got their name from a hack or taxi driver running the meter. Dances took place in a formal dance hall setting with a live band or orchestra performing. The male patron was expected to purchase tickets that he turned over to the dancer when finished; she in turn redeemed them for cash, less attendant costs. Dances were short, running a couple of minutes and the band only briefly paused between songs. Like a taxi's meter, a lighted counter was placed above the band indicating how many dances had taken place. "Because the dances were so short, and the band hardly paused between them," reports historian Elizabeth Clement, "a series of lights above the orchestra indicated to the dancers how many dances had gone by." It is reported that it took a man between five and eight dances to ejaculate.[211]

Paul Cressey, a 1920s University of Chicago sociologist, pioneered the study of the taxi-dance hall. He was fascinated by the social phenomenon of "transient associates." He believed such dancing involved three forms of sexual alliance. One involved conceiving the dancer as a mistress embodying "well-understood standards of loyalty and faithfulness"; the man "pays the rent" or "buys the groceries" and the alliances may last for months. A second form of association involved the dancer in a part of a plural alliance: "the girl enters an understanding by which she agrees to be faithful to a certain three or four men, who many even come to know one another." The third involved the one-night stand or overnight date; it was "a rather frequent practice . . . [that] quickly takes on the character of clandestine prostitution."

Cressey found that, "actually, however, the professional prostitute is seldom discovered in a taxi-dance hall. While promiscuous sex behavior and extramarital alliances of varying types are all to frequent, prostitution of the old forms is not common." Nevertheless, in 1931 in response to a mounting moralist outcry over the questionable standards at New York dance halls, fifteen taxi-dance hall proprietors formed the Five Boro Ballroom and Dancing Academy Owners' Association to self-regulate the industry. In the summer of '31, the NYPD took over licensing and inspecting dance halls.[212]

What made these establishments remarkable was that, by the 1920s, they had become identified with interracial mixing, especially between white women and Asian and other immigrant men. In cities like New York, San Francisco, and Chicago with significant Chinese, Filipino, and Japanese immigrant communities, along with Italian and Spanish-language immigrants, taxi-dance halls provided one of the only social venues for immigrant men to associate with women, particularly white women, however limited and exploitive they might have been.

In Gotham, men could have fun and obtain sexual release at the same time and at a relatively low price. Taxi-dance clubs like the Rainbow Garden on East 125th Street as well as the Sunbeam Dance Palace, Happyland Dance Academy, Lincoln Square Dancing, and Goldman's Dance Hall welcomed all. Numerous reports document how these men were overcharged, insulted, and taken advantage of. Yet, these dance halls were among the few public venues that single, immigrant men could socially (let alone sexually) engage with women. And they did so for as little as $2 to $3 compared to what it cost to have sex with a prostitute; $6-plus for a black prostitute and $10-plus for a white prostitute. Some of these clubs persisted into the '50s and '60s, most notably the Parisian Dance Land at 49th Street and Broadway and Orpheum Dance Palace at 46th and Broadway.[213]

The female theatrical performer—and, indirectly, the American woman—was slowly being sexualized in the decades between the Civil War and the Great War. "Girl shows" were one of terrains of illicit sex engagement during post-WWI America. They first appeared as a sideshow act at the 1893 Chicago Exposition and quickly became a feature of touring circus midway sideshows, carnivals, truck, and railroad shows. These shows crisscrossed the nation, bringing live entertainment to small-town and rural America where anti-vice rules were more lax. These shows developed out of burlesque, which had thrived in the United States from the 1860s, and were contemporaneous to other popular forms of sexually provocative entertainment, including vaudeville, tabloid shows, and revues. Girl shows were pegged as a lower-cost alternative because of their more explicit erotic presentations. During the Depression, low-cost admissions helped propel burlesque into the nation's most popular form of entertainment. They introduced the still popular G-string.[214]

Between 1902 and 1920, the number of girl shows operating across the United States jumped from seventeen to an estimated two hundred. During its heyday, the traveling girl show fell into two distinct categories—revue shows and cooch shows. "Girl shows in carnivals were classified by carnies as revue shows," notes A. W. Stencell, in his marvelous study *Girl Show*. They were large burlesque shows featuring chorus lines, comedians, variety acts and female dancers. It was not uncommon for one of the strippers to disrobe to a G-string and pasties. Cooch shows, on the other hand, usually had only two or three girls, but according to Stencell, they rarely disappointed men who had come out to the midway to see naked women.[215] "One of these [revues] was that in nearly all cooch shows there were no seats," Stencell reports, "the guys just stood around the small stage." He evocatively describes the scene: "The girls would strip down to just their G-strings. Then it cost more to see them nude. Also, the cooch show rarely had comics or novelty acts. And, while the revues and most girl shows never went nude, the cooch always did."[216]

Bill English, who ran Gold Medal Shows during the pre-WWII period, explains how his show worked. "The girls [would dance] onstage in front of a curtain. They would remove their tops and finish topless." He would then come on stage and introduce a "special" show, nude female performance—and only for an additional fifty cents. "We would raise the curtain on the first stage and the girls would dance nude on the stage behind." When the performance ended, "the girls would ding the crowd themselves, saying they would do something extra special for the tips. This turned out to be the same nude dance repeated."[217] Whatever other "extra special" the performers would do for paying customers is not reported.

While the female performers at these shows appear to have had very little use for S&M or other traditional fetish devices, they were nonetheless very inventive in their use of props and, most especially, costumes to enhance their overall appeal. The elaborate burlesque costumes were an essential feature of the review show and often served at the starting point of presentation for the cooch show. Perhaps the most famous props were the fans and feathers pioneered by Faith Bacon and Sally Rand, respectively.[218] At the end, however, nipple-tassels or pasties and the G-string were the final barriers to the total female nudity demanded by male fantasy.

These female performance artists used still other props to squeeze a little bit more money from the male audience or "mark." Baby powder was applied by the mark to the back and front of her naked body, and then she rubbed against him, leaving a unique memento. The performer sometimes applied peanut putter to her breasts that, as one reports, "I would go boom-boom with my tits and leave peanut butter all over his face, nose and hair." Some performers placed a lit candle on the stage floor before the audience, squatted down over it and blew it out. Even money was exploited, as Stencell reports, "Many girls would get the guys to fold a dollar bill lengthwise and they would pick it up from the stage with their sex." But perhaps the biggest hit was the use of an egg. As Stencell notes, "Sometimes the girls would put an egg inside themselves in the dressing room and come out onstage and squat down and drop the egg from between their legs."[219]

By the mid-'50s, many of the leading burlesque stars saw the proverbial handwriting on the wall and started accepting offers to perform in popular outdoor and traveling venues. Legendary strippers like Gypsie Rose Lee, Georgian Sothern, Crystal Ames, Tirza, Vicki Wells, and Blaze Fury were major attractions at these traveling shows. They helped make the '50s the zenith of this unique American institution of live illicit performance.

Female impersonators were a unique feature of many traveling girl shows. "For many gay men and women, too, it was a safe world where you were judged only on the job you did," Stencell observes. Male-to-female transsexuals and transvestites performed what were then called a "half-and-half." Among such performers were Hedy Jo Star, a transsexual burlesque stripper; Jaydee Easton, a regular at the larger "10-in-1" carnival side shows; and George West and Cleo Renew, who Easton recalls as "two old drag queens." In the era before silicon implants, impersonators had doctors inject "water tits" into their chests to simulate breasts; they lasted for only about one month. Hiding their male genitalia for onstage performance required ingenuity. "You got rid of your male sex by looping an elastic piece around your penis and pulling it back and up," Easton admits. "The elastic band holding everything back was attached to a small rubber ball that was inserted in your anus. . . . Done properly you could even turn around and show your backside."[220] No sacrifice was too great for one's art.

Lewd

In April 1955, New York City's license commissioner, Edward T. McCaffrey, ruled against permitting Thomas Phillips, executive director of the Burlesque Artists Association, from presenting a burlesque show at Brooklyn's Orpheum Theater at 574–78 Fulton Street. In no uncertain terms, McCaffrey argued, "to the mind of

most citizens the current meaning of the word burlesque is synon-
ymous with the strip and the tease, the bump and the grind and the
dialogue of double meaning of unvarnished salaciousness." Phillips
insisted his show was "true American burlesque," popular during the
first-quarter of the twentieth century and distinguished by "a satire
on events . . . with real low-comedy situations, a good chorus, an all-
star cast and no nudity." He also explained that "exotic work"—such
as the striptease—would be "part of the night club routine." Phillips
appealed the commissioner's decision.

A month later, and to the surprise of many, New York Supreme
Court Justice Aron Steuer directed the city's license commissioner
to permit Phillips to stage the show, "but without strip teases, run-
ways and exotic dancers." The judge said that Phillips could use the
term "burlesque," which had been officially banned in 1940 by Mayor
LaGuardia. He argued that such a ban "amounts to a censorship without even the merit of reasonable grounds for belief that was to censored
would be objectionable." However, ever cautious with regard to abuse
of the ruling, Steuer added, "this does not mean that we do not have an
adequate means of preventing lewd or indecent exhibitions."[221]

In the late '40s, midtown jazz clubs, many located on West 52nd
Street, started promoting strip shows to attract customers. In March
1948, *Time* bemoaned the fate of 52nd Street. "Where nightclubs
in sorry brownstones crowd each other like bums on a breadline,
an era was all but over. Swing was still there, but it was more hips
than horns. Barrelhouse had declined." It went on to note: "Burlesque was back. . . . There was little jazz left on 52nd Street. Even
the customers had changed. There were fewer crew haircuts, pipes
and sports jackets; more bald spots, cigars and paunches."[222] In
1951, Arnold Shaw made a survey of West 52nd Street clubs and
found that "the strip joints outnumbered the jazz clubs by seven to
three." On one side of the block, strip clubs included the Flamingo
at 38 West, the Club Nocturne at 54 West, and Club del Rio at 60
West; on the other side of the street were the Club Ha-Ha at 39 West
(featuring Sherry Corday and Toy Carol), the Lido at 41 West, the
Harem at 57 West, and the Moulin Rouge (hosted by Melba, "the
Toast of the Town"). Other clubs featuring strippers included the

French Quarter, Club Pigalle, the Flamingo, Club Nocturne, Club del Rio, and Henry Fink's Club Samoa with its South Pacific theme. Shaw found that "the police department constantly received reports that girls were brushing against customers and seating themselves at table uninvited."[223]

In '54, *Playboy* featured a special spread about 52nd Street and what it dubbed "novelty strippers." "There was a time when a girl could count on an enthusiastic audience by simply peeling down to her birthday suit. Not so today," it reported. "The modern male is a jaded animal." That same year, *Newsweek* reported that fifty nightclubs in the city featured striptease acts. An established venue like Leon & Eddie, at 33 West 52nd Street, highlighted Sherry Britton whose act "was only mildly risqué and gave no offense to the family-type audience that frequented the club." Britton also performed at the Club Samoa, at 62 West. However, Leon & Eddie's big headliners were Lili St. Cry, Winnie Garrett ("the Flaming Redhead"), and Georgia Sothern ("the Wow Girl"). Even the Famous Door featured Camille, who was billed as "the Six Foot Sex Girl." The Three Deuces showcased Zorita who performed with a live snake. And the grand old man of burlesque, Harold Minsky, recalls seeing Sothern perform: she "did six minutes of bumps and grinds to the fast music of 'Hold That Tiger' and generally came offstage needing oxygen."

"'Top Banana': Burlesque Not Dead Yet," read the *New York Herald Tribune* the front-page story of October 28, 1951. Johnny Mercer, the legendary lyricist, songwriter, and entertainer, authored the piece and wrote the music and lyrics for the new production. Mercer asks a key question: "Is burlesque too specialized a facet of the entertainment world to sustain a Broadway musical? We don't think so." By "we" he was referring to Phil Silvers, the song-and-dance comic, and the other performers and producers of his old-fashioned Minksy-style show.[224]

More than burlesque and strip shows took place in the midtown west's honky-tonk.* In '55, the TV producer Bernie Brillstein was a regular at the Club Samoa and tenderly recalled it as "a bust-out joint

---

* See "Honky-Tonk."

on Fifty-second Street where guys could pick up broads. We'd eat club sandwiches and drink Cokes, and be treated like kings while the girls jerked off their other customers under the table." Philosophically, he admitted, "The girls would pretend they wanted to meet these losers later, but they never did." Jess Stearn, author of the 1956 book *Sisters of the Night*, reports that an increasing number of "B-girls" called 52nd Street home. He said that during the '50s, young amateurs, most notably struggle actresses and dancers, replaced traditionally more "professional" prostitutes. He claims they got $500 to a $1,000 an hour for services rendered.[225]

Cabaret magazine dated 52nd Street's nadir to 1953. In 1955, it reported "the demise of West 52nd as a nitery center was hastened by the police. Many of the places were hauled up on the carpet for permitting women employees to mingle with the guests, for providing insufficient illumination, for fast B-girl practices, and for other infractions. Licenses were suspended for months or permanently." Shaw dates its demise to July 4, 1960, when the State Liquor Authority cancelled the licenses to sell alcoholic drinks of seven 52nd Street clubs in one day. An era was coming to an end.

The Honky-Tonk entertainment scene was facing a crisis. The public exhibition of live, erotic performance took shape during the Roaring '20s and survived the Great Depression and WWII. Now, New York was being restructured due to the creation of a truly national market economy and suburbanization. Times Square was suffering, and live—and especially sexually risqué—entertainment helped draw business. A wink-and-a-nod acceptance existed between club owners (and performers) and law-enforcement agents (police and courts). The new Honky-Tonk, one with a national character, incubated a new live experience.[226]

SEX

FLESH TRADE

POLLY ADLER, 1900–1962

Sin City

Daily media reports often headline tantalizing stories of the New York Police Department arresting streetwalkers, breaking up a prostitution ring, and closing storefront massage parlors offering other, more genital, services. Sin still sells. However, between 2008 and 2012, the state Division of Criminal Justice Services reported the NYPD arrested only 5,834 people for patronizing a prostitute. On average, that's only 1,167 arrests per year—twenty-two or so a week—and that's in a city with millions of adult residents and visitors (e.g., businesspeople and tourists) prowling the city streets every day and night.[229]

In 2012, the city's police commissioner, Ray Kelly, championed yet another program to curb the oldest profession, Operation Losing Proposition; one can only wonder who "brands" these undertakings. Like similar programs before it, this one targeted the customers, the johns. It was armed with the latest, high-tech "solutions" that taxpayers' dollars could pay for, using decoys armed with remote audio systems; "arrest teams," and undercover officers providing backup. The NYPD—along with other local police forces and DAs across the nation—regularly holds press conferences promoting their latest prostitution busts.[230]

These police efforts mostly target what is best understood as the low-hanging fruit of the flesh trade. Columbia University sociologist Sudhir Venkatesh makes this clear in a revealing 2011 study, "How Tech Tools Transformed NY's Sex Trade." His findings are simple: the flesh trade is big business in the Big Apple. "The economies of big cities have been reshaped by a demand for high-end entertainment, cuisine, and 'wellness' goods," he notes. "In the process, 'dating,' 'massage,' 'escort,' and 'dancing' have replaced hustling and street-walking. A luxury brand has been born. These changes have made sex for hire more expensive."[231]

Venkatesh segments the city's commercial sex business into four groups, with the respective terms of services "for traditional inter-course." A streetwalker got a $75 fee and her pimp's cut was 25 per-cent (30 percent on weekends). Self-employed hookers got $150 per session and pocketed it all, but "she has to pay for online marketing, transportation, security, bribes to shopkeepers, and drugs for cli-ents." "Blue-collar" escort services charged $350 per outcall session and the sex worker got 60 percent, but the service "pays for adver-tising and on-call security officers. The client covers the hotel room and drinks." Finally, for upscale escort services—like that used by former New York governor Eliot Spitzer and other high-rollers—the sex workers are paid separately; "if one gets the standard $2,000, the other gets the same. The client covers expenses." What a great tax write-off.[232]

The structure of the Big Apple's flesh trade suggests the finan-cial, social, and sexual organization of commercial sex operating throughout the country. A quick Google search of "prostitution" and "prostitution arrests" lists innumerable stories about sexual exchanges taking place everywhere and all the time throughout the country. However, according to the most recent FBI data, only 44,090 people were arrested in 2011 for "prostitution and commercialized vice"; this represents a 50 percent drop in arrests from the 2004 total of 87,872. The FBI offers no explanation as to why this remarkable decline has taken place.

Going to Polly's?

For a quarter century, "Going to Polly's?" was a popular question among late-night partygoers in the know. Before his election to mayor in '26, Jimmy "Beau James" Walker visited Polly Adler's sex salon, as did many late-night partygoers. Regulars included Robert Benchley, George S. Kaufman, and even Dorothy Parker of the Algonquin Round Table gang; Adler fondly recalled Benchley as "the kindest, warmest-hearted man in the world."[233]

Adler was born Pearl Adler, the daughter of Gertrude (Koval) and Morris Adler in Yanow, Belorussia, near the Polish border in 1900. Just before World War I broke out, her parents sent their fourteen-year-old daughter to live with family friends in Holyoke, Massachusetts. She arrived aboard the *Naftar* and began a new life in a new world; she did not see her parents and siblings again until 1928 when they, too, immigrated to the United States.[234]

Looking for better opportunities, she moved to Brownsville, Brooklyn, living with cousins and working in a shirt factory. In 1916, Margaret Sanger opened the first—and short-lived—birth control clinic, not far from where Adler lived.* When she was seventeen, the factory foreman raped her. While rape may have been all too common in early-twentieth-century Gotham (like it is today), Adler found herself pregnant and undertook the bold move of having an abortion. Her family and the tight-knit patriarchal Jewish community of Brownsville shunned her because of her decision. In defiance—and through a classic topsy-turvy immigrant story—Pearl relocated to Manhattan, renamed herself Polly, and became part of city folklore. The life she created mirrored the city's commercial sex scene during the first half of the twentieth century.

Adler, a small woman standing only four feet eleven inches, was a spitfire who found her way into the prostitution racket by chance. Landing in Manhattan from the wilds of Brooklyn, good fortune enabled her to move in with a young woman living in an apartment on Riverside Drive, on the Upper West Side. There she met actresses,

---

* See "The Pill."

showgirls, and gangsters, forever breaking with her past. In 1922, Adler was hired by a bootlegger to procure women for the flesh trade; a quick learner, she started to freelance. "Soon I was meeting a lot of money men and when I saw the way they flung dough around I thought to myself: Why shouldn't some of it be flung my way?" she reflected. She continues, "So I gave my address to the one who I thought would be discreet, and it wasn't long before three girls were coming in several nights a week to entertain acquaintances I had made along the Great White Way."[235]

Early in her career, Alder was busted in a police raid for running a "disorderly house." This, her first arrest, shook her up and she tried to go straight, opening a lingerie shop that, unfortunately, failed. She returned to the flesh trade. From the Roaring '20s until the early '50s, Adler ran a number of Gotham's most celebrated, upscale bordellos, sometimes called "parlor houses" or brothels. She was a distinct city character, a very New York outsider. One of the sex resorts Adler ran was on West 54th Street and it hosted early-morning live jazz performances by a young Edward "Duke" Ellington and his band. Duke, Sonny Greer, his drummer, and other band members played once or twice a month on Sunday mornings. "We'd show up around 5 o'clock," Greer recalled. "Polly would see we got breakfast, and we'd work until around nine in the morning. It was nothing to leave with fifty or sixty dollars in tips. One of the girls took such a liking to Duke, she started seeing him on the side."[236] Adler even opened a brothel in Saratoga Springs, New York, the summer retreat for Gotham's sophisticated racetrack set.

During her heyday, Polly's operations were ostensibly "protected" by the police and gangsters, and she provided the required kickbacks of hospitality, cash, and sex services. Nevertheless, Adler was busted thirteen times, a casualty of what she called "quota raids." These were the formal prostitution arrests that cops had to make to prove they were doing their job, like recent stop-and-frisk busts. Known to the local fuzz, Adler was a perfect catch when they couldn't make their quota.[237]

Adler enjoyed the uptown city life and was a regular in the Harlem party scene. She visited jazz clubs as well as the more private, intimate buffet parties, a unique part of Prohibition-era, late-night entertainment. In her 1953 memoir, *A House Is Not a Home*,* she recounts visiting a party run by a woman known as "Sewing Machine Bertha" at which upper-class white visitors out for a night of slumming "would be shown lewd pictures as a preview to the performance of the same tableaux by live actors, white and colored." She reports, "money also supplied reefers and cocaine and morphine so that the 'upper clawsses' could have themselves a real low-down time."[238]

Her bordellos welcomed an assortment of notables including a US Senator, famous male and female writers, movie stars, prominent men-about-town, and even "a member of the White House inner circle." And they came for more than sex. One night, after hosting a grand dinner party, Adler brought on the night's entertainment that included "three queer boys who were completely in drag, with wigs, false eyelashes, high-heeled pumps and beautiful evening gowns."

The follow-up act "was their opposite number, 'Mabel,' a big fat colored girl clad in white tie and tails." "Mabel" was likely the notorious Gladys Bentley, the Clam House's headliner. She was the only performer to publicly exploit her lesbian identity. The 250-pound alto singer, dressed in top hat and tuxedo, belted out lyrics richly enhanced with double-entendres. Her repertoire of popular songs included "My Alice Blue Gown," "Sweet Georgia Brown," and most famous, "My Subway Man"; she encouraged audiences to join in, especially during the lewd choruses. "If ever there was a gal who could take a popular ditty and put her own naughty version to it," observed one journalist, "La Bentley could do it."[239]

During WWII, Adler was as patriotic as the next person, but in her own way. "As a result of the shortage of hotel accommodation," she admitted, "men who had previously engaged hotel suites in which to entertain now brought their parties to my house, and my bar did a thriving business." However, in '43, she was yet again busted. She was warned not to entertain enlisted men but, she admitted, she "resented the police warning and ignored it." When the cops

---

* Ghostwritten by Virginia Faulkner.

raided her apartment, she was bedridden with pleurisy and ended up in Bellevue Hospital's psychiatric ward. She had self-medicated herself with opiates and was mistakenly diagnosed as a drug addict. When her case was came to trial, it was dismissed. Looking back on the experience, she reflected: "While I cannot say that I enjoyed my sojourn in the psychopathetic ward, I did learn that there are no crazy people—only sick ones."[240]

With the war's end, city life all seemed so unexciting, so over. The edge that had kept Adler *in the life* for a quarter-century seemed to be spent. In an era before the popular adoption of psychotherapy, she turned for advice to one of the few people she trusted: her lawyer, Mrs. Gottlieb. Her next stop was Los Angeles and a new life in the sun. Adler attended college at age fifty and published her memoir, which inspired a 1964 movie starring Shelley Winters and a hit song in the same year written by Burt Bacharach and Hal David and sung by Dionne Warwick. She wisely opined, "Prostitution exists because men are willing to pay for sexual gratification, and whatever men are willing to pay for, someone will provide." Adler died in 1962.

Sexual Pleasure

On January 19, 1959, Edward R. Murrow hosted a remarkable CBS Radio broadcast, "The Business of Sex," a sensational exposé on the flesh trade. Five years earlier, Murrow had defeated Senator McCarthy in a now-legendary TV encounter. In his new program, Murrow took on a different target—moral hypocrisy. He revealed that US companies used prostitutes to further their business interests, including keeping some on their payrolls. Murrow claimed that there were some thirty thousand hookers operating in New York who helped lubricate the wheels of commerce. "We discovered that call girls come from all walks of life," he declared. "They are secretaries, receptionists, school-teachers, models, society girls, fledgling actresses, or housewives in need of extra money."[241]

Murrow's exposé raised serious questions about the moral integrity of not only American business, but also its male corporate leaders. One of the executives Murrow interviewed admitted using sex "is a very common thing in our line of business." He then went on to explain: "We feel that it helps to create the most personal kind of relationship and has lots of advantages. . . . And certainly I would say that this is much more normal than having to pay a bribe to someone in order to accomplish a result. And much more palatable from our viewpoint."[242]

In the '50s, traditional brothels and "call girl" services persisted, but they were increasingly being augmented by a new generation of prostitutes operating out of escort or dating services, nude photographic galleries, massage parlors, and even as sex therapists or surrogates. Sex was slowly being accepted as part of the new normal. This change in commercial sex enabled sex workers easier access to more (male) customers through ads placed in weekly "underground" newspapers and other outlets. However, prostitution remained illegal in New York and nearly every state and local police harassed, demanded bribes from, and arrested hookers. The oldest profession modernized but still remained immoral and illegal, a sin.

In 1971, two sociologists, Charles Winick and Paul Kinsie, published a revealing study of the postwar flesh trade, *The Lively Commerce: Prostitution in the United States*. It documented a major change in the American male's erotic sensibility of sexual pleasure. "Prostitutes and madams report substantial more customers who are seeking oral satisfaction ('muff divers' or 'face men')," they found. Assessing the commercial sex industry, they report, "The trend toward greater orality has been continuous, with a substantial increase after World War II." Their findings were based on extensive first-person interviews with professional sex workers and the annual surveys conducted by the American Social Health Association. The society found that in the postwar period, "nine out of ten customers [of prostitutes] now want some form of oral satisfaction in contrast to the 10 percent requesting it in the 1930s."[243]

During the postwar era, many considered oral sex a "perversion," as some people do even today. Sexual standards then were based on two premises. First, sexual intimacy (especially intercourse) was reserved for married couples with pleasure as a means for procreation. Sexual intercourse involved the classic missionary position; oral sex was shunned. Second, female prostitutes provided the principal means by which heterosexual men could experience what was considered unacceptable sexual pleasures. Alfred Kinsey confirmed this. In his landmark 1948 study, *Sexual Behavior of Human Male*, he found that "Men go to prostitutes to obtain types of sexual activity which they are unable to obtain easily elsewhere." However, he noted, "Few prostitutes offer any variety of sexual technique" other than the conventional intercourse positions, particularly the missionary position. A select few offered mouth-genital contacts and "experience[s] for the sadist or the masochist, and for persons who have developed associations with non-sexual objects (fetishes)." Finally, some provided an opportunity for "males who have participated in sexual activity in groups."[244]

Adding greater texture to the nature of what was commonly understood as deviant sex, Winick and Kinsie point out that "[a]n active prostitute may be exposed to a wide range of 'perversions.'" They note, "some customers like to cry and wear makeup. Others enjoy sexual intercourse with a prostitute while she is tied to a bed or a chair. Still others attach a collar and leash to a prostitute and have her walk around the floor on all fours." The researchers identified other secret indulgences prostitutes facilitated. "Some customers engage in sexual intercourse with a prostitute *a tergo* [from behind], while she is eating from a dish or lapping milk from the floor." Stockings seemed to have a particular fascination. A prostitute who wore only stockings turned on a good number of fetishists; other men masturbated while the hooker seductively removed her stockings; and some johns simulated strangling a prostitute with a stocking. The sociologists discovered "some brothers had a small funeral chamber in which the prostitute would be laid out as if she were about to buried, complete with recorded funeral music and candles at either end of the casket." They add, "the prostitute would be instructed not to move while the customer had intercourse with her."

Some customers sought to fulfill still more specialized desires. Some asked the woman to whip them or wanted to whip her; some wanted to be tied up or to tie her; others brought specific items of clothing, often lingerie, for the woman to wear. Feathers, often ostrich feathers, and clothing made of red or black velvet were other items to adorn the female sex worker. Some clients enjoyed a woman nude adorned only in furs, while others dressed her in nothing but long black gloves or slippers. The hooker biting, scratching, clawing, or punching turned on some others. In conclusion, the researches noted, "The women who meet such specialized requirements are likely to get extra pay. Among the most enthusiastic clients are sadists and masochists, who are likely to be older than the general clientele."[245]

During this period, there were very few male homosexual brothels—or what were called "peg houses."[246] Only two were reported operating in New York during the early '50s. From one eyewitness account, they do not seem to be very attractive, erotic venues of pleasure. Male brothels were "very modest apartments, with several boys in each apartment, sitting around waiting for clients," reported the sociologists. "In the larger [of the two] apartment, two bedrooms were available for the use of the prostitutes and their customers. Most of the boys were wearing service uniforms—Army, Navy, and Marines."[247] If requested, many heterosexual brothels supplied male homosexual prostitutes. "Scarcely a madam of a 'house' exists (or existed, at least recently) who doesn't have a boy available of just about the right age, type, and proclivity the male customer might dare to designate—all for a price, of course," they reveal. Going further, they noted that such service is "often at an even higher fee than that charged for the girls, because, alas, the males cannot perform their functions with full satisfaction as often in a given period."[248]

Other researchers of the period confirm this assessment. Dr. Harry Benjamin and R. E. L. Masters, writing in their "definitive report," *Prostitution and Morality* (1964), found that "many individual prostitutes and some brothels cater to almost the entire gamut of sexual deviations." They distinguished a wide-range of unorthodox sexual "deviations":

> Men who wish to be beaten by women, or to beat them; men who wish to be bound by women, or to bind them; fetishists who desire

partners wearing garments of rubber, leather, or fur; other fetishists who want partners in boots, in high heels, in masks, or partners with large breasts or long hair; transvestites, who want to have intercourse while dressed as women—or, sometimes, simply to converse while dressed as women; exhibitionists and voyeurs; persons—coprophiles, urolagniacs, etc.—whose predilections involve urine and feces; necrophiles satisfied by a partner simulating a cadaver; these are by no means the only deviants among the prostitutes customers.

Never losing sight of the commercial exchange at the heart of this, the oldest profession, Benjamin and Masters noted, "In general, the more extreme the deviation, and the more dangerous or painful for the prostitute, the higher is the fee demanded of the customer."[249] The women who provided such services, especially sadism and masochism, tended to be older. Winick and Kinsie confirmed this assessment, noting that "perhaps because with age they realize that such service yield more money, or because 'straight' customers become more difficult to find."[250]

Helping to further illuminate the extremes of sexual pleasure, Benjamin and Masters pointed out that there are "some men who are attracted to maimed or deformed women, to dwarfs and giantesses, to women who are pregnant, who are lavishly tattooed, who have unusual skin conditions or scars, and so on." They identified the unique appeal of women with various amputated limbs or breasts as well as hunchbacked women. "In the United States," they observed, "the demand for these unusual physical specimens apparently greatly exceed the supply."[251]

The Oldest Profession

As the truism goes, prostitution is the oldest profession, and hookers in the Big Apple date from the earliest Dutch settlement. The city's first madam is reputed to be Griet or Grietje ("Little Pearl") Reyniers, a lively *bawd* or *doxie*. In 1668, when taunted by seamen on a departing sloop with the cry, "Whore! Whore! Two pound butter's whore!" She allegedly responded accordingly: lifting her petticoat, she pointed to her naked backside, replying: "*Blaes my daer achterin.*" Repeatedly assailed by respectable citizens, she thumbed her nose at them, insisting, "I have long been the whore of the nobility, now I want to be the rabble's whore."

Reyniers was born in Amsterdam (some say Wesel, Germany) in 1602 and died around 1669 in Gravesend, Breuckelen (now Brooklyn). According to some researchers, her name indicates that her family was of Huguenot descent. She sailed to New Amsterdam in '1629 aboard the *De Zoutberg* ("Salt Mountain") and, according to some accounts, plied her trade with male passengers and seamen alike. Some aboard were scandalized when Reyniers pulled "the shirts of some of the sailors out of their breeches." In addition to settlers, the ship she sailed on would likely have carried livestock, wagons, plows, tools, clothing, food seeds, firearms, and cheap goods for trade.[252]

The Fort Amsterdam she found is really unimaginable today. It was a tiny port enclave with a population of about 270 Dutch folk and some Lenape Indians. Over the next three decades, the town's population grew exponentially, reaching about 1,500 people in 1664 when the English seized it, renaming it New York. A few years before Reyniers arrived, in 1625 or '26, the settlement witnessed the arrival of eleven slaves. These African men had been seized by Dutch privateers from Spanish or Portuguese ships and had names like John Francisco, Antony Portugsee, and Simon Congo. The Dutch claim to New Amsterdam was part of larger territory that stretched along the East Coast known as New Netherlands. It stretched from Gloucester, New Jersey, to Albany, New York, and into Brooklyn. In the 1698 census, the city had nearly five thousand inhabitants.[253]

As a young woman in Amsterdam, Reyniers reportedly worked at Peter de Winter's tavern, but was argumentative and was fired for acting discourteously to customers. The tavern mistress claimed to have seen her in a back room, "her petticoat upon her knees." Nevertheless, she was married twice, the first time to Aelbert Egberts, a twenty-year-old tailor from Haarlem, in September 1626. A widow in December 1629, she married Anthony Jansen Van Salee [Jansz], a seaman from Cartagena; some reports say they married while sailing to the New World, while others claim they met and married in New Amsterdam. In May 1647, she was reported still married and the mother of four daughters.

Quickly making the port home, Reyniers apparently loved to walk-the-walk up the Big Apple's first "ladies mile," the East River shoreline meeting-place known as the Strand (now Pearl Street). On these strolls, she is reported to have often hiked her petticoats to display her wares to passing sailors. Many of the goodly settlers of New Amsterdam were staunch Calvinists, members of the Reformed Dutch Church, and were deeply offended by her conduct. They organized a banishment campaign that led to the Common Council expelling her from New Amsterdam; adding insult to injury, she was forced to pay the cost of the trial.[254]

In the three centuries following the Dutch arrival, the tavern was the nexus of New York—and American—civic life. It rivaled the church, functioning as the leading secular institution, housing the first governments and serving as a cultural venue. People didn't drink local water for fear of infection and the local alcohol drinking hole was often more popular than the house of worship. It was a venue promoting alcohol consumption and civil sociability. It was often a second home for prostitutes.

During the colonial era, taverns, often located in a private residence, met important social needs. They were business venues offering congregation for locals and hospitality for travelers. The colony- or locally licensed public house welcomed qualified individuals, men (and occasionally women) who were judged to be respectable and sober. These establishments offered meals, beverages, and lodgings at fixed rates. They served as meeting places for elected officials, gathering places for the sharing of information and gossip, the reading of broadsides and political debate. They were also venues for entertainment, be it fiddle playing or storytelling. They provided travelers a primitive form of hospitality, offering questionable meals, dubious drink, and a shared bed for visitors; many provided food and shelter for a guest's animals. More importantly, they offered wayfarers the opportunity to socialize with fellow travelers and locals. Women-of-the-night often came unescorted.

Following the Civil War and the horrendous 1863 Draft Riot, the city's districts of ill repute moved farther uptown. The movement followed two trajectories: one up the west side, the other up the East Side. Going west, the first stop on this caravan was Greenwich Village, sometimes called "Little Africa" because of the black people who lived there, located between Bleecker Street and Washington Square, and home to fashionable prostitutes. A quarter-century later, at the turn of the twentieth century, the trade moved farther uptown to the Tenderloin, between 23rd to 42nd Streets and Fifth and Eighth Avenues. It was home to "parlor houses" and bordellos located near upscale hotels and theaters on Broadway. First-class sex establishments serviced "gentlemen," while second-class brothels served clerks and mechanics. Below this level, a host of venues operated in working-class neighborhoods throughout the city providing the commercial sex engagement that met the needs of the poor and ethnic/racial minority males.

The Tenderloin was home to some of the city's finest restaurants—the Fifth Avenue Hotel, the Hoffman House, and Delmonico's—as well as Madison Square Garden and the Ladies Mile, the fashion district. At night this district was known as Satan's Circus, home to innumerable saloons and sexual resorts. Among the leading dance halls were the Tivoli (West 35th Street near Broadway), the Bohemia (West 29th Street), Star and Garter (West 30th Street and Sixth Avenue), and Sailor's Hall (on 30th Street), as well as Heart of Maryland, the Broadway Gardens, Stag Café, Paddy Pig's, Pig's Head, White Elephant, and the Chelsea. Buckingham Palace, on West 27th Street, was "the handsomest dance house in the city." It was a two-story building, "gaudily decorated," with an orchestra performing and a balcony running along the second floor with tables and chairs and where anything went. "The women present are the inmates of the neighboring houses of ill-fame and street walkers," reported James McCabe. Another popular venue was the Cairo, located at 36 West 39th Street, decorated in an exotic "Turkish" style and where sexual solicitation was common. Still another unique attraction was the French Madam's resort on West 30th Street, just off Sixth Avenue, famous for its dancing girls who performed a nude cancan in a private cubicle for a dollar a show—other exotic performances were charged accordingly. The area was also home to innumerable sexual resorts, including the White Elephant and the Cremorne. The Cremorne, located in a basement of a building on West 32nd Street, was named after a legendary London nightspot and offered very cheap drinks; it was dubbed, "one of the bawdiest resorts in the Tenderloin."[255]

In the early twentieth century, prostitution was identified as both a symptom and a cause of the moral decay allegedly corrupting the nation. Traditionalists and progressives joined in common cause to fight for its suppression. In 1910, Christian moralists secured the passage of the Mann Act outlawing interstate sex commerce. Prior to the outbreak of WWI, they succeeded in closing approximately 125 "red-light" districts located throughout the country under the requirements of "war discipline."* They got legislation passed that led to the arrest, forceful medical testing, and/or imprisonment of some thirty thousand women for allegedly being carriers of venereal disease and, thus, being "domestic enemies" undermining the war effort.

Naturally, it was poor, working-class, racial minority, and immigrant women who maintained the entire edifice. These women had few if any options and bore the brunt of social scorn and arrest, physical illness, and drug addiction, sometimes even beatings and death to keep the industry functioning. "All too often, a woman had to choose from an array of dehumanizing alternatives," the historian Ruth Rosen astutely observed. These choices included "to sell her body in a loveless marriage contracted solely for economic protection; to sell her body for starvation wages as an unskilled worker; or to sell her body as a 'sporting woman.'"[256] Whatever the choice, some form of prostitution was involved. Respectable society was not kind to these women then, and that remains very much the same today.

---

* The term "red light" is apparently derived from the early days of prostitution in Kansas City when a railroad brakeman posted a red light outside a whorehouse while he was engaged inside; see Ruth Rosen, p. 105.

Commercial Sex

In the Big Apple at the end of WWII many different types of female—and some male—sex workers plied their trade. The women were referred by a host to different—and often demeaning—names, ranging from "call girl," "hooker," "hustler," pony," "puella," "strumpet," "trull," "bawd," "harlot," "biffer," "pos," "prossie," "she-she," "pig-meat," to—in the case of heavy women—"blimps." Their customers were known as "johns," "suckers," or simply "trade." The far fewer males engaged in the sex trade were known as "hustlers" and "hustitutes."[257]

The shift from a war economy of austerity to one of postwar peace and prosperity transformed commercial sex. During the war, military authorities—seeking to prevent a syphilis outbreak among servicemen similar to the one that had occurred during WWI—imposed relatively stiff restrictions on off-base sexual liaisons between servicemen and prostitutes. "By 1945 commercialized prostitution in the United States had reached an all-time low as a result of the high degree of law enforcement by local, county, and state authorities," Winick and Kinsie observed.[258] Of particular note, the long-standing but illegal brothel disappeared from the sexual landscape. For more than a century, brothels, or houses of ill repute, had been one of the principal venues for commercial sex in the United States—especially for young men and single workingmen, novices in the ways of pleasure. It was not uncommon for a father, older brother, or other male relative to bring an inexperienced young male to a neighborhood brothel to have his first sexual experience.

The disappearance of the brothel was due to a confluence of factors. Military authorities were relatively successful preventing sexual engagement by men in uniform with prostitutes given the number of soldiers stationed on restricted US bases and oversees. Nevertheless, an underground sex trade continued, as evident in Polly Adler's experience. With the war's end, America was restructured. Commercial sex was transformed with the rise of the automobile society, mass relocation to the suburbs, and the increase in TV-based consumer culture. A new sexual ethos was emerging, one appealing to

middle-aged and middle-class white men epitomized by the growing popularity of Hugh Hefner's *Playboy* magazine launched in 1953.
This transformation challenged traditional values, precipitating the
postwar culture war. The period's sex-crime and loyalty crises legitimized anti-sex campaigns by local law enforcement, both police
and the courts. The climate of sexual secrecy, with its accompanying
sexual underground, intensified. Yet, faced with repression, illegal
sexuality flourished throughout the country, including an apparent
increase in sexual commerce.[259]

Sex workers ranged from the lowest to the highest level, from
streetwalkers, to bar girls, to call girls ("pony girls" or "party girls"),
to brothel prostitutes, and to private practitioners of special fetishisms or perversions. Female sex workers included "taxi dancers" in
ten-cent-a-dance halls; "corncrib" girls who rented tiny rooms with
cot, chair, and washstand for very quick (e.g., fifteen-minute) sessions; hotel whores who worked out of cheap hotels; masseuses in
massage parlors; and a newly emerging group of prostitutes who conducted their business in automobiles and were sometimes referred
to as "streetwalkers on wheels." Some sex workers conducted business at "fleabag" hookups or, according to one authority, "the lowest
of the low in the hierarchy of whoredom," including impoverished
elderly women servicing skid-row men. Still others included interracial prostitutes who served "unpopular and/or segregated minorities"; "animal" prostitutes working with specially trained dogs, small
horses, and other animals that performed with a female in erotic
exhibitions; and, following Christine Jorgensen's 1953 sex change
operation, transsexual prostitutes.[260] High-end practitioners ranged
from out-call girls and brothel prostitutes to "kiddy freaks" and
excrement fetishists.

But who were these female sex workers? And why did they take up
this, the oldest profession? Jess Stearn, a New York writer of the day,
expressed the dominant attitude. Writing in his 1954 exposé, *Sisters
of the Night*, Stearn identified prostitutes as troubled, unhappy, and
self-loathing women. Not unsympathetic to their plight, he reported
that most were young girls, often innocent as to the ways of the
world, trapped by poverty and moral failing into selling themselves,

be it in a brothel, or as a call girl or streetwalker. Most saw the skin trade as temporary work and all hoped they would get married and leave the life behind them—and some did, but, unfortunately, most did not. Stearn shared the assumption that no matter how much they made financially, these women were burdened by guilt and shame that no amount of money could assuage. In stark disagreement, Beverly Davis, a well-known Hollywood madam who ran a number of successful "sporting clubs" or brothels in the '50s, argues most emphatically that prostitutes go into the life (at least within a brothel or call house) "because they want to."[261]

Prostitutes who were busted, like Adler, ended up at the New York's Women's Court. It was located on the second floor of the Criminal Courts Building in lower Manhattan, a "high-ceilinged, somber and austere room." Most of the women who appeared were identified as streetwalkers, the lowest rung of the commercial sex trade. Most had been busted in a targeted police sweep. In the late '50s, the Women's Court processed some two thousand cases annually, nearly all streetwalkers. "We do not reach the high-class prostitutes at all, they are well hidden and well protected," admitted John Murtagh, the chief magistrate. "The ones we get are the unfortunates who walk the streets. All we do is just try to make the city look clean and pure."[262]

In the Women's Court, justice sometimes triumphed over punishment. Monroe Fry describes a remarkable trial in which a good-hearted cop and kindly judge looked past the law and acquitted a girl-of-the-night. At the trial for solicitation, an undercover cop reported making eye contact with a stylish woman on Central Park South and Sixth Avenue. They smiled at one another; exchanged pleasantries; and the cop asked what he could do for her? She said he could give her a present of $20. Accompanying her to her apartment, he hands her the cash, she undresses and he arrests her. Most remarkable, the judge reviewed her background and discovered that she had no prior arrests, did not have a venereal disease, and was a divorcée raising two children. He turned to the cop and asked: "Think she deserves a break?" The cop answered, unequivocally: "Yes!"[263]

Jewish Jezebel

One evening in November 1930, Polly Alder, Gotham's most infamous madam, received an anonymous phone call, apparently from one of the city's finest. As she later recounted, "the moment I picked up the receiver and even before I could say hello, a man's voice blurted out, 'Hurry, Polly, get out of your house. They're on their way to serve you with a subpoena.' . . . I never found out who called me."[264] Quickly packing an overnight bag, she skedaddled from her East Side apartment, not to return for four months. The subpoena demanded she appear before the Seabury Commission, a state committee investigating municipal corruption. It was one appointment she was not going to keep.

Polly was the talk of the town, a celebrity that only the Roaring '20s twin movements of moral rectitude—alcohol temperance and sexual abstinence—could produce. Over the preceding decade, she had run some of the city's most notorious brothels. To keep her houses of ill repute operating, she regularly offered payoffs, whether in cash or sexual favors, to New York vice cops, politicians, and gangsters—which they all gladly accepted. Adler began her career during the '20s and now, with the onset of the Great Depression, she remained a media darling.

Her East Side phone number (Lexington 2–1099) was a whispered secret among those in the know, whether cop, politician, playboy, gangster, or one of the Algonquin Round Table gang. Adler was a self-made woman who found fame and fortune following a path well trod by others, including Sophie Tucker and Mae West. These women were often daughters of immigrants arriving in the United States around the turn of the twentieth century. They matured to adulthood as part of an historical wave of "new women" who redefined acceptable sexuality and built careers promoting female sexuality. But Adler, as distinguished from Tucker and West, sold the sexual favors of other women as opposed to selling herself, whether as raw talent or a suggestive fantasy. Tucker and West successfully pushed the limits of popular culture to establish a new female aesthetic standard; Adler's career promoted commercial sexual exchange that, nearly a century later, still remains illegal, with the rare exception of parts of Nevada.

In true *Godfather* or *Boardwalk Empire* fashion, Adler's contributions to the payoff grab bag were filtered upward through the police apparatus and the Tammany machine. She knew how to play the game and how to keep secrets. Everyone also knew of her close, professional and personal, relations with some of the city's mob bosses, including Arthur Flegenheimer (a.k.a. "Dutch Schultz") and Charles "Lucky" Luciano.[265]

"I had to get out of town because I wasn't going to talk," Adler later explained. "I am not an informer," she insisted.[266] She would not testify before a special commission set up by Governor Franklin Roosevelt to investigate municipal corruption.* More so because the call came amid front-page stories about the murder of one of the commission's other star witnesses, Vivian Gordon (a.k.a. Benita Franklin Bischoff). She was a thirty-one-year-old divorcée who was, as Adler admits, "in the same business." Shortly after Gordon's strangled body was found in the Bronx's Van Cortlandt Park, her sixteen-year-old daughter committed suicide. Gordon, a former stripper who'd worked for the Minskys, had already provided background testimony about the police vice squad's frame-up scheme of women for alleged prostitution and was about to go public. Rumors circulated that cops killed her. Adler's name was among those found in her phonebook.[267]

Adler knew she could not testify, could not face a judge, a state commission, and the public. She could not have the most intimate aspects of her life splattered across tabloid headlines. Nor could she be put under oath and reveal the workings of her racket, a racket as old as recorded history yet involving some of the city's leading politicians, police, and celebrities. In true Hollywood style, she skipped town, hopping from Newark to Pittsburgh before landing on the sunny sands of Miami.

---

* The investigation was popularly known as the Seabury Commission after Judge Samuel Seabury, the presiding investigator.

When Adler finally returned to Gotham, the heat was off and she agreed to appear before the commission. In May '31, the *Times'* reported, "Polly Adler, alleged keeper of a disorderly house, was enabled, by the system of bribery and corruption in Women's Court, to escape punishment time after time while other innocent women were sent to prison on fabricated evidence covering fifty-five printed pages." Her appearance was anticlimactic: she refused to name names and the commissioners didn't really push her. As the *Times* noted, she "has been defiant under questioning."

During the few gravy years that followed, she lived in an elegant, twelve-room apartment in the heart of "cafe society country," the fashionable East Side, at 35 East 55th Street, between Fifth and Madison Avenues. The bordello had four bedrooms painted in peach and apple green with accompanying baths. "The living room," she later wrote, "was Louis XVI, but not arbitrarily so." It was painted a soft gray, had pale green satin drapes and was decorated with jade lamps. Her apartment even had a taproom sporting a masculine, "military motif" in red, white, and blue, with red leather bar stools. She was especially proud of a "cozy paneled library, the walls were lined with shelves displaying my fine collection of books."

Adler kept four "hand-picked young ladies" who earned a minimum of $50 a night (about $850 in 2015 dollars), before tips. She admitted, "much of the business was after 4:00 a.m., when the city's saloons closed. Free food was served, and the bar did a flourishing business." She ran an upscale enterprise, insisting, "at no time would I allow off-color conversation or the practice of unnatural sex." The ladies-of-the-night were permitted only two drinks while on duty. Sexually speaking, things were pretty tame.

"Strangely enough," Adler found, "the notoriety I had received during the Seabury investigation, instead of alienating my upper-crust clientele, acted as a magnet." New York and the nation, she swooned, was "Polly-conscious," with "money people" flocking to her door for entertainment. Perhaps most surprising, she began to receive women as guests, notably women "who were so rich or so famous or so intellectual or so uninhibited that they could go anywhere." She found herself operating a "coeducational bordello."[268]

In 1935, things began to change for Adler. Under pressure from yet another state investigation of municipal vice and racketeering, this one appointed by Governor Thomas Dewey, she was an easy target. She was subject to an unofficial but apparently organized campaign involving repeated raids, tapping her phone, placing undercover agents as employees in her apartment building and, finally, a serious bust. However, the most frightening event was the assassination of the Dutch Schultz. The good times were over.

In early March, Adler—using the alias "Joan Martin"—was busted as part of a new anti-vice campaign. The *Times* describer "the Adler woman" as "short, stocky, with heavily rouged lips and cheeks and brightly tinted finger nails" who, when released, wore "an expensive fur coat." The police claimed her brothel "had a notorious reputation." She faced two charges. One was for running a "disorderly house" and keeping three young women as "inmates," Eva Coo, Dorothy Walker, and Yvonne Moore; the second was for possessing "indecent" moving pictures. Perhaps more significant, her personal phonebook was seized. She was released after posting $4,000 bond. In classic tongue-and-cheek fashion, she brushed off the charges: "[I've been] the fall guy in so many investigations I'm beginning to feel like a rubber ball."[269] Police commissioner Lewis Valentine did not pull any punches as to the significance of the bust. "I am very much elated over the arrest of the notorious Polly Adler. She is one woman I wanted to see brought in," he opined. "The police who have been working on her case have been doing so for the paste four months, but they could never get her in the place until this morning. We wanted her as the keeper of a disorderly house."[270]

However, when Adler trial final took place, she was convicted of only running a brothel, the "blue movie" episode and her address book were not discussed. As she later admitted, "it would give my customers more confidence in me if they saw that I would go to jail rather than stand trial and be cross-examined about the people named in my 'little black book.'" She received a thirty-day sentence and a $500 fine. Shortly after her conviction, the feds came down on her for income tax evasion, putting a $16,000 lien on her assets.

Adler received unexpected support from the *Daily News*. In an editorial, the paper noted:

> Here is a woman who keeps an expensive house of ill fame, conducting it on the quiet, without complaints from the neighbors, and with every regard for outward decency. . . .
>
> The police tap the woman's wires, set spies on her and in other ways keep her under surveillance as if they suspected her being the Lindbergh kidnapper. . . .
>
> It is this crusading against personnel and private habits and instincts—the sex instinct, the deed-rooted human fondness for gambling as shown by the prevalence of policy gamesters—which is futile and sickening, just as the prohibition of drinking liquor was.[271]

The editorial didn't keep Adler from jail.

Her thirty days at the city's women's jail at the Jefferson Market Women's Court were remarkably uneventful.[272] Unfortunately the jail sentence didn't stop continued police harassment. Respectful cops would show up at her door and advise her to move on. "We hate to do this," one or another would say, "well, take a friendly tip and move." And so she did, jumping from the East Side to the West Side and back, including apartments in West 50s near Seventh Avenue, at 59th Street and Madison Avenue, 77th Street and Amsterdam Avenue as well as spots on West 83rd Street and West 54th Street.

In 1939, *Forbes* magazine published a special issue on the World's Fair that spotlighted Adler. Feeling redeemed, she gloated, "I entered the Valhalla of the American executive." The issue profiled the great pleasures of Gotham, identifying Adler, along with Peggy Wild and Diane B., as running some of the finer "sporting houses." Nevertheless, while agreeing that there had been a shift in the nation's "moral standards," she objected to two of the article's findings. First, she insisted that she ran a house for the "upper bracket" and, second, "my business *never* fell off, regardless of depression or anything."[273] *Fortune* noted that Adler's parlor was "on Central Park West in the Sixties," likely her place at 69th Street and Columbus Avenue.

Physical Pleasures

"Nothing in New York yet compared to Caesar's Retreat," reported Gay Telese in his memorable tale *Thy Neighbor's Wife*. Located on East 46th Street,* Caesar's was the city's most lavish massage parlor. It opened in 1972, the high point of massage parlors as a venue of illicit sexual pleasure. "Thousands of dollars had obviously been spent by its owner—a Bronx-born onetime stockbroker named Robert Scharaga—in decorating, the man private rooms, the sauna, the circular baths, the plaster-cast Romanesque statuary and fountain," Telese noted. It offered free champagne, $20 massage with herbal oils, and even a $100 champagne bath—accompanied by three lovely damsels—for the more adventurous customer.[274]

Talese pioneered "new journalism," a style popular in the 1960s and '70s, opening up news writing to greater literary expression, what was dubbed narrative nonfiction. His accounts of New York massage parlors, like his visits to sex clubs in Southern California, have a participant-observer's critical eye for detail along with a novelist's imaginative flair. He knew what he was writing about. His depiction of a massage parlor's physical environment and working conditions is worth quoting at length:

> After the customer had paid the fee to the manager, and selected the masseuse of his choice, she escorted him through a hall into one of the private rooms, carrying over her a starched sheet she had gotten from the linen closet.
>
> Closing the door and spreading the sheet over the table, she waited until the man had completely nude before she began to remove her clothing. It was the belief of most studio managers that, if the customer happened to be a plainclothes police officer, the masseuse could not be prosecuted for immorality if the policeman had preceded her in exposing himself. While this assumption had yet to be tested in court, it was nonetheless adhered to in most parlors.

---

* John Heidenry places it on East 54th Street; see Heidenry, p. 85.

Although the majority of customers were old enough to be the masseuse's father, there was a curious reversal of roles after the sexual massage had begun: It was the young women who held the authority, who had the power to give or deny pleasure, while the men lay dependently on the backs, moaning softly with their eyes closed, as their bodies were being rubbed with baby oil and talc.[275]

For the services provided, the young female masseuses usually received about one-third of the fee for the session—as well as tips for additional services rendered. Most often, the masseuse provided some form of a full-body massage as well as either a "hand-job" (i.e., masturbation) or a "blow job" (i.e., fellatio). These young women earned between $300 and $500 per week, a relatively good salary for the period.

Massage emerged as a venue for physical therapy during the post-war era as many men returned from the war suffering a wide variety of ailments. During this period, massage underwent a fundamental split, dividing between those seeking to legitimize their practice through professionalization (including licensing boards, trade associations, conventions, etc.) and those, more enterprising, who saw providing physical contact and stimulation, including genital release, as a business opportunity. The line between these two tendencies sometimes blurred and the split between physical therapy and sexual satisfaction continues to define the massage business to this day.

The erotic massage "parlor" as a venue of physical, sexualized pleasure emerged in the West Coast during the mid-'50s. "Visitors were admitted by appointment only, and the masseuses, invariably refined-looking women, often wore starched nurses' uniforms that were covered with a white smock while administering a massage to a naked man on the table," Talese reported. "To be fully massaged and finally masturbated by one of these white-gowned professionals was, to many men, a highly erotic experience."[276]

Success killed the massage parlor. By the early '70s, they moved from the sexual underground to the cutting-edge mainstream; parlors—like Caesar's—got hip, one aspect of the '60s sexual revolution.[277] This transformation was due, in significant part, to the growing acceptance and popularity of once discreet, illicit, sexual indulgences. Public morality was changing and so too the sexual culture. Nudity was increasingly more acceptable, especially as evident in magazines, movies, and even Broadway plays. A shift in values among many young, college-aged women, feeling less guilt or shame about sexual promiscuity, provided an ample supply of highly effective workers to "man" the parlors. A growing number of entrepreneurs seemed willing to invest the often relatively modest capital needed to open a parlor; with time, more elaborate and expensive facilities opened. Equally important, local police and judiciary increasingly tolerated—or could be bribed—to ignore these fairly transparent sexual enterprises. Finally, there was an abundant supply of men, particularly more respectable, middle-age men, eager to engage in safe sexual acts—and had the money to do so.

By the early '70s, numerous parlors operated in the city. One of the first to open was the Pink Orchard, on East 14th Street, and its success led to opening of others. Among these were the Perfumed Garden, on West 23rd Street; the Secret Life Studio, on East 26th Street, described as "four dimly lit mauve rooms"; the Casbah East and Casbah West, which resembled "an ultramodern cave"; the Middle Earth Studio, on East 51st Street, which resembled "a hippie commune, having beaded curtains, madras pillows, and incense burning in the rooms"; the Stage Studio, on East 18th Street; and the Studio 34, on West 34th Street. West 42nd Street's Deuce was home to a number of parlors, including the Palace (at 410, formerly Club Za-Za that featured live sex shows), the Geisha House (at 414), and French Model House (at 436).[278]

In twenty-first-century New York, adult sexual relations take one of three forms—consensual, commercial, or involuntary. Each is a terrain of moral and political conflict, with ongoing battles over the meaning of each term. Consensual sex seems simple enough. It involves "adults" (e.g., eighteen years or older) who are fully "rational" (i.e., able to make a coherent decision) and agree to have sex without a financial (or other) exchange involved. Commercial sex involves a "consensual" relation with a financial (or other) exchange and entered into "voluntarily." And involuntary sex involves all non-consensual sex practices, whether rape, pedophilia, child porn, trafficking, or lust murder.

However, with the rise of the culture wars during the George W. Bush administrations, the distinction between sex work and sex trafficking blurred. Moralists of both the right and left, like Christian activist Linda Smith, founder of Shared Hope, and anti-porn feminist academic Gail Dines, effectively turned all forms of "non-consensual" sex into trafficking, redefining "consensual" commercial sex as a form of sex slavery. Their well-intentioned if misconceived efforts to expand the definition of trafficking serves only to reinforce policies of sexual repression.

Sex is a primordial human need and, like nearly all needs under capitalism, can be turned into a commercial exchange: the human (mostly male) "need" for sex is mediated through the marketplace turning both buyer and seller of sexual favors into commodities. Prostitution operates across the United States as variegated as the marketplace. There are "legal" bordellos operating in parts of Nevada; easily arranged hookups through "escort" services; one-on-one sessions with professional sex workers found through the Internet; local massage parlors and health "spas"; and added services at strip clubs and other illicit sexual venues. But at the bottom of the flesh trade pyramid—and usually most easily targeted in police sweeps—remains the streetwalker.

LAVENDER PERIL

LIBERACE, 1919–1987

Tipping Point

Has the United States reached a "tipping point" over the issue of homosexuality? From a once-hanging offense or pathology, it is now conceived as part of the human condition, with gay marriage accepted by a landmark June 2015 Supreme Court decision.[279] The decision follows a June 2013 court ruling in favor of New York's Edith Windsor who challenged federal tax laws following the death of her wife, Thea Spyer. It rejected parts of the 1996 Defense of Marriage Act permitting legally married gay couples to the same federal benefits as heterosexual married couples. This comes amid a fundamental change in sexual values in which once formerly unacceptable sexual "perversions"—like porn, sex toys, transvestism, S&M, B&D, water sports, and fetish outfits—are, today, enjoyed as a normal expressions of "sexual wellness" by a growing number of adults, especially women.

Sometimes court decisions lead popular opinion, like the '54 *Brown* decision desegregating US schools, or the '73 *Roe* decision legalizing abortions; other times they follow changes in the public mindset, like with the '65 *Griswold* ruling overturning state bans of on the use of contraceptives and with the '67 *Loving* decision permitting interracial marriage. On the issue of same-sex marriage, US courts are following—and giving official blessing to—public sentiment; most important, they are not seeking to block the inevitable. Up until the Court's June 2015 decision, thirty-seven states had legalized gay marriage. A Pew Research Center survey found that 49 percent of Americans favor same-sex marriage, while 41 percent oppose it; a decade earlier, in 2004, it found that 60 percent of Americans opposed gay marriage while 31 percent supported it. Perhaps most revealing, the *Washington Post* reported in 2013 that 81 percent of people under thirty years of age support same-sex marriage.[280]

Same-sex marriage is no longer a "hot button" culture-war issue. A decade ago, it divided the nation, almost as bitterly as abortion and the wars in Afghanistan and Iraq. While the war against a woman's right to choose and the permanent war complex grind on, homosexuality is no longer a sin, a psychopathology, or a criminal offense. As of mid-2015, the US military formally accepts homosexuals; a increasing number of celebrities, athletes, CEOs, and politicians are "out"; and more and more families have a relative, friend, coworker, or neighbor who is openly gay.

A Man's Man

On September 25, 1953, Liberace performed to a sold-out audience at New York's legendary Carnegie Hall. Since boyhood, he had dreamed of this moment—and it had finally come true. In the '50s, Liberace was a national celebrity, a unique entertainment persona—with flamboyant attire, effeminate airs, and an oversized grand piano with glittering candelabra. And audiences loved him.[281]

Liberace was America's first truly national gay entertainer and TV celebrity—and he denied the very homosexuality that fashioned his public persona. This contradiction affected his personal life and most acutely reflected the sexual culture of the postwar era. His remarkable popularity signified a deepening crisis over masculinity that accompanied the consumer revolution. His popular acceptance was a form of mass denial; he represented the cultural legitimization of the sexual subversive—the "homo," "fag," or "deviant"—that threatened the nation's moral order. He was the voice of homosexuality denied, one that was not uncommon before the 1969 Stonewall riot and the rise of the gay liberation movement.

Born Wladziu Valentino Liberace in West Allis, Wisconsin, in 1919, he was the child of a respected musical family. Considered a child prodigy, his official biography claims that he received praise from Ignacy Paderewski, the legendary Polish pianist and composer. However, rumors abound that he got his start performing in Milwaukee's gay establishments in the post-Prohibition period.[282] His sexual denial would be the basis for the scandals that came to haunt his life.

In 1940, Liberace moved to New York and began performing as an intermission pianist at the Plaza Hotel's celebrated Persian Room. Mystery still surrounds the fact that he did not serve in the US military during WWII, a period in which most able-bodied men were called up. Nevertheless, by the late '40s, he had established himself as a unique public personality. He made his movie debut as a honky-tonk pianist in H. Bruce Humberstone's *South Sea Sinner* (1950), costarring MacDonald Carey and Shelley Winters. He released a number of popular recordings through Columbia and made numerous guest appearances on radio and TV shows. His efforts peaked in '52 when he secured his own TV program, *The Liberace Show*. In '56, he starred in a sold-out concert at the Hollywood Bowl celebrating his twenty-fifth anniversary in show business.

In '56, Liberace was invited to England to give three Royal Command Performances. In London, rumor became scandal. An entertainment-gossip columnist for the tabloid, the *Daily Mirror*, "Cassandra" (William Connor), implied that Liberace was gay: "the summit of sex, the pinnacle of masculine, feminine, and neuter." The writer went on, "Everything that he, she, and it can ever want . . . a deadly, winking, sniggering, snuggling, chromium-plated, scent-impregnated, luminous, quivering, giggling, fruit-flavored, mincing, ice-covered heap of mother love."[283] Liberace sued the *Daily Mirror* for libel. He testified in court, insisting that he was not a homosexual, nor had he ever engaged in homosexual acts. Liberace won! Yet, victory need not always bring success. While Liberace fought the good fight in England, he paid dearly in the States. Public scandal popped the bubble of social denial. He lost personal and TV appearances and his record sales dropped off considerably.

Liberace was but one of many reputed homosexuals who, during the '50s, sought the safety of the "closet" of public denial to protect their personal and professional identities. It was a tactic employed by innumerable men (and women) seeking to hide an unacceptable form of sexual identity. Among other well-known celebrities who sought such privacy, especially Hollywood movie stars, were Montgomery Clift, Rock Hudson, Sal Mineo, Roddy McDowell, and Tab Hunter. Many of the actors, like Clift, Hudson, and Hunter, were widely known within the movie industry as "pretty boys," a common term for homosexuals. Rumors of sexual deviance also circulated about Greta Garbo and Marlene Dietrich, James Dean and Marlon Brando.

A national sex panic of the '50s took place in parallel to the House Un-American Activities Committee (HUAC) blacklists of alleged Communists and fellow travelers like the Hollywood Ten. It was in the interest of the movie studios to present their stars in the best light, as upstanding heterosexuals. The studios wanted to safeguard their investments; respectable stars sold tickets. Nevertheless, revelations often occurred, many trumpeted in *Confidential* and other gossip magazines known as the "scandal press." These revelations ruined people's lives.

Questions about the masculinity of a public personality were not limited to Hollywood stars. Rumors were regularly whispered about J. Edger Hoover's transvestitism; Joseph Alsop, the noted media pundit; New York's Archbishop, Cardinal Frances Spellman; and the affections shared by Senator Joseph McCarthy and his two aids, Roy Cohn and David Schine. Similar suspicions were raised about Whitaker Chambers, a former Soviet spy who identified Alger Hiss, a State Department official, as a Communist. Stories circulated that John F. Kennedy engaged in a *ménage à trois* with Michael Butler, a noted socialite and bi-sexualist.[284] These were but a few of the men whose masculinity was questioned during the '50s sex panic.

No Gotham rumor was so popular and, simultaneously, so emphatically denied by both the Catholic Church and the *New York Times* than the sexual predilections of Cardinal Francis Joseph Spellman. He held his position from 1939 until his death in 1967, vehemently denouncing Communists and sexual deviants, especially homosexuals. Yet, among the city's gay and more hip underground scenes, Spellman was known as "Franny," "Telma," or "Nellie Spellbound," a closeted homo. In his 1984 biography, *The American Pope*, John Cooney found that "many felt—and continue to feel—that Spellman the public moralist may well have been a contradiction of the man of the flesh." In the early '40s, rumors circulated that Spellman sent his private limo to Broadway to pick up a young man who was in the chorus line of the musical *One Touch of Venus*. Cooney reported that numerous priests and others he interviewed took Spellman's homosexuality for granted.[285]

Perversion

At a posh party at New York's glamorous Plaza Hotel in 1958, corporate executives, celebrities, and government officials comfortably rubbed shoulders. Drinks were imbibed and well-wishes exchanged. The social worthies attending the gala ranged from Lewis S. Rosenstiel, chairman of Schenley Industries, a leading liquor company, to Roy Cohn, former counsel to Senator McCarthy, and FBI director Hoover, the nation's top lawman.

As gossip has it, during the evening Hoover hosted a private get-together in his suite where he made a most dramatic appearance. Susan L. Rosenstiel, the wife of the Schenley chairman, attended the private soiree. As she reported, "he [Hoover] was wearing a fluffy black dress, very fluffy, with flounces and lace stockings and high heels, and a black curly wig." She added, "he had makeup on and false eyelashes." She claimed that Cohn introduced Hoover to her as "Mary" and he allegedly responded, "Good evening." She also insists that she saw Hoover go into a bedroom and take off his skirt where "young blond boys" had sex with him in bed.[286]

Hoover's reputed transvestitism is part of popular American folklore like the sex scandals involving Thomas Jefferson relationship with his slave, Sally Hemings; James Buchanan's homoerotic love affair; Warren Harding's out-of-wedlock child; and John Kennedy's endless affairs.[287] Hoover's "deviance" is much debated and—whether real or myth—provides a unique vantage point into the sexuality of the tumultuous '50s. Tales of Hoover's transvestitism have their roots in Anthony Summers's 1993 book, *Official and Confidential: The Secret Life of J. Edgar Hoover*. Summers presents Rosenstiel's story about Hoover's black dress and tells other tales in which the FBI director is reputed to have engaged in sex with young men. Rosenstiel claimed that she attended a follow-up gala at the Plaza in '59 and this time Hoover wore a red dress with a black feather boa wrapped around his neck. She also claimed that Hoover, holding a Bible, had one of his attending young blond men read a passage as another played with his exposed penis.

Conservatives have long fought this depiction of the nation's top cop, somehow thinking his mean-spirited, tough-guy pose was compromised by his alleged transvestitism or homosexuality. Ronald Kessler, in *The Bureau: The Secret History of the FBI*, presents the most compelling defense of the former FBI chief. He argues that Rosenstiel was a less-than-credible witness, having served time at New York's municipal prison, Riker's Island, in 1971 for perjury. He reports that New York's long-term district attorney, Robert Morgenthau, found her a questionable witness, if not mentally incompetent. She believed that Hoover had conspired against her during her divorce proceedings. Finally, Kessler objects to Summers's conclusion that the Mafia blackmailed Hoover because of his fetishistic predilections, effectively halting federal criminal investigations; he insists that the prosecution of legendary mob money-man, Meyer Lansky, demonstrates Hoover's independence. Anyone who has seen Francis Ford Coppola's classic *Godfather* series may well beg to differ.[288]

While the concerns raised by those defending Hoover's reputation may be true or the evidence questioning Hoover's reputation unsubstantiated, one simple fact stands without question: Hoover's life partner was Clyde Tolson. A fellow FBI agent, Tolson and Hoover were inseparable for more than forty years. They shared a house, dressed in similar outfits, vacationed together, and, which says more than anything, are buried alongside one another. Like legendary female "spinsters" long living together, what the relationship meant to Hoover and Tolson remains very much a personal mystery.[289]

The threat of homosexuality took innumerable forms. It could be a political smear, like the alleged homosexuality of public figures ranging from Hoover to Senator McCarthy and Senator and presidential candidate Adlai Stevenson (D-IL). Such smears were directed against Chip Bohlen, nominated to be ambassador to the Soviet Union, as well as Chambers.[290] Similar accusations accompanied the widespread arrest and prosecution of mostly men for allegedly engaging in homosexual acts in Washington, DC, and other cities. Nevertheless, homosexual women and men fashioned a sexual—but also cultural and political—community that enabled them and other sexual deviants to not only survive, but strengthen their personal and social identities. These outsiders contributed to what, in the '60s, became the counterculture and the women's liberation and gay-liberation movements.

Lavender Peril

On March 21, 1958, at two in the morning, Benito Feliciano approached Joseph Curry in front of a Turkish bath at 10 Saint Marks Place, a popular spot among gay men. Looking provocatively at Curry, Feliciano placing his cupped hand on Curry's crotch and offered to give him a blow job. Curry was an undercover cop and busted Feliciano for violating the city's penal law, section 722, subdivision 8, engaging in disorderly conduct. At trial a week later, the Magistrate's Court judge overturned the arrest because it lacked proof that the encounter intended or actual breached the peace.[291]

No one knows just how many male and female "homosexuals" called Gotham home in the postwar decades. In '58, the sympathetic sex researcher, psychiatrist Albert Ellis, and Tony Segura, a

Mattachine Society activist, estimated that only about 5 percent of homosexuals were "obvious."* In 1964, Wardell Pomeroy, a Kinsey collaborator, estimated that 15 percent of male and 5 percent of female homosexuals were "obvious." The rest of the homoerotic populous remained essentially invisible, "passing," indistinguishable from heterosexuals.[292]

Another indicator of homosexuals in the city in the '50s is suggested by the annual arrests for sodomy and other sex crimes. William Eskridge, a Yale Law School professor, provides a thorough assessment of homosexuals and American law enforcement during the postwar decades, "Privacy Jurisprudence and the Apartheid of the Closet." He speculates, "The years 1946 through 1961 represented the high point for enforcement of both sodomy and disorderly conduct and degeneracy prohibitions in New York City." He adds, "Annual sodomy arrests regularly exceeded 200, and degeneracy arraignments exceeded 3,000 for several years before declining to between 1,000 and 2,000 for most of the 1950s."[293]

Eskridge analyzed three sex-crime categories in terms of arrests and complaints from 1958 to 1966—non-rape felonies (including "forcible sodomy and sodomy with a minor"); sex misdemeanors (including "consensual sodomy"); and sex offenses/degenerates (included "consensual sodomy"). In '58, non-rape felony arrests totaled 419 and complaints were 468; in '66, non-rape felony arrests were 425 and complaints were 517. Similarly, in '58, sex misdemeanor arrests were 2,103 and complaints were 2,693; in '66, sex misdemeanors arrests were 2,275 and complaints were 3,856. However arrests and complaints of sex offenses/degenerates showed a marked shift: in '58, male arrests of offenses/degenerates were 1,142 and complaints were 776; in '66, male offenses/degenerates arrests dropped to 363 and complaints were 402.

The drop in these numbers reflects the fact that the '50s were marked by a slow-motion battle over sexual morality. In New York and other states, there were differences between local law enforcement,

---

* The Mattachine Society was established in 1950 as a "homophile" civil rights organization.

district attorneys, and court judges over what was morally unacceptable. It was a fight over the proper application of "breach of peace," "disorderly conduct," and "vagrancy" statutes with regard to homo-erotic encounters. Nevertheless, homosexuals were charged with anal or oral sex crimes, often felonies. Until the 1950s, engaging in anal sex was consider a crime: anyone—male or female—who "'carnally knows any male or female person by the anus or by or with the mouth; or voluntarily submits to such carnal knowledge' . . . is guilty of sodomy." In 1950, the state reclassified consensual—anyone who "voluntarily submits to such carnal knowledge"—sodomy to a misdemeanor, making the maximum penalty a six-month sentence. However, among homosexuals, the man who inserted his penis into the anus of another man could be guilty of sodomy, while the other man could at most be guilty to being an accomplice.[294] In the same spirit, the vagrancy law prohibited loitering "for the purpose of inducing, enticing or procuring another to commit lewdness, fornication, unlawful sexual intercourse or any other indecent act." As Eskridge explains, "these charges typically involved a complainant when the intercourse resulted from force, intoxication, or relations between an adult and a minor."

Less serious sex crimes (often misdemeanors) included solicitation, indecent liberties with a child, indecent exposure, lewd conduct, attempted sodomy, and disorderly sexual conduct. In addition, dancing, kissing, and holding hands with someone of the same sex in public were considered misdemeanors. They violated various statutes involving lewdness, indecency, or disorderly conduct. Cross-dressing was also a criminal offense. Men could be busted for wearing a "disguise" or "masquerade" that included women's clothes and makeup; women were subject to what was known as the "three-piece" rule—a woman in trousers could beat the disguise statute if she wore three pieces of women's clothing (e.g., bra, panties, and stockings).

The NYPD pursued those suspected of engaging in illegal homosexual practices through its vice squads. Each consisted of about a dozen officers and employed a variety of tactics in the pursuit of illegal homosexual practices. Investigations ranged from a complaint to the police or an officer's direct observation of (alleged) criminal conduct. Police regularly conducted undercover surveillance or spying of "cruising" venues like public restrooms—popularly known as "tearooms"—in bars and subways as well as bathhouses, deserted parking lots, and beaches; the city's most famous outdoors cruising area was the Ramble in Central Park. The police frequently employed what was dubbed the "jump raid," a raid to disrupt male socializing in bars and other venues. Eskridge noted, "two police officers typically huddled in or above a toilet booth and watched oral intercourse by men in adjoining booths." Police also used entrapment: "reasonably attractive policemen operated as decoys and loitered at a homosexual hangout to arrest men who proffered explicit passes such as verbal invitations or fondling of the decoy's genitals," Eskridge found. There were far fewer arrests and prosecutions of lesbians because they engaged in far less public sex than male homosexuals. In addition, the NYPD had far fewer female officers to act as decoys.

Homo Panic

The 1950s sex panic led to a new vocabulary to demonize those deemed unacceptable. Old-fashioned and more religious terms like "sin" and "immorality" gave way to more medical, scientific, and secular concepts. "The terms sexual psychopath, sex criminal, deviant, and homosexual came to be used almost interchangeably in discussing the situation," reports historian John Loughery.[295] George Chauncey, another historian, is even more to the point: "Like the term abnormal, the term deviant made any variation from the supposed norm sound ominous and threatening, and it served to conflate the most benign and the most dangerous forms of sexual nonconformity." He adds: "People who had sex outside marriage, murdered little boys and girls, has sex with persons of the same sex, raped women, looked in other people's windows, masturbated in public or cast 'lewd glances' were all called sex deviants by the press."[296] In effect, social authority did not simply demonize homosexuality as a threat to male self-identity, it suspected all forms of sexual difference to be both crimes and challenges to be moral—and political—order.[297]

"The 'homosexual' became a particular target of persecution in America," Lillian Faderman observes. "He or she presented an uncomfortable challenge to the mood that longed for obedience to an illusion of uncomplicated 'morality,'" she pointedly adds.[298] With an inverse irony that only *realpolitik* can engender, no less an authority—and later practitioner—of the mechanics of state power than Arthur Schlesinger, Jr., warned against the spreading feminization of the American male. In one of his historical studies of the period, he tied together—with a psychophysical (if not eroticized) aesthetics unique to such scholarship—the challenges facing the United States. Communism was "something secret, sweaty, and furtive like nothing so much, in the phrase of one wise observer of modern Russia, as homosexuals in a boy's school."[299]

Congressional hearings—along with innumerable local- and state-government probes—were directed at homosexuals and other perverts. Among such deviants were "pornographers," specifically publishers of paperback pulp fiction, comic books, and photo-magazines as well as moviemakers, distributors, and exhibitors. Representative A. L. Miller (R-NB) wrote special language into the 1950 Security Act legitimizing the investigation of what was called "perverts."[300] That same year, the Senate conducted a wide-ranging investigation into the presence of "homosexuals and other perverts" employed by the federal government. Advocating the removal of all homosexuals from government employment (both civilian and military), the Senate warned that a pervert "tends to have a corrosive influence upon his fellow employees. These perverts will frequently attempt to entice normal individuals to engage in perverted practices. This is particularly true in the case of young and impressionable people who might come under the influence of a pervert." It concluded with a dire warning, "One homosexual can pollute a Government office."[301]

Congressional legislation and investigative hearings served to embolden local police and other moral authorities. In the early '50s, a series of highly publicized assaults on consenting adults took place in Washington, DC, during which an estimated one thousand people were arrested annually. The local vice squad publicly estimated that there were some 3,500 "sex perverts"—i.e., homosexuals—working in the government, three hundred to four hundred in the State Department alone. Between January 1947 and November 1950, some 574 civilian employees were investigated for allegedly being perverts.

The national sex panic intensified with the adoption of President Harry Truman's Executive Order 10241 issued in 1951; it barred prostitutes, paupers, the insane as well as ideological undesirables and homosexuals from government employment. In '53, Congress passed and President Dwight Eisenhower signed the now-infamous Executive Order 10450, "Security Requirements for Government Employment," legalizing the firing of federal employees for committing "any criminal, infamous, dishonest, immoral, or notoriously disgraceful conduct, habitual use of intoxicants to excess, drug addiction, sexual perversion." As a result, between May 1953 and June 1955, an additional 837 investigations of alleged sex perverts took place.[302]

The purging of a demonized population went far beyond the halls of Congress and the Executive Branch. In '54, US military established the Armed Forces Disciplinary Control Board to investigate alleged homosexuality among service personnel. The agency's sole purpose was to weed out "deviants" from the (nearly) all-male military. During the '50s, the number of men (and some women) in uniform discharged for homosexuality skyrocketed. Whereas in the '40s, such discharges averaged annually about one hundred cases, in the '50s they topped two thousand per year.[303]

Nevertheless—or perhaps, in fact, because of such hostility—some of these selfsame perverts began to create political organizations and publicly protest their abusive treatment. Most important, the Mattachine Society, representing males, and the Daughters of Bilitis, representing females, were formally established in 1950 and 1955, respectively. "The attacks on gay men and women hastened the articulation of a homosexual identity and spread the knowledge that they existed in large numbers," historian John D'Emilio observes. He adds, "ironically, the effort to root the homosexuals in American society made it easier for them to find one another."[304] The creation of the Mattachine Society and the Daughters of Bilitis formally established the modern gay-rights movement. They made an important difference. Unfortunately and not unlike the NAACP, these groups adopted a civil-rights agenda that led to, in the words of Jennifer Terry, "at times, broader claims for sexual and political diversity [being] submerged through the imperative to seem normal and adjusted."[305]

Resistance

The most radical sexual community of the 1950s may well have been working-class lesbians living underground lives in cities throughout the country. Elizabeth Lapovsky Kennedy and Madeline D. Davis reveal that in Buffalo, New York, "lesbians should be placed alongside civil-rights and labor activists as forces representing a strong radical resistance to the dominant conservatism [of the period]." This applied equally to lesbians in the Big Apple. Wherever they called home, they were outsiders.

Kennedy and Davis argue in their invaluable study, *Boots of Leather, Slippers of Gold: The History of a Lesbian Community*, that during the postwar decades, lesbians (along with gay men) confronted significant repression from federal, state, and—especially—local law-enforcement authorities. The medical community, especially psychiatry, mirrored this repression in the treatment of homosexuals. "Despite state repression, working-class lesbians in the 1950s continued developing lesbian community and culture and were able to break new ground toward ending secrecy and defending themselves," the authors note. More insistent, they propose that "the effect of state repression and violence on the street was to make lesbians resistance more defensive, but it did not disrupt the expanding presence of lesbians."[306]

Within the social context of the '50s, lesbian personal and public expression found articulation in two principal roles, the "butch" and the "fem.''* "Butch-fem roles were both like male-female roles in the heterosexual world and different," observe Kennedy and Davis. They provocatively add: "just as lesbian relations were like hetero-sexual marriage but also very different."[307] While formally appear-ing to duplicate traditional heterosexual gender power relations in the public arena, lesbian roles inverted heterosexual roles in matters relating to sexual passion. Mirroring traditional heterosexual male roles, butches were tough and explicit in declaring their sexuality. "Their carefully cultivated masculine appearance advertised their difference and indicated a woman's explicit sexual interest in another woman."[308]

But the butch subverted the traditional heterosexual male's goal in sexual intimacy in terms of sexual conquest—satisfying oneself at the expense of the other, the female partner. As the scholars make clear, "the butch's foremost objective was to give sexual pleasure to a fem." And the fem? "She not only knew what would give her phys-ical pleasure, but she also knew that she was not the receptacle for someone else's gratification." This does not mean that the butch did not achieve pleasure serving a fem: "Many butches were and remain spontaneously orgasmic. Their excitement level peaks to orgasm while the make love orally or digitally to a woman."[309]

In the '50s, lesbians encountered public repression in Buffalo, New York, and other cities. Ever adaptive, working-class butches and fems were forced to conduct their public lives at the margins of civil society, the sexual underground. Too small a community of their own, they were often required to mix with other social minorities in run-down "street bars." According to Kennedy and Davis, these bars "were a meeting ground for diverse elements at the sexual fringe. Their clientele was mixed." It included lesbians and gay males, pros-titutes and pimps, straight men and people of color. Because of the often-fractious nature of social relations at these bars, fighting was endemic—and this required many customers, including butch lesbi-ans, to be prepared, including carrying a switchblade knife.[310]

---

* Audre Lorde called these relations "mommies and daddies"; see Natasha Kraus pp. 30–56.

Few lesbians of the postwar era appeared to have accepted or engaged in non-traditional sexual practices, often adhering to conventional gender roles. Yet, many butches subverted traditional desire by actively seeking to serve and satisfy the fem. For example, while lesbians experimented with "sixty-nine," "threesomes," and "daisy chains," according to Kennedy and Davis, they usually ended without full, mutual satisfaction. Nor did they play with dildos and other sex toys. Many butches wore their cloths during sex and even insisted on having sex with the lights on. The community rejected women whose sexual performance was "not consistently butch or fem." Women who engaged in "ki-ki" (neither-nor) or "AC/DC" roles were often ostracized. The full consequence of living out such fiercely prescribed roles was realized in the lives of these women. As the authors painfully acknowledge, "the social ideal of the stone butch meant many lesbians of this period never experienced mutual lovemaking."[311]

The male writer, Jess Stearn, offers a different insight into lesbian life in *The Grapevine: A Report on the Secret World of the Lesbian*. It is a follow-up to his earlier exposé of male homosexuals, *The Sixth Man*, identifying lesbians as the "fourth sex." Employing a popular journalist style, Stearn hides his sympathetic if moralist perspective behind fast-paced interviews with only first-named alleged lesbians. He notes, "there were all types of lesbians," both "masculine stereotype" (i.e., "butch," "dike," "bull-dagger," "big-diesel," "stompin' butch" and "baby butch") and the "feminine counterpart" (i.e., "femme," "doll"). Attending a Daughters of Bilitis meeting in San Francisco, he found, "Professionally the girls were a cross-section of society" and included "teachers, social workers, clerks, secretaries, shop owners, draftsmen, [and] engineers." He also noted that these women often used personal ads in newspaper "Agony Columns" to connect with one another.

Stearn grouped the lesbians he considered into a half-dozen made-up categories. "Bisexuals" were women with a "lingering desire for the opposite sex"; "transgressors" are women of "culture and refinement [who] intimately rub elbows in dirty bars with girls they wouldn't hire as maids"; "lace-curtain" women who "would cheerfully die before admitting their lesbianism even to their closest friends"; the "Hollywood sex symbols" included starlets "whose femininity is a household word [and] are frankly lesbians in the private lives"; "bachelor girls" who are "disillusioned and disappointed in lesbian romance" and now live alone; and "married" couples, women who are informally committed to one another and have "the same passions, desires, and aspirations as conventional couple . . . and some even had children to raise, the product of previous marriages with men." In New York, he reportedly witnessed a lesbian marriage in Greenwich Village on—where else?—Gay Street as well as a bust at a Village gay bar led by a NYPD female undercover officer of a woman "fondling" another women that the cop acknowledged as "both above and below, if you know what I mean."[312]

No commercial establishment played a more significant role in the formation of a self-identified community, the modern gay movement, than gay-friendly bars. Other licensed commercial establishments—including bathhouses, massage parlors, adult bookstores (often with backroom peepshows), and grind house movie theaters—encouraged sexual encounters, most often anonymous ones between men. Bars, like the Stonewall in Greenwich Village, facilitated social and sexual engagements. Many served either an exclusively gay, mostly male but with some female and transgender, clientele or catered to a predominantly heterosexual clientele but were gay friendly or gay tolerant. Of these, the ones that catered to lesbians, cross-dressing "fairies," leather and other distinct sub-groupings were few in number but played an especially important role.

New York long prohibited bars and restaurants from serving homosexuals. Nevertheless, a resourceful lesbian could patronize a discreetly operating bar in nearly every large city as well as many smaller ones throughout the country. While many lesbians, let alone heterosexual women, did not drink alcohol or felt uncomfortable going to a questionable place in a seedy part of town, a remarkable number of women—both black and white—appear to have done so. In the Village, she could visit Julius, a bar dating from 1864 and located on 159 West 10th Street, off Waverly Place. Long a gay hangout, it gained national press when, three years before Stonewall, on

April 26, 1966, four "homophile activists" staged a "sip in" challenging the state Liquor Authority. The protest was comparable to civil rights sit-ins in the South and it helped ignite the gay liberation movement.[313]

The Bagatelle at 86 University Place was another Village lesbian hotspot. According to scholar Lisa Davis, it "was a lesbian bar and hangout well into the 1950s." She gives some flavor to the festive scene: "Saturday night was the big night when dykes slicked back their hair, and Sunday afternoon sessions were an added treat. There was a backroom for dancing, and a warning light that flashed on as a signal to stop when somebody dangerous came in up front." Audre Lorde, the radical bisexual lesbian writer, was a regular and well understood the bar's culture. "If you asked the wrong woman to dance, you could get your nose broken in the alley down the street by her butch, who had followed you out of the Bag for exactly that purpose," she recalled. "And you were never supposed to ask who was who, which is why there was such heavy emphasis upon correct garb. The well-dressed gay girl was supposed to give you enough cues for you to know."[314]

A second area with a vital gay nightlife was the uptown East Side, on Third Avenue between East 45th and 52nd Streets. Unimaginable today with work on a new Second Avenue subway underway, the Third Avenue subway was the last elevated railroad line to operate in Manhattan, running until 1955. The neighborhood around the "El" was a rundown, working-class neighborhood. To those in the know, it was dubbed the "Bird Circuit" for the cluster of local gay bars like the Golden Cockerel, the Yellow Cockatoo, the Swan, the Golden Pheasant, and the Blue Parrot.

The sexual liberation movement that emerged during the late '50s radically transformed the scope of self-identity. Traditionally, those socially stigmatized as perverts sought anonymity, hiding in the proverbial closet. Anonymity ensured private pleasures and avoided public scandal, if not jail. The most explicit articulation or self-representation of sexuality was often limited to, among women, prostitutes and showgirls and, among men, fairies and drag queens. During the '50s, an increasing number of once-illicit sexual proclivities found expression; they would begin to find social acceptance in the '60s and '70s.

Underground

An underground of sexual deviants survived and thrived amid the 1950s culture war. This radical sex community was formed through the voluntary association of self-selected individuals, men—and some women—seeking to fulfill idiosyncratic sexual indulgences. Many were into simply homoerotic pleasures. Others sought to fulfill leather, bondage, sadomasochism (S&M), or other fetishes. Remarkably, they discreetly sought out—and found—like-minded individuals, whether heterosexual or homosexual, who shared their particular fantasy. Some might have been readers of magazines like Bob Mizer's *Physique* or John Willie's *Bizarre*, others subscribers to the *Caprice Catalog* or were Bettie Page devotees. They met through personal ads placed in, for example, the Sunday *New York Times* or magazines like the *Saturday Review* as well as more explicit publications.[315] Through these and other means, deviants found ways to meet—be it one-on-one or in groups either at private, initiation-only "parties" or public venues like bars and bathhouses.

Improvisation and creativity were the watchwords of these sex radicals. "Chains could be purchased in hardware stores, and a hose covered with black electric tape and a condom served as a dildo," Loughery notes. "More specialized items were trickier to find." One shop caught his attention. "Uncle Sam's Umbrella Shop off Times Square, for instance, sold whips and paddles," he reports, "because it was a theatrical supply store in the theater district, though many of Uncle Sam customers never acted in a play."[316]

The sexual practice engaged in at each setting may have been different, yet—if successful—it would culminate in the same erotic fulfillment. For example, bus stations were recognized settings for anonymous sexual encounters because of the presence of a large transient population. They were an especially popular point of convergence for soldiers and recently released veterans. Their men's rooms were notorious for the presence of "glory holes," a unique innovation of anonymous male sexual practice. A report about the activities of a seventeen-year-old white youth is illustrative of this hidden culture: "[He] returned to the bus station on a number of occasions and performed fellatio on 'maybe thirty or forty men, maybe more' up to about age 35." The researchers report that "twice he fellated men who stuck the penis through the hole between the toilet stalls, and whose faces he did not see. . . . He was also excited by the 'mystery' of sucking a penis when he knew nothing about the appearance of the man to who it was attached."[317]

One of the most extreme underground sexual subcultures of the period was the gay male S&M leather sex party. The anthropologist Gayle Rubin found that "sex parties had been critical to the development of leather social life at least as far back as the late forties. Before there were leather bars, there were S/M parties." These parties were usually held in private homes and apartments, hosted by one or two individuals, and populated by means of informal networks of referrals. Samuel Steward, a '50s gay fetishist who taught English at a Catholic college near Chicago, hosted such informal parties at his Chicago apartment; they also took place in New York and other cities. These parties helped the early gay leather, S&M community diversify and grow. "The contacts made through these networks in the late forties and early fifties led to the establishment of the first leather bars," Rubin observed.[318]

By the '50s, the S&M scene among homosexual men seems to have advanced only modestly. According to Loughery, "the world of arousal by way of masters, slaves, whips, chains, paddles, tough talk, and black leather was in its infancy in the 1950s." He notes, "At least one bar in New York City was known to let patrons change into their outfits in the back after six p.m. A man in leather on the streets was sure to be stopped by the police."[319] In Los Angeles, Thom Magister was among the earliest "outlaw bikers." "In those days there were no ready-made leather shops with on-the-rack and off-the-shelf kinky items," he recalled. "If you wanted a dildo you carved it. A harness was created by visiting the local saddle shop and improvising. Leather pants and jackets came from Harley-Davidson. Caps came from western shops as did boots and vests." Nostalgically, he mused, "each item was made with care and imagination."[320] As Rubin reports, "The earliest gay leather bars and motorcycle clubs appears in the midfifties, in New York, Los Angeles, and Chicago."[321]

Brando was the new male. In the 1953 film *The Wild One*, he was a tough, uncompromising yet vulnerable, exemplifying the postwar new-breed masculinity, the American antihero. He fashioned a new aesthetic vocabulary for the male pose—what Linda Beltran calls "a new renegade image of leather-clad bikers."[322] It helped recast male identity. It became the image of resistance combined with brooding intelligence, of sexualized youth standing resolute against the tyranny of corporate and religious moral order. Yet, it was at once a shadow with little substance, combustible but not incendiary. Collapsing Baudelaire and Billy the Kid, the outsider renegade would haunt the mythology of the suburban white male of the postwar era.

This eroticized social iconography was seized upon by, among others, the younger male gay community. Many were WWII or Korean War veterans who did not experience their "homosexuality" as the *lack* of "masculinity." Quite to the contrary, these men began to fashion a super-masculine imagery that challenged popular stereotypes of—but not "out"—homosexuals like Liberace. It was adopted as the iconic image of male heterosexuality as well, most symbolically represented in the Marlboro Man.* With a voice not heard in the United States since Whitman, the audacity of this new sexual imagery was no better captured than by the then-youthful Alan Ginsburg in *Howl.* These were men

> who let themselves be fucked in the ass by saintly motorcyclists, and
>   screamed with joy,
> who blew and were blown by those human seraphim, the sailors,
>   caresses of Atlantic and Caribbean love,
> who balled in the morning in rosegardens and the grass of public parks
>   and cemeteries scattering their semen freely to whomever come
>   who may . . .[323]

---

* One of the last Marlboro Men, Darrell Hugh Winfield, was gay and died at age eighty-five in March 2015.

Life in the Closet

Liberace died in 1987 from cardiac arrest due to AIDS. He never admitted to being homosexual and his foundation and website continue the fiction. Like other celebrities before Stonewall and the launch of the gay liberation movement, he lived a successful, if secret, life.

The early to mid-1950s were Liberace's gravy years. In the post-WWII era, he became a popular figure in both Las Vegas and Los Angeles. In the early '50s, songs like "The Impossible Dream," "Send in the Clowns," "Theme from Love Story," "Close to You," and "Raindrops Keep Falling on My Head" were American favorites. In 1952, he hosted a popular TV series, *The Liberace Show*. In '54, he played sold-out concerts at Carnegie Hall, Madison Square Garden, the Hollywood Bowl, and Soldier Field in Chicago. He relocated to Las Vegas, building a grand mansion that—until 2010—hosted his museum. He maintained dozens of fan clubs, receiving thousands of fan letters and numerous marriage proposals. And as he proudly claimed, "My costumes have become my trademark and trademarks are hard to come by in show business."[324]

In 1956, Liberace was making a grand tour of Britain and "Cassandra," a columnist for the British tabloid, the *Daily Mirror*, wrote a savage attack on him. He called the American popular entertainer "the biggest sentimental vomit of all time," insisting that the entertainer was a homosexual. In '57, Liberace sued Cassandra for libel, swearing under oath in public testimony that he was straight, and won. He collected £8,000 damages and £14,000 costs; equivalent to $217,000 and $378,000 in 2015 dollars. It would prove a pyrrhic victory.

In '57, two popular gossip magazines ran scandalous exposés about Liberace that brought the British scandal home. In May, *Hush-Hush* published "Is Liberace a Man" and, in July, *Confidential* published "Why Liberace's Theme Song Should be 'Mad About the Boy.'" *Confidential*'s attack was part of the magazine's campaign against Hollywood stars, homosexuals, Communists, organized crime figures, and people engaged in interracial sex. Robert Harrison was the magazine's publisher, and one of its principal writers was Howard

Rushmore, an anticommunist investigator who had worked for William Randolph Hearst's New York *Journal-American* and had earlier been a CP member and regular contributor to the *Daily Worker*. He had testified before HUAC, naming Edward G. Robinson, Charlie Chaplin, Clifford Odets and Dalton Trumbo as Communists. In addition to outing Liberace, it also suggested that Tab Hunter, Rock Hudson, Van Johnson, Anthony Perkins, George Cukor, Johnnie Ray, tennis star Bill Tilden, Dorothy Dandridge, Maureen O'Hara, and Marlene Dietrich as well as New Deal official Sumner Welles, Walter P. Chrysler, Jr., Peter Orton, heir to the Vanderbilt fortune, and Sweden's King Gustav V were sexual deviants. Liberace and Dandridge sued the magazine and settled out of court.

In his biography of Liberace, Darden Asbury Pyron reports on how some Hollywood celebrities like Hudson, Perkins, and Cukor lived in the "deep closet" to avoid professional ruin. Pyron quotes an unnamed closeted gay person, "You couldn't be too careful in those days. In those days, if you had sex with a man, that put you in a category from which you could not deviate. You were a fruitcake, and destined to be that all your life." Another gay man recalled Hudson's situation: "He always had two phone lines when he lived with someone, and made sure his roommate never answered his phone. He was careful not to be photographed with a man. On the set, if he met someone, they would exchange phone numbers with the stealth and caution of spies passing nuclear secrets. Rock would wait until one in the morning to make the call. If it was all right, he would drive to the person's house, park two blocks away, look around furtively and then run to the door."[325]

Liberace lived long and successful in the closet and, only slowly in the '60s, as cultural values began to change, became more "out" in his public performances while insisting on not being gay. During the early days of his life in New York during the mid-1940s he got a gig as the intermission pianist at the Plaza Hotel's Persian Room, and it is unlikely that he didn't stop by the hotel's legendary Oak Room. It was a popular haunt for upscale, sophisticated East Side gentlemen of good taste, and it was not alone. Other discreet nightspots catering to the gay gentry included Spivy's Roof, the penthouse of a building at 57th Street and Lexington Avenue; the Astor Hotel, at Seventh Avenue and 45th Street; the Savoy-Plaza Bar at Fifth Avenue and 58th Street; and Tony's on West 52nd Street. Another upscale gay cruising haunt was the Metropolitan Opera House that Liberace visited regularly.[326]

Liberace spent much of his professional life on the road, performing throughout the United States and the world. Leaving New York in 1947, he moved to Los Angeles, settling in Sherman Oaks and Palm Springs. In 1966, he relocated to Las Vegas, purchasing a house that he called home until his death in '87. During these four decades he had innumerable sexual hookups, including cruising Mexican youths on Sunset Boulevard; picking up body builders; seducing young men performing in the chorus line of his shows; and group sex parties at his Palm Springs home. He also engaged in relations with a variety of young men, including Rock Hudson, John Rechy (author of *City of Night*), and Scott Thorson, Liberace's live-in lover for the five years preceding his death.

Pyron offer a valuable insight into Liberace's sexuality. Behind his exaggerated finery and apparent feminine mannerisms, Liberace was never not in control. "He was the aggressor; he called the shots; he determined the length and duration of sex," Pyron asserts. "His sissy persona notwithstanding, he was the pursuer, the hunter, the initiator—the 'man,' as traditionally defined—in relations." Reflecting on Liberace, he concludes, "the more feminine appearing a man, the more likely he is to be the 'top.'"[327]

Liberace's relation with Thorson is at the heart of Steven Soderbergh's well-received 2013 HBO biopic, *Behind the Candelabra*, starring Michael Douglas and Matt Damon.[328] Thorton, an eighteen-year-old dog trainer, was introduced to Liberace after one his shows at the Las Vegas Hilton. He was invited to help care for the performer's poodle and moved in. They lived together for five years and Thorton, serving as lover and chauffeur, was ultimately deeply offended by Liberace's promiscuity, his visits to gay bars and adult sex shops, and his endless view of porn. They broke up in 1982 when Liberace replaced him as a lover with an eighteen-year-old male dancer.

Rebellion

At around 3:00 a.m. on Saturday, June 28, 1969, the Stonewall Riot in Greenwich Village erupted. It marked a major step in the transformation of the gay rights movement and New York's sexual underground culture. Gotham has a long history of bars catering to those deemed the "lowlife," including wayward youth, gay men, lesbian women, and transgender people.[329] And like such bars throughout the country, New York's gay bars were for the most part clandestine venues facilitating discreet encounters, including sexual assignations—and run by organized crime, the Mafia.[*]

During the '50s, the mob controlled the illicit bar scene, especially in the Village. As the historian Martin Duberman observed, "the Washington Square [bar] was owned by the Joe Gallo family, which also controlled Tony Pastor's and the Purple Onion (whereas the Genovese family operated the Stonewall, Tele-Star, the Tenth of Always, the Bon Soir on Eighth Street, and—run by Anna Genovese—the Eighty-Two Club in the East Village featured drag shows for an audience largely composed of straight tourists.)"[†][330] As part of the ritual of illegal gathering places, repeated police harassment—with its attended payoffs, sex services, closures, and arrests—threatened not only the clientele, but the mob as well.

The Stonewall, located at 51–53 Christopher Street, near Sheridan Square, was a pretty seedy place.[‡] Charles Kaiser remembers it as "not an elegant place; it did not even have running water behind the bar."[331] But it did attract a wonderfully diverse clientele. As Kaiser adds, "the crowd was unusually eclectic for a gay place in this era." It attracted a good number of underage gay youths, lesbians, and drag queens, including people of color.

The city's dailies screamed front-page headlines about the Stonewall riot: "Homo Nest Raided: Queen Bees Are Stinging Mad," *New York Daily News*, June 28th; "Village Raid Stirs Melee," *New York Post*,

---

[*] See "Underworld."
[†] On Club 82, see "Illicit Performance" and "Underworld."
[‡] In June 2015, the Stonewall received New York City landmark status.

June 28th; and "4 Policemen Hurt in Village Raid," *New York Times*, June 29th. The uprising exploded the myth of homosexual passivity in three ways. First, it forcefully demonstrated that "homos," and in particular stylized effeminate drag queens and lesbians of color, were not passive; the riot showed they could fight. Second, it marked a new stage in what had been a more formal, legalistic political movement of self-identified male and female "homophiles"; the riot showed they—"homos"—could be a militant social force. And, third, individual homosexuals no longer needed to hide in the proverbial closet; the riot showed they could come out and be their real selves, however she or he manifested it. Stonewall was a rebellion by heretofore "deviant" sexual outsiders. It initiated the politicization of a new sexual culture, rendering acceptable previously unaccepted boundaries of sexual deviance or perversions, like homosexuality, transsexuality, and fetishisms. Four years later, in 1973, the American Psychiatric Association reclassified homosexuality, no longer a mental disorder; the once forbidden became what psychologists identified as "deviance without pathology."[332]

The sexual outsiders, including many drag queens, transsexuals, and young men of color, who partied at the Stonewall that hot Saturday night knew the rules of the game. And, when push came to shove, they broke them. A guest pays the doorman to get in and the barman for drinks; the operator pays the mob boss who makes the appropriate awards to cops and politicians. It's an art of city life perfected over a century of municipal corruption. That night, the queers said no more.

The Stonewall riot was, initially, a popular act of resistance and not political. Like a classic wildcat strike, it started out as an act of rage, the great historic shout: "Fuck No!" It was an act of the new urban proletariat, of wayward youth, lesbians, transvestites, and people of color. It crystallized a national gay-rights movement that— over time and many battles—changed America. A once-shunned minority would no longer endure their social stigma, their shame. They gained legitimacy through defiance.

Political activity, including rioting, is but one manifestation of a self-identified community. Such activity helps coalesce a group of people seeking to accomplish or resolve a deeply felt grievance. Many of those who could be broadly identified as part of the movement for sexual liberation during the '50s thru '70s participated in a network of both public and private forms of association, including clubs, bars, bathhouses, and invitation-only parties. These associations often functioned as pre-political formations, setting in place a social infrastructure of shared intent from which political actions emerged.

On June 22, 2014, thousands of leather fetishists and others gathered along West 27th Street between Tenth and Eleventh Avenues to celebrate the Folsom Street East Fair. Started in 1997, it is New York's version of San Francisco's legendary Folsom Street Fair that is organized to celebrate "sexual freedom." On September 21, 2014, San Francisco hosted the thirtieth Folsom Street Fair, the world's largest gathering of gay and straight folks into leather, S&M, and other sexual proclivities. An estimated four hundred thousand fetishists, their admirers and voyeurs—many sporting provocative outfits or simply parading naked—meandered up Folsom celebrating consensual, age-appropriate sexual perversions. The Sunday Fair is the capstone gathering of Leather Pride Week, with every night featuring a special deviant-themed event.[333]

Folsom is the centerpiece of a growing number of gatherings of formally illicit or deviant sexual practices that are taking place across the country. For heterosexuals, such get-togethers include Hedofest (Washington, Texas), Couples Choice (Eagle Nest, New Mexico), the Orlando International (Orlando, Florida), and Life Style West (Las Vegas), a four-night extravaganza. Gay-centric but hetero-friendly events including the Key West Fantasy Fest, the International Leatherman (ILM, Chicago) and the Mid-Atlantic Leather Association (MLA, Washington, DC).

These public gathering are but a small sampling of what adult sexual adventures, from Christian romantics to the most radical, secular atheists, are engaged in. These sexual adventures also include the private noncommercial liaisons between single people, married, other couples and groups that involve all manner of formerly forbidden sex play. This expanded sexual palette also includes commercial exchanges easily arranged through free newspaper ads, online websites and email promotions. The sexually once forbidden has become the new normal.

IDENTITY CRISIS

MILTON BERLE, 1908–2002

American Century

Henry Luce, founder of *Time* magazine, first proclaimed the "American Century" seventy-five years ago, in early 1941. It was a period in which the United States was finally recovering from the Great Depression and world war was still far away in Europe and Asia. Isolationism was the national sentiment and principal foreign-policy strategy. Luce's American Century proclaimed a counter strategy: an internationalist agenda based on joining—and winning—the war against Fascism. It was a war for democracy that suggested a domestic agenda, one promoting a better quality of life for all, the American Dream. In the wake of Pearl Harbor, the isolationist bubble burst and turned Luce's words into the nation's war chant, "the 20th century is the American Century." An enormously expanded federal government, a government that guaranteed the war effort and profitability of corporate America, underwrote both the international and the domestic campaigns. The American Century defined life in the United States for a half century.[334]

Today, the American Century is over—and Americans know it. The decades of the American Century were marked by significant gains in the quality of life enjoyed by an unprecedented number of ordinary Americans. The life of the vast "middle class" improved in terms of key historical markers, including living standard, infant mortality rate, life expectancy, household income, and educational attainment. Accordingly, during this era the birth rate declined (to 13.0 per 1,000 in 2010 from 24.1 in 1950) while the divorce rate rose (to 3.4 per 1,000 in 2009 from 2.6 in 1950). This suggests that people felt more secure about the survival of their offspring.[335]

An increasing number of children of the post-WWII American Century are having a hard time, with no prospects of a better tomorrow. Three in ten have used food stamps while a third have taken food from a charity. According to the *Times*, "They are unhappy to be out of work and eager to find new jobs. They are struggling both with the loss of income and a loss of dignity. Their mental and physical health is suffering."

Amid this malaise, cynicism is deepening. Americans no longer take for granted the mystification fed to them, whether as news, advertisements, or public statements by government and corporate officials. More and more people consider themselves cynics—suspicious, dubious, questioning official government and corporate press-release hype. They know that they are being lied to, with false messages coming from all sides. The most telling evidence of this growing cynicism was the 2014 Congressional elections: the 2014 voter turnout was the lowest since World War II; just 36.4 percent of the voting-eligible population cast ballots—and 75 percent of those voting were white. Younger voters aged eighteen to twenty-nine, a core part of the Democratic base, made up 13 percent of the national electorate this year, compared to 19 percent in 2012.[336]

For average Americans, much has changed over the last half century particularly in terms of personal identity, of one's sense of self, even something seemingly as definite as one's gender. In the '50s, one's masculinity or femininity, what it meant to be a "man" or "woman," seemed clearly defined, with each apparently secure in their gladly accepted role. But was this the case?

A Man's Man

During the early 1950s, Milton Berle hosted America's most popular, primetime Tuesday night TV show, *The Texaco Star Theatre*. From 1948 to 1956 it ran on the NBC network at 8:00 p.m. and captured a huge share of TV viewers. It turned Berle into "Mr. Television" and "Uncle Miltie."

Berle, born in 1908, was a child performer by the age of five; during the '30s and '40s, he was a vaudeville, radio, and movie star. Publicly, he may have been the first entertainer to perform in drag, as a female impersonator, on the new—and heavily regulated—family-entertainment medium of television. Privately, he was considered a stud, a man's man who had four wives (twice with the same woman) and many lovers, ranging from the silent-screen stars Theda Bara and Pola Negri, to the evangelist Aimee Semple McPherson and figure-skating queen Sonja Henie, to Hollywood stars Lucille Ball, Veronica Lake, Rita Hayworth, and Marilyn Monroe. He had innumerable hookups with prostitutes and was a regular at Polly Adler's houses of ill repute. According to his son, William, Berle was into kinky sex (e.g., piss play and blow job with ice cubes in the woman's mouth) and had "reputedly the biggest penis in the history of show business."[337] He was a manly man who entertained in drag. He never reported having sex with another man.

Berle's twin personalities—heterosexual stud and drag performer—frame the changing meaning of sexual identity, of masculinity and femininity, during the '50s. It was an era of Christine Jorgensen's sex-change procedure, the anti-homosexual "Lavender Peril" and the censorship of comic books and adult pornography.* Many leading academics and popular writers of the period—ranging from David Riesman and C. Wright Mills to Helen Gurley Brown and Betty Friedan—warned that Americans were facing a crisis of sexual self-identity. The '50s is more than how it's remembered.[338]

---

* See "Introduction," "Lavender Peril," "Comic Book Corruption," "Obscene Image" and "Prurient Word."

Berle was born Mendel Berlinger in Harlem on July 12, 1908, and grew up in the Bronx, at 957 Tiffany Street.[339] In his breezy 1974 autobiography, *Milton Berle*, he mentions how traumatized he was when, at age five, his family was evicted from its apartment. Berle's father, Moses, an apparently emotionally weak, non-ambitious man—clinically depressed?—who worked at a series of low-paying jobs, including house painter, door-to-door salesman, and night watchman, was blamed for the family catastrophe. His mother, Sarah—who later renamed herself Sandra and who Berle reverentially called "Mama"—was a department-store detective who worked at Lord & Taylor, Saks & Co., and John Wanamaker. She was a true "stage-door mother" who pushed her son to stardom.

In 1913, the Berlinger family was in crisis. "My father became the mother and she [mother] became the father," Berle admitted. "He stayed home and she went out to work." For the next half century, Mama became an active—and often controlling—part of Berle's professional and personal life. She took him to his first audition to model for shoes and his first lines were, "My name is Buster Brown, I live in a shoe. This is my dog, Tiger, he lives there, too."

In the early '50s, TV shows were produced live, in real time for over-the-air broadcast and many hosted live studio audiences. Mama attended nearly all of Berle's New York shows and accompanied him to out-of-town engagements, including to Chicago and Los Angeles. Nearly a half century earlier, at six years old, young Berlinger—soon to be rebranded "Berle"—debuted in a silent movie serial, *The Perils of Pauline*; as a child actor he performed with stars like Charles Chaplin, Douglas Fairbanks, and Mary Pickford. He first appeared on Broadway at age twelve, performing as one of the Florodora Boys in the musical comedy, *Florodora*, and, a decade later at twenty-one, he headlined at the legendary Palace Theatre. He also performed in Earl Carroll's *Vanities*, George White's *Scandals*, and Florenz Ziegfeld's *Follies*. *Time* described him as "a six-foot-long banana with bedpan ears, Bugs Bunny teeth, a rubbery leer that threatened to meet at the back of his neck, and the energy of a wildebeest stampede." Over eight decades, Berle performed in more than fifty movies and his last appearance was at age ninety-two in the 2000 made-for-TV movie, *Two Heads Are Better Than None*.[340]

Texaco sponsored programs on NBC radio in the '40s and, as TV took hold, the network proposed that the sponsor underwrite a new weekly TV variety show, *Texaco Star Theatre*. Berle, who had appeared on Texaco-sponsored radio programs, was invited to be one of the rotating hosts. When first broadcast on June 8, 1948, TV was a new medium, reaching an estimated half-million TV households throughout the country. Berle, drawing on his decades of vaudeville comic experience, stole the show, becoming the single host and fashioning the model format for early TV's entertainment programs. He clowned around with leading entertainers like Harpo Marx, Dean Martin, and Jerry Lewis, and even welcomed the hot, young Elvis Presley in June '56, three months before Elvis appeared on Ed Sullivan's show. Most provocative, Berle often dressed in outrageous drag outfits, most memorably as Carmen Miranda, Cleopatra, and Mae West. Berle brought vaudeville to television, the stage to the TV screen. However, over the next five years as the new medium of television took shape, it generated new on-air stars who captured viewers' attention; Berle's show went off the air in '56. He twice tried to reinvent the show, first on NBC as *Kraft Music Hall* (1958–1959) and then on ABC as *The Milton Berle Show* (1966–1967), but neither caught an audience.[341]

Berle's autobiography is a classic rags-to-riches yarn, the story of how a nice Jewish immigrant "mama's boy" from the Bronx becomes a star—rich and famous and slept with some of the country's sexiest women. Like all such tales, it's a self-serving historical record of assimilation. It's filled with the usual name-droppings, adventure tales, and self-proclaimed *mea culpas*. He admits that during his early days in vaudeville he performed in blackface not unlike other young entertainers, including Jewish performers like Sophie Tucker. Perhaps most surprising, his Texaco show was among the first TV programs to invite African American talent to appear, including the Step Brothers, Bill "Bojangles" Robinson, and Lena Horne—and this was in the early '50s. While headlining at Chicago's Palace in 1933, he was invited to perform for someone he couldn't say no to, Al

Capone. Driving to Cicero, Illinois, he appeared at the Cotton Club, the gangster's joint. Getting no initial response from Scarface, Berle upped the ante, telling an endless stream of raunchy jokes that got the don roaring. He refused to accept payment for his performance, asking only for a favor sometime in the future. He never called in the request.[342]

Though seeming like very much a Gotham FDR liberal, Berle was not particularly political. He was thirty-three years old when WWII was declared in 1941 and, while he never mentions it, he—like most men aged twenty-one to forty-five—probably registered for the draft. Like Liberace, Berle did not volunteer or serve; other entertainers did, including Jimmy Stewart, Mel Brooks, Lenny Bruce, and Josephine Baker. Berle did perform at numerous war-related fundraisers and benefits. He was a gambler who loved to play the ponies, bet big-time at racetracks and with local bookies. He also reports that he was among those—including city policemen—who forcefully broke up a pro-Nazi bund rally in '39. He was apolitical and skirted the anticommunist witch hunts led by HUAC and McCarthy. In the wake of the appearance of *Red Channels* in '50 that listed the political (i.e., possible Communist) affiliations of entertainers and others, Berle reports, "I screamed and pleaded but I couldn't get my friend John Garfield on the show." NBC also blacklisted Gertrude Berg, who starred in *The Goldbergs*, from appearing on his show. Berle befriended those hounded like Jack Gilford.[343]

Sexuality was in play during the '50s and Berle—along with other popular entertainers Bob Hope and Jack Benny—put on a dress, a wig, and make-up to impersonate female characters. These female impersonators were comparable to old-style performers in blackface, which Berle had done during his early vaudeville days. But what if such gender roleplaying by a male-in-drag was a form of subversive titillation like "cheesecake" or "beefcake" magazines and some comic books? Most distinctive, these female impersonators were not "drag queens." Though decked out in outrageous costumes, they were never not males; they were not like the drag queens that performed at Club 82.

In the '50s, female impersonators challenged conventional notions of gender identity, and they took one of two forms, the "masculine" male-in-drag and the "feminine" transvestite or drag queen. Berle may well have been the first male-in-drag TV personality, followed by a legion of entertainers including Tony Curtis, Jack Lemon, Flip Wilson, Dustin Hoffman, and RuPaul as well as Dennis Rodman, the NBA basketball player. Such males-in-drag never lost their masculinity. The male transvestites, like those who performed at the Club 82, were female-identified impersonators. A third, and far more contentious, meaning of gender identity was represented by Jorgensen's sex change operation.[*]

The '50s saw an apparent increase in bisexuality. Michael Butler, a Chicago businessman who reportedly engaged in a *ménage-a-trios* with a youthful John Kennedy, was possibly a genuinely bisexual, one fulfilled sexually with people of both genders. Another form of bisexuality involved self-identified homosexuals who sought to accommodate their "deviance" to acceptable norms through marriage. Many known homosexuals married people of the opposite sex, including two notable Harlem Renaissance figures, Richard Bruce Nugent and Gladys Bentley.[344] And then there was what can best be described as the homosexual family man; he was a devoted husband and father in public and in his personal life, but someone else in his most private life. Three such men were the conductor Leonard Bernstein, historian Edward Sagarin, and author Paul Goodman.[345]

Bernstein was a renowned composer and conductor of the New York Philharmonic from 1958 to '69. In 1951, he married Felicia Montealegre Cohn and they had two children. In the mid-'50s, he collaborated with Jerome Robbins, Arthur Laurents, and Stephen Sondheim in the creation of *West Side Story* (1957). Charles Kaiser, in *The Gay Metropolis*, dubs their collaboration: "four gay Jewish men, all working at the very top of their craft." Laurents recalled Bernstein as simply "a gay man who got married. He wasn't conflicted about it at all. He was just gay." Equally important, Bernstein's score captured New York's vitality stressed by a deepening social

---

[*] See "Outsiders" and "Illicit Performance" for more on Jorgensen and Club 82, respectively; one author claims Berle visited Club 82; see St. Sukie de la Croix, *Chicago Whispers*, p. 239.

crisis. As Kaiser notes, Bernstein's "synthesis of Broadway, jazz, Latin rhythms, and Aaron Copland perfectly captured the city's astonishing spirit."[346]

Sagarin, writing under the penname Donald Webster Cory, published *The Homosexual in America* (1951), one of the most groundbreaking studies of the era. Before becoming an academic and professor at the City University of New York, he worked in the perfume and cosmetics industry. He was married and a father of one child, but appears to have maintained discreet sexual relations with men. His book, released a couple years after Alfred Kinsey's groundbreaking study of male sexuality (1948), offered a sympathetic, political defense of homosexuality. While he saw it as a "perversion" requiring treatment, he believed homosexuality should not be a criminal offense, nor should homosexuals be discriminated against. He was one of the founders of the city's chapter of the Mattachine Society, but became increasingly conservative about gay activism, especially in wake of the '69 Stonewall riot.[347]

Goodman was a maverick intellectual during the quarter-century spanning the '40s to '60s. He authored more than forty books, including poetry, plays, novels, short stories, and nonfiction work, and published regularly in leading progressive publications like *Commentary*, *Dissent*, *The Nation*, and *Partisan Review*. His most popular work, *Growing Up Absurd* (1960), a critique of youth in the organizational society, had considerable influenced on the '60s counterculture and New Left. He was a psychotherapist and founder of the gestalt therapy movement. And he was married, a father of three children, and a notorious bisexual who regularly picked up male students and other men. He never denied his sexual proclivities; there is no evidence that he had sexual relations with any woman other than his wife. In the heady '60s, he joined Allen Ginsburg arguing that homosexuals were the new "niggers."[348]

The masculinity of Bernstein, Sagarin, and Goodman represents a different sexuality. They chose to marry women, have children, and raise families—and have sexual relations with men. In each case, their respective wives seem to have known of their husband's "infidelity" and accepted it—up to a point. How these men, their wives and families lived out this social contradiction was something shared by others of the day—as it is today.

Masculinity Crisis

A half century before *Mad Men* aired on cable TV, Sloan Wilson's 1955 novel, *The Man in the Gray Flannel Suit*, identified the malaise of the postwar consumer revolution. It sold 100,000 copies and, a year later, a movie adaptation was released starring Gregory Peck and Jennifer Jones. The story came to define a generation.[349]

The story's main character, Tom Rath, is a WWII hero who returns to postwar prosperity only to find his future stuck on the corporate treadmill. He's a white-collar executive at a Manhattan media company who enjoys his lunchtime martinis and dutifully returns to his suburban "castle" in Connecticut to his wife, Betsy, and their three children. The couple feels stuck, suffocated by the tedium of work and domesticity, at a dead end.

The Raths' story reveals how conformity breeds the loss of initiative, the erosion of selfhood. While Tom settles into the grind of his midtown office, Betsy suffers the meaninglessness of simply seeking fulfillment through consumerism. In an argument with Tom, she laments, "I wanted you to go out and fight for something *again*— like the man I married. Not to turn into a cheap, slippery yes-man." The book and movie hinge on Tom's marital infidelity and the child he fathered while stationed in Italy during the war. How the couple comes to accept Tom's infidelity is the story's dramatic resolution. However, the resolution cannot change the objective situation they live in. Leading magazines of the day identified with Rath's plight. *Look* noted that "nearly every white-collar man" was in the same situation as Tom and *Life* dubbed it the "Gray Flannel Trap."[350] Something was wrong with the American Dream.

Warnings about trouble in paradise had begun in 1950 with the release of *The Lonely Crowd*, a study by David Riesman, Nathan Glazer, and Reuel Denney.[351] They argued that the twin forces of the postwar recovery—the white-collar corporation and the suburban

lifestyle—were eroding the traditional distinction between masculinity and femininity. A generation of men hardened by Depression and war were now required to accept organizational consen-
sus and domestic partnering. Women, who had been forced from
Rosie-the-Riveter self-sufficiency into homemaker, were acquiring
new senses of personal power; where the office and factory had a
glass ceiling, the family and the checkbook offered a new kind of
authority. Male and female role models were in flux.

The postwar reconstruction of the American way of life required
a new notion of selfhood, whether masculinity or femininity. The
sociologist C. Wright Mills dubbed this new subjectivity, "feminization," and it involved the remaking of traditional male identity.
Where once the American male was defined as a producer, a worker,
a provider for "his" family, he was now an office functionary, paper
pusher, and a household partner. Male selfhood or personal identity was shifting from the urban or rural cash-and-carry breadwin-
ner to the suburban, credit-worth consumer. This process mirrored
the transformation of corporate and government organization from
industrial manufacturing and national economy to monopoly capitalism and international marketplace.[352]

The "feminization" of masculine identity posed a special challenge to male—and female—heterosexual sexual practice. In essence,
a heterosexual male had to be strong, assertive, and virile, yet sensitive, without being *feminine,* a pansy. The new male had to function successfully in the growing organizational bureaucracy as well
as being fully domesticated, a suburban home- and car-owning husband, parent, and sex partner. Of particular import, he could not honestly express, let alone contemplate, desire for unconventional sexual
practices, including those with other men. Nevertheless, this "new"
male was increasingly interested in a wider range of sexual practices,
in particular oral sex—whether received from his wife, a girlfriend, a
prostitute, or another man. Orality was an insurgent form of desire, a
new and increasingly popular expression of male "perversion." It challenged traditionalist notions of both masculinity and heterosexuality.

Millions of male war soldiers returned to the factory floor,
small businesses, and offices, while women faced an equally trying

situation. The displaced legion of Rosie-the-Riveters and other women (some lesbians) who had served in the nation's war effort, some in factories producing war goods, some nurses at the front, found themselves driven into the all-white suburban ghettos. They had to navigate the new consumerism, one based on TV shows and the giddy purchasing of "affordable" goods.*

Dr. Kinsey's Diagnosis

Alfred Kinsey has been the subject of numerous biographies and a successful Hollywood movie starring Liam Neeson. His name is identified with Sigmund Freud, Wilhelm Reich, William Masters & Virginia Johnson, Margaret Sanger, and Gregory Pincus (inventor of "the Pill") as someone who helped define modern sexuality. He paid dearly for his effort.

Mainstream postwar Americas were shocked, *shocked*, by the revelations about male sexuality revealed in Kinsey and his associates' now-classic 1948 study of male sexuality. His findings—most of which are accepted today as part of national folklore yet remain still contested by religious fundamentalists and others—precipitated a near crisis of social conscious. Moralists, politicians, and the medical establishment could no longer conceal the deepest private truths of American male sexual life that Kinsey's research revealed.

To everyone's—including Kinsey's—surprise, his 804-page scientific tome, *Sexual Behavior in the Human Male*, became a bestseller, quickly selling over 200,000 copies; it rose to the top of the *New York Times* bestseller list in spite of the fact that the *Times* refused to carry advertisements for the book and failed to review it when it first appeared. As one commentary of the day observed, "If present laws concerning sexual crime and misdemeanor were in force, 95 percent of all adults would be or would have been at some time, in prison."[353]

---

* For more on female identity during the '50s, see "Lavender Peril" and "The Pill."

Kinsey's team found that 70 percent of men had visited prostitutes; 40 percent of married men were "unfaithful" to their wives; 37 percent of men (and 19 percent of women) had had at least one homosexual contact; and one farmhand in six had sexually experimented with an animal.[354] With the notable exception of indulgences of farmhands, little seems to have changed over the last half century other than the acceptance of the obvious.

Based on approximately 18,000 interviews conducted between 1938 and 1953, Kinsey's twin studies—*Sexual Behavior of Human Male* (1948) and *Sexual Behavior of Human Female* (1953)—represent a landmark in not only empirical research, but moral philosophy as well. He sought to apply a research model that he had pioneered as a noted entomologist* to the study of sexuality. By presenting the findings from a database drawn from detailed sexual histories of a relatively large sample, Kinsey sought to make it impossible to continue to deny the full range—or "individual variation," as he referred to it—of sexual practices engaged in by American white men and women. His studies provide not only an invaluable snapshot of America's pre- and postwar sexual landscape, but insight into the deeper historical forces that conditioned the development of modern sexuality.

Kinsey recognized that the then-conventional sexual values did not accept the difference between sex for procreation and for pleasure. Perversion was understood as a sexual practice that subverted the goal of reproduction. "Sodomy laws are usually indefinite in their descriptions of acts that are punishable; perversions are defined as unnatural acts, acts contrary to nature, bestial, abominable, and detestable," he noted. Looking deeper, he found, "Such laws are interpretable only in accordance with the ancient tradition of the English common law which . . . is committed to the doctrine that no sexual activity is justifiable unless its objective is procreation."[355]

---

* Kinsey was a PhD. entomologist, a tenured professor at Indiana University, and author of two pioneering works, *The Gall Wasp Genus Cynips: A Study in the Origin of Species* (Bloomington, 1930) and *The Origin of Higher Categories in Cynips* (Bloomington, 1936). For portraits of his scientific background, see Gathorne-Hardy, pp. 100–19, and Jones, pp. 141–47, 197–226.

Looking at sexual arousal and erotic techniques, he presented detailed and quite revealing information about common fantasies, kissing habits, nudity, breast and genital manipulation, various positions during heterosexual and homosexual intercourse, and oral eroticism. In terms of heterosexual intercourse, he advanced a radical materialist approach, arguing "that positions in intercourse are as much a product of human cultures as language and clothing." He invoked this perspective to directly confront the dominant—what would later be called "patriarchal"—practice represented in the supine position in which the male is on top of the front-faced female. For Kinsey, resistance to variation in sexual positions—as with, for example, the woman on top of the man—is associated directly with the dominant male cultural fear "that the female becomes masculine while the male becomes effeminate in assuming such a position, and that it destroys the dignity of the male and his authority in the family relationship."[356]

Kinsey struck the deepest societal nerves with his analysis of two sensitive topics, childhood sexuality and adult homoerotic practices. Focusing specifically on adult homoeroticism, he stated, "a considerable portion of the population, perhaps the major portion of the male population, has at least some homosexual experience between adolescence and old age." Underlying this assessment was a radical definition of homoerotic activity: "persons who have had physical contacts with other males, and who were brought to orgasm as a result of such contacts." Pushing the boundary of acceptable scientific—let alone social—assessment, he acknowledged: "Males do not represent two discrete populations, heterosexual and homosexual. The world is not to be divided into sheep and goats. Not all things are black, nor all things white." Going further, he argued: "It is a fundamental of taxonomy that nature rarely deals with discrete categories. Only the human mind invents categories and tried to force facts into separated pigeon-holes." He concludes, asserting: "The living world is a continuum in each and every one of its aspects.*"[357]

---

* Kinsey's own "bi-sexuality," and especially its impact on his research, has been a major point of contention between his two principal recent biographers; see Gathorne-Hardy, pp. 334, 354–59, 367–69, 372–73; Jones, pp. 169–71 and 384–96.

Kinsey and his team revised the popular tri-part model of human sexuality—i.e., heterosexual, homosexual, and bisexual—into a seven-point range that ran from zero to six in terms of sexual proclivity, or heterosexual-to-homosexual scale based on the reported sexual practices of his subjects. Each point delineated a very imprecise distinction between men engaged in exclusive heterosexual to exclusive homosexual acts and—with any bell-curve—the greatest segments of the population concentrated somewhere in the middle. For Kinsey, there were no "homosexuals" or, for that matter, "heterosexuals"—only men engaged in sexual acts that were labeled the one or the other.

Denial

The empirical truths revealed in Kinsey's first study disturbed many, provoking widespread criticism among religious, academic, and civic leaders. No less a would-be moral authority than Billy Graham attacked the work, warning, "It is impossible to estimate the damage this book will do to the already deteriorating morals of America."[358] Other religious leaders, like conservatives Normal Vincent Peale and liberals Reinhold Niebuhr and Henry Pitney Van Dusen, head of Union Theological Seminary, joined the chorus of criticism. Prominent sex researchers, most notably Gershon Legman, assailed the report as did leading psychologists and psychoanalysts like Lawrence Kubi and Edmund Bergler. Even progressive thinkers, most notably Margaret Mead, Ashley Montagu, and Karl Menninger, challenged the study's findings.[359]

In 1953, Kinsey and his associates published an even more massive work—842 pages—as the second volume of their monumental study, this one focused on the sexuality of American white women. Seeking to address a number of the statistical and medical-scientific criticisms raised against the first study, Kinsey subjected his empirical database to far more rigorous statistical analysis. In addition, he paid more attention to the role of such biological issues as neural mechanisms and hormonal factors among women than he had considered when analyzing males. Nevertheless, like the first volume, the focus of this study was the reported sexual practices of his sample, in this case some 6,000 women.

As he had argued in the first volume, Kinsey found that childhood and adolescents were periods strongly defined by sexual curiosity and desire.[360] Turning to adult women, he carefully analyzed the same six types of sexual activity—petting, masturbation, marital and extramarital intercourse, and homosexual and animal contacts—he employed with males. Of the six possible types of sexual activity, the greatest number of females engaged in heterosexual petting before marriage. After marriage, the largest proportion of women engaged in coitus. The second greatest number of females, both before and after marriage, engaged in masturbation.

Looking more carefully at masturbation, Kinsey noted one small but profound difference between females and males. "Some 2 percent of the females in the sample had reached orgasm by fantasying erotic stimulation, without tactilely stimulating their genitalia or other parts of their bodies," he reports. (No males reported such an ability to reach orgasm through fantasy alone.) He identifies other masturbation techniques used by about 11 percent of the women surveyed: "Some had rubbed their genitalia against pillows, clothing, chairs, beds, or other objects. Douches, streams of running water, vibrators, urethral insertions, enemas, other anal insertions, sado-masochistic activity, and still other methods were occasionally employed, but none of them in any appreciable number of cases."[361] Going still deeper into the complex phenomenon of female masturbation, Kinsey noted that among about half of his sample "fantasies had occurred in connection with most of their masturbation." He adds: "Masturbation fantasies may concern heterosexual, homosexual, animal, sado-masochistic, or still other sorts of sexual contacts." And may involve one or more than one such fantasy together.[362]

Kinsey found that marital coitus "is socially the most important of all sexual activities" and that "the married female reaches orgasm in only a portion of her coitus . . . [S]ome 10 per cent of all females in the available sample had never reached orgasm at any time, in any of their marital coitus."[363] Looking specifically at coital techniques, Kinsey found "nearly all the females in the sample recorded that they had most frequently used a coital position in which the male was above while the female lay supine beneath, facing the male." Soberly assessing female sexuality, he reflected, "the near restriction of coitus in our European-American culture to a single position must represent a cultural development rather than a biologically determined phenomenon."

Examining other forms of female sexual fulfillment, Kinsey found that extramarital coitus, homosexual engagements, and animal contacts were modestly practiced. Concerning extramarital relations, Kinsey noted such affairs were a function of age and years married: From "the total sample the active incidence [of extramarital intercourse] had begun at about 6 per cent in the late teens, increased to 14 per cent by the late twenties, and reached 17 per cent by the thirties." However, "they reached their maximum of 26 per cent by forty years of age."[364]

With regard to homoerotic encounters, such contact was a function of age and marital status—i.e., single women (some proportion of which must have been lesbians, but are not identified as such) having a statistically higher and longer-sustained incidence of homosexual engagement. "The number of females in the sample who had made specifically sexual contacts with other females also rose gradually . . . from the age of ten to about thirty. By then, some 17 per cent of the females had had such experience," Kinsey reported. "By age forty, 19 per cent of the females in the total sample had had some physical contact with other females which was deliberate and consciously, at least on the part of one of the partners, intended to be sexual."[365]

Based upon the extensive research on female sexuality, Kinsey expanded his seven-point "heterosexual-homosexual" rating scale to include a new category—those having no erotic response. As he specified, there are individuals who "do not respond erotically to either heterosexual or homosexual stimuli, and do not have overt physical contacts with individuals of either sex in which there is evidence of any response." This condition differs significantly between females and males: "After early adolescence," he reported, "there are very few males in this classification, but a goodly number of females belong in this category in every age group."[366]

In 1954, the House's Reece Committee issued the Dodd Report that attacked some of the nation's leading private foundations. It singled out the Rockefeller Endowment for supporting Kinsey's research. The report argued that the research Rockefeller and others were funding threatened social order, what would today be called "national security." The Congressional report came out following the 1953 publication of Kinsey's study of female sexuality.* Kinsey was first funded, in 1941, by a Rockefeller subsidiary, the National Research Council. He believed that the Foundation had made a truly long-term commitment to his research effort—sometimes estimated at securing 100,000 interviews. Prior to the House report's release, the Foundation informally notified Kinsey that it planned to cease funding his research. In '53, Dean Rusk, the Foundation's recently appointed director and future Secretary of State under President Kennedy, formally pulled the plug. Kinsey felt betrayed; his long-term scientific research halted and unable to fully refute his popular and academic critics.[367]

Commie Psychos

"Communists are such liars and cheats that even when they apparently recant and testify against someone else for his communist convictions, my first reaction is to believe that the accused person is a patriot," warned President Dwight Eisenhower. The labeling of Communists (or alleged Communists) as "liars and cheats" was part of a broad attack on radicals, their personalities or psychologies. As the historian Tony Perucci observes, "The Communist was always seen to be acting, while the anti Communist American was transparently truthful."[368] Part of the Cold War hysteria articulated by psychologists, politicians, and the popular media invoked personality issues as a determining factor leading essentially unhappy—and dishonest—people to become subversives.

---

* House Special Committee to Investigate Tax-Exempt Foundations and Comparable Organizations; Norman Dodd was the committee's chief investigator.

Robert Lindner, with a PhD from Cornell, was a popular '50s psychologist and author of the 1944 book, *Rebel Without a Cause: The Story of a Criminal Psychopath*, upon which the film was based. In '54, he released *The Fifty-Minute Hour*, a case study of an average working-class guy, "Mac," who was a Communist Party member. Linder identified Mac's problem as being "afraid of his penis" due to being raised by a domineering grandmother. He joined the party as "a weapon, a tool for revenge" for this mistreatment and, following therapy with the good doctor, "Mac quit the Party. He no longer needed it." Therapy worked not only to address psychological or personal problems, but the appeal of subversion as well.

Psychological portraits of alleged Communists saturated much of the mass media during the Red Scare. In March 1947, *Look* magazine published a sensational piece, "How to Spot a Communist," by Leo Cherne.* "Because the whole Communist apparatus is geared to secrecy, it is not always easy to determine just who is a Communist," he warned. "But whether he is a Party card-holder or a fellow traveler, the American Communist is not like other Americans. To the Communist, everything—his country, his job, his family—take second place to his Party duty." Cherne insisted, "Even his sex life is synchronized with the obligations of The Cause."

Don Siegel's popular 1956 quasi-sci-fi thriller, *Invasion of the Body Snatchers*, starring Kevin McCarthy and Dana Wynter, revealed alien "pods" subverting an all-American community while locals pay little attention to the threat. John Frankenheimer's 1962 political thriller *The Manchurian Candidate*, with Frank Sinatra, Laurence Harvey, Janet Leigh, and Angela Lansbury, takes the psychological threat to its logical conclusion. In this drama, an American soldier and Korean War hero, who had been a prisoner-of-war and "brainwashed" by Russian and Chinese Communists enemies, becomes an unwitting assassin out to execute a presidential candidate. In '51, the pulp mystery writer Mickey Spillane has his fictional detective, Mike Hammer, take on a supposed commie in *One Lonely Night*. Hammer

---

* President Ronald Reagan awarded Cherne the Presidential Medal of Freedom from in 1984.

reveals that the supposed Communist, Oscar, is an escaped mental patient. Hammer rages: "That's why you were a Commie, Oscar, because you were batty. It was the only philosophy that would appeal to your crazy mind."[369]

Politicians and pundits picked up on this theme of psychological problems leading to a person's susceptibility to Communism. Most famously, Senator Joe McCarthy declared, "practically every active Communist is twisted mentally or physically in some way." Perhaps more telling, Arthur M. Schlesinger, Jr., then at Harvard, authored the influential 1949 work *The Vital Center*, which argued, in part, only psychologically damaged people were Communists. "America has its quota of lonely and frustrated people, craving social, intellectual and even sexual fulfillment they cannot obtain in existing society," he noted. "Communism fills empty lives." This "emptiness" was reinforced by sexual deviance. Schlesinger argued that Communism's appeal was due to the "some what feminine fascination with the rude and masculine power of the proletariat." He went so far as to insist that Communists were "reminiscent of nothing so much as the famous scene in Proust where the Baron de Charlus and the tailor Jupien suddenly recognize their common corruption," their homosexuality.[370]

Deviance

Those in political and moral authority took it upon themselves to arm the body politic against this new sex threat challenging traditional American values. The most intimate aspects of private life and the physical body had to be policed at a level equivalent to that used to contest international Communism. The principal vehicle in this battle was the medical-psychiatric profession, the nation's leading authority on mental health. Its power was buttressed by the nation's leading religious institutions, media outlets, and government agencies in a battle to maintain moral order.

During the postwar era, the American psychiatric establishment adhered to a "medical" definition of mental health and sexual normalcy. The definition combined elements from biomedicine and an appropriated version of Freudian psychoanalysis. This model strongly influenced law enforcement as to what was acceptable sexual conduct, i.e., what was normal. The model served as a mental-health equivalent to the McCarthy-era loyalty oath: A violation of the rules of anticommunism could land one in jail; a violation of standards of normalcy could doom one to a psycho ward, if not worse.

The legacy of European *fin de siècle* sexology, especially Freudian psychoanalysis, casts a long shadow over American psychiatry. Freud visited the United States only once, in 1909, to give his now-legendary Clark University lectures. During the following five decades, psychoanalysis was Americanized and, as recounted by Eli Zaretsky and others, the more radical aspects of Freud's theoretical analysis were neutralized or removed.[371] Zaretsky maps out the process by which American psychoanalysis came increasingly under the control of medically trained practitioners. A quarter century after Freud's Clark lecture, "all candidates for psychoanalytic training were expected to have completed a psychiatric residence in an approved [medical] institution." This proved so effective that by World War II, as Zaretsky notes, "psychoanalysis was being institutionalized in the United States."[372]

Psychiatry's bible, the *Diagnostic and Statistical Manual of Mental Disorders* (*DSM*), was first introduced in 1952. Psychiatry was then in thrall to the psychoanalytic model, especially when it came to the notion of perversion. As Paul Friedman states in the 1959 *American Handbook of Psychiatry*: "Broadly speaking, we designate as sexual deviation or perversions any patterns of sexual behavior which differ from normal coitus and serve as major sources of sexual gratification rather than as foreplay to coital activity." The key phrase—"sexual gratification rather than as foreplay"— locates perversion as an end in itself and, thus, a threat. Among the "special" psychopathological conditions Friedman identified are coprophilia, exhibitionism, fetishism, overt homosexuality, necrophilia, pedophilia, sadomasochism, transvestitism, voyeurism, and zoophilia.[373]

In the postwar period, the Americanized medico-psychoanalytic paradigm confronted a set of diverse challenges that contributed to its ultimate eclipse. One challenge came from sex researchers like Alfred Kinsey and Evelyn Hooker who presented empirical data that undermined conventional notions of perversion. Hooker, a UCLA literature professor, published "The Adjustment of the Male Overt Homosexual" in 1957, a landmark in critical analysis. A different challenge came from those championing alternative forms of psychology. They included behaviorists advocating aversion therapy, popularized by Albert Ellis and Aaron Beck, as well as psychologists Erich Fromm, Carl Rogers, Gordon Allport, Rollo May, and Abraham Maslow who put forward an approach broadly understood as "humanist" or "existential" psychology. They were revisionists of Freud, stripping his ideas of primal conflicts, thus making psychology more palatable to the American public.[374]

A medical challenge to the dominant notions of perversion came from those who believed that a person's abhorrent mental conditions and/or criminal actions were physiological based and, therefore, should be treated like any other biophysical malady. They challenged the more psychologically oriented psychiatry and involved a variety of often-conflicting approaches. One called for surgical intervention to fight perversion and was most aggressively represented by proponents of the lobotomy, especially the frontal lobotomy pioneered by Walter Freeman and James Watt; Freeman claimed that between 1936 and 1967 he performed 3,439 lobotomies. So acceptable was this procedure that its innovator, Egan Moniz, received the 1949 Nobel Prize for medicine.[375] A second medical approach involved shock therapy, either as insulin shock (i.e., insulin potentiation therapy or insulin coma therapy [ICT]) or electroconvulsive therapy [ETC]. Both found strong support within the medical field; however, while ICT died out in the early '60s, ETC (originally developed by Harold Sachheim) faced significant popular resistance in the '60s yet is still used today. Finally, the use of antipsychotic drugs, especially Thorazine (i.e., chlorpromazine) first introduced in 1954 by SmithKline, represented still another approach that found widespread acceptance; it is claimed that by 1964 more than fifty million people worldwide had used the drug.[376]

Still another challenge came from those questioning psychiatry's understanding of Freud and the Freudian model, or its theoretical underpinnings. Wilhelm Reich* advanced the most controversial strand among those "rereading" Freud.[377] Herbert Marcuse advanced a more influential critique in his 1955 work, *Eros & Civilization—A Philosophic Inquiry into Freud.* He combined Freud's psychoanalytic critique and Marx's social analysis with Martin Heidegger's phenomenological method to fashion a work that celebrates the inherent radicality of eros, of free libido within a human society and personal relations. It remains the most utopian, visionary work of the postwar era.[378]

Together, these varied empirical, psychiatric, medical, and theoretical challenges to the dominant medico-psychoanalytic paradigm contributed to the reconceptualization of the then-dominant notion of perversion. They helped set the stage for the American Psychiatric Association landmark 1973 decision removing homosexuality from its list of psychiatric disorders.

---

* For more on Reich, see "Sex Panic."

SEX PANIC

WILHELM REICH, 1897–1957

Sex Trafficking

President Barack Obama proclaimed January 2013 National Slavery and Human Trafficking Prevention Month. "This month, we rededicate ourselves to stopping one of the greatest human rights abuses of our time," he declared. "Around the world, millions of men, women, and children are bought, sold, beaten, and abused, locked in compelled service and hidden in darkness. They toil in factories and fields; in brothels and sweatshops; at sea, abroad, and at home. They are the victims of human trafficking—a crime that amounts to modern-day slavery."[379]

Two months later, the White House announced plans for strengthening its commitment to fight trafficking. "The Administration will also present new private sector partnerships in support of law enforcement efforts to combat child sex trafficking in three major jurisdictions, as well as research and tools to help law enforcement better identify children sold online," it announced. It subsequently promoted a variety of new initiatives.[380]

Human trafficking is a worldwide phenomenon, postmodern slavery. Reports about victims of trafficking, whether taking place internationally or in the United States, regularly appear in the media.

Horror stories and photos of young victims and testimonials from "rescued" victims appear in news articles, TV shows, movies, websites, academic reports, and government publications. These depictions emphasize the human suffering of near-powerless "slaves" forced to work in agriculture, manufacturing, construction, retail, and domestic service. The most exploited are those involved in commercial sex, especially young women and underage girls. It is a horrendous practice and fuels justified outrage among people—and politicians—the world over.

How extensive is trafficking in the United States? A February 2013 report by the Congressional Research Service (CRS), "Trafficking in Persons: U.S. Policy and Issues for Congress," estimates that "as many as 17,500 people are believed to be trafficked into the United States each year, and some have estimated that 100,000 US citizen children are victims of trafficking within the United States." The CRS notes: "Trafficking victims are often subjected to mental and physical abuse in order to control them, including debt bondage, social isolation, removal of identification cards and travel documents, violence, and fear of reprisals against them or their families." Sex trafficking is a horrible practice. Victims are forced to perform in a variety of venues, including residential brothels, "hostess clubs" or "room salons," fake massage studios, outcall escort service, strip or "gentlemen's" clubs and in old-fashioned street prostitution.[381]

Historically, the FBI did not investigate prostitution but left it to state and local law enforcement. Under President Bill Clinton, Congress passed the Victims of Trafficking and Violence Protection Act (TVPA) that established, within the State Department, the Office to Monitor and Combat Trafficking in Persons. According to Ronald Weitzer, a sociology professor at George Washington University, neither the Clinton administration nor the Act "distinguished forced and voluntary prostitution, did not link prostitution to trafficking, did not claim that legal prostitution increases trafficking into a country, and resisted mandatory sanctions against nations with poor records in combating trafficking."[382]

In 2011, the CRS issued a revealing report, "Sex Trafficking of Children in the United States: Overview and Issues for Congress."

It warns, "The exact number of child victims of sex trafficking in the United States is unknown because comprehensive research and scientific data are lacking." Nevertheless, the report identifies a number of factors contributing to trafficking, including runaway and "thrown-away" children as well as a young person's prior history of child sexual abuse and child sexual assault; poverty; the presence of large numbers of unattached and transient males; gang membership; organized crime; and foreign trafficking into the United States.[383] America faced a new sex crisis.

In 2013, the FBI reported that its war against trafficking included "66 dedicated task forces and working groups throughout the U.S. involving federal, state, and local law enforcement agencies working in tandem with U.S. Attorney's Offices." It spearheaded repeated street-level campaigns against prostitution and sex trafficking, most notably Operation Cross Country (OCC). The Justice Department estimated that, each year, nearly 450,000 children run away from their homes and that one-third of teenagers living on the street will be lured into prostitution. Clearly, underage prostitution—whether "consensual" or due to sex slavery—is a real problem.[384]

The CRS' 2011 report is most revealing when assessing the fate of those young people "rescued" from the sex trade. In no uncertain terms it states: "Of note, specialized services and support for minor victims of sex trafficking are limited. Nationwide, organizations specializing in support for these victims collectively have fewer than 50 beds. Other facilities, such as runaway and homeless youth shelters and foster care homes, may not be able to adequately meet the needs of victims or keep them from pimps/traffickers and other abusers."[385] Trafficking victims are forced from the frying pan into the fire.

Officials and activists have begun to rethink sex trafficking by shifting the focus to the underlying factors that lead many young people to get trapped in the sex racket. First, officials are seriously considering decriminalizing sex work involving both adult consensual commercial sex and trafficked youths. Officials are considering the "regulation" of commercial sex as a means both to protect the health and safety of sex workers and to restrict—if not eliminate—sex trafficking. Regarding underage sex slavery, a dozen states, including

New York, Minnesota, Connecticut, and Massachusetts, have passed what are known as "Safe Harbor laws" that decriminalize young people arrested for prostitution. Some officials seek to divert resources from the periodic street-level stunts like the FBI's OCC to address the issue of household domestic violence that seems to be the leading indicator of young people running away from home and ending up in the sex trade. Such action could help Americans get beyond the periodic sex panics that have distorted healthy sexual life for the last four centuries.[386]

Book Burning

On August 23, 1956, agents of the Federal Drug Administration (FDA) seized six tons of scholarly literature from a Greenwich Village warehouse, transported it to the New York Sanitation Department's Gansevoort Street incinerator and burned it. This burning followed one that took place a few weeks earlier near Rangeley, Maine, at which the FDA destroyed 251 volumes and other materials. The books burned were the works of Wilhelm Reich.

No two adversaries were more poorly matched. Where the FDA brought the full weight of an increasingly Cold War paranoid US government to bear against him, Reich stood resolute with limited resources, a handful of supporters and a commitment to a belief in the fundamental rights of free speech and scientific research. In essence, Reich went on trial and, after his final appeal to the Supreme Court failed, to prison for refusing to accept the FDA's authority to regulate what he insisted was legitimate scientific research. A twentieth-century Galileo? He refused to honor an injunction to stop selling the "orgone accumulator," an apparently harmless medical device for the treatment of cancer and other ailments. He was found guilty of contempt of court.

The punishment meted out to Reich—a two-year prison sentence and a $10,000 fine—was perhaps the clearest example of just how right he was about what he called the "emotional plague," the sex panic. He originally introduced the concept of the emotional plaque in his classic 1930s psychoanalytic text, *Character Analysis*, and reintroduced it in 1953 in *The Murder of Christ*. The plague was the sociopolitical paranoia that originally gripped Germany and, in the '50s, threatened the United States. His analysis and practice led to a federal investigation, prosecution, judgment, imprisonment, and his death in a federal penitentiary in '57. While the FDA might have thought it could suppress Reich's message about sexual and emotional health, he—and his insights—would come back with an unanticipated vengeance when embraced by the counterculture generation of the tumultuous '60s.

Reich was one of the most original, idiosyncratic, and tragic outsiders of the twentieth century. Born on March 24, 1897, in Galicia, a region within the Austro-Hungarian Empire, Reich lived many lives. He was an early disciple of Sigmund Freud, a radical Marxist, a pioneering sexologist, a believer in UFOs, and the discoverer of "orgone" energy. He claimed it was the life force, the essence that unites humans with nature, the psyche with the body, and individuals together with others in a healthy society. His motto was simple: "Love, work, and knowledge are the wellsprings of our lives, they should also govern it."[387]

The burning of Reich's works was the first state-sanctioned campaign of destruction of scholarly material, ostensibly First Amendment–protected publications, in New York in nearly a quarter-century. Shortly after Fiorello LaGuardia became mayor in 1934, he promoted an anti-obscenity campaign targeted at the Times Square entertainment district. He closed down burlesque houses, pinball arcades, and sex paraphernalia shops and burned what he deemed "obscene" publications. This mirrored Anthony Comstock's single-minded campaign a half century earlier to purify New York and the nation of obscene materials; Comstock claims to have destroyed fifteen tons of books, 284,000 pounds of printing plates, and nearly four million pictures. In the '40s, comic book burnings took place throughout the country.[*]

---

[*] See "Comic Book Corruption."

"Sometime during the early morning of November 3 [1957]," Myron Sharaf, Reich's first biographer, reports, "Reich's vital spark, his orgone energy, could not bounce back. He had been pushed beyond the limits of his endurance." In other words, Dr. Reich was dead. He died in the federal penitentiary at Lewisburg, Pennsylvania, following nearly eight months of a two-year sentence for crimes related to the promotion and sale of an innovative medical treatment device, the orgone accumulator. According to Sharaf, "He died of heartbreak."[388]

Reich first settled in New York following his immigration to the United States in 1939 to escape the Nazi terror. He relocated from New York to his summer research facility near Rangeley, Maine, in '52. He went on trial in Portland, Maine, at 10 a.m. on May 3, 1957, along with his colleague, Dr. Michael Silvert, a psychiatrist who ran Reich's New York operations out of his Village apartment. Both men had refused to honor a court order to appear for trial and were arrested on May 1, Reich in Washington, DC, and Silvert in the city. Federal agents brought both men to Portland in handcuffs on May 2; the defendants spent the night before the trial in jail.

Reich served as counsel for both defendants. Three days of legal proceedings followed, with both Reich and the state prosecutor, Joseph Maguire, examining and cross-examining a dozen or so witnesses. The judge, George C. Sweeney charged the jury to decide, not the merits of scientific research, but whether the defendants had committed contempt by violating the injunction to stop selling an unproven medical device, the orgone energy accumulator. He insisted on keeping the trial's focus narrow and the jury decided accordingly. Taking only ten to fifteen minutes to deliberate, the jury came back with guilty verdicts for both men.

After a hopeless appeal to the Supreme Court was rebuffed, Reich went first to the Danbury, Connecticut, penitentiary, then to the Lewisburg, Pennsylvania, facility. At the Pennsylvania prison, he worked in the library and likely crossed paths with some other notable early '50s lawbreakers. Two of the more well known were David Greenglass, Ethel Rosenberg's brother, and Samuel Roth, America's leading pornographer. Reich did not show up for roll call on the morning of November 3 and was found dead in his cell.

Sex Panic

During the postwar period, the United States was besieged by a sex crime "panic." It started in the late '40s and peaked in the mid-'50s. In 1947, FBI director J. Edgar Hoover warned, "the most rapidly increasing type of crime is that perpetuated by degenerate sex offenders. . . . [It] is taking its toll at the rate of a criminal assault every 43 minutes, day and night, in the United States."[389] In '48, the *Saturday Evening Post* writer, David Wittels, claimed that sex crimes were conducted by "psychopathic personalities" and estimated that "at least tens of thousands of them are loose in the country today."[390]

The panic was based, in part, on an ill-defined concept of a "sex crime." One commentator claimed it "originated when, after a series of brutal and apparently sexually motivated child murders, major urban newspapers expanded and, in some cases, sensationalized their coverage of child molestation and rape." Between 1953 and 1955, federal statistics indicate that the number of sex crimes increased 17 percent, from 46 to 54 per 100,000. The statistics appear to cover all sex-criminal arrests, including prostitution. The increase contributed to a nationwide hysteria about crimes involving "sexual psychopaths" attacking children and youths.[391]

The '50s panic drew force from more dangerous, disturbing criminal incidents. Throughout the nation there were reports of violent sexual attacks, especially rapes of women and girls, and even lust murders. The most notorious was the "Black Dahlia" case in Los Angeles, involving the murder and dismemberment of Elizabeth Short.[392] It was a sexually titillating story, a national headline grabber, and the source for many novels and movies.

New York was the site of two headline-grabbing teen murder stories. The first took place in August 1954 and involved four white, Jewish Brooklyn youths—Jerome Lieberman, Melvin Mittman, Jack Koslow, and Robert Trachtenberg—arrested for murdering Willard Mentor, a thirty-four-year-old black man. Mentor, who worked at a local burlap bag factory, appears to have been drunk and sleeping off his hangover in a public park when the teens attacked, beat, and threw him into the East River where he drowned. Koslow, in his defense, insisted that sleeping in a park was vagrancy and drunks like Mentor were social parasites.

At trial, it was alleged that the foursome had earlier killed Reinhold Ulrickson, another local alcoholic. Equally titillating, the youths were accused of attacking neighborhood girls walking in local parks, whipping them with a bullwhip that was ordered from a comic book classified ad. Koslow admitted that he was a regular comic book reader, inspired by the series, *Nights of Horror*. Dr. Fredric Wertham, a Department of Health senior psychiatrist, was called in to determine the youths' sanity. The media branded the teens the "Brooklyn Thrill Killers" and they became the poster boys of juvenile delinquency. A growing chorus insisted that comic books contributed to this social evil.[393]

The second incident took place in August 1959 and is known as the "Capeman" murders. Two white youth—Robert Young and Anthony Krzesinski—were killed in a street fight with a Puerto Rican youth gang. The fight took place in a Hell's Kitchen school playground and one of the busted Puerto Ricans was Salvador Agrón, sixteen years old. He drew media attention because he wore a Dracula costume, a black cape with a red lining, and was a member of the Vampires street gang.[394] The murders took place two years after the Broadway opening of *West Side Story*.

After the suspects were arrested, a mob of mostly neighborhood white residents protested outside the precinct house, shouting, "Kill the spics, kill the spics." Officials, both civic and community, mobilized to head off a race riot. A collation of 162 organizations established the Puerto Rican Self-Help Program and announcing, in full page *New York Times* ad, "We too fight delinquency," promoting a "crash program to fight delinquency." In January 1998, four decades after the Capeman murders, an $11 million musical on the incident opened on Broadway. The play, written by Paul Simon and Derek Walcott, was based on Agrón's life. It opened at the Marquis Theatre to poor reviews and ran for only sixty-eight performances.

The panic was further fueled by an increasing number of reported incidents of "pedophilia." In the '50s, pedophilia covered both the sexual molestation of a "child" as well as youthful or teenage boys and girls, what is now referred to as "ephebophilia." A series of sex crimes involving older men and youthful boys became national scandals. One alleged assault involved the former tennis star Bill Tilden and a fifteen-year-old boy. However, the most infamous criminal homoerotic episodes took place in Boise, Idaho, and Sioux City, Iowa. In Boise, three men were arrested for having sex with youths. The arrests led local authorities to investigate some of 1,500 residents to determine how widespread were such practices. In Sioux City, the abduction, sexual assault, and murder of two children, one twenty-two months old, led to the arrest of nearly two-dozen men charged with pedophilia and homosexuality, but who had nothing to do with the original crimes.[395]

Numerous criminal sodomy cases were reported in New York, many involving older men with boys. Among the stories that captured headlines was one that involved a teacher of twenty-five years at a school for boys accused of sodomizing a twelve-year-old student (*People v Doyle*, 1952); another involved a fifty-nine-year-old man accused of sodomizing—and then being sodomized by—a sixteen-year-old youth (*People v. Maggio*, 1962). Equally important, the state court debated the meaning of both oral and anal sex. It held that "only the one whose penis is inserted into a body orifice of another" is guilty of sodomy. The ruling drew much dissent; many argued that anal and oral sex were not the same sex acts even though both involved the male penis.[396]

A more benign expression of this panic involved the nationwide outbreak of panty raids at college campuses. Long forgotten, these raids constituted the first incidents of civil disobedience (and sometimes violence) by college students. "In the spring of 1952, as the police action in Korea dragged on and as support for Eisenhower's presidential candidacy grew," the historian Beth Bailey reports, "college campuses throughout the nation erupted in violence. Windows were smashed, buildings were briefly occupied." She adds, "students fought police—and one another—while the media breathlessly reported each new riot." Students at Princeton marched through the campus chanting, "We want girls! We want sex! We want panties."[397]

"White slavery," prostitution, was another arena in which the panic played out. Regular reports of violation of the federal Mann Act, a 1910 Comstock law that prohibited the interstate "trafficking" of females for commercial sex, drew front-page media headlines. Violations involved "any woman or girl [transported] for the purpose of prostitution, or debauchery, or for any immoral purpose." However, as two contemporary researchers, Harry Benjamin and R. E. L. Masters, warned, "to the extent that 'White Slavery' existed in the West in recent times—and that extent was very greatly exaggerated—the women involved were not necessarily prostitutes."[398] They were workingwomen, yet another commodity.

The most threatening "deviant" of the postwar era was the male homosexual and, to a lesser extent, the female lesbian. The "faggot's" shameless behavior—sexual desire for a same-gender partner—challenged heterosexual male masculinity. Many American men felt deeply insecure, even threatened, by the changes remaking society. "In the more sexualized post-war era, even bachelorhood was suspect, and marriage became more than an emotional, economic, and procreative arrangement," notes the writer John Loughery.[399] For women (and particularly for lesbians), the expanded social freedoms afforded during WWII, both in the civilian labor market and within the Armed Forces, were being curtailed. No wonder, as the historian Lillian Faderman observes, "the 'homosexual' became a particular target of persecution in America." Going further, she pointedly adds: "He or she presented an uncomfortable challenge to the mood that longed for obedience to an illusion of uncomplicated 'morality.'"*[400]

A New Home

Reich landed in New York on a hot, humid day in August 1939 and was welcomed by Walter Briehl, a child psychoanalyst, and Theodore Wolfe, a professor of psychiatry at Columbia, who put up the $5,000 guaranteeing his immigration visa. Briehl showed him the

---

* See "Lavender Peril."

sites, taking him to a jazz club in Harlem and to Jones Beach on Long Island. Reich was smitten. "New York is huge and totally different from Berlin, simpler and more impressive," he wrote a friend in Germany. "People are quiet, not rushed, as I expected; they are friendly and courteous; in a word, they are not yet disappointed and corrupted."[401] Reich seemed never to have returned to these sites, but did regularly dance the waltz with his wife, Ilse Ollendorff, at their favorite Forest Hills nightspot.

Reich arrived in the new world carrying a unique pedigree. In the '20s, Freud and other early founders of the then-fledgling discipline of psychoanalysis saw him as a promising analyst. At age twenty-three, he was admitted as a regular member of Vienna Psychoanalysis Association and, in 1930, he was a founding member of the Berlin Psychoanalysis Association. Reich is the author of *Character Analysis*, one of the classical texts in the psychoanalytic canon, and dozens of other important works. But whereas Freud accommodated the needs for theoretical revision and was liberal with regard to the political status quo, Reich was an orthodox adherent to Freud's first principal, a radical materialist contesting social power. In '35, he was expelled from the official psychoanalytic movement.

His expulsion was pushed for two reasons—one theoretical, the other political. First, Reich challenged two principals of psychoanalytic orthodoxy. He refused to abandon Freud's original biological determinism; he believed that underlying biological and physiological drives, the living body, and its sexual fulfillment, determined character and behavior. Second, he rejected Freud's notion of the death instinct; he argued, particularly with regard to masochism, the need for healthy physical intimacy were fulfilled through self-hating behavior and not, as Freud speculated, a death wish. Going further, Reich believed that achieving full orgasmic potency through satisfying heterosexual genital sex was the most basic human drive. This principal guided his professional and personal life.

Reich was also expelled from the official psychoanalytic movement because of his political activism. For him, ideas were more than theories or diagnoses; they were practices—both with regard to a patient and with regard to the larger society, the working class. The psychoanalytic leadership assailed Reich's involvement with Austrian and later German Communists, particularly his establishment of "sex-pol" clinics for working-class adults and, most threatening, young people. In the face of the mounting social crisis of the late 1920s and early 1930s, Reich was one of the earliest—and the most analytically rigorous—proponents of a radical intellectual current that would profoundly affect European and American intellectual life in the postwar era, the attempt to synthesize Freud and Marx, self and society, being and class.

Reich joined the medical wing of the Austrian Communist Party following what is known as "the bloody day" of July 15, 1927, a day that saw eighty-nine workers killed in a pitched battle with a neo-Nazi militia. Throwing himself into the workers' struggle, he sought to achieve the reconciliation of personal-psychic and social-economic life by combining theory with practice through sexual hygiene clinics. Following his move to Berlin in 1930, he joined with other radicals to set up clinics to provide sex education to the proletariat. These clinics spoke directly to the needs of working-class men and women, adults and youths—advocating for abortion on demand (including abortions for unmarried women and girls), supporting free distribution of contraceptives (especially to youths), affirming childhood masturbation, and supporting nudism, among other controversial positions.

Reich's reputation preceded him to the United States; it helped him get a temporary appointment at the New School for Social Research. Its "University in Exile" was established in 1933 as a haven for European intellectuals fleeing the Nazis. Among its émigré faculty were philosophers Hannah Arendt, Alfred Schutz, Leo Strauss, and Aron Gurwitsch; economist Gerhard Colm; political scientist Arnold Brecht; sociologist Hans Speier; anthropologist Bronisław Malinowski; and psychologist Max Wertheimer, who helped develop Gestalt, or cognitive, psychology. Among the courses Reich taught in 1940 and '41 were "Character Formation: Biological and Sociological Aspects" and "Clinical Problems in PsychSomatic Medicine."[402]

Reich remained peripheral to the larger expat community; he actually refused to go to concerts fearing crossing paths with former colleagues from Vienna.[403] He was building the future, not looking back on the past and all that was lost. Over the nearly two decades he called the United States home, Reich retained few if any friends or professional associates from the "old world." However, he maintained a strong, long-term personal and professional relationship with English educator A. S. Neill, founder of Summerhill, the legendary experimental school.

Settling in Forest Hills, Queens, Reich quickly fashioned a new life. He first rented a house at 7502 Kessel Street and, in 1941, bought one at 99–06 69th Avenue, a block from the Forest Hills Tennis Stadium. He gathered acolytes, recruited students, started treating patients, conducted "primary" research, and published learned pieces. He had divorced his first wife, Annie Reich, in 1933, with whom he had two daughters and who all lived in the city. Shortly after settling in Queens, he met Ollendorff, a German émigré, and they were together for fourteen years; they were legally married in 1941—for immigration purposes—and had a son, Peter.[404]

In 1940, and as part of his research, Reich constructed an "accumulator" to try to measure a heretofore unidentified force of nature, "orgone" energy. Sharaf describes it as a "boxlike apparatus . . . [It] had metal walls on the inside backed with organic material on the inside. . . . One panel of the apparatus had an opening with a lens through which possible manifestations of the presumed energy could be observed by the researcher from the outside."[405] Using this research instrument, Reich believed he had discovered the life force, energy separate from matter.

In late December 1940, Reich wrote Albert Einstein, America's foremost German émigré and the world's leading scientist, to get his support for his groundbreaking discovery. In what became known as "The Einstein Affair," Reich visited the physicist at his home in Princeton, New Jersey, on January 13, 1941, spending between four and five hours discussing orgone theory. Enthusiastic after the meeting, Reich sent Einstein a number of different accumulators, hoping for his scientific blessing. After two weeks of analysis, Einstein wrote a critical assessment: "I hope this [explanation] will awaken your sense of skepticism, so that you will not allow yourself to be deceived by an illusion that can be easily explained. Please have someone pick up your instruments, since they are of some value. They are undamaged. With friendly greetings, A. Einstein."

Disappointed but not disillusioned, Reich pressed on with his orgone research. In 1941, he applied the accumulator to the treatment of people suffering from cancer. Drawing upon his earlier sexology theories, he argued that cancer was a physical manifestation of a deeper, psychosexual disorder, or what he termed the "cancer biopathy." According to Sharaf, Reich "felt that basic cause of such degenerative diseases [like cancer] was a chronic malfunction of the organism's biological energy." As Reich insisted most emphatically: *"Cancer is living putrefaction of the tissues due to the pleasure starvation of the organism."*[406]

Reich's treatment regime included the use of "larger, man-sized accumulators." Sharaf, who worked with Reich and experienced an accumulator, described it as follows:

> They were about two feet six inches square in floor area and about five feet high, so that when a person sat down inside he or she was surrounded closely by the metal walls, without actually touching them. An aperture in the door, about one foot square provided ventilation. . . . [W]alls made of alternating layers of celotex and sheet iron (later, layers of glass wool and steel wool were used for additional concentration) increased the accumulation strength. The early accumulators were built of only a few layers, up to five fold.[407]

Over time, Reich fashioned a variety of orgone accumulators, ranging from the famous "box" to a blanket. The resulting orgone therapy would help treat a patient's "body armor," freeing him or her to better experiences the deeper bodily processes, most especially sexual orgasm. The patient would, therefore, be in touch with the body's processing of the life force, orgone energy.

The originality of Reich's research during this period cannot be denied. He was, put simply, asking a very different set of questions than other researchers. As Sharaf notes, "It is easy to overlook the fact that no one in his time was seeing and doing what he was seeing and doing." No one sought to link the mind to the body, to the body politic, to social being, and to the natural, organic, world.[408] More than a half century later, scientific researchers—let alone ordinary people—are still trying to answer this question.

In December 1941, Reich's political past caught up with his new life in Queens. About a week after the Japanese attack on Pearl Harbor and a few days after Germany declared war against the United States, FBI agents knocked on Reich's door at two in the morning. He was seized—along with thousands of other men—as an "enemy alien." Much like the roundup of "Muslims" following 9/11, Reich spent about a month at a detention center on Ellis Island; he was released on January 5, 1942. Following his release, FBI agents paid him a visit, inspecting his library and seizing three "un-American" works: Hitler's *Mein Kampf*, Trotsky's *My Life*, and a Russian alphabet for children. When questioned as to why they were in his library, stupefied, Reich reminded them that as a scholar, a *scientist*, he had to understand his subjects of study. Later that year, Briehl, who was a student of Reich's in Germany and then a New York psychiatrist, urged him to take the New York State medical licensing examination to preserve his status as a doctor; Reich refused.

One group that did not overlook his research was the US Food and Drug Administration (FDA). In 1947, disturbed by rumors that the accumulator was being sold as a "sex box" to enhance sexual potency, the FDA began investigating Reich. Over the next decade, the FDA would conduct an extensive campaign against him, culminating in Reich's arrest, conviction, imprisonment, and death.

A Lost Life

It is unclear why, after the war, the *New Republic* singled out Reich for attack. In December 1946, the magazine published a very critical review by the psychiatrist, Dr. Fredric Wertham, of the recently released English version of Reich's classic text, *The Mass Psychology of Fascism.** Originally released in '33, it is considered a breakthrough

---

* A decade later, Wertham would play a critical role in the comic book wars; see "Comic Book Corruption."

Freud-Marx analysis linking character formation with political practice; it links the authoritarian personality with totalitarianism, the
Nazi regime. In the late '40s, the *New Republic* was under the edi-
torship of Henry Wallace, FDR's former vice president and who the
Democrats unceremoniously dropped for the '44 election, replacing
him with Harry Truman. Some insist that Michael Straight, whose
parents founded and owned the magazine, orchestrated the attack
on Reich. Straight attended Cambridge University in the '30s and
became close to those known as the Cambridge spy ring.[409] Wertham's review of *The Mass Psychology of Fascism* reflected what was
then recognized as a "Stalinist" analysis, accusing Reich of "utter
contempt for the masses." Wertham insisted that Reich embraced
bourgeois values, particularly notions of mysticism and a belief that
people were really not capable of political freedom. Most tenden-
tiously, Wertham argued that Reich was an enemy of the working
class and an advocate of "psycho-fascism."

Less than six months later, in May 1947, the *New Republic* featured a follow-up exposé of Reich's psychiatric practice, "The Strange
Case of Wilhelm Reich," by Mildred Edie Brady. In April '47, she
gained attention with *Harper's* publication of a provocative article,
"The New Cult of Sex and Anarchy." Brady was long associated with
progressive causes, including helping found Consumers Union.
Reich rarely gave interviews to the press, but granted one to Brady.
She presented Reich as a quack, a mad scientist who built orgone
energy accumulators "which are rented out to patients who presum-
ably derive orgastic potency from it."[410] She urged the psychoanalytic
community to repudiate him.

The article led to a firestorm of rumors and accusations about
Reich and his practices. The orgone accumulator was mocked as a
sex machine and his clinical method vilified; Reich was accused of
promoting masturbation as part of therapeutic practice. Ironically,
Reich's lawyer, Arthur Garfield Hays had advised him not to sue the
magazine or the author for slander; Reich appears to not have known
that Hays was a Consumers Union sponsor.

Over the next few years, a steady stream of articles came out
against Reich, many simply restating the questionable assertions

claimed in Brady's original pieces. The story was picked up by a number of popular publications, including *Consumer's Reports* as well as *Colliers, Mademoiselle, Everybody's Digest*, and the *New York Post*, then a liberal tabloid. The most serious attack came in March '48 when the Menninger Clinic, in its *Bulletin*, printed Brady's article in full, thus giving it scientific legitimacy. Brady's findings were also reported in the *Journal of the American Medical Association* and the *American Journal of Psychiatry*. In 1950, the well-respected *Antioch Review* ran a piece by Martin Gardner, an influential liberal thinker, that marginalized Reich as a well-meaning, if misguided fool. *Time* magazine joined the circus, publishing an article provocatively entitled, "The Marvelous Sex Box." However, *Politics* and *The Nation* gave, in the words of Reich's biographer Christopher Turner, "enthusiastic accounts of his sexual theories."[411]

This media attention may have drawn the FDA's scrutiny to Reich. In July 1952, FDA inspectors paid an unannounced visit to Reich's Maine research center, "Orgonon," and seized a number of accumulators. The agency sent one of the devices to the well-respected Mayo Clinic for assessment and Dr. Frank Krusen undertook an independent analysis. His August 1953 report to the FDA was emphatic: "It was very difficult for me to bring myself to take the time to prepare this report because of the fact that this quackery is of such a fantastic nature that it hardly seems worthwhile to refute the ridiculous claims of its proponents."[412]

During this period, Reich's line of inquiry shifted beyond the maladies of the body and the unconscious. Against the background of the Korean War and mounting anticommunism, he began investigating atomic energy. He sought to determine whether orgone energy could suppress the effects of nuclear poisoning. He acquired a small amount of radioactive isotopes from the Atomic Energy Commission (AEC) and conducted a series of test of the isotope placed inside an orgone accumulator. At his Maine retreat, many of his colleagues, including his son, suffered mild cases of radiation poisoning.

At this time, Maine farmers were suffering a draught and Reich took up the challenge. Pushing his own boundaries, Reich tested whether an orgone accumulator could be a "cloud-buster" or rainmaking devise. He constructed what can only be called an orgone gun, with one end consisting of a series of long metal pipes pointed to the sky and the other end made up of a cable anchored in a deep well. He conducted rainmaking experiments at his Rangeley compound as well as in the Arizona desert and in New York and Boston. In '53, Reich pushed further the limits of rational scientific research, applying himself to the study of flying saucers, UFOs. His interest in unidentified objects seems to have started in '52 when people at his Maine facility reported seeing shining objects in the sky. He was influenced by a then recently published work by Donald Keyhoe, a decorated World War II fighter pilot, *Flying Saucers from Outer Space*; Keyhoe also published the '50s blockbuster *The Flying Saucers Are Real*.

On February 10, 1954, the worlds of Reich's scientific research collided with the FDA's authority to regulate medical procedures. Maine's US attorney filed an injunction against Reich and, going further, the US attorney general enjoined Reich and his associates from the interstate shipping of accumulators. The die was cast. Reich held such authorities in contempt, insisting only fellow scientists could judge him. A couple of years later, Reich met his fate.

One of the great ironies of Reich's later years was that while he was being demonized by the more establishment press, rejected by the scientific community, and hounded by federal authorities, he was discovered, then celebrated, by late '50s hipsters and the '60s counterculture. Reich had a strong following among a core group of true-believers, some medical doctors, and scientific researchers, who tried to uphold the master's official, orthodox wisdom. Parallel to these believers, some psychologists, therapists, and others passed through Reich's orbit and, subsequently, established more acceptable practices like bioenergetics. At the same time, Reich was discovered by the bohemian, hipster culture, and his ideas and practices transformed into a hedonism that shocked him.

Paul Goodman, an anarchist libertine made famous for his classic study, *Growing Up Absurd* (1960), introduced Reich to the hip scene. This was the period when the Beats gave way to folkies and the hippies—and the counterculture movement began to spread throughout the country. He wrote a glowing tribute about Reich's sex theories that Dwight McDonald published in *The Nation*.[413] Reich was embraced for his vision of human freedom, one in which the mind and the body are unified, not separate domains. He was a true outsider, embraced as much for his contributions of classical psychoanalytic work as for his sex-pol movement, fighting fascism during the '20s, and the accumulator of the '50s. For Goodman, Reich offered a post-Freudian alternative to more conventional psychiatry and psychology, a rereading of the post-WWII consumer revolution. For Goodman, Reich celebrated the radical or utopian spirit of physical, sexual life, of the living body—and his own bisexuality. Allen Ginsburg and other Beat writers embraced Reich as did the founders of the Living Theatre, Julian Beck and Judith Malina. He was seriously read by the literary set, including Norman Mailer, JD Salinger, and Saul Bellow. Some even underwent "Reichian" therapy with an accumulator. Goodman once visited Reich at his Forest Hills home and was lambasted for misreading his work. Reich insisted he was neither a libertine nor into free love; he was an orthodox materialist, a true Freudian. Against his intentions, Reich became one of the "fathers" of a movement he would have embraced as a spirited youth but rejected as a defeated adult.

Reich suffered deeply during the last years of his life. He was mocked and persecuted; his works were burned; he was arrested, tried, and convicted; he died in prison. In the years before prison, he turned increasingly to drink, favoring brandy; he had odd, if not perverse fetishism like taking showers wearing his underwear. He struck out against those closest to him, repeatedly hitting his ex-wife and various lovers. Toward his patients and colleagues, he increasingly appeared as an autocratic, paranoid, pathetic man. He remained vehemently homophobic, but neither a racist nor anti-Semitic.

As government pressures mounted, Reich increasingly turned to exaggerated claims, including that he offered a cure for cancer, was a rainmaker, had weapons to fight extraterrestrials, and was protected by the president and Air Force. A lifetime earlier in interwar Germany, Reich had been peripherally involved with the Frankfurt School, a group of radical anti-Stalinist Marxist academics and others, including

Herbert Marcuse. His assessment of Reich is the most telling: "The critical sociological insights contained in Reich's earlier writings are thus arrested; a sweeping primitivism becomes prevalent, foreshadowing the wild and fantastic hobbies of Reich's later years."[414]

Over the last century, the United States has witnessed three culture wars. The first took place during the early twentieth century and was waged over alcohol, prostitution, and the new women; the second occurred during the '50s and targeted sin, sex, and subversion; and the current war took shape as a political and moral response to the Supreme Court's landmark 1973 decision, *Roe v. Wade*, and peaked during the Bush II administration.

Abortion—a woman's right to terminate an unwanted pregnancy—remains the most passionate and enduring issue, but other concerns have drawn support from religious leaders, politicians, and conservative activists. These issues include a wide range of consensual adult sexual engagements, including homosexuality and same-gender sexual relations; premarital and extramarital sex; birth control and teen sex education; commercial sex; and pornography. However, the new normal draws the line at nonconsensual physical, sexual engagements.

Over the last decade-plus, the United States has seen an on-again, off-again battle over Internet porn filtering. In 1996, Congress passed the Communications Decency Act (CDA), part of the Telecommunications Act. It was designed to block Internet transmission of sexually explicit materials to minors under eighteen years. It prohibited materials "that, in context, depicts or describes, in terms patently offensive as measured by contemporary community standards, sexual or excretory activities or organs." A year later, in *Reno v. American Civil Liberties Union*, a federal district court ruled the CDA unconstitutional, and the Supreme Court led the ruling stand.

In 2000, and at the height of the culture wars, Congress passed the Children's Internet Protection Act (CIPA). It required public libraries that receive federal funds to install computer-based filters blocking access to Internet pornography. Librarians and others challenged the Act but, in 2003, the Supreme Court ruled it did not violate First Amendment rights. It's the filtering law of the land.

THE PILL

MARGARET SANGER, 1879–1966

Abortion Wars

On July 13, 2013, Purvi Patel, a thirty-three-year-old woman, went to the ER at St. Joseph Hospital in Mishawaka, Indiana, seeking medical help for bleeding from her vagina as a result of a premature delivery. Shortly thereafter, another trauma befell her, this one likely to ruin the rest of her life.

The police were notified and she was arrested. Homicide detectives interrogated her, then searched her home and downloaded her cell phone messages. The police claimed that, in an email to a friend, she admitted buying—and taking—a drug from a Hong Kong company to abort an unwanted pregnancy. However, a blood test revealed no drugs in her system at the time of the miscarriage. She admitted that she had given birth to a dead fetus and, in desperation, placed it in a bag and dropped it in a dumpster behind a nearby store. On March 31, 2015, Patel was sentenced to twenty years in prison for feticide, the fetal murder of her unborn child and of having a baby that she allowed to die.[415]

Patel was the second Indiana women to be prosecuted for feticide. The first was Bei Bei Shuai, a Chinese migrant, in 2010. She was arrested after taking rat poison in a failed attempt to commit suicide. She was charged with the death of the fetus that was born a girl, named Angel, and died two days later. She was kept in jail for more than a year awaiting trial for feticide before a plea deal finally freed her in 2013.[416]

The anti-abortion movement is tightening its grip on a woman's pregnancy. According to the National Conference of State Legislatures, at least thirty-eight states have introduced fetal homicide laws. These laws are ostensibly designed to protect the fetus, an unborn person, by criminalizing pregnancy. They have been used against mothers in Alabama, Mississippi, South Carolina, and other states.[417] The *New York Times* reported that the Patel case "demonstrates how unsparing the criminal-justice system can be to women whose pregnancies end in (or otherwise involve) suspicious circumstances." It warns, "If one lesson of the case is about the legal risk of inducing your own late-term abortion, another is about the peril of trying to get medical help when you are bleeding and in pain."[418]

In 1873, the US Congress enacted the most draconian laws involving sexuality in the nation's history, popularly known as the "Comstock laws." They were named after Anthony Comstock, the nation's leading moralist who spoke for a new generation of American Puritans, whose efforts resulted in the 1873 law, "Suppression of Trade in, and Circulation of, Obscene Literature and Articles of Immoral Use." It was followed, in 1910, by the Mann Act barring interstate sexual commerce and, in 1919, the adoption of the Eighteenth Amendment establishing Prohibition. These modern Puritans were a powerful force.

The 1873 Comstock law stands as the most sweeping, omnibus anti-sexuality law in American history, covering all interstate commerce and communication. It singled out birth control, targeting "any article or thing designed or intended for the prevention of conception or procuring of abortion."[419] To enforce the law, Comstock was appointed a special officer of the US postal system and given the power to seize what he labeled as obscene materials as well as arrest those he identified as pornographers, including those advocating birth control.

A century later, in 1973, abortion was legalized when the then all-male Supreme Court voted 7–2, in *Roe v Wade*, to overturn a Texas law making it a crime to assist a woman to have an abortion. The Count found the law violated a woman's due process rights. While *Roe* formally remains the law of the land, it is being systematically eroded in a last-ditch effort by the Christian right. Richard Nixon was the president at the time of the decision and supported abortion, but in limited cases: "There are times when an abortion is necessary. I know that. When you have a black and a white or a rape." The subsequent Republican administrations of Ronald Reagan and the two Bushes supported anti-sex and anti-abortion campaigns. Over the last decade, their efforts suffered major defeats with regard to the normalization of homosexuality, birth control, and teen sex education.

Since taking control of both houses in January 2015, Republican legislators have introduced twenty-nine separate bills to restrict a woman's right to an abortion, thirteen in the Senate and sixteen in the House. None has yet passed.[420] According to the Guttmacher Institute, between 2011 and 2014, states enacted 231 abortion restrictions. The Kaiser Family Foundation found that in just the first month of 2015, more than one hundred bills had been introduced to restrict a woman's right to an abortion in innumerable ways. They include: requiring parental notification, a father's permission, watching an anti-choice video, requiring a seventy-two-hour waiting period, prohibiting second-trimester terminations, banning abortions after twenty weeks, and requiring abortion providers to have hospital admitting privileges or meeting hospital surgical-procedural requirements to provide services. For the anti-choice movement, if you can't convince people, especially women, that abortion is "wrong," then you use the state to impose moral discipline. The anti-abortionist group, Operation Rescue, reports that between 2009 and 2014, the number of abortion facilities declined by 188, or nearly a quarter, from 739 to 551. It also reports that in 2014, 73 facilities were closed for all or part of the year.[421]

Woman Rebel

In 1950, Margaret Sanger attended an intimate dinner party at the Park Avenue apartment of Dr. Abraham Stone, medical director of the Clinical Research Bureau (a.k.a. the Margaret Sanger Research Bureau) and a longtime birth control advocate; his deceased wife, Dr. Hannah Stone, had been a strong supporter of Sanger's work. Now living in Tucson, Arizona, she was visiting the city and had come to meet one of the other guests, Gregory Pincus, a Harvard University PhD biologist and a pioneering fertility researcher. As Pincus later recalled, "she asked, 'Gregory, can't you devise some sort of pill for this purpose [birth control]?' I said I'd try."[422] A decade later, in May 1960, the Food and Drug Administration (FDA) approved the first simple-to-use, foolproof, and safe oral contraceptive method, "the Pill." It changed America in ways the woman rebel never anticipated.

When Sanger and Pincus met, Sanger was seventy-one years old and no longer the radical she had been four decades earlier. On October 16, 1916, she—along with two other women, her sister, Ethel Byrne, a nurse, and Fania Mindell, a receptionist who spoke Yiddish—opened the nation's first birth-control clinic on Amboy Street in the predominantly immigrant, Jewish neighborhood of Brownsville, Brooklyn. It dispensed birth-control literature, provided helpful information, and supplied contraceptive devices (e.g., pessaries, condoms, and douching solutions) to the predominately immigrant and working-class women of the neighborhood. The clinic operated for ten days, serving some 488 women, before the police closed it down. Sanger and Byrne were arrested for violating Comstock laws; found guilty, the sisters each served thirty days in jail; Byrne went on a hunger strike and was force-fed. They were imprisoned with prostitutes and drug addicts, and spent time educating these women on birth control and other "women's issues."[423]

Sanger was born Margaret Louisa Higgins on September 14, 1879, to Irish-immigrant parents in Corning, New York; she died almost eighty-eight years later on September 6, 1966. In her youth, she struggled alongside radicals like Emma Goldman, Elizabeth Gurley Flynn, and Havlock Ellis; in her maturity, she was on a first-name basis with world figures like Eleanor Roosevelt, John D. Rockefeller, Jr., and Mahatma Gandhi. Her life's trajectory defines the integration of "birth control" from the margin to the mainstream of social life. As David Halberstam observed, "She was an American samurai, and she spent her life on a wartime footing."[424] She moved from an outsider to an insider.

In 1910, Sanger moved with her husband, William Sanger, an architect and artist, and their children from the placid suburbs of Westchester, New York, to the city and plunged into the rich intellectual, cultural, and political life that Ann Douglas called "mongrel Manhattan."[425] She joined the Socialist party, wrote columns for *The Call*, and was a regular at Mabel Dodge's legendary salons. Others who attended these memorable get-togethers were political figures like John Reed and Bill Haywood, the artists Arthur Davis, Charles Demuth, and Max Weber, and renowned intellectuals like Will Durant and A. A. Brill. Within such a stimulating environment, the obligations of marriage and family became restraints on her desire to live a passionate life.

Sanger challenged the powerful traditionalist convention that a married mother without means (i.e., a rich husband or inherited wealth) should not lead an autonomous life, become a public figure separate and distinct from her husband. Fully exploiting the knowledge and experience gained as a nurse in Westchester, she became an articulate spokesperson on what was then called "women's issues," particularly family planning and birth control. She founded and edited *The Woman Rebel* and published two critical pamphlets, "What Every Girl Should Know" and "Family Limitation," that directly challenged US obscenity laws. In August 1914, Comstock indicted Sanger for sending birth control information through the US mail. Fearing a possible forty-five-year prison term, she fled to Europe to avoid the trial. During her absence, Comstock went to the Sanger home and, posing as a father seeking birth-control assistance, bought a pamphlet from William Sanger, and arrested him; Sanger served a month in jail.[426]

Sanger's 1916 arrest and trial took place amid the mounting hysteria that accompanied the United States' entry into World War I.

The war caused a fundamental schism within the progressive community. While some supported the war effort, many of her more radical comrades, most notably Goldman, stood in pacifist opposition to US involvement. Sanger took a third course. She claimed neutrality, insisting that a women's right to birth control was above the war and the polarizing positions it engendered. Sanger's compromise would guide her efforts during the subsequent decades of her long and distinguished life.

Sanger's position allowed her to escape the right-wing revenge executed against the most radical progressives during the postwar Red Scare. While the Palmer Raids and the subsequent deportations of radicals (including Goldman, her oldest comrade-in-arms and rival for influence) were underway, Sanger organized the nation's first birth-control conference. Held in 1921, it drew distinguished guests such as Winston Churchill and Theodore Dreiser, as well as many medical and academic dignitaries. As Ellen Chesler, her principal biographer, notes, "The conference reestablished Margaret as the country's preeminent spokeswoman for birth control."[427]

Sanger sought to reconcile political belief with practical action. Birth control not only offered a woman greater power over her life— her body and her pregnancy—but also provided a means by which she could experience greater erotic pleasure, an experience separate from procreation. Sanger's political activism and intellectual forcefulness were matched by a strong sexual passion. She advocated for sexual freedom and also practiced it. She appears to have really enjoyed sexual relations with her two husbands as well as affairs, if not of the flesh than of the mind, with some of the leading intellectuals of her day, including Ellis, H. G. Wells, and Lorenzo Portet.[*] Her relationship with (and subsequent marriage to) Noah Slee, a millionaire manufacturer, started in 1921 (while still married to Sanger) as she organized her first US birth-control conference. With its success

---

[*] Portet was a disciple of Francisco Ferrer, Spain's leading reformer and educator who was assassinated by Spanish monarchists in 1909. Sanger may well have had a homoerotic encounter with Janet de Selincourt, the wife of one of her lovers, Hugh de Selincourt; see Chesler, 186.

and her marriage to Slee, she abandoned both her radical socialist roots and sexual liaisons outside of marriage as well. As Chesler describes it, the marriage deteriorated into a sad, bitter relationship as the stock market crash and Depression destroyed Slee's fortune and selfhood. Her sexuality seemed to have been rekindled in 1933 when she met Angus Sneed MacDonald, once again finding sexual intimacy with a man other than her husband.[428]

In 1930, Sanger provoked one of the twentieth century's major confrontations over a woman's right to birth-control materials, this time as a free speech issue. She "illegally" imported Japanese condoms, a violation of the Comstock laws. In 1936, the Supreme Court, in *U.S. v One Package of Japanese Pessaries,* struck down the prohibition because the material, as information and devices, served medical purposes, protecting the patient's life. During the following two decades, and especially among WWII servicemen stationed away from home or overseas, condoms became the principal means to prevent catching a sexually transmitted disease (STD).

A City's Shame

During January 1956, bags containing pieces of the dismembered body of Jacqueline Smith, a twenty-year-old fashion designer, were discovered in litter baskets along Broadway between 72nd and 80th Streets. All told, the city police found fifty bags containing her remains. Smith had moved to the city from Lebanon, Pennsylvania, a year earlier and ended up living at 224 East 27th Street with her new boyfriend, Thomas G. Daniel, a twenty-four-year-old salesman at a riding equipment shop.

In December '55, Smith discovered that she was five to six weeks pregnant and asked Daniel to marry. He refused, but said he would arrange for her to have an abortion. He secured the assistance of Leobaldo Pijuan, a forty-six-year-old Bushwick Hospital attendant who lived at West End Avenue and 69th Street; he received between $100 and $125 to perform the abortion. However, things went badly and Smith was unresponsive following the procedure. Pijuan asked a friend, Dr. Ramiro Morales, a twenty-six-year-old intern at Bronx's Lincoln Hospital, to check her out. Examining Smith, Morales reported that she was dead; he departed but did not report the death. Over the following week or so, Daniel and Pijuan discarded Smith's body parts along Broadway.

On December 30, Smith's father, Chester Smith, came to visit but couldn't locate his daughter. Accompanied by Daniel, he went to the police station to report her missing. Under intense questioning by a female officer, Daniel claimed that Smith had been so distraught over his rejection of her marriage proposal that she committed suicide, stabbing herself while in the bathroom. He claimed he threw her dead body into the Hudson River. Under further interrogation, the police learned about Pejuan and, searching his apartment, found over eight hundred stolen medical instruments. Pejuan pleaded guilty and testified against Daniel. Pejuan was sentenced to seven and a half years in prison; Daniel received eight years.[429]

Throughout the '50s, the New York police actively went after abortionists and "rings" were regularly busted operating throughout the city. In April 1951, seven people were arrested in Brooklyn for running a ring that the authorities claimed took in an estimated $500,000 annually. Interestingly, in 1942, the state had passed a law that made the doctor who gave information about abortion to a woman or referred a woman to an abortionist "equally guilty."[430] In '54, a ring was busted in the Bronx and, like the Smith case, this one involved a woman's death during an illegal abortion. The abortion took place at 3753 Sexton Place and the woman who died was Mrs. Gertrude Pinsky, thirty-five years old and from Brooklyn.[431] In July '59, eight people were arrested for being part of a "city-wide" ring and all were from Manhattan. At a press conference, District Attorney Frank Hogan noted, the "clientele was diversified and ranged from a college girl from an exclusive school to a Federal Government employee and chorus girls."[432]

During the '50s, police crackdowns of illegal abortions were part of the culture war against sin, sex, and subversion. According to historian Leslie Reagan, author of *When Abortion Was a Crime*, it was a "near impossibility of obtaining birth control in the fifties and sixties" and this "raised the danger of intercourse and the fears felt by single women." She found that "physicians and birth control clinics refused to provide contraceptives to unmarried women." She also found, "fewer abortionists practiced in New York City in 1955 than had in 1940." This led to a tripling in the fee charged for the procedure, with fees ranging from $200 to $500.[433] It also led to the entry of unlicensed practitioners like Pijuan and Francese into the field.

In the '50s, abortions included both "legal" and "illegal" procedures. In New York State, a legal abortion was defined as a "therapeutic" procedure undertaken for the sole purpose to save the woman's life. Other states had wider definitions of a legal abortion, including efforts to preserve the mother's "health" or "safety" and to prevent "serious or permanent bodily injury to her." No one knows the total number of abortions performed in the United States, let alone in New York City, during this period.

Jonathan Eig, author of *Birth of the Pill*, points out, "Year after year in the 1950s, the nation became more fertile."[434] More pregnancies—who knows how many were unwanted?—led to more abortions. In January 1956, Mrs. Eugene Mayer, wife of the chairman of the board of the *Washington Post* and *Times Herald*, gave the keynote address before Planned Parenthood's Committee on Mothers' Health Center. She estimated that 750,000 "criminal abortions were performed annually" in the United States. (By "criminal" she meant non-therapeutic abortions.) She argued that these abortions were "obtained by married women with three or more children." She identified poverty and ignorance of birth control methods as primary causes for women turning to abortion and called for more birth control education and "the incorporation of contraception into the material welfare program." Planned Parenthood estimated that the number of illegal abortions taking place annually during the 1950s and '60s ranged from 200,000 to 1.2 million. In '58, the Kinsey Institute released its third installment in the pioneering *Sexual Behavior* series, *Pregnancy, Birth and Abortion*, by Paul Gebhard, et al., and offered a more sobering assessment. It estimated that 120,000 unmarried women had abortions annually.[435]

City authorities were concerned about an apparent abuse of therapeutic procedures used to circumvent legal restrictions prohibiting abortion. In the 1940s, city physicians performed an average of 710 therapeutic abortions per year; by the early '60s, the number had dropped to fewer than three hundred due to strict enforcement to anti-abortion laws. Between 1943 and '62, the rate of therapeutic abortions dropped by 65 percent. During this two-decade period, white women received more than 9 out of 10 (91 percent) of legal abortions. Those who suffered the most with the cut in legal abortions were the city's poor, including whites, African Americans, and Puerto Ricans. City public health officials pointed out, "the disparity . . . between ethnic groups has been widening over the years" and believed it a "medical responsibility . . . to equalize the opportunities for therapeutic abortion."[436]

At Sloane Hospital for Women, New York–Presbyterian Hospital's obstetrics and gynecology unit, a similar pattern was evident. Reagan notes that between 1951 and 1960, "half of the private patients who had therapeutic abortions had them for psychiatric reasons, compared to less than 20 percent of the ward patients." Dr. Robert E. Hall, of Columbia University, found that at Sloane, "private-paying patients received four times as many therapeutic abortions as did nonpaying ward patients." Most revealing, while "ward" patients were racially mixed, including African Americans, Asians, and whites, "private" patients were nearly exclusively all white. Very few therapeutic abortions were performed on low-income ward patients. Dr. Hall found that a ward patient who received a therapeutic abortion was sterilized "twice as often" as a private patient. Reagan decried "these coercive sterilization proposals, based in racist stereotypes and designed to be punitive, were aimed at low-income black women." She also notes, "some physicians carded [carried] out the implied social policies by sterilizing black women without their consent."[437]

The most revealing disclosure about therapeutic abortions came from Dr. Alan F. Guttmacher, chief of obstetrics and gynecology at Mount Sinai Hospital. Writing in the August '59 Redbook, he reported that 90 percent of legal abortions performed at the hospital during the preceding six years were technically illegal and, in a follow up interview, he said a "majority" of such abortions performed in US hospitals, excluding Roman Catholic hospitals, were illegal. At Mount Sinai, between 1953 and '58, 147 therapeutic abortions were performed—39 percent for psychiatric reasons, 31 percent to prevent birth of an abnormal child, 10 percent due to past or present cancer in mother and 10 percent due to other physical problems. Dr. Glenn Craig of San Francisco, head of the American College of Obstetrics and Gynecology, confirmed his assessment, insisting that these illegal abortions were "morally and medically correct."[438]

The outcome of the campaign against both illegal and legal abortions was devastating. According to Reagan, "by the early 1960s, abortion-related deaths accounted for nearly half, or 42.1 percent, of the total maternal mortality in New York City." She adds, "When skilled practitioners performed this procedure, the mortality rate was lower than that for childbirth. Abortion deaths were almost completely preventable."[439]

The Pill

At the time that Sanger met Pincus in 1951, American medical research was engaged in what can best be described as the "pill race," the search for a safe and inexpensive form of oral contraception. Behind the high-minded pronouncements of Sanger and other birth-control advocates, a fierce battle was going on between leading scientists, backed by pharmaceutical companies and wealthy benefactors, over how to control pregnancy. It was a battle that Sanger and her associates ultimately won, but led to consequences she neither anticipated nor likely wanted.

Pincus—often called "Goody" because his middle name was Goodwin—was the child of Russian Jewish immigrants and grew up in Woodbine, New Jersey, and the Bronx; he graduated from the Bronx's Morris High School. He won a scholarship to Cornell University, studied biology, and went on to Harvard for graduate work. He received a master's and PhD for his research on mammalian sexual

243

physiology and taught at the university. Pincus's innovative work on achieving in-vitro fertilization of rabbits led to a national scandal in which he was derided as a new "Dr. Frankenstein." the *New York Times* sensationalized and falsified his research The, comparing him to the mad scientist in Aldus Huxley's *Brave New World.*[440] In 1936, Pincus published a breakthrough work, *The Eggs of Mammals*, which was widely praised among the scientific community. Nevertheless, Harvard denied him tenure; he was too hot.

Pincus was invited by a former Harvard associate, Hudson Hoagland, to join the biology department at Clark University in Worcester, Massachusetts.* It was a tenuous position that led the two to establish, in 1944, the Worcester Foundation for Experimental Biology, an applied research company. Min Chueh Chang, a Chinese-born and Cambridge-educated biologist Pincus had met lecturing in England, joined the team. One of their earliest clients was the pharmaceutical company G. D. Searle & Co. and they researched the use of synthetic progesterone to block ovulation in animals. Another scientist, Carl Djerassi, working in Mexico for a competing company, Syntex, synthesized progesterone in '51; Syntex did not pursue the development of a contraceptive.

Sanger had long sought a safe and convenient birth-control method and was impressed by Pincus's research into the use of hormones as a contraceptive. To support his further study, Sanger turned to a longtime supporter of birth control, Katharine Dexter McCormick. Coming from the Dexters, one of Chicago's most prominent families (the family dates from the Mayflower), she was no ordinary member of the late-nineteenth-century grand bourgeoisie. Her father was a prominent lawyer, active in the antislavery movement; her mother championed women's rights and social reform. Both encouraged their daughter to excel in her education and she was the second woman to graduate from MIT, majoring in biology.

Katharine Dexter married Stanley McCormick, an heir to the International Harvester fortune, in 1904. A few years after their

---

* In 1909, Clark University hosted Sigmund Freud, accompanied by Carl Jung, in a legendary lecture series, his only US presentation; Emma Goldman attended the lectures.

marriage, he suffered increasing bouts of schizophrenia and she devoted much of her life to his care. Part of this care involved supporting biological research into schizophrenia and she funded a program at Harvard to study the problem. In 1909, her husband was declared legally incompetent and died in 1947.

McCormick was an imposing and impressive woman. She stood six feet tall and sat on a sizeable fortune. She was an ardent suffragist, vice president and treasurer of the National American Woman Suffrage (before the passage of the Nineteenth Amendment), and vice president of the League of Women Voters (after the Amendment passed). McCormick was also a strong backer of birth control. She first met Sanger in 1917 at a speech she gave in Boston and, now, three decades later, they were about to change the world. On June 8, 1953, Sanger took McCormick to the Worcester lab to meet Pincus; she would ultimately provide $2 million for the development of the first safe oral contraceptive.

The final member of the team was Dr. John Rock, a well respected Harvard obstetrician and gynecologist. Pincus, a research biologist, could not conduct human trials and needed to work with a clinical physician. Rock was a practicing Catholic who had, in 1949, coauthored a popular book, *Voluntary Parenthood*, that addressed birth control. He also backed control and he operated what Eig calls, a "rhythm clinic." One of his personal adages was: "Religion was a very poor science." Rock had been testing progesterone to address the problem of infertility, of how to stimulate pregnancy. Including Rock was also seen as a way to blunt the Catholic Church's anticipated hostility, especially the charge that contraception was a Jewish conspiracy.[441]

Together, this remarkable team—consisting of an activist, a philanthropist, scientists, and a doctor—transformed American (and worldwide) birth practices, sexuality, and the moral order. In '54, the team began conducting human trials of the new contraceptive. The first trial involved between fifty and sixty women who attended Rock's fertility clinic; the trial proved a success with ovulation blocked in all the women. A second trial took place at Worcester State Hospital involving two-dozen or so female and male psychiatric patients; it's not clear how many patients participated "consensually." In '55, Pincus, accompanied by Sanger, made the first formal announcement of the progesterone trial at the Fifth Annual International Planned Parenthood League conference in Tokyo. Not surprisingly, the announcement received little attention in the United States. However, things changed when, a couple of months later, Rock gave a formal paper on the progesterone trial at a leading endocrinology conference in Canada.

Pincus and Rock sought FDA approval for a large-scale human test of Searle's version of the progesterone-based pill. Because of strict anti–birth control regulations in many US states, including Massachusetts, the team selected Puerto Rico, a US territory where local officials backed population control efforts. In April '56, they started the trial in San Juan and 830 women were recruited as subjects. After an initial round of success, the researchers faced their first setbacks involving the drug's numerous side effects, including nausea, dizziness, headaches, pain, and vomiting. They determined, unfortunately, that the progesterone Searle provided (named Enovid) was contaminated with synthetic estrogen. After further testing, the researchers reformulated the mixture into what became the Pill. Additional large-scale human trials took place in Haiti and Mexico City. In '57, they received FDA approval for the Pill, but as a medication to address severe menstrual problems, not as a contraceptive. Finally, three years later, the Pill was approved as an oral contraceptive.[442]

Race Purification

Today, the notion of race purification is associated with Nazi Germany, especially their "centers of applied eugenics" like the Auschwitz concentration camp. Often forgotten, the "scientific" theory of eugenics was originally put forward in 1893 by the British scientist Francis Galton, a cousin of Charles Darwin. It was envisioned as a theory of "race" improvement. Galton argued, "Eugenics is the study of agencies under social control that may improve or impair the racial qualities of future generations, whether physically or mentally."

In the *fin de siècle* period, race determined humanity, structuring a hierarchy of social order, and eugenics became the ideology of the Gilded Age and its aftermath. It was a period when the American elite championed Social Darwinism, a self-serving misreading of Charles Darwin's biological concept of the "survival of the fittest." The theory was transferred onto social relations to legitimized race and class hierarchy. Social Darwinists believed that biology was destiny and that the white race sat atop the thrown of human evolution, defining civilization. Not surprisingly, many of the elite also believed that those least "developed" were doomed by heredity to be not merely biologically inferior but were also socially unfit. Galton wanted eugenics to be a religion, the science of breeding, and with it, race improvement for the betterment of civilization.

The "science" of eugenics was founded on the shared belief among the social elite that human evolution culminated in the Anglo-Saxon "race." All other races lacked the spiritual, mental, and physical capabilities of the white man. This belief system, or worldview, was shared by many "leading" people of the day, including politicians, industrialists, ministers, college professors, scientists, journalists, and social activists. Most remarkable, both church and science concurred. Adherents to the Social Gospel saw eugenics as a scientific proof that would usher in the Kingdom of God on earth.

To appreciate the mindset of those advocating eugenics a century ago, it's useful to cite one of its leading theorists on race purification. In 1911, Dr. Charles Benedict Davenport authored the then influential book, *Heredity in Relation to Eugenics*. Shocked by the massive influx of Eastern and Southern Europeans to American cities, Davenport warned: "[T]he population of the United States will, on account of the great influx of blood from South-eastern Europe, rapidly become darker in pigmentation, smaller in stature, more mercurial, more attached to music and art, [and] more given to crimes of larceny, kidnapping, assault, murder, rape and sex-immorality." Most telling, he predicted, "the ratio of insanity in the population will rapidly increase." His analysis did not include African Americans, Jews,

Asians, Middle Easterners, Hispanics, and Native Americans, who likely only further polluted the race pool.

The eugenics movement was as much a symptom of Gilded Age ruling-class arrogance as a reflection of the real threats it perceived from a nation undergoing profound social change. Between 1890 and 1920, America was transformed. The population nearly doubled, jumping to 106 million from 62 million, thus reshaping the nation's demographic character. Some 23 million European immigrants, many of them Catholics and Jews, joined 2 million migrating Southern African Americans and whites to recast the cities of the North and Midwest. In New York, the black migration culminated in the legendary Harlem Renaissance. However, migration was driven, in part, by the South's punitive Jim Crow laws, the rise of the Ku Klux Klan, and a series of lynchings, race riots, and other violence that swept the nation in the years preceding and following the Great War. This was also the era of the 1925 "Scopes monkey trial" immortalized in Stanley Kramer's classic 1960 movie, *Inherit the Wind*.

Many within the American gentry, both nationally and locally, enthusiastically backed eugenics. It received strong and uncritical support from progressives like Sanger and McCormick as well as notables like Theodore Roosevelt and Woodrow Wilson. With backing from the Carnegie, Rockefeller, and Harriman fortunes, eugenics was legitimized as a science and used to justify the draconian Immigration Restriction Acts of 1921 and 1924. The first legal state-sanctioned sterilization in the United States took place in Indiana in 1907. In 1924, Virginia passed a sterilization law and, in 1927, Carrie Buck, a seventeen-year-old, became the state's first person to be sterilized. A state-appointed agency was given the authority to determine who was feeble-minded, imbecilic, and a suffering epileptic; it ordered Buck sterilized. In 1927, the Supreme Court decided that state-sanctioned sterilization was legal. Justice Oliver Wendell Holmes ruled against Buck, writing most memorably: "It is better for all the world, if instead of waiting to execute degenerate offspring for crime or to let them starve for their Imbecility, society can prevent those who are manifestly unfit from continuing their kind . . . Three generations of imbeciles are enough."[443] The new law of the land led to an increased use of sterilization throughout the country. Obviously, the definitions of "imbecile" and "feeble-minded" were essentially arbitrary, morally and politically motivated, thus legally meaningless.

In October 1950, Sanger, living in Tucson and reported ill at age seventy-one, decided not to attend the Planned Parenthood Foundation's thirteenth annual meeting at the city's Roosevelt Hotel. She asked her son, Dr. Grant Sanger, to deliver her message. As reported in the *Times*, she urged the "sterilization of feeble-minded and victims of transmissible, congenital diseases. "Sanger's message was intended to "save innocent children from the cruelty of being born to such parents."[444] Sanger represents what can best be described as the "new" eugenics movement. Her most recent biographer, Eig, argues, "Sanger and McCormick were both elitists, to be sure, and they grew more elitist as they got old and wealthier, but there's little reason to believe either one of them was racist." He goes on to define her position: "Sanger never joined the eugenicists who argued that rich, educate, white people should be encouraged to have *more* children. Nor did she single out race when she identified people who she felt ought to be having fewer children. . . . Race never seemed to be the driving factor in her deliberations."[445]

In 1952, there were 1,401 sterilizations in the United States. An estimated 60,000 people were sterilized as biologically inferior humans (i.e., "mental defectives") in the seven decades that eugenics was legal in the States. As the noted scientist, Stephen Jay Gould, observed: "Sterilization could be imposed upon those judged insane, idiotic, imbecilic, or moronic, and upon convicted rapists or criminals when recommended by a board of experts." Add to this list the feeble-minded, promiscuous women, and homosexuals. Sterilization was most often imposed on youths, the poor, women and African Americans.[446]

The "new" eugenics represented by Sanger reflected three interlinked factors. First, it was based on a genuine belief that women needed better control over their pregnancies. Second, it sought to address one of the great dilemmas of the postwar era, alleged over population: "the population bomb." Third, it became a core component of US Cold War foreign policy, backed by the government and leading foundations. These factors influenced the ultimate acceptance of the Pill that followed FDA approval in 1960.

During the '50s, there was an intense scientific—and political—debate over an alleged population crisis. Two demographers, Pierre Desrochers and Christine Hoffbauer, frame the debate in stark terms: Malthusians vs. Cornucopians. "Malthusians" are followers of Thomas Malthus, the British economist who argued that population growth would increase faster than agriculture's ability to feed people. "Cornucopian" refers to the mythical Greek "horn of plenty," or cornucopia, that the world's bounty meets human's need. Looking back from 1999, the journalist Nicholas Eberstadt found, "In no small part, the structure, outlook, and policies of today's 'population movement' trace their lineage to institutions, initiatives, and individuals sponsored by the community of American foundations." In 1954, the Hugh Moore Fund published a pamphlet, "The Population Bomb," that argued: "There will be 300 million more mouths to feed in the world four years from now—most of them hungry. Hunger brings turmoil—and turmoil, as we have learned, creates the atmosphere in which the communists seek to conquer the earth."[447] (In 1968, the Sierra Club published, *The Population Bomb*, authored by Paul and Anne Ehrlich.)

One of the leaders of the "new" eugenics movement was John D. Rockefeller, III, one of the nation's leading philanthropists. He joined with, Fairfield Osborn, author of *Our Plundered Planet* (1948), which warned of an imminent population crisis, and John Foster Dulles, soon-to-be President Eisenhower's secretary of state, to established the Population Council in '52. That year, he convened a retreat, the "Conference on Population Problems," held under the auspices of the National Academy of Sciences at Colonial Williamsburg, a national park.[448] (Williamsburg's restoration had been one of his father's, JDR, Jr., greatest accomplishments.) Much of the conference focused on India and, as a delegate reported, Cold War politics was ever-present:

At luncheon today I raised the question as to why it was that almost everybody who spoke this morning talked about India. . . . And I think unconsciously we are scared, and I think we have a right to be. [India] is where the ferment is taking place. That is where the pressure is the greatest. And that is where the situation is being taken care of by the Communist propagandists who are filtering into the villages . . . . If India's poverty could not be solved within the country's current political system, the Indian people would turn to Communism in search of a solution.[449]

The Ford Foundation made its first population grant in 1952. As rumor had it, the grant was awarded "to appease two trustees' wives who happened to be 'Planned Parenthood nuts.'" In 1955 and for three years after, the Population Council funded *Eugenics Quarterly*; as Barbara Gordon found, the fear of a population explosion was driven by "desire to cut the birth rate of the poor, particularly non-whites, in the United States."[450]

The ideology or political acceptance of population control underwent a significant shift between the late '50s and the mid-'60s. Nothing better epitomized the transition in moral values than that expressed by two presidents. In '59, President Eisenhower declared that he "could not imagine anything [i.e., population control] more emphatically a subject that is not a proper political or governmental activity." A few short years later, in 1965, President Lyndon Johnson proclaimed, "five dollars invested in population control is worth a hundred dollars invested in economic growth."[451]

Unanticipated Consequences

Betty Friedan's *The Feminine Mystique* opens with a memorable passage: "The problem lay buried, unspoken, for many years in the minds of American women. It was a strange stirring, a sense of dissatisfaction, a yearning that women suffered in the middle of the twentieth century in the United States. . . . 'Is this all?'" The question gave voice to the "modern" or second-wave women's movement.[452]

Norton published Friedan's book in '63, but it had taken her five long years to write. She graduated from the then all-female Smith

College, one of the "Seven Sisters," in 1942. She relocated to the city where she hung out in the Village, flirted with Communism, and made a living as a freelance writer. But marriage, three kids, and suburbia reordered her life. In the mid'-50s, she came back, publishing in *Harper's* and *McCall's*. She pitched a provocative article exploring the apparent alienation among many privileged, college-educated white women. The leading "women's magazines" of the day, *McCall's*, *Ladies' Home Journal*, and *Redbook*, rejected her radical thesis. However, when the book came out, *McCall's* and *Ladies' Home Journal* excerpted selections for publication.[453]

The '50s was an era of feminist gestation or what the sociologist Verta Taylor called "abeyance."[454] A generation earlier, women activists, both conservative and progressive, were committed to a wide range of social causes, whether temperance, the vote, birth control, or sexual experience. Many stood as the fierce last rampart protecting traditional family values; others embraced the "new woman," the flapper with a shorter skirt, no corset, lipstick, who smoked, had a job and money in her pocket. Their efforts culminated in the passage of the Eighteenth and Nineteenth Amendments. During the '40s, a generation of women had served their country in the military (as nurses) and in war-related jobs. Those days were over.

Postwar economic "reconversion" involved the transition from a war to a peace or consumer economy, from a pay-as-you-go marketplace to one of plenty based on credit-worthiness and debt. It also involved the conversion from a more gender-open society to a gender-closed one. An "open" society is one in which structural factors create new opportunities, *spaces,* for those traditionally shut out, whether due to gender, race, ethnicity, or immigration status. WWII created such a space; with men required for the war effort, new opportunities opened for women. When the war ended and men returned victorious (and with the GI Bill), gender space closed.

As opportunities contracted, a new vision of domestic life opened up. After a decade-and-a-half of suffering, of the Depression and war, Americans were promised prosperity and happiness. It was very appealing; seductive to many. The dominant media—including commercials or advertisements (in all forms), radio, TV and movies, and magazines and newspapers—endlessly invoked a vision of the new "new" woman. Women were defined by their new roles in society, as wife, mother, homemaker, and consumer. And it worked for white, middle-class women, at least for a while. As Gordon observed, "Women's biological capacity for motherhood made it improper for them to attempt any other career."[455] Until Friedan and other women began to ask: "Is this all?"

During the '50s, the nation's demographic makeup was transformed. Women got married earlier; in 1950, the average age for marriage was 20.3 years, down by one full year from 1930. And the fertility rate jumped. The number of first births in the 1930s was about 2.5 million per year, but by the '50s it was over 5 million annually. In the 1930s, American women had, on average, 2.2 children during her lifetime; the birth rate peaked in 1957 at 3.7 children, the highest in US history. Women who did not define their lives in terms of home and children were, in Taylor's words, "considered deviant."

The Bureau of Labor Statistics found that, in 1950, the total female labor force participation rate was at 33.9 percent, and only about 24 percent of married women had paying jobs; by '59, the number of married women in the labor force had increased to about 31 percent. During this period, those women in the labor force held lower-paying jobs as waitresses, secretaries, factory workers, nurses, and teachers. Taylor notes that, in 1957, "80 percent of the respondents to a national poll believed that people who chose not to marry were sick, immoral, and neurotic."[456]

But all was not well with the American Dream. Rumblings of women's discontent were being voiced, most importantly with the 1952 US publication of Simone De Beauvoir's *The Second Sex*; it came out in '48 in France. "We are not born woman, we become it," she acknowledged.[457] As Vanessa Martins Lamb found, "During the 1950s, psychiatrists, analysts and doctors noted that the housewife's syndrome seemed to be increasingly pathological; malaise, fatigue, nervousness, sleeping troubles were becoming heart attacks, suicides, bleeding ulcers, hypertension and other serious diseases." She adds, "Emotional distress was becoming a psychotic breakdown." An occasional article about women's discontent, including references to reported increases in obesity and alcoholism, appeared in the popular media. Such stories ranged from *McCall's* "The Mother Who Ran Away" (1956) and "Boredom Bad for You?" (1957) to *Redbook's* "Why Young Mothers Are Always Tired" (1959). In addition, there were reports of increased rates of adultery and divorce.[458]

Taylor's notion of "abeyance" is an illuminating insight. "Abeyance is essentially a holding pattern of a group which continues to mount some type of challenge even in a nonreceptive political environment," she argued.[459] No social movement, like second-wave feminism, comes from nowhere. Each movement has its own roots that often date back generations. She points out that the '50s was a bleak political period for women: "Although women's organizations succeeded in having 236 bills pertaining to women's rights introduced into Congress in the 1950s, only 14 passed." She noted that feminism was nurtured, kept alive if in a dormant state during the era, by three tendencies: (i) those more legalistic, often associated with the Women's Bureau of the Department of Labor; (ii) those more political, often associated the women's divisions of the Democratic and Republican parties; and (iii) those more activist, represented by National Woman's Party (NWP), which was founded in 1916 and, during the suffrage struggle, claimed a membership of 60,000.[*] In the decades following passage of the Nineteenth Amendment, the NWP pushed for an Equal Rights Amendment (ERA) and its membership dwindled.[†] By 1945, it had 4,000 "general" members but, by '52, its membership shrank to 1,400; most distressing, in '47 it claimed 627 "active" members and, in '52, its activist members declined by two-thirds to only two hundred.[460]

---

[*] Taylor does not include left-wing radicals like Friedan in the early development of the women's movement. According to historian Daniel Horowitz, "At least from 1940 until 1953 [Friedan] inhabited a world where Communists and their sympathizers held influential positions, where she witnessed redbaiting, and where she encountered the ideology of American Communists, especially in their Popular Front appeals." (see Daniel Horowitz, *Betty Friedan and the Making of the Feminine Mystique*, p. 135) and Joanne Boucher, "Betty Friedan and the Radical Past of Liberal Feminism," *New Politics*.

[†] The Equal Rights Amendment secured Congressional passage in 1972, but by '79 failed to be adopted by two-thirds of the states.

The Pill received FDA approval in 1960, and it's unlikely that Sanger or her colleagues who invented it anticipated the "sexual revolution" that would transform the nation later that decade and the next. Sanger seems to have gotten more prudish with age. Self-servingly forgetting her own abortion and extramarital affairs, she came to tell women that "sex belongs to love and love belongs to marriage." According to Gordon, Sanger "consistently opposed masturbation and insisted that will power could get rid of the habit."

Nevertheless, the Pill quickly became the country's leading form of contraception. "Many women found swallowing a small tablet once a day for twenty days each month to be more appealing than fumbling with a diaphragm and jelly or persuading their partners to wear a condom," Elizabeth Siegel Watkins notes. In 1962, and even though a doctor's prescription was required to get the Pill, over one million American women were taking it; that number more than doubled in '63, reaching 2.3 million women; and by '65, it nearly tripled again, topping 6.5 million women on the Pill.[461]

"Sanger and the pill did not quite ignite the sexual revolution, but they didn't have to," Eig observed. "The fire was already burning; the pill only accelerated it."[462] The Pill separates reproduction from sex, changing the nation's moral order. In 1962, Helen Gurley Brown published *Sex and the Single Girl* that loudly proclaimed a new era for female sexuality. "Theoretically a 'nice' single woman has no sex life. What nonsense!" he insisted. "She has a better life than most of her married friends. She need never be bored with one man per lifetime." In '65, Brown became editor of *Cosmopolitan* ("Cosmo"), turning a traditional women's magazine into the voice for a generation of "new"—and younger, unmarried—women. In July 1965, she published, "Oh What a Lovely Pill!" which argued, "The new pill that makes women more responsive." She later described the role of the Pill as follows: "To me, the most important thing about it was that if you weren't worried about getting pregnant, you could enjoy yourself more in bed."[463]

For women, and especially married women who could get a prescription, the Pill forever changed their birth-control practice and, for many, their sexual experience. However, there is little empirical data linking the Pill to the '60s sexual revolution. While younger, college-age women were at the forefront of the "revolution," few had access to "legal" contraceptives; one needed a doctor's prescription to get the Pill and doctors usually restricted such prescriptions to married women. Indeed, the revolution was very much driven by heterosexual male desire, symbolized by Hugh Hefner's *Playboy* magazine. It was an era marked by a sexual double standard, especially with regard to women engaged in premarital sex, let alone dealing with an unwanted pregnancy. However, a second—and more feminist—women's movement later emerged, further revolutionizing the revolution with a new sexuality. As Gordon noted, "The modern women's liberation movement has reaffirmed both celibacy and multiple sexual partners for women."[464] It's a sexuality based on consent and, in the twenty-first century, consent has become the first principle of the new normal.

SUBVERSION

RED SCARE

ETHEL ROSENBERG, 1915–1953
JULIUS ROSENBERG, 1918–1953

National Security

Edward Snowden joined a growing list of the new Most Wanted when he released the first trove of National Security Agency (NSA) documents in June 2013. He is one of a growing number of well-intentioned whistleblowers that put public wellbeing above private gain or the fiction of national security. They are not traitors; they do not sell government secrets to the highest bidder or to another state. Rather, they freely publicize the secrets of unjust federal and other government agencies so the American people will see the truth and, hopefully, put an end to the questionable practices. Other whistleblowers include Thomas Drake, NSA employee; Shamai Leibowitz, FBI translator and linguist; Chelsea (Bradley) Manning, Army private; Stephen Kim, State Department analyst; John Kiriakou, CIA officer; and Jeffrey Sterling, CIA officer. Each has been assailed as disloyal, a criminal, a traitor, someone who aids and abets the enemy. Each was marked as a Public Enemy.[465]

Among the loudest of those assailing Snowden was former president George Bush. "He's not a whistleblower, by the way, because a whistleblower actually wants the rule of law to be enforced," he insisted. "He copied documents and he made a run for it. He may be actually aiding our enemies." Looking deeper, he insisted, "I think he is very dangerous, because he has information in his head, he's making threats [and] he's on the loose." Bush added, "We don't know what other documents he copied, and we don't know who else he's talking to."[466]

September 11 changed everything. During the two decades following the collapse of the Soviet Union in 1991, what President Eisenhower identified as the military-industrial complex faced a crisis. The Cold War was over; the enemy had been defeated and the complex's very rationale for existence was put in doubt. Many Americans demanded a peace divided and sought to shrink the bloated military budget. In the post–Cold War era, with no foreign enemy to fight, the sole purpose of the military-intelligence corporate complex was to defend the nation. It failed on 9/11.

In the wake of 9/11, no expense was spared in the war against terrorism. This war, more so than WWII and Vietnam, was fought on two fronts—military muscle and intelligence knowhow. An endless stream of manpower and the latest weaponry (culminating with drones) poured into the vast black holes of Afghanistan and Iraq; that this weaponry was eventually demobilized to serve civil ends—and ended up in Ferguson, Missouri, and other cities to combat local popular unrest—should come as no surprise. Precise figures on total federal spending on intelligence, both foreign and domestic, is hard to determine. In 2010, Senator Dianne Feinstein (D-CA) acknowledged that the total intelligence budget had doubled since 2001. The *Washington Post* reported, based on a Snowden release, that the intelligence budget for 2013 was estimated to be $52.6 billion, including $14.7 billion for the CIA and $10.8 billion for the NSA.[467]

Snowden's revelations confirmed many Americans' worst suspicions about the US's ever-expanding, two-headed security state. One "head" consists of the formal law-enforcement, security juggernaut that includes the vast network of federal, state, and local entities that are duly, "legally," constituted to maintain law and order and protect national security. This apparatus maintains state power. The second "head" is a parallel policing force consisting of local and national corporate entities that use legal—if often questionable—practices to undermine popular democracy, most notably capturing and commercially exploiting a citizen's personal information. This apparatus helps maintain corporate power. Together, the public-state and private-corporate security system is gaining ever-greater control over the lives of ordinary Americans. Together, they constitute the postmodern, twenty-first-century security system.

The revelations by Snowden and other whistleblowers confirm many people's worst fears: once-lauded principles of American democracy and personal privacy are in jeopardy. People feel they are being constantly tracked, monitored, and surveilled. Aspects of daily life that Americans long took for granted, especially their communications, are being exhaustively subject to government and corporate scrutiny. Vast amount of ostensibly personal communications are being collected, whether calls or emails, online searches and purchases, or Facebook and Twitter posts. Cars are also tracked through networks of CCTV cameras on city streets as well as highway and bridge tollbooths. News that the US postal system digitally records all mail shipments only adds to the concern. An endless assortment of government agencies and private corporations are gathering, processing, retaining and monetizing an unprecedented amount of information about every American.

Show Trial

Julius and Ethel Rosenberg were the first civilians in American history to be executed for espionage, electrocuted at the Sing Sing Prison in Ossining, New York, on Friday, June 19, 1953. The couple was, according to the *New York Times,* "stoic and tight-lipped to the end." They "went to their deaths with a composure that astonished the witnesses," it reported.[468]

In the week preceding the executions, Justice Department officials visited the couple in prison and informed them "that confessions could win them a reprieve from death." In an unprecedented action, prison officials setup a special telephone line to the Justice Department in Washington, DC, in case one of the Rosenbergs agreed to confess and name names. The *Times* reported, "Both Julius and Ethel Rosenberg, however, maintained they were completely innocent and had nothing to confess."[469]

Julius Rosenberg was the first to face execution. He entered what was described as the "white-walled death chamber" wearing white trousers, a brown T-shirt, and leather slippers, his familiar mustache shaved off and glasses removed. The prison chaplain, Rabbi Irving Koslowe, accompanied him, chanting the twenty-third Psalm, "The Lord is my shepherd, I shall not want." A mask was hung over his face and he was placed in the oak electric chair. At 8:04 p.m., he received the first of three jolts of 2,000 volts of electricity; at 8:06 p.m., Dr. H. W. Kipp pronounced him dead.[470]

Shortly following the removal of Julius's body from the death chamber, Ethel Rosenberg was brought in. The *Times* notes that she "wore a dark green dress with polka dots and . . . [h]er hair was close-cropped on top to permit contact with an electrode." Days earlier, Ethel's mother, Tessie Greenglass, visited her at the death house and, allegedly, suggested she divorce her husband and name names. "You'll burn," Mrs. Greenglass warned. Two women accompanied Ethel to the death chamber, Mrs. Helen Evans, a prison matron, and Mrs. Lucy Many, a prison telephone operator and former matron. Most moving, Ethel grasped Evans's hand and "drew her close and kissed her lightly on the cheek." According to the *Times*, Evans "choked up at the final farewell and left the room quickly." Rosenberg shook Mrs. Many's hand, a final farewell, and she departed. Rabbi Koslowe intoned the fifteenth and thirty-first Psalms. He turned to Ethel and asked, "Julius is gone. Do you have any names?"; she insisted she had none. Sitting placidly in the electric chair, guards placed a leather mask over her face and, at 8:11 p.m., she received three successive jolts of electricity. However, the initial three 2,000-volt shocks did not kill her and she required two additional jolts before, at 8:16 p.m., Ethel Rosenberg was pronounced dead.[471]

Traditionally, the state carried out executions at 11:00 p.m. However, because the Rosenbergs' executions were scheduled for a Friday night, performing it so late meant it might take place during the Jewish Sabbath. The presiding judge, Irving Kaufman, consulted a rabbi as to the exact time when the Sabbath began and it was determined to be at 8:51 p.m.; the judge scheduled the executions accordingly. (Joseph Frances, New York State's executioner, was paid $150 per execution.)

The Rosenbergs' executions took place on their fourteenth wedding anniversary. Earlier that day, the couple was informed that both the Supreme Court and President Dwight Eisenhower had rejected the final appeals to spare their lives. Their meals for that day were simple: for breakfast, cereal (with milk and sugar) and coffee; for lunch, frankfurters with sauerkraut and boiled potatoes; and for dinner, meat with tomato sauce, mashed potato, bread with apple butter and iced tea. They were permitted to spend two ninety-minute sessions together, in the afternoon and early evening, but remained separated by a wire fence. At 7:30 p.m., they were returned to their respective cells and prepared for execution. The *Times* reported, "Because of the rapid developments in the case they did not get the special dinner normally granted to prisoners about to die."[472]

Rumors circulated that thousands of protesters would ring the prison, challenging the execution. Warden Wilfred Denno ordered extra guards—totaling 385—to, as the *Herald Tribune* warned, "barricade prison property against any possible encroachments by pro-Rosenberg demonstrators." A State helicopter circled overhead. No protest took place.[473]

President Eisenhower eloquently articulated the Cold War rationale for his refusal to halt the Rosenbergs' executions. "I am convinced that the only conclusion to be drawn from the history of this case is that the Rosenbergs have received the benefits of every safeguard which American justice can provide," he noted. Clarifying his argument, he added: "There is no question in my mind that their original trial and the long series of appeals constitute the fullest measure of justice and due process of law." For him, as for many Americans, there was an intimate link between morality and loyalty, a link that defined politics. "When democracy's enemies have been judged guilty of a crime as horrible as that of which the Rosenbergs were convicted: when the legal processes of democracy have been marshalled to their maximum strength to protect the lives of convicted spies: when in their most solemn judgment the tribunals of the United States has adjudged them guilty and the sentence just. I will not intervene in this matter."[474]

The Rosenbergs case has haunted the American conscious for a half century. Were they guilty of conspiring to deliver US atomic secrets to the Soviet Union? Was only Julius the conspirator and Ethel an innocent foil to force her husband to confess? And, even if convicted, were their executions a miscarriage of justice? Was the trial and execution of the Rosenbergs—like Haymarket (1886) and Sacco and Vanzetti (1921)—a show trial, a legal spectacle? Was it an American version of the Moscow Trials of 1936–1938, in which the accused's guilt or innocence was never in doubt, the outcome determined in advance?[*] Was it a modern-day version of 1630s trial of Galileo Galilei over his support of Copernicus's theory that the earth revolves around the sun, or the Salem witch trials of the 1690s? Was the goal of the Rosenbergs' trial really about securing a public confession, a recantation, the naming of names, or an abject lesson for all those suspected of being a subversive?

Federal agents arrested Julius Rosenberg on June 17, 1950, on suspicion of conspiracy to engage in espionage. It took place after his brother-in-law, David Greenglass, a former machinist at Los Alamos atomic bomb development site, named him as passing secret information—including a crude sketch of an implosion-type nuclear weapon design—to the Soviet Union through a courier, Harry Gold.[†] Two months later, on August 11, 1950, Ethel was arrested. The Rosenbergs' conspiracy trial—along with their codefendant, Morton Sobell—commenced on March 6, 1951, at the US Courthouse

---

[*] In December 1952, following a classic show trial that found them guilty of treason, eleven Jewish members of the Czechoslovakian Communist Party, were hung in Prague—all had been charged with conspiring in Zionist plots against the government.

[†] Miriam Moskowitz, who recently turned ninety-eight, was another victim of Gold's false testimony; see "98-year-old New Jersey woman loses in bid to erase McCarthy-era conviction," *Guardian*, December 14, 2014.

at Foley Square, now named after Justice Thurgood Marshall. The defendants were found guilty March 29, and on April 5 Judge Kaufman imposed the death sentence on the Rosenbergs and a thirty-year prison sentence on Sobell. Two years later, on June 19, 1953, the Rosenbergs were executed. Ethel spent a total of 801 days on death row at Sing Sing, while Julius spent 767 days; the Justice Department reported that costs associated with the trial and executions totaled $34,618.51, with overall costs at $150,000; $1.3 million in 2015 dollars.[475]

In 1995, the US government released what is known as the Venona documents, files from a fifty-year-long program run by the US Army Signal Security Agency to monitor Soviet telegram traffic. Sam Roberts, writing in the *New York Times* in 2008, reported that Venona "incriminated Julius. . . . Ethel's role in the entire affair remains less certain." The files revealed that an estimated 350 Americans had worked for the Soviet Union. Roberts pointed out that Sobell said, "the true reasons for Ethel's arrest are at least partly accurate, as the prosecutors had hoped that threatening her with a death sentence would eventually pressure Julius to confess." Most disturbing, during the Rosenbergs' trial, the federal government had the Verona information and neither provided it to the defense nor presented it in court. In all likelihood, the information would have spared both Rosenbergs' lives, with Julius serving a long prison term. Also in 2008, Greenglass, who served ten years of a fifteen-year sentence, recanted his trial testimony, claiming he perjured himself.[476]

Current scholarship suggests that Julius Rosenberg was likely a Soviet operative who worked with Greenglass to provide the Soviet Union with US technical information; both were low-level agents with no access to top atomic-bomb information.[*] More so, Edith was a prewar Communist and, while generally knowledgeable about and sympathetic to what her husband was doing, seems to have been only marginally involved in his clandestine activities. The plotline of this Cold War drama was pretty straightforward. In February 1950, a senior atomic bomb scientist, Klaus Fuchs, was arrested in London and charged with espionage. He named names, particularly the information courier, Gold. In May '50, the FBI arrested Gold who, in turn, named Greenglass, who was picked up in June. A month later, Julius was arrested and, in August, his wife was seized. Neither Rosenberg named names.

Victor Navasky notes in his study, *Naming Names*, "the Rosenberg case split the Jewish community." The American Jewish Committee (AJC) was a leading organization defending Jewish people, but strongly anticommunist. Arnold Foster, AJC general counsel, warned, "There was an evident quotient of anti-Semitism in the McCarthy wave of hysteria." He added, "Our evaluation of the general mood was that the people felt if you scratch a Jew, you can find a Communist." In order to fight this development, the group's leadership distributed an internal memorandum in 1950, "Public Relations Effects of Activities of Jewish Atom Spies," and, in '53, funded a study by S. Andhil Fineberg, an AJC staffer, called *The Rosenberg Case: Fact and Fiction*.[477] Making this a particular New York story, all the principals were Jewish, including the judge, Kaufman, and the prosecutors, Irving Saypol and Roy Cohn, as well as the defendants. However, not a single Jewish person was allowed to serve on the jury

A few days before the scheduled execution, a threatening call was made to Judge Kaufman's home at 1185 Park Avenue (between 93rd and 94th Streets). While the judge and his family were out of town, the caller warned that the apartment building would be blown up. The police took the threat in stride and did not conduct a search of the building. Nevertheless, the threat was widely reported and the judge received a security detail for the remainder of the trial. In delivering his sentence, Kaufman heaped scorn on the defendants:

> I consider your crime worse than murder. . . . I believe your conduct in putting into the hands of the Russians the A-bomb years before our best scientists predicted Russia would perfect the bomb has already caused, in my opinion, the communist aggression in Korea, with the resultant casualties exceeding 50,000 and who knows but that millions more of innocent people may pay the price of your treason.

He concluded, "Indeed, by your betrayal you undoubtedly have altered the course of history to the disadvantage of our country."[478]

The Rosenbergs and Sobell were put on trial for conspiracy to commit espionage. Kaufman condemned them to death and a long prison term, respectively, for engaging in treason—i.e., aiding and abetting an enemy. During the long Cold War, the United States rounded up Communists but never formally declared "war" against the Soviet Union. Still more troubling, Kaufman blamed the couple for helping start the Korean War yet, the United States only formally entered the war in June, the same month Julius was arrested.

The Rosenbergs' trial is a classic all-too-noir morality tale. Every one accused of espionage named names—except the Rosenbergs. During the trial, they held fast to their Fifth Amendment right against self-incrimination; they refused to name anyone, even in the face of death. Reflecting on his conviction and sentence, Julius Rosenberg warned:

> This death sentence is not surprising. It had to be. There had to be a Rosenberg Case because there had to be an intensification of the hysteria in America to make the Korean War acceptable to the American people. There had to be hysteria and a fear sent through America in order to get increased war budgets. And there had to be a dagger thrust in the heart of the left to tell them that you are no longer gonna give five years for a Smith Act prosecution or one year for Contempt of Court, but we're gonna kill ya![479]

The Rosenbergs went to their death proclaiming their innocence and refusing to name names. They also, as reported by the *New York Herald Tribune*, "died paupers," leaving their children only some books and painful memories.[480]

The Rosenberg case, especially their five-time delayed executions, was an international *cause célèbre* and provoked popular protests in New York and throughout the country. Fearing violent demonstrations in Europe, the State Department reinforced guards at US embassies in Paris, Brussels, and Vienna. In Rome, representatives from the Italian Communist Party and the labor movement presented a petition to Ambassador Claire Booth Luce urging clemency for the Rosenbergs. In London, leading intellectuals and artists, including Sean O'Casey and Dylan Thomas, signed a similar petition urging the president to spare the couple's lives.[481]

The case occurred during a period when the Red Scare gripped New York and the nation. The city was witness to a half-dozen major anticommunist showdowns during the tumultuous late '40 and early '50s that set the stage for the Rosenbergs trial. In '48, the HUAC held hearings in the city that witnessed a clash between Representative Richard Nixon (R-CA) and Alger Hiss, the president of the Carnegie Endowment and a former senior State Department official, over his alleged Communist ties. In a sensational media event, the FBI arrested Judith Coplon (Socolov), a Justice Department employee, on March 4, 1949, for passing secret information to the Soviet Union; following two drawn out trials and conviction, all charges were finally dropped.[482] In '49, the Smith Act trials of eleven CP members began and dragged on until '58; all defendants were found guilty. Then there were the Peekskill riots, two violent '49 showdowns between supports of pro-CP groups and the entertainer, Paul Robeson, against anticommunists and racist local residents, some of whom were reported to be members of veterans groups and police forces. In '50, the State Department revoked Robeson's passport and, in '53, Senator Joe McCarthy held hearings about Communist writers, most notably Howard Fast.*

During the final months of the Rosenbergs' trial, three pivotal international events took place that likely influenced the trial's outcome. First, the Soviet Union detonated its first atomic bomb on September 23, 1949; second, on October 1, '49, the communists claimed victory over the Kuomintang-led government in the long-drawn-out Chinese civil war, a conflict that started in 1927; and third, the Korean War started in June 1950 and ended with a truce in March '53. US postwar global hegemony was being challenged, setting the stage for the next half century's Cold War.

The city was tense in the days leading up to and following the executions. Much of the effort to defend the couple was organized by the National Committee to Secure Justice in the Rosenberg Case,

---

* See "Freedom Fighter" and "Radical Voices."

cofounded by Emily and David Alman and William A. Reuben. A June 14 demonstration drew seven thousand people to Washington, DC, including the Rosenbergs' children and Julius's mother, Sophie Rosenberg. On June 18, some two thousand Rosenbergs supporters took trains from midtown's Pennsylvania Station to DC to demonstrate in front of the White House, urging the president to spare the couple's lives.[483]

At 6:30 p.m. on the night of the execution, five thousand people assembled at the north end of Union Square at 17th Street for a "prayer meeting." Demonstrators carried signs reading, "The Rosenbergs Are Innocent," and a truck with a load speaker broadcast angry comments from various speakers. "The crowd was whipped to fever pitch by speeches that alternatively denounced the President and members of the Government," reported the *Times*. Speakers "praised the Rosenbergs as 'freedom-loving people' who were to die for world peace and American democracy." The crowd accompanied a young woman singing the Negro spiritual "Go Down Moses." However, the police were on special alert, warned about the possibility of "demonstrations, disorder, vandalism and other attempts to disturb the peace or damage property." They ordered the loud speaker shut off and the crowd dispersed in an orderly manner, with no violence reported.

Following the execution, the city saw an enormous outpouring of grief. The Rosenbergs funerals were held at the I. J. Morris, Inc., funeral parlor at 9703 Church Ave., at Rockaway Parkway, in East Flatbush, Brooklyn. Between 9:00 p.m. on Saturday, June 20, and 1:00 p.m. on Sunday, an estimated 1,800 people filed passed the coffins. The funeral took place on Sunday at 2:00 p.m. with some 350 people gathered in the chapel, including both Julius's and Ethel's mothers, Sophie Rosenberg and Tessie Greenglass, respectively, and Julius's brother and two sisters as well as Helen Sobell, the codefendant's wife. In addition, a crowd estimated at 10,000 people milled on the street outside the funeral parlor and were reported to be "quiet and well behaved." The police had 184 officers on standby including mounted police. Maurice Erstling, a cantor, conducted the ceremony. The Rosenbergs' attorney, Emanuel Block, gave a eulogy that noted, "America today is living under a heel of a military dictatorship garbed in civilian attire." Rabbi Abraham Cronbach, a professor emeritus at the Hebrew Union College in Cincinnati, Ohio, offered a sermon stating, "We must eschew hatred, we must disdain rancor, we must keep our hearts clean of vindictiveness." Some in the audience hissed the rabbi.[484]

Following the ceremony, a funeral cortege consisting of 7,000 autos drove to the Wellwood Cemetery in Pinelawn, Long Island, for a ceremony that began at 4:30 p.m. It was a hot June day, with the temperature at 93 degrees. A number of people gave brief speeches at the gravesite, including Emily Alman, cofounder of the support committee, and W. E. B. DuBois who read the twenty-third Psalm. The Rosenbergs were buried in "rough-hewn oak" coffins; first Julius was interned at 5:25 p.m., followed by Ethel. In an irony that did not escape the *Herald Tribune*, the cemetery was located a few miles from the Brookhaven National Laboratory, an atomic research site.[485]

Red Scare

On Saturday, August 7, 1948, HUAC convened a special hearing, "Regarding Communist Espionage in the U.S. Government," at 10:30 am in room 101 at the Federal Courthouse in Foley Square and Representative Nixon presided. The hearing followed one two days earlier at which Alger Hiss categorically denied the he had ever known an individual by the name—or by a photographic image—of Whittaker Chambers. The principal witness on the seventh was Chambers, a senior *Time* editor, a former CP member from 1925 to 1937 who became a leading anticommunist witness and writer. His exchange with Nixon set the stage for one of the most combative trials of the Cold War era.

Nixon raised a key issue that would haunt the case as it made its way through the US courts and the court of public opinion:

NIXON: During the time that you knew Mr. Hiss, did he know you as Whittaker Chambers?
CHAMBERS: No. He did not.

NIXON:	By what name did he know you?
CHAMBERS:	He knew me by the party name of Carl.
NIXON:	Did he ever question the fact that he did not know your last name?
CHAMBERS:	Not to me.
NIXON:	Why not?
CHAMBERS:	Because in the underground Communist Party the principle of organization is that functionaries and heads of the group, in other words, shall not be known by their right names but by pseudonyms or party names.
NIXON.	Were you a party functionary?
CHAMBERS:	I was a functionary.[486]

Chambers seems to have never called himself "Carl" and his actual birth name was either Jay Vivian Whittaker Chambers or David Whittaker Chambers.

Nixon recognized the relative flimsiness of Chambers's assertions and had him reveal more personal information about Hiss to substantiate his claim that he could identify Hiss and that Hiss was a Communist. Nixon grilled the witness as to Hiss's mannerisms, habits, pets, and vacations. One aspect of Hiss's life drew special attention, apparently revealing Chambers's familiarity with him. He revealed that both Hiss and his wife, Priscilla, were amateur ornithologists, bird watchers. According to the witness, "They used to get up early in the morning and go to Glen Echo, out the canal, to observe birds. I recall once they saw, to their great excitement, a prothonotary warbler." Unbeknownst to either witness, Nixon arranged a secret confrontation between the two antagonists at the Commodore Hotel, near Grand Central Station. Following the "accidental" meeting, Hiss admitted that he recognized Chambers as "George Crosley," a man he sold an old car to in the mid-'30s.

On August 25, a showdown between Chambers and Hiss took place at a televised HUAC hearing at the Cannon Caucus Room in Washington, DC, with Nixon as ringmaster. The two witnesses could not have been more mismatched. Hiss was the classic New Deal "brain truster," a Harvard Law School graduate who had clerked for

Justice Oliver Wendell Holmes, an associate to Dean Acheson and John Foster Dulles, an adviser to President Roosevelt at Yalta and who served as Secretary General at the 1945 San Francisco meeting at which the UN was founded. Chambers was a former CP member and admitted Soviet spy as well as *Time* editor, and an admitted homosexual. Under oath, Hiss denied he knew Chambers, that he was a Communist, or that he passed State Department documents to Chambers; the documents were revealed by Nixon as microfilms hidden in Chambers's pumpkin patch, thus dubbed the "Pumpkin Paper." Based on Chambers's testimony and "evidence," Hiss was indicted for perjury by a grand jury at the Foley Square federal courthouse. His first trial ran from May to July '49 and ended in a hung jury; a second trial ran from November '49 to January '50 and he was found guilty. He was sentenced to five years in prison; Hiss always maintained his innocence.[487]

The Hiss affair raised a troubling question: how deep had the Soviet threat penetrated the US government? Many conservatives, in particular Republicans, questioned whether Communist spies had infiltrated Roosevelt's New Deal committees and their possible role undermining the Fair Deal of an "unelected" Truman administration; Harry Truman assumed the presidency when FDR died on April 12, 1945. The pivotal '48 election pitted Truman against the insurgent Progressive candidate, former vice president Henry Wallace, and Republican candidate, New York governor, Thomas Dewey. It was a bitter election campaign in which the Republicans dismissed Wallace as a Communist and charged Truman with being soft on Communism at home and overseeing an ineffective foreign policy of Soviet containment. Dewey was expected to sweep the election. Truman's unexpected victory was made famous by the *Chicago Tribune*'s front-page headline, "Dewey Defeats Truman."*

WWII broke out in Europe on September 1, 1939, when Germany invaded Poland. Five days later, on September 6, FDR issued an oral

---

* The '48 election also saw three minor parties—and their respective presidential candidates—split the vote: State's Rights (J. Strom Thurmond), Progressive (Henry Wallace), and Socialist (Norman Thomas).

presidential directive "providing that the Federal Bureau of Investigation of the Department of Justice should take charge of investigative work in matters relating to espionage, sabotage, and violations
of the neutrality regulations." Under FBI director J. Edgar Hoover's
supervision, the agency engaged in a far-reaching surveillance campaign of those it identified as subversive or radical; the campaign
persisted into the late '60s under what was dubbed the counterintelligence program (COINTELPRO).[488]

The Cold War was formally launched on March 5, 1946, when
Winston Churchill made his famous "iron curtain" speech in Fulton, Missouri. Over the following decade, the issue of domestic and
international Communism came to play a critical role in US politics.
In '46, Republicans seized on Churchill's warning and railed against
the Democrats allegedly being "soft" on Communism to spearhead
a victorious Congressional campaign, enabling the party to capture
both houses of Congress. Senator Robert Taft (R-OH) accused Truman of promoting "a policy of appeasing the Russians abroad and
of fostering Communism at home." Anticommunism was a major
campaign issue for Nixon's '46 Congressional campaign and McCarthy's '47 Senate campaign.

Amid the growing anticommunism climate, Truman and the
Congressional Democrats sought to outdo the Republicans with calls
for patriotism. In November '46, the president appointed a Temporary Commission on Employee Loyalty that issued a report on
the threat posed by subversion. In March '47, Truman issued Executive Order 9835 that formally established the loyalty commission
and created the Attorney General's List of Subversive Organizations
(AGLOSO). The list included groups ranging from the Abraham
Lincoln Brigade to the National Negro Congress. Also in '47, Attorney General Tom Clark proposed a train that would travel across the
country displaying "documents of liberty." Truman visited the train
in Washington, DC, in November '47, urging Americans to reflect
on their WWII sacrifices and rededicate the nation to its founding
principles. The train operated until January '49, coinciding with Truman's inauguration. More significant, Congress passed and the president signed the National Security Act of 1947 that established the

U.S. Air Force, the Department of Defense, the National Security Council, and the Central Intelligence Agency.[489]

Having lost control of both houses of Congress to Republicans, the Democrats pushed anticommunist legislation to show how tough they could be. Senator Patrick McCarran (D-NV) promoted the Internal Security Act of 1950 that established the Subversive Activities Control Board (SACB) intended to force the CP to register as a Soviet Union–controlled organization. The SACB required all groups to register that were: (i) domestic "communist-action organizations" substantially under the control of "the world-wide communist movement"; and (ii) domestic "communist-front organizations" defined as substantially under the control of "communist-action organizations." During the period from April 1951 to July 1952, the SACB held hearings to determine whether the CP was a "communist-action" organization. The CP fought registration all the way to the Supreme Court that ruled, in 1961, that the Act was Constitutional and the party had to register.[490]

In 1952, McCarran upped the anticommunist fervor with the passage of the Immigration and Nationality Act (i.e., the McCarran-Walter Act) that revised laws relating to immigration, naturalization, and national-origin quotas in an effort to allegedly prevent Communist infiltration. It also gave the government the power to deport subversives. In September '52, McCarran's Senate Internal Security Subcommittee (SISS)—analogous to HUAC—held hearings in room 1305 at the federal court building in Foley Square in an effort to expose Communists in the city's public schools and colleges. Senators interrogated current and former Brooklyn College faculty, among others, who had been earlier called by the state's Rapp-Coudert Committee or otherwise identified as communists.* In '54,

---

* Between September 1940 and December 1942, the New York State legislature held hearings through the Joint Legislative Committee to Investigate the Educational System, a.k.a. Rapp-Coudert Committee, to investigate the city's public universities, especially City and Brooklyn colleges. Approximately five hundred faculty, staff, teachers and student were subpoenaed and interrogated about their political beliefs, required to name names of subversives. See "Rapp-Coudert Committee."

the liberal Senator Hubert Humphrey (D-MN), who had backed the 1950 Internal Security Act, introduced the Communist Control Act of 1954 that sought to suppress the party.[491]

In August 1956, the FBI established COINTELPRO designed "to expose, disrupt, misdirect, discredit or otherwise neutralize" groups and individuals it categorized as subversives, opposed to the national interest. By '59, more than four hundred New York FBI agents were assigned to fighting "Communism." By the early '60s, the agency expanded its intelligence mission to neutralize civil rights, anti-war, and other "radical" groups, arguing that they were "communist front organizations." Hoover was insistent: "Communists have been trained in deceit and secretly work toward the day when they hope to replace our American way of life with a Communist dictatorship. . . . They utilize cleverly camouflaged movements, such as peace groups and civil rights groups to achieve their sinister purposes. While they as individuals are difficult to identify, the Communist Party line is clear." In 1960, the FBI established a parallel program, the Communist Infiltration Program (COMINFIL), which sought to prevent radicals from infiltrating "legitimate mass organizations" like the Boy Scouts and the NAACP. Under COMINFIL, the FBI investigated the Socialist Workers party (1961), "White Hate Groups" (1964), "Black Nationalist Hate Groups" (1967), and the "New Left" (1968).[492] In the wake of the attacks of September 11, 2001, the latent power of the security state became manifest, unleashing historically unprecedented surveillance procedures on all Americans, whether alleged "terrorist," merely Muslim or simply having a telephone.

Red City

The Rosenbergs came of age during what can best be called New York's "red" period. The decade-and-a-half of the Depression and WWII witnessed the ostensible integration of radicals, including the CP, into mainstream political life. The CP-backed two American Labor Party members who won seats in the House: Vito Marcantonio, from East Harlem, who served seven terms from 1934 to 1950, and Leo Isacson, from the Bronx, who served as a replacement during 1948–'49.* Two CP members served on the city council. In '39, Peter Cacchione was elected from Brooklyn, holding the seat until his death in 1947. In 1943, Harlem elected Benjamin Jefferson "Ben" Davis to the council; he served until he was expelled in '49 for being indicted by the federal government for violation of the Smith Act and, in 1951, was convicted and sentenced to five years in prison.

Esther Ethel Greenglass was born on September 28, 1915, and Julius Rosenberg was born on May 12, 1918. Both were children when the stock market crashed in '29, setting in motion the Great Depression; both were in their twenties when WWII broke out, setting the stage for a new world order; and both were in their mid-thirties when executed in 1953, the Cold War in full force. Both Rosenbergs were children of immigrant Jewish parents, both were born and grew up in the Lower East Side, and both graduated from the local Seward Park High School. After graduation, and not uncommon for the period, Ethel went to work and Julius went to college.[493]

At Seward, Ethel began studying acting and performed in a number of school productions. Graduating in '31 as the Depression deepened, she took a job at the National New York Packing and Shipping Company on West 36th Street to help support her family. She continued her acting studies at the Clark Settlement House and also studied music, joining the Schola Cantorum that performed at Carnegie Hall and the Metropolitan Opera House. Working conditions at her job and the general social tumult of the Depression radicalized her and she joined the Young Communist League (YCL). In August '35, the Shipping Clerk's Union called a strike at her company and Ethel served on the four-person strike committee, the only woman. When the strike ended, Ethel and the other committee leaders were fired; the union appealed to the National Labor Relations Board (NLRB) and won its claim.

---

* In 1948, Paul Robeson narrated a ten-minute documentary promoting Marcantonio "that was shown during street meetings from the back of a truck." See Gerald Meyer, *Vito Marcantonio*, p. 99.

After Seward Park, Julius Rosenberg attended City College of New York and earned a degree in electrical engineering in 1939. In the '30s, he joined the YCL, and, in '36, met Ethel singing at a Seaman's Union benefit. The couple married in June 1939 and had two sons, Michael (born in 1943) and Robert (born in 1947). In the first years of their marriage, the couple lived in the Lower East Side at the Knickerbocker Village on Monroe Street; Emily and David Alman also lived in the complex. In 1940, he took a job with the Army Signal Corps where he worked on radar equipment. In 1942, the Rosenbergs became members of the CP, but a year later they both dropped out. According to the FBI, the Rosenbergs "discontinued their open affiliation with the Communist Party because he [Julius] had always wanted to do more than just be a Communist Party member."[494] In '45, the Signal Corps fired Julius due to his earlier CP membership. He then worked with the Emerson Radio and Phonographic Company until their arrest in 1950.

The Depression led to a significant increase in CP membership. In '29, it had an estimated 10,000 members; by '36, membership jumped to 40,000; and, by '43, it reached its peak of 83,000. Perhaps more significant, the proportion of female members tripled during this period, increasing from 15 percent in the early 1930s to over 45 percent in 1943. Once the war was over, the old war against Communism was renewed.

In the early '30s, "class war" was breaking out in the city with CP members often in the leadership. In early March 1930, a CP rally in Union Square drew 35,000 people. The *Times* reported, "communist leaders, defying warnings and orders of the police, exhorted their followers to march on City Hall and demand a hearing from Mayor [James] Walker." It vividly described the ensuring battle:

> Hundreds of policemen and detectives, swinging night sticks, blackjacks and bare fists, rushed into the crowd, hitting out at all with whom they came into contact, chasing many across the street and into adjacent thoroughfares and rushing hundreds off their feet. . . . From all parts of the scene of battle came the screams of women and cries of men, with bloody heads and faces.

During this period, Communists and other radicals did more than hold rallies; many engaged in a variety of militant actions. Some fought to stop evictions, often returning the evicted tenant's furniture back to their apartment and engaging in bitter street fights with city marshals and police officers. The *Times* describes an incident that took place in the Bronx in February 1932: "Women shrieked from the windows, the different sections of the crowd hissed and booed and shouted invectives. Fighting began simultaneously in the house and the street. The marshal's men were rushed on the stairs and got to work after the policemen had driven the tenants back into their apartments." One study claims that 77,000 evicted New York families got their homes back through such activism. Some responded to utility companies' turning off a tenant's gas and electric by turning the gas back on and stringing electric wires that bypassed the meter. The CP led the effort to organize the unemployed, actively recruiting at factory gates, breadlines, flophouses, and relief offices. Historians Frances Fox Piven and Richard Cloward note, "Communists themselves often took the lead in confrontations with police; comrades were exhorted to stand firm and defend other unemployed workers when the police attacked, as they often did."[495]

In 1940, as tension over the coming war increased, President Roosevelt signed the Alien and Registration Act (a.k.a. Smith Act), originally proposed by Representative Howard Smith (D-VA). It required all foreign-born aliens over fourteen years of age to register in terms of their occupational status and political beliefs. Within four months of the Act's adoption, nearly five million aliens registered. In addition, it required those advocating the overthrow of government to register as well. People required to register included those "knowingly or willfully advocate, abet, advise or teach the duty, necessity, desirability or propriety of overthrowing the Government of the United States or of any State by force or violence, or for anyone to organize any association which teaches, advises or encourages such an overthrow, or for anyone to become a member of or to affiliate with any such association." It was the first statute since the Alien and Sedition Acts of 1798 to make advocacy of ideas a federal crime.[496]

In the immediate postwar period, a strike wave erupted during 1945 to '46 involving workers across the industrial spectrum and across the country. The bloodiest battles of the Cold War were fought out on the shop floor and in the classroom, in the mines and waterfronts across the country. In response, between 1946 and 1950, the Congress of Industrial Organizations (CIO) implemented a purge of Communists and other radicals.

Between 1949 and '58, Smith trials took place in Baltimore, Boston, Cleveland, Denver, Detroit, Honolulu, Los Angeles, Minneapolis, New Haven Philadelphia, Pittsburgh, Seattle, San Juan (Puerto Rico), Saint Louis, and New York. While the principal targets were CP members, over two hundred people were indicted, including Trotskyite members of the Socialist Workers Party, anarchists, and Nazi sympathizers. In '48, eleven CP members were indicted in New York, including Eugene Dennis and Henry Winston (national leaders), Gus Hall (Ohio leader), John Gates (editor, the *Daily Worker*), and Ben Davis (city council member). The trial opened on November 1, 1948, at the Foley Square courthouse, with four hundred police officers standing guard. In 1951, a second round of indictments was served on twenty-one more party leaders, including the legendary radical Elizabeth Gurley Flynn. One can imagine that the Rosenbergs were well aware of these indictments and trials, and may have personally known some of the accused.[497]

The Rosenbergs, individually or as a couple, may well have participated in party-related activities. Many young New Yorkers, like Joseph Papp, who grew up in Brownsville, Brooklyn, joined the YCL, attracted by its militancy.[498] One can only wonder if the Rosenbergs and Papp crossed paths at the Jefferson School of Social Science, the party's leading educational and cultural institution. Popularly known as the "Jeff School" that operated from 1944 to '56 in a renovated nine-story former furniture warehouse at Sixth Avenue and 16th Street; it grew out of the earlier Workers School and School for Democracy. Its popularity peaked in the late '40s, reportedly attracting upward of 10,000 students a year; it operated branches in Brooklyn, the Bronx, and Harlem named the George Washington Carver School: A People's Institute. All permanent workers, including teaching faculty, were members of Local 555, State, County, and Municipal Workers of America.

The Jeff School drew on a diverse and highly respected group of teachers, many who had lost their positions as a result of the blacklist imposed following the state's Rapp-Coudert hearings. The school's faculty ranged from leading Marxist scholars like Herbert Aptheker, Irene Epstein (a.k.a. Eleanor Flexner), and Philip Foner to former US diplomat William E. Dodd and Frederick Vanderbilt Field, the scion of a wealthy family who underwrote the school's renovation; mystery writer Dashiell Hammett and legendary music professionals Mark Blitzstein and Lee Hayes; and dancers Edith Segal and Ana Sokolow as well as the cartoonist Ad Reinhardt. The school offered innovative courses like those in psychiatry, taught by two psychiatrists, Joseph Wortis and Joseph B. Fürst, MDs; in '51, it offered courses on "romantic love and its limitations under capitalism" and "Marxist sexual morality"; and a course for women only taught by Isabel Johnson, Alger Hiss's future wife, "Beauty and Fashion Clinic: Making the Most of Your Appearance." It also offered special children's programs.

Fees were relatively affordable, initially at $5 for a ten-session course but were later raised to $7 and $8; scholarship aid was available for "veterans, Negro men and women and those active in trade union and community work." In addition, the school hosted regular lectures and conferences. According to historian Marvin Gettleman, "FBI agents (many of whom were African Americans) planted in Party Schools sought evidence to buttress the Bureau's contentions (later to convince much of the rest of the government, and the public as well) that Communists were engaged in a Moscow-directed conspiracy."[499] The most consequential gathering was held in 1956 and was only for CP members. Leon Wofsy, a YCL leader, read aloud Nikita Khrushchev's revelations about Stalin's horrors.

In the wake of 9/11, the United States faced a wave of antiterrorist "hysteria" reminiscent of the post-WWII Cold War. It saw the mass roundup of supposed Muslims, arrests and trials of both alleged and actual terrorists, the persecution and prosecution of whistleblowers alike, and the execution of an American citizen, Anwar al-Awlaki. He was assassinated under special provisions of the Authorization to Use Military Force (AUMF), signed into law by President Bush on September 18, 2001, which permits the president and US military to bypass First and Fifth Amendment due-process rights to meet national security requirements. No matter how far the US has come since the '50s, so little seems to have changed.[500]

FREEDOM FIGHTER

PAUL ROBESON, 1898–1976

Racial Injustice

On July 17, 2014, Eric Garner, a Staten Island resident, was going out for dinner to a local sports bar, Buffalo Wild Wings, with a good friend, Ramsey Orta. At 202A-Bay Street, at the intersection of Bay Street and Victory Boulevard, he met his untimely death. Stopping to break up a fight between some local youths, New York Police Department (NYPD) officers grabbed him, accused him of selling "loosies" (i.e., individual untaxed cigarettes), and attempted to arrest him. Garner, a forty-three-year-old African American father of six, was a big man, standing 6'3" and weighing 350 pounds. A swam of six officers in undercover gear jumped him, even though he had not committed a crime. They forced him to the ground with one officer grabbing his neck. Garner repeatedly moaned, "I can't breathe, I can't breathe," and died at the scene.

What distinguished Garner's death from innumerable police killings of people of color—especially men—that take place every year in the US was the video recording of the incident made by his friend, Orta. The police's "blue wall of silence," common to all-too-many incidents involving the death of a civilian in police custody, was punctured by the video recording. It showed policeman Daniel

Pantaleo forcefully holding Garner by the neck, effectively killing him.

When the video of the killing was shown on TV and the Internet, a firestorm of public outrage broke out. The city's black community was incensed, as were civil-liberties advocates and other New Yorkers of all races. Mayor Bill de Blasio admitted to being "very troubled" by the video and mentioned that he had had "the conversation" (about being stopped by cops) with his black teenage son, Dante, infuriating the police unions. Pantaleo was initially ordered to turn in his badge and gun. The four emergency medical (EMS) workers who responded to the scene—and were ordered by NYPD officers not to intervene—were suspended without pay.

The NYPD's killing of Garner came at a propitious moment, one linking past and present. It recalled innumerable recent police killings of innocent people of color, including Carlos Alcis and Kimani Gray in 2013, Sean Bell in 2006 and Amadou Diallo in 1999. It also linked a local incident to similar killings taking place across the country, the most explosive being the August 2014 shooting of the unarmed eighteen-year-old Michael Brown in Ferguson, Missouri, but also Walter Scott in North Charleston, South Carolina, as well as incidents in Madison, Wisconsin, Los Angeles, California, Phoenix, Arizona, Pasco, Washington, and Baltimore, Maryland, among other cities.[*] Protests erupted in the wake of these killings and were further fueled when grand juries in both Staten Island and Ferguson decided not to indict the officers involved the killings of the unarmed black citizens. (The SI District Attorney, Daniel Donovan, Jr., a conservative Republican in a predominately conservative borough, won a Congressional seat vacated by the previous, convicted representative, Michael Grimm.) These street-level police killings of mostly unarmed and innocent men of color are a postmodern form of lynching. Such killings—and their official cover ups—will not likely end soon.[501]

---

[*] The website *Killed by Police* documents 2,718 "police lynchings" of civilians during the period of 2013 (768), 2014 (1,106) and 2015 (844, as of September 15, 2015); see http://killedbypolice.net.

For many New Yorkers, the police killing of Garner was yet another example of consequences of the NYPD's "stop, question and frisk" policy. In the 1990s, NYPD Commissioner Bill Bratton embraced the policy, making it part of police practice. Its ostensible purpose was to, according to the New York Bar Association (NYBA), "reduce violent crime, a means of keeping guns off the street and improving the quality of life in the neighborhoods most affected by crime." Remarkably, between 1990 and 2010, the city's rate of violent and property crime fell by more than 50 percent, to 456,202 from 1,144,874. Little of the decline can be attributed to stop-and-frisk.[502]

The program's ostensible purpose was to recover weapons but, over the last decade, only about 6 percent of police stops resulted in arrests and in only about 2 percent was a weapon seized. Most alarming, the NYBA found that "85 percent of those stopped are black and Latino, and are overwhelmingly male." The New York Civil Liberties Union found that since 2002 the police conducted four million stops. In 2002, 97,296 stops were conducted, of which 82 percent of those stopped were innocent; a decade later in 2012, the police made 532,911 stops and 89 percent of those stopped were innocent. In August 2013, US District Judge Schira Scheindlin ruled in a case brought by the Center for Constitutional Rights that stop-and-frisk was a form of racial profiling and violated New Yorkers' constitutional rights. In 2014, stops dropped by more than 90 percent to 46,235 and 82 percent of those stopped were found to be innocent.[503]

Six decades ago, on January 5, 1951, a solemn rally was planned for Harlem to protest a police killing of an unarmed black man, John Derrick. He was a twenty-four-year-old US Army serviceman wounded in Korea, and people were furious. A month earlier, Derrick and a couple of buddies had met at a Harlem tavern to celebrate his medical discharge and he was killed leaving the bar. Organized by the local NAACP chapter, leading black and white New Yorkers planned to attend to rally, including Senator Jacob Javits, Congressman Adam Clayton Powell, Jr., labor leader A. Phillip Randolph, baseball legend Jackie Robinson, and boxing middleweight Sugar Ray Robinson. The *Amsterdam News* insisted,

"[The] people of Harlem will be able to show the police, the district attorney and the grand jury that police brutality in the community will be tolerated no longer."

Warrior

On May 9, 1958, Paul Robeson, having just turned sixty years old, headlined a celebratory concert marking his return to Carnegie Hall and the sold-out audience welcomed him joyfully. After nearly a decade blacklisted from the stage, screen, records, radio, and TV and barred from foreign travel, Othello the Moor was finally back. The *New York Times* reported that he was "dressed in a dinner jacket, instead of the customary tails of the recitalist." Accompanied by pianist Alan Booth, he performed songs in English, German, Russian, Hebrew, Yiddish, and Chinese. He interspersed the songs with a number of theatrical monologues, including from Shakespeare's *Othello*, and personal commentary. The audience gave him three standing ovations and, as an encore, Robeson sang "Joe Hill," about an executed labor organizer, only to be drowned out by further applause. Some twenty policemen were stationed outside the hall to prevent disturbances. But, as the *Times* reported, "Their presence was unnecessary. The audience, which filled the hall, was orderly, and there were no demonstrations outside. And so the police went home about 9:15 p.m." Robeson's spirit was invigorated.[504]

According to Robeson's biographer, Martin Duberman, "His only disappointment was that the hall had mostly been filled with whites." Robeson scheduled a follow-up concert for May 23rd and, to ensure that more black people would attend, he had hundreds of tickets distributed through Louis Michaux's National Memorial Book Store, just off 125th Street at 2107 Seventh Avenue, and other uptown outlets.[505] Robeson made his Carnegie Hall debut in 1929 and now, nearly three decades later, his life had come full circle.

Over the preceding decade, Robeson's personal, professional, and political lives were under attack. He was once considered

America's foremost African American personality, yet anticommunist proponents singled him out for special treatment. They railed against his race and celebrity in the United States and abroad; for some, he was an "uppity nigger." They were threatened by his unceasing defense of civil rights, trade unions and the Communist Party (CP). And they felt he was committing treason for his support of the Soviet Union and anticolonialist struggles in Africa and other parts of the world. In the late '40s, his unflinching stances brought him widespread denunciations from both the white media establishment and the "Negro" leadership. He was blacklisted, with innumerable concert engagements cancelled. In 1941, the FBI placed Robeson under surveillance and, by the '50s, FBI agents followed him everywhere, even tapping his phone. He and his wife, Eslanda (Essie) Goode Robeson, were subpoenaed to testify, individually, before House and Senate anticommunist hearings, respectively. In 1950, the US State Department revoked his passport, and even prohibited him from crossing the border to Canada, because he refused to sign a loyalty oath. In a court filing in February '52, the Department revealed what it most feared with regard to Robeson:

> Furthermore, even if the complaint had alleged, which it does not, that the passport was canceled solely because of the applicant's recognized status as spokesman for large sections of Negro Americans, we submit that this would not amount to an abuse of discretion in view of the appellant's frank admission that he has for years been extremely active politically in behalf of the independence of the colonial people of Africa.[506]

Now, six years later, he was about to regain his full stature; nevertheless, the Cold War had taken its toll.

Robeson and his family were victims of the postwar anticommunist witch hunt. He intermittently separated from his wife, Essie, and reportedly suffered bouts of depression (and was even diagnosed as bipolar).[507] A month after the Carnegie concert and as the anticommunist hysteria subsided, the Supreme Court ruled in a related case that the State Department could not seize a citizen's passport.* Robeson finally got his passport back. But he had paid dearly.

The turning point in Robeson's fate took place in early 1949 while he was on a concert tour of Europe. The trip came shortly after Henry Wallace's disappointing presidential campaign of '48, for which Robeson had worked tirelessly; President Harry Truman won the tight race. In Europe, Robeson performed to packed houses in England, France, Norway, and other countries. While in France in April '49, he joined W. E. B DuBois, Pablo Picasso, Pablo Neruda, Julian Huxley, and two thousand other delegates from sixty countries at the Paris Peace Conference, sponsored by the Soviet Union's Communist Information Bureau (Cominform). The conference followed a similar Cominform-backed gathering at New York's Waldorf-Astoria Hotel held a month earlier that the CIA calls "one of the strangest gatherings in American history." Some eight hundred leading literary and artistic figures, including Lillian Hellman, Aaron Copland, Arthur Miller, a young Norman Mailer, and Russian composer Dmitri Shostakovich, joined in what the CIA reports as a "call for peace at any price with Stalin."[†508]

At the Paris gathering, an Associated Press (AP) dispatch misquoted Robeson's remarks, reporting the following:

> We [colonial people] denounce the policy of the United States government, which is similar to Hitler and Gobbels. . . . It is unthinkable that American Negros would go to war on behalf of those who have oppressed us for generations against a country [Soviet Union]

* W. E. B. Du Bois, Rockwell Kent, Charlotta Bass, Howard Fast, Albert Kahn and Lisa Sergio were among those who had their passports revoked; see Barbara Beeching, "Paul Robeson and the Black Press," p. 342.

† In 1950, the Congress for Cultural Freedom was launched with CIA backing; among the American delegates were Sidney Hook, James Burnham, James T. Farrell, Tennessee Williams, Arthur Schlesinger, Jr., and Robert Montgomery. The CIA also financed the National Student Association in the late '40s; See Louis Menand, "A Friend of the Devil," a review of Karen Paget's *Patriotic Betrayal*," pp. 85–90.

which in one generation has raised our people to the full dignity of mankind.*

When publicized in the United States, Robeson's misquoted comments led to a firestorm of criticism. National politicians and the establishment press branded him a traitor. Many leading African Americans, including Walter White (head of NAACP), Representative Powell, and Mary McLeod Bethune (president of the National Council of Negro Women) joined the chorus of denunciation.[509]

Robeson did not return to the United States until mid-June and, by then, it was too late to correct the misquote; the damage had been done. On June 19, he addressed a rally organized by the Council of African Affairs, a CP-backed group, at the Rockland Palace at 155th Street in Harlem. "I defy any errand boys, Uncle Toms of the Negro people to challenge my Americanism because by word and deed I challenge this vicious [US] system to the death," he railed. He added, "How Sojourner Truth, Harriet Tubman and Frederick Douglas must be turning in their graves at this spectacle of craven, fawning, despicable leadership." (Following the rally, Robeson went to the wedding of his son, Paul, Jr., to a fellow Cornell student, Marilyn Greenberg, a white, Jewish young woman from Queens.) In its report on the rally, the *Times'* headline the next morning was clear: "Loves Soviet Best, Robeson Declares"; the *Amsterdam News* carried a UK-originated story, "Why Doesn't Paul Robeson Give More to His Own Negroes Instead of Russian Reds."[510]

Over the next couple of months, the rage against Robeson intensified. In July, HUAC called a special hearing on Robeson's misquoted comments, inviting a number of African Americans to testify, most notably Jackie Robinson. Robinson was the hearing's star attraction, but he was far less forceful in his denunciation of Robeson, calling his comments "silly." "He has a right to his to his personal views, and

---

* Duberman reports that Robeson argued, "the wealth of America had been built 'on the backs of white workers from Europe . . . and on the backs of millions of blacks'" and that he concluded, "'Our will to fight for peace is strong. . . . We shall not make war on anyone. . . . We shall not make war on the Soviet Union'"; see Duberman, p. 342.

if he wants to sound silly when he expresses them in public, that is his business and not mine." He went on to praise US liberties, especially religious freedom, and argued that Negros could win the battle against racial discrimination "without the Communists and we don't want their help."*[511]

As the year wore on, things only got worse for Robeson. In late August, a planned concert featuring Robeson in Peekskill, New York, was forcefully prevented by local anticommunists; a follow-up concert on September 4th was violently attacked as local and state police stood by and gloated.† He was blacklisted and eighty-five scheduled concerts were cancelled. Local authorities, often the fire department, in Detroit, Cincinnati, and Akron prevented him from performing; in Los Angeles, newspaper ads assailed Robeson as a traitor. However, an estimated ten thousand supporters turned out for him when he performed at Chicago's Wrigley Field. Later in September, he attempted to testify at the federal trial at the Foley Square courthouse in defense of the eleven CP members for violating the Smith Act; they refused to sign the loyalty oath. The presiding judge, Harold Medina, who had been one of Robeson's Columbia law professors, severely restricted his testimony.

In 1950, the Cold War caught up with Robeson. That year, Senator Joe McCarthy announced his list of 205 Communists in the State Department and the Korean War started. NBC cancelled his appearance on Eleanor Roosevelt's popular radio talk show to debate Powell.[512] Julius and Ethel Rosenberg were arrested and Robeson's passport revoked.‡ It would be eight long years before he regained his passport and his proud voice.

---

* Robeson had a testy relationship with Robinson. In December 1951, Robeson was with an interracial group at Harlem's Smalls Paradise, a legendary nightspot, when he saw Robinson seated with fellow black Dodger Don Newcombe and sent a waiter to invite them to his table. Robinson reported sneered, "Fuck Paul Robeson," and the two ballplayers left; see Dorothy Butler Gillman, *Paul Robeson*, p. 158; Duberman, p. 396.

† For more on the Peekskill riots, see "Radical Voices."

‡ For more on Rosenbergs, see "Red Scare."

Police Lynchings

On December 7, 1950, three African American buddies were making their way home from a Harlem tavern celebrating the medical discharge from the US Army of John Derrick, a twenty-four-year-old serviceman wounded in Korea. Derrick's two friends were Zach Milline, a thirty-five-year-old grocery store owner, and Oscar Farley, a thirty-two-year-old military private. Two city patrolmen, Louis Palumbo and Basil Minakotis, stopped the group, ordering them to raise their hands. Shots were fired. The policemen insisted Derrick pulled a gun; none was found. Milline and Farley insisted that the two cops, without warning, started shooting, killing Derrick. The district attorney's office found that the two patrolmen were "properly performing their duties" and the county grand jury found "no basis for an indictment."[513]

The Derrick shooting followed a February '46 incident that took place in Freeport, Long Island, and involved the four Ferguson brothers. They were returning home after celebrating Charles's reenlistment in the Army Air Force when, stopping at the local bus terminal's tearoom, they were refused service due to their race. Charles Ferguson accused the operator with holding a "Jim Crow attitude." According to witnesses, a rookie policeman, Joseph Romeika, lined the brother against a wall, kicked two of them in the groin and shot and killed twenty-seven-year-old Charles Ferguson, a father of three and the Airman. Also shot was twenty-five-year-old Alfonso Ferguson and Joseph Ferguson, twent-two, was wounded from a ricocheted bullet that had killed Charles. Adding to the miscarriage of justice, Richard Ferguson, the fourth brother, was arrested, charged with disorderly conduct, found guilty, and fined $100. Romeika insisted that Charles Ferguson had a weapon and the other brothers threatened him. No gun was found and no charges were brought against the officer.

The Derrick killing incensed many New Yorkers. The Harlem establishment, led by the *Amsterdam News* and the NAACP, called for a mass rally of protest on January 5, 1951. The New York CP pushed the analysis of the incident further. It argued that the shootings were a Northern version of Southern lynching; police brutality replacing the Klan. Writing about the Derrick killing in the CP's paper, *Daily Worker*, Abner Berry railed, a "Negro army veteran only 12 hours out of uniform was lynched by two white policemen in Harlem on Pearl Harbor Day." The historian Clarence Taylor argues, "Among the most active groups in the fight against police brutality was the American Communist Party."[514] The party had fought against lynching for decades, most significantly during the legendary Scottsboro Nine case of the 1930s; its efforts made the case an international *cause célèbre*, ultimately saving the young men from the death penalty.

In 1951, Robeson, on behalf of the Civil Rights Congress (CRC), a CP-affiliated organization, was among a group to present a petition, "We Charge Genocide," to the United Nations (UN). The report protested police brutality and charged the United States with violating Article II of the UN Genocide Convention by failing to prevent the lynching of African Americans. It detailed the killings of blacks (particularly men) in Atlanta, Birmingham, Chicago, Cleveland, Detroit, Los Angeles, Memphis, New Orleans, and Washington, DC, among other cities. It documented fifty-seven cases involving—among the "hundreds" of reports of police brutality—"police shootings and beatings of African Americans in New York City." Four years earlier, in October '47, the NAACP submitted a petition, "An Appeal to the World," to the UN accusing the US of systematic racial discrimination.[515] Little has changed over the last half century.

A Life Fully Lived

Robeson was the son of William Drew Robeson and Maria Louisa Bustill. His father was a North Carolina plantation slave and, not unlike Frederick Douglass, escaped as a teenager through the Underground Railroad, relocating to New Jersey and becoming a pastor. Robeson's mother was the great-great-granddaughter of Cyrus Bustill, a founder of the Free African Society, the first African American mutual aid organization established in 1787.[516]

Robeson was born in Princeton, New Jersey, in 1898 and, in 1915, he won a scholarship to Rutgers College, only the third black student to be accepted to the school. In his freshman year, he tried out for the football team that had no black players. At 6'2" and 190 pounds, he was a forceful presence and confronted staunch racism. At a scrimmage, white players piled on him, dislocating his shoulder, tearing away his fingernails and breaking his nose. After recovering, he went out to redress his mistreatment, targeting a ball carrier. "I was to smash him so hard to the ground that I'd break him right in two," he admitted. No further incidents occurred. He was twice named an All-American in football and also won letters in baseball, basketball, and track. He graduated in 1919 as the class valedictorian, was a debater and, in his junior year, was invited into the honors society, Phi Beta Kappa. Robeson then attended Columbia Law School, graduating in '23, but his tenure practicing law was short lived. He was the only black attorney at the prestigious firm of Stotesbury and Miner, but quit in the face of racial prejudice. He met and married Essie in 1921 and, although separating periodically due to his infidelities, they remained a part of each other's life for the next forty years.[517]

Spurred on by Essie and an innate showmanship, Robeson turned to the stage for a new career. In 1920 and while at Columbia, he performed at the 135th Street YMCA in Ridgely Torrence's *Simon the Cyrenian*; Torrence, together with Robert Edmond Jones and Kenneth Macgowan, founded the legendary Provincetown Players.[518] His fortunes changed in '24 when he costarred with Mary Blair, a white woman, in the Eugene O'Neill play *All God's Chillun Got Wings*. It was a scandalous performance, threatened with violence on opening night. The play was an uncompromising critique of the "miscegenation" taboo; it centers on a white woman who not only loves and marries a black man, but has sex with. In 1925, he began his singing career performing Negro spirituals.

In 1927, the couple moved to London and became the toast of the town. The following year, Robeson received sensational reviews performing "darkie" classics like "Ol' Man River" in the popular musical *Show Boat*. In March '30, he performed as Othello at the

Savoy Theatre, opposite the twenty-two-year-old white actor Peggy Ashcroft as Desdemona. In *Othello*, he once again crossed the great invisible taboo separating the races. "She loved me for the dangers I had passed," Shakespeare has Othello say, "and I loved her that she did pity them." The play was a success and ran for 295 performances. (Robeson and Ashcroft had an affair that deeply upset Essie.) Nevertheless, at the pinnacle of his success and at the Savoy Hotel grill, an upscale nightspot he'd been to before, he confronted good old American racism head on. As he wrote to the *Manchester Guardian*, he and Essie were invited to the club "at midnight for a drink and a chat. It was a nightspot he had visited many times." He then adds, the manager "informed me that I could not enter the grill room because I was a negro, and the management did not permit negroes to enter the rooms any longer." An American party of white big-spenders insisted that no blacks be permitted. Robeson never returned to the club.[519]

Robeson discovered radical politics, both as practice and theory, while in London. The onset of the Depression took an ever-deepening toll on British workers, most notably coal miners. He performed in fundraising events and studied Marxism and the Russian language. He was exposed to a different black population, this one more international, Caribbean and African. During this period, he also studied several African languages and became friends with Emma Goldman. A decade earlier, she and Alexander Berkman had been expelled from the United States and resettled to the Soviet Union and—as an anarchist who challenged the Leninist state-socialist model—she wrote a pointed critique, "There is no Communism in the U.S.S.R."; they fled the Soviet Union in 1921.[520]

Robeson was particularly troubled by the growing threat posed by the Nazis in Germany. He first visited Berlin in 1930 and wrote to Essie, "It's a marvelous city." Four year later he again visited the city as a stopover on his way to Moscow and had a very different experience. Accompanied by Essie and Marie Seton, the couple's white friend, to the train station, he was threatened by a crowd, including storm troopers. They started to surround them, incensed by a black man with a white woman. As he later admitted, he "read the hatred in their eyes" and felt he was facing a lynch mob. "I took a step forward," physically asserting himself; he recalled, "they could read something in my eyes." The crowd let the party board the train. "I never understood what fascism was before," he admitted. "I'll fight it wherever I find it from now on."[521]

His trip to Russia was a very different experience. Sergei Eisenstein, the legendary filmmaker, and others of the Moscow artistic elite embraced him warmly during his two-week stay. According to Robeson's biographer, Dorothy Butler Gillman, "He was even more impressed by the lack of racial prejudice he found in the Soviet Union." She adds, "Children embraced him, showered him with affectionate names, and Russians everywhere accepted him 'as a human being.' It was quite a contrast to Berlin." This experience would resonate in him for the rest of his life; he would never criticize the Soviet Union. Two of Essie's brothers, John and Frank Goode, were part of a small group of black Americans then living in the Soviet Union. John worked as a bus driver and Frank, a big man, performed as "Black Samson" in traveling wrestling and circus shows. Their lives were materially difficult under Soviet austerity and Essie helped out by giving them money.[522]

As the European crisis mounted, the Spanish Civil War became the site of a showdown between Soviet Union–backed Republicans and Nazi-supported Fascists. Back in London, Robeson took up the Republican cause, performing in a number of benefits. In early '38, he and Essie traveled in Spain, visiting Barcelona and other war-torn cities. US and British soldiers affiliated with the International Brigade warmly embraced him. Looking back on his short visit to Spain, he recalled it as "a major turning point in my life. . . . I have never met such courage in a people."[523]

In 1939, the Robesons returned to New York and lived in an apartment at 555 Edgecombe Ave., at West 160th Street, in Harlem's Sugar Hill. It was home to the black gentry, including Walter White, Roy Wilkins, and Thurgood Marshall.[524] It was a pivotal year, witness to Marian Anderson's legendary performance at the Lincoln Memorial. The Daughters of the American Revolution (DAR) barred her from performing at Constitutional Hall because she was black. In response, Eleanor Roosevelt secured the Memorial and publicly quit the DAR. More troubling, in August '39, Germany and the Soviet Union signed what is known as the Hitler-Stalin nonaggression pact that permitted both to carve up Poland. The alliance lasted until June '41 when Germany invaded the Soviet Union and its line again shifted. Robeson initially embracing the dubious CP line supporting the pact and became an antiwar militant, speaking out against US intervention in Europe. However, when Germany invaded Russia, his position changed, not unlike that of the party. It was a period in which Robeson deepened his relationship, both intellectually and personally, with DuBois, the father of modern Afro-American intellectual thought.

During the war, Robeson was an enthusiastic patriot. He encouraged Americans, particularly African Americans, to support the war effort; he urged them to participate in bond drives, blood drives, and patriotic concerts. He was also a fixture of the city's most sophisticated nightlife, a regular at Café Society, a truly hip jazz club. Opened by Barney Josephson in 1938, it was located in Sheridan Square, in the heart of Greenwich Village, and was noted for its great jazz—and accepting interracial mixing. It featured renowned talents like Lena Horne, Sarah Vaughn, Josh White, and Zero Mostel. Which doesn't mean racists incidents didn't take place, including one involving Robeson.

In October 1943, Robeson opened on Broadway starring in *Othello*. Like his earlier London performance, his costar was a white woman, Uta Hagan. (He had an affair with her, too.) One night, likely following a performance of the play, he and Hagan ended up at Café Society and confronted an ugly scene. Another partygoer, a white Southerner, "drunk as a skunk," was seated nearby and yelled out to Robeson that his name was also "Robeson" and said, "Your daddy was probably one of my daddy's slaves. You probably belong to me." Robeson jumped to his feet, ready for a fight; Josephson, a friend, intervened.[525] During the war, Robeson also remained true to his deepest belief, African American equality, and appeared at many concerts and mass meetings, some in the South, in defense of black civil rights. This was a risky action.

The world changed when WWII ended. A new Cold War between the two superpowers began, one that would define the next half century. And Robeson was caught in the anticommunist hysteria, his life turned upside down. In '52, he was invited to address the annual convention of the International Mine, Mill and Smelter Workers Union of British Columbia in Vancouver, but he couldn't cross the border. To circumvent the travel restrictions, he addressed the convention by telephone and gave a performance on May 18 at the Peace Arch Park located in Blaine, Washington, a few feet from the Canadian border. At the park, he stood atop a flatbed truck parked on the grounds and, using a loudspeaker, sang to a crowd of over 40,000 Americans and Canadians. The rally became an annual event for next four years until the travel ban to Canada was finally lifted. He also used long-distance telephone hookups to address the Soviet Writers Conference of '54; the Afro–Asian Conference held in Bandung, Indonesia, in '55; the Welsh Miners' annual celebration of '57; and a popular London rally, "Let Paul Robeson Sing," in '57.[526]

Race and the City

New York is a city of many cities, of distinct neighborhoods based as much on class as race, culture, or ethnicity. In 1950, the city's population stood at 7.9 million and 9 out of 10 (7.1 million) were white, but drawn from different nationalities, ethnic backgrounds, and religious affiliations. Blacks were the second-largest segment, representing less than 10 percent, or 747,000 people; most had relocated from the South during the "Great Migration," but there was a growing Caribbean community. "Others" stood at 27,909 people. According to the US Census, Puerto Ricans were included in "white and Negro Totals" categories, but were estimated at 246,303 people; there were only 21,400 Asians reported living in the city.[527]

Harlem became the Black Mecca during the Roaring '20s, fueled by the massive exodus of poor black (and some white) people from the rural South to cities of the East and Midwest during the *fin-de-siècle* decades. It was a migration spurred as much by the promise of economic opportunity in the North as by a desire to flee post-Reconstruction Jim Crow racism and Southern poverty. As Gilbert Osofsky bitterly points out in his classic study, *Harlem: The Making of a Ghetto*, "There were more Negroes lynched, burned, tortured and disenfranchised in the late eighties, nineties and the first decade of the twentieth century than any other time in our history." This migration remade Chicago, Detroit and, most importantly, Gotham.

Three unrelated developments helped concentrate blacks in Harlem, setting the stage for it becoming the Black Mecca. First, the Great Migration (and immigration from the Caribbean) radically increased the city's black population. Second, the old-world village of Harlem, long known as a city suburb, went through a speculative housing-development boom and bust. The white gentry who were expected to fill the new apartment buildings and townhouses never arrived, leaving a significant glut in the housing stock. Third, the city extended the subway system uptown into Harlem, thus providing affordable transportation farther north.

Between 1900 and 1930, the black population of New York exploded fivefold and, by 1930, African Americans accounted for 12 percent of the city's 6.9 million population.[*] In the short-lived recession that occurred in the wake of the WWI, Harlem was filled with many empty apartments. Enterprising black real estate agents welcomed both the older, established leaders of the "black bourgeoisie" and the young turks of the new cultural movement setting the stage for the flowering of the Harlem Renaissance. The old guard consisted of such legendary figures as DuBois, James Weldon Johnson, and Marcus Garvey; the "new bloods" included writers like Langston Hughes, Wallace Thurman, Zora Neale Hurston, and Claude McKay.

Many of these uptown "New Negroes" shared with their bohemian brothers and sisters downtown in the Village a new, radical aesthetic sensibility. They shared a critique of industrialization and

---

[*] The city's black population has steadily grown in terms of both numbers and relative proportion: 1900, 60,666 (1.8%); 1950, 747,608 (9.47%); and 2010, 2,088,510 (25.5%); see Demographic history of New York City.

of machine culture, with its mass production, uniformity, and standardization of life, as well as a desire to invent new forms of creative expression, especially in art, music, and literature. Not surprising, many embraced the ideas of Marx and Freud, Stravinsky and Picasso, Einstein and Joyce. Consciousness, in all's it magnitude, required a new sensibility, one that invoked the long suppressed proletariat, the unconscious, the primitive. For many of the '20s, the "Negro" embodied this new sensibility.

The United States seized the island of Puerto Rico in the wake of the Spanish-American War of 1898 and maintains it as a colony, a possession, to this day. The first Puerto Ricans settled in Gotham in the mid-nineteenth century and the 1910 Census placed the total number of Puerto Ricans at only 554. During WWI, the United States needed soldiers and adopted the Jones Act of 1917 granting Puerto Ricans US citizenship so they could serve in the military; nearly 18,000 did so. By 1920, the city's Puerto Rican population totaled nearly 7,500 and, by 1940, it topped 61,000. A decade later, near a quarter-million "Nuyoricans" would call the city home.[*] In 2010, there were 2.3 million Hispanic/Latinos in the city, accounted for nearly 30 percent of the population.

In 1948, the island's legislature passed the infamous Law 53, a gag law—*ley de la mordaza*. It outlawed expressions of nationalism, including promoting island independence through speech and writing; displaying the Puerto Rican flag; singing a patriotic song; or meeting with others to consider independence. Conviction could mean ten years in prison and/or a $10,000 fine. (It was repealed in '57.) In anticipation of the United States's further integration of Puerto Rico into the American orbit, Pedro Albizu Campos and other militant nationalist spent 1949 and '50 preparing for an armed independence uprising. A decade before the Cuban Revolution, on October 30, 1950, some two thousand rebels seized the town of Jayuya, along with Peñuelas, Mayagüez, Naranjito, Arecibo, and Ponce. As

---

[*] The terms "Nuyoricans" seems to have been coined by Guillermo Cotto-Thorner in *Tropico en Manhattan* (1952), a novel about Puerto Ricans in New York; it gained its current usage in the early 1970s; see "Nuyoricans."

one account determined: "By the end of the local revolts there were 28 dead—7 police officers, 1 national guardsman, and 16 Nationalists. There were also 49 wounded—23 police officers, 6 national guardsmen, 9 Nationalists and 11 non-participating bystanders."[528]

In the United States, a failed uprising in a far-off Caribbean island was not big news. However, two days after the rebellion on the island was put down, November 1, 1950, two militants from the Bronx, Oscar Collazo and Griselio Torresola, attempted to assassinate President Harry Truman in Washington, DC. According to the Truman Library, "They thought the assassination would call attention to Puerto Rico and advance the cause of Puerto Rican independence."[529]

Four years later, four independence fighters—Lolita Lebron, Irving Flores Rodriguez, Andres Figueroa Cordero, and Rafael Cancel Miranda—stood in the public gallery of US House of Representatives while Congress was in session and opened fire with automatic pistols. Five Congressmen were injured; all survived. In the din, Lebron—"wearing bright lipstick and high heels, dangly earrings, a stylish skirt and jacket, a kerchief around her neck" waving a Puerto Rican flag, according to the *Washington Post Magazine*—reportedly shouted, "Puerto Rico is not free!" The revolutionaries were captured and served long prison terms but never recanted their deeds.[530]

In 1955, the NYPD established the Bureau of Special Services (BOSS), popularly known as the "Red Squad." Like similar groups operating in Los Angeles, Detroit, and other cities, its goal, in the words of the state's chiefs of police was "to drive the pinks out of the country." Two undercover female police officers and numerous FBI agents infiltrated the CP and various municipal agencies (e.g., schools); it kept a file on Dorothy Day and the Catholic Worker from 1955 to 1968.[531]

In July 1959, HUAC held hearings held in New York and San Juan on "Communist activities among Puerto Ricans in New York City and Puerto Rico." More than a dozen witnesses were subpoenaed; most of the alleged Communist witnesses refused to testify. An NYPD BOSS officer, Detective Mildred Blauvelt, an NYPD officer testified. "I became a member of the New York City Police

Department in December of 1942, and upon entrance into the department was assigned by them to infiltrate the Communist Party as an undercover agent," she revealed. Her actual infiltration of the party is a bit unclear: "I succeeded in doing so by becoming a member of the Communist Party in April of 1948. I was expelled from the Communist Party in September 1943, but gained reentrance into the party once again in April of 1944, and stayed in the Communist Party until my expulsion in November of 1951."

A series of FBI memos from 1960 shed light on its COINTELPRO (i.e., Counter Intelligence Program) that operated from 1957 to '71. During this decade-and-a-half, it targeted the CP, Puerto Rican nationalists, "white hate groups," the New Left, and the Black Panthers. According to the FBI, "It is believed that upon instituting a counterintelligence program in this field, efforts should be directed with the following aims" that included: (i) "disruption and discord"; (ii) "creating doubts as to the wisdom of remaining in the independence movement"; and (iii) "causing defections from the independence movement." Singling out Puerto Rican nationalists, the agency notes, "Factionalism is a common fault within pro-independence groups and it is believed that this existing element can be developed, enlarged and exploited." Ward Churchill and Jim Vander Wall, authors of *The COINTELPRO Papers*, found that the "Bureau engaged in intensive investigation of *independentista* leaders both on the island and in New York in order to ascertain their (real or arguable) weaknesses in terms of "morals, criminal records, spouses, children, family life, educational qualifications and personal activities other than independence activities."[532]

Are You Now?

The most distressing question raised during the Cold War was: "Are you now or have you ever been a member of the Communist Party?" HUAC and other federal and state investigations as well as numerous conservative politicians and the media often asked the question. Failure to answer the question, particularly in the negative, even under the Fifth Amendment protection against self-incrimination, could get one denounced in the press, backlisted, or in jail. The scenario was most notably played out at HUAC's October 1947 hearings involving the Hollywood film industry where ten notable professionals were found guilty of contempt and received prison sentences. It was a question that plagued Robeson for decades: was he a Communist?

The Depression helped legitimize the CP in the United States; it often served as the more militant wing to the labor and civil-rights movements. During the period from 1935 to '39, known as the "Popular Front," it aligned with progressive organizations in opposition to rising fascism in Europe. Earl Browder, the CP leader, declared in '36, "Communism is 20th Century Americanism." However, following the '39 Hitler-Stalin pact, its political "line" shifted and it became strongly anti-interventionist, losing many members. That same year, President Roosevelt signed a directive for the FBI to undertake illegal actions against the party.[533] WWII forged an alliance between the United States and Soviet Union, and party membership peaked just after the war at between sixty and eighty thousand. In '51, over half its members are reported to be located in the New York area. However, as Cold War tensions mounted and the party was attacked, it took a more accommodating position with regard to the Democrats, fueling a bitter dispute with Representative Vito Marcantonio and the American Labor Party, undercutting his East Harlem Congressional seat. By '57, membership shrank to ten thousand. During this period, Howard Fast was one of the party's leading public spokespersons.[*534]

Robeson was one of a dwindling number of prominent African Americans to wholeheartedly embrace the CP's Hitler-Stalin antiwar policy.[535] By '41, he was under FBI surveillance. The WWII United States–Soviet Union "hot" war alliance led to a reordering of political priorities and the easing of anticommunism hysteria. Robeson moved closer to the party, party-affiliated groups, and party members. In '43, he became chairman of the Council of African Affairs

---

* For more on Fast, see "Radical Voices."

(CAA), which the FBI considered a Communist-front organization. At a CAA fundraising event at the Waldorf-Astoria, he spoke eloquently about his trip to the Soviet Union, insisting that he found "new life, not death, freedom, not slavery, true human dignity, not inferiority of status."[536] In '45, he was elected vice president of the CRC. He also developed close personal relations with leading black CP members, including Ben Davis (a city council member), Revels Cayton (a California trade union leader), and Max Yergan (a CAA leader who became a prominent anticommunist).

In September '47, HUAC issued a study, "Report on Civil Rights Congress as a Communist Front Organization," that singled out Robeson for special rebuke. "Paul Robeson will be remembered as one who has been outspoken in his defense of the Communist Party on numerous occasions," it argued. It went on to acknowledge, "He has defended Gerhart Eisler and Leon Josephson, active international Communist agents." Most troubling, it noted, "he [Robeson] refuses to affirm or deny membership in the Communist Party, [although] he has participated in official Communist gatherings on March 17, 1941, March 17, 1947, and on May 8, 1947." It concluded, "He has long been an ardent apologist for the Soviet Union, where his son was resided and was educated."[537]

Between 1953 and '55, HUAC held a series of hearings on "communist activities" that focused on the CP and "Negros" in New York. The first round took place on March 16, May 6, and June 15, 1953; a second round took place two years later, on July 28 and 29 and August 1, 1955. Dozens of alleged former CP members testified, many staunchly anticommunist. On January 13 and 18, 1954, it held separate hearings on what it identified as "Communist methods of infiltration (entertainment)"; Robeson is mentioned only in passing.

For Robeson, the question of his political affiliations came to a head when he was subpoenaed to testify for before HUAC on June 12, 1956. Chairman Francis Walter (D-PA), Representative Gordon Scherer (R-OH), Representative Bernard "Pat" Kearney (R-NY), and Richard Arens, chief counsel, interrogated him. Their interchange often got very bitter, reflecting Robeson's resolute principles. As to the primary question, his Communist affiliation, the opening exchange set the tone for the day's session.

ARNENS: Are you now a member of the Communist Party?

ROBESON: Oh please, please, please.

SCHERER: Please answer, will you, Mr. Robeson?

ROBESON: What is the Communist Party? What do you mean by that?

SCHERER: I ask that you direct the witness to answer the question.

ROBESON: What do you mean by the Communist Party? As far as I know it is a legal party like the Republican Party and the Democratic Party. Do you mean a party of people who have sacrificed for my people, and for all Americans and workers, that they can live in dignity? Do you mean that party?

ARNENS: Are you now a member of the Communist Party?

ROBESON: Would you like to come to the ballot box when I vote and take out the ballot and see?

ARNENS: Mr. Chairman, I respectfully suggest that the witness be ordered and directed to answer that question.

WALTER: You are directed to answer the question.

(*The witness consulted with his counsel.*)

. . .

ARNENS: I respectfully suggest the witness be ordered and directed to answer the question as to whether or not he honestly apprehends, that if he gave us a truthful answer to this last principal question, he would be supplying information which might be used against him in a criminal proceeding.

(*The witness consulted with his counsel.*)

WALTER: You are directed to answer that question, Mr. Robeson.

ROBESON: Gentlemen, in the first place, wherever I have been in the world, Scandinavia, England, and many places, the first to die in the struggle against Fascism were the Communists and I laid many wreaths upon graves of Communists. It is not criminal, and the Fifth Amendment has nothing to do with criminality. The Chief Justice of the Supreme Court, Warren, has been very clear on that in many speeches, that the Fifth Amendment does not have anything to do with the inference of criminality. I invoke the Fifth Amendment.

The hearing came to a climax with the following memorable exchange:

WALTER:	Just a minute, the hearing is now adjourned.
ROBESON:	I should think it would be.
WALTER:	I have endured all of this that I can.
ROBESON:	Can I read my statement?
WALTER:	No, you cannot read it. The meeting is adjourned.
ROBESON:	I think it should be, and you should adjourn this forever, that is what I would say.[538]

After six grueling hours, Robeson was excused. Most remarkable, and in distinction to what happened to the Hollywood Ten and Fast, he was not charged with contempt. Two years later his passport was returned and, in July '58, he left for a celebratory tour of Europe, appearing at sold-out engagements in England, France, East and West Germany, Czechoslovakia, and the Soviet Union. In England, he once again performed *Othello*, this time at Stratford-on-Avon. In 1959, he met with by Nikita Khrushchev at the Kremlin. In 1960, he toured Eastern Europe and, in November, was warmly received in Australia and New Zealand. He died in relative obscurity in 1976, living a modest life with his sister in Philadelphia.[539]

Robeson is being rehabilitated. In 2015, two plays were successfully staged celebrating his life and accomplishments. In New York, Daniel Beaty wrote and stars in *The Tallest Tree in the Forest*; in Los Angeles, Keith David performs in Phillip Hayes Dean's *Paul Robeson*. The British filmmaker, Steve McQueen, who directed the Academy Award–winning *12 Years A Slave*, is developing a biopic about Robeson.

The Cold War is over; the Soviet Union has collapsed and China has been integrated into the global capitalist market. In the United States, Communism is no longer a geopolitical or an ideological issue; inequality—the tyranny of the 1 percent—has replaced class war. Nevertheless, the unanswered question remains: Was Robeson a Communist?

To satisfactorily address this question, one must ask, what was a "communist" during the bitter Cold War era? For anticommunists like HUAC, McCarthy, and other politicians as well as establishment opinion makers, the term involved three different notions that were often collapsed into a single condemnation. First, a Communist could be an agent of the Soviet Union, a spy, most notably represented by Julius Rosenberg; second, a Communist could be a member of the party, like Fast; and third, a Communist could be anyone adhering to a radical analysis and practice with regard to US domestic and/or foreign policies, best represented by Robeson. Each was perceived as a threat.

Robeson appears to have never been a CP member. Although he was repeatedly denounced as a "communist," the FBI and HUAC never brought formal charges against him and he repeatedly refused to sign the loyalty oath. Rather, as the historian David Caute notes, he was a "fellow traveler," someone who was not a party member but adhered to its—and Moscow's—"line."[540] He never publicly addressed the Hitler-Stalin Pact, the '56 invasion of Hungary, or Khrushchev's revelations about Stalin's political terror. He represented a radical's great Cold War moral choice: US capitalism or Soviet Union Communism? During the '50s, there were few third options; pick your poison.

Robeson was mid-twentieth-century America's leading black personality, a renowned entertainer and a committed radical. He never joined the party, never came under its hierarchical—Stalinist—structure. The party needed him as much as he needed it. He was the nation's most progressive voice, one that for three decades spoke a very different truth than the white mainstream or the black leadership. Robeson adhered to most party positions and was personally close to several black members. He also needed an international force that supported anticolonialist struggles in Africa and other parts of the third world. That force was the Soviet Union.

Robeson spoke a very different truth. He was, first and foremost, an African American, the son of a father born a slave. He had reached the pinnacle of American success, including college sports, higher education, the theatre, concerts, movies, and public opinion. Robeson unceasingly championed civil and labor rights at home and fought colonialism abroad. He identified with the plight of the disposed, what in 2015 is conceived as the 99 percent. And he fought the good fight at home and abroad. He supported the Soviet Union as an ideological wedge, a counterweight, the world's only anticolonialist power, one that could contain, if not contest, US hegemony. It served both as a promise of what was possible, a social fiction, and a military force fostering a middle space for national liberation movements, especially in Africa. The complexities of Robeson's creative and political engagements were unique to American history.

RADICAL VOICES

HOWARD FAST, 1914–2003

National Security

In May 2015, Jeffrey Sterling, a former CIA officer, was sentenced to a forty-two-month federal prison term for violating the 1917 Espionage Act. He was convicted of leaking classified information to James Risen, a *New York Times* reporter, which was then revealed in Risen's 2006 book, *State of War*. The US government initially demanded Risen testify that Sterling was the source of his information. The *Times* initially refused to publish Risen's original story, buckling to US government pressure over "national security" claims; it only capitulated to publish the story when his book was to be released.

President Barack Obama is a Harvard Law School graduate, former editor of its prestigious *Review* and a self-proclaimed student of the *Constitution*. Whatever his overall political legacy will be, the Obama administration will be long remembered as the presidency that most used the Espionage Act to pursue government whistleblowers, those who leaked "classified information" to journalists. A study by *ProPublica* found that, since 1945, the US government has used the Act eleven times to prosecute government employees; under Obama, it's been used seven times. Among those charged in addition to Sterling are: Thomas Drake, NSA employee; Shamai

Leibowitz, FBI translator and linguist; Bradley Manning, Army private; Stephen Kim, State Department analyst; John Kiriakou, CIA officer; and Edward Snowden, NSA contractor.[541]

The First Amendment does not protect all speech. Unprotected speech involves a wide assortment of forms of expression the meaning of which has been fought over since the nation's founding. Among the speech not protected by the First Amendment are: (i) issues concerning national security, including treason, sedition and security; (ii) obscenity, including adult and child pornography; (iii) corporate secrets, including patents; and (iv) personal harm, including libel. The definition of these concepts has been repeatedly argued by the Supreme Court. Free speech is a terrain of struggle.

Four decades ago, the *New York Times* published Daniel Ellsberg's whistleblower exposé, the *Pentagon Papers*, a.k.a. *United States—Vietnam Relations, 1945–1967: A Study Prepared by the Department of Defense*. The federal government sought to block the publication on the grounds of national security. The Supreme Court ruled that the government had not met its burden of proof to require an injunction blocking the publication; it was a best seller and helped end the Vietnam War.

During the Cold War era of the mid-1940s thru the mid-'50s, innumerable Americans were arrested, tried, and went to prison for refusing to "name names." Many writers, filmmakers, actors, union officials, educators, and others were subpoenaed to testify before both federal and state government investigatory committees; the most notable was the HUAC. While the current federal effort to suppress whistleblowers like Sterling is highly focused, the Cold War campaign was more widespread, indicating a deeply shared anticommunist panic that gripped the nation. Howard Fast's experience confronting what one writer named "the great fear" illuminates the phenomenon.[542]

A God That Failed

A front-page story in the *New York Times* of February 1, 1957, was definitive: "Reds Renounced by Howard Fast—Writer Traces Party

Break to Khrushchev Speech." In a guarded interview, Fast admitted breaking with the Communist Party (CP) and Communism. But it was a qualified break. "I am neither anti-Soviet nor anti-Communist," he said, "but I cannot work and write in the Communist movement."[543]

Fast is remembered today for *Spartacus*, the 1960 movie directed by Stanley Kubrick based on his 1951 novel and with a screenplay by Dalton Trumbo. It had an all-star cast featuring Kirk Douglas as a rebellious Roman slave along with Laurence Olivier, Peter Ustinov, Charles Laughton, Jean Simmons, and Tony Curtis; it won four Academy Awards. Its release signaled the end of the Hollywood Red Scare, for which both Fast and Trumbo (one of the Hollywood Ten) had been blacklisted during the '50s witch hunts. The film was released after the memorable 1960 Kennedy-Nixon presidential election and, most telling, JFK, the president-elect, crossed an anticommunist picket line to see the film.

Fast was a prolific writer, author of forty novels along with countless articles (many for the CP's *Daily Worker*), plays, movies, and TV scripts, and two autobiographies, *The Naked God: The Writer and the Communist Party* (1957) and *Being Red* (1990). A New Yorker from birth, he was the son of an old-fashioned artisan laborer who worked first as a skilled ironsmith and then as a patternmaker in the garment trade. Fast grew up at 504 West 159th Street, just off Amsterdam Avenue, in a mixed neighborhood of Jews, Irish, and Italian immigrants; he lived just north of Harlem, the center of the city's African American community. He graduated from George Washington High School at age sixteen and didn't attend college but always wanted to be a writer. He published his first short story, "Wrath of the Purple," at age eighteen in *Amazing Stories* in October 1932.[544]

During World War II, Fast worked in the Office of War Information (OWI) as a scriptwriter for Voice of America (VoA) radio. In 1943, he joined the CP and published his first major work, *Citizen Tom Paine*. Success got him assignments for *Collier's, Coronet, Esquire, Jewish Life, Saturday Review*, and *Woman's Day*. This was the period in which the Soviet Union—and the CP-USA—shifted its official line with regard to the war. The 1939 Hitler-Stalin Pact, a nonaggression agreement allowing both to plunder Poland and avoid hostility with each other, was over. In 1941, after being attacked by Germany, the Soviet Union aligned with the England, France, and, ultimately, the United States in common cause against the Axis powers. Not since the Depression-era '30s had Communism been accepted as a (relatively) legitimate movement promoting social justice. According to one estimate, just after WWII, CP membership was pegged at between 60,000 and 80,000 and, in '51, over half were located in the New York City area; by '57, membership shrank to 10,000. During this period, Fast was one of the party's leading public spokespersons.[545]

The world changed following the war. Europe—along with much of the rest of the world—was carved up within contesting spheres of influence. Winston Churchill named the split between the United States and the Soviet Union a "Cold War" in a speech in Fulton, Missouri, in 1946, helping launch the twentieth century's second Red Scare, traumatizing the nation. Internationally, it was marked by the Soviet's dropping of an atomic bomb in August '49; Mao Zedong's forces capture of China in October '49; and the start of a bitter Korean hot war in June '50. A half century of saber rattling between the two superpowers had begun. Domestically, the decade was scarred by a disturbing state-of-siege mentality, with political and cultural dimensions. It witnessed government and corporate collusion—supported by mainstream trade unions—to restrict labor rights through loyalty oaths and background checks. A form of workplace tyranny was imposed on federal and state employees, school and college teachers, factory and office workers, publishers and writers, scientists and technicians, musicians and filmmakers, and dissidents of every persuasion.

Fast was one of those targeted during the Red Scare. He was a prominent public figure who did not deny his CP association. Many Communists broke with the party following the Hitler-Stalin pact. However, during WWII, with the Soviet allied with the United States militarily, the CP had become more respectable. It created front groups or aligned with legitimate organizations in an effort to increase its membership and influence. Fast joined the party's during its populist upswing, a presence felt most strongly in New York.

Fast was ordered to testify before the HUAC in 1946 regarding the activities of the Joint Anti-Fascist Refugee Committee (JAFRC), a CP front group for which he served as a board member. The fund sought to help orphans of American veterans of the Spanish Civil War, and Eleanor Roosevelt was allegedly one of its supporters. Fast refused to answer questions regarding fund backers and was held in contempt of Congress, receiving a three-month sentence at a federal penitentiary in 1950. For his literary work and support of the Soviet Union, Fast was awarded the '53 Stalin International Peace Prize, the Soviet's version on the Nobel Prize.[546]

The hearing and imprisonment took its toll on Fast, professionally and personally. He was blacklisted and couldn't get work writing for major magazines or get his books published. In response, he started a self-publishing company, Blue Heron Press, funded by presales and contributions, foreshadowing today's crowdfunding financing model. "I had no money with which to publish the book, but I had friends and I knew that over ten million people in America had read my books," he later wrote. "I wrote to these friends. I asked them to buy in advance, sight unseen, a novel called *Spartacus*, which I would publish if and when enough of them sent me five dollars for a subscription to it." He originally conceived the book while in prison and, as Phillip Deery reports, he sold 48,000 copies during the book's first three months after release.[547]

Fast took his party membership seriously, both formally (as a spokesperson) and ideologically (as a writer). However, the blacklist had bitter consequences in terms of his personal life, his health, and his intellectual rigor. Isolated and endlessly attacked, he apparently suffered bouts of depression and became more doctrinaire, more ideologically Stalinist. Writing for *Literature and Reality*, a Marxist journal, he rejected most contemporary American literature, including novelists, poets, and critics, as reactionary and degenerate while championing Soviet writers. Holding his nose, he said John Steinbeck "reeks" with "cheap, phony sentimentalism" and denounced George Orwell as a "crass" and "inept" propagandist, responsible for "childish and wicked little opium dreams" that reflected the interests of Wall Street.

His break with the CP came after years of soul searching and bitter intraparty disputes. His disillusionment began in the late '40s over issues involving aesthetics and what was then known as the "Jewish question." He claimed that the party wanted to expel him as early as 1948 because of his "Jewish nationalist point of view" which expressed in the novel, *Glorious Brothers*; only the intervention of party leaders saved him from expulsion. His aesthetic literary style was distinguished as "socialist realism," yet he had pitched battles with V. J. Jerome, editor of *Political Affairs* and chairman of the CP's cultural commission. Another battle took place over Fast's 1950 play, *The Hammer*. Party leaders insisted, in keeping with its anti–Jim Crow casting policy, that the son of a small, slender, Jewish father be played by the six foot two, deep-throated African American actor, James Earl Jones. Fast was outraged, but lost. According to one account, "The mostly Yiddish-speaking audience laughed."

In 1957, as the *Times* pointed out, Fast has "generally been considered the leading Communist writer in this country." Fast later admitted that in 1952, "I hated the Communist Party . . . remaining in it only because I was a goddam hero and there was nowhere else to go." However, in the wake of Nikita Khrushchev's revelations about Joseph Stalin's purges, gulag, and anti-Semitism, Fast could no longer associate with the party or write for the *Daily Worker*. Khrushchev's revelations were first made in Moscow in February 1956 at the twentieth party congress and they slowly began to leak out to European party officials before being publicly revealed in the United States by the *Daily Worker* in June '56. The party's political situation grew more untenable in the wake of the Hungarian uprising of October '56 and the Soviet military invasion of Hungary in November.[548] Now, a year after Khrushchev's original revelations, Fast finally broke with the party. As he later admitted, "the edifice that I had become a part of thirteen years earlier came crumbling down in ashes—ashes of grief, horror and helplessness." He swore, "Never again will I remain silent when I can recognize injustice. . . . Never again will I fail to question, to demand proof. Never again will I accept the 'clever' rationale." He concluded, "And with this said, I feel better—better than I have felt in a long time."

The party savagely attacked Fast following his public *mea culpa*, castigating him as an apostate. He claimed that party leaders treated him "like a pack of wolves" and subjected him to a "particular brand of character assassination." However, in the postwar era, Fast was not the only one to break with the party. An earlier, 1949 *mea culpa*, *The God That Failed* documented the respective breaks from the party by Louis Fischer (United States), André Gide (France), Arthur Koestler (Germany), Ignazio Silone (Italy), Stephen Spender (England), and Richard Wright (United States). Shortly after Fast's story appeared in the *Times*, he appeared on NBC's *Today* show with David Garroway, and the *Look Here* show with Martin Akronsky. In 1958, Fast began working with Kirk Douglas and Universal Studios on the film script of *Spartacus*. He was being rehabilitated.[549]

Blacklist

Arthur Miller's *The Crucible* opened at Broadway's Martin Beck Theatre on January 22, 1953—the same week Eisenhower was inaugurated president. The play recalls the witch trials that gripped Salem, Massachusetts, in the 1690s, and explores how religious hysteria breeds repression, including the hanging of women (and some men) deemed to be witches. Critics and the audience recognized Salem as a metaphor for the postwar Red Scare, the anticommunism hysteria fueled by HUAC and Senator McCarthy. Three years after the play's premier, HUAC subpoenaed Miller to testify. The date picked for his appearance, June 21, 1956, was eight days before his well-publicized and long-scheduled wedding with Marilyn Monroe on the twenty-ninth. According to Miller, HUAC Chairman Francis Walter (D-PA) offered to dismiss the playwright's testimony if he could pose with the actress.[550]

Miller was considered an unfriendly HUAC witness and refused to name names. He insisted, "I could not use the name of another person and bring trouble on him." In May '57, he was found guilty of contempt of Congress and sentenced to a $500 fine or a thirty-day prison term and the loss of his passport; his conviction was reversed in '58. But he was also blacklisted, barred from working in movies and television, but not on Broadway.

For a decade-and-a-half, from 1947 to 1961, the Red Scare terrorized the nation, especially the entertainment fields and, most notably, Hollywood. In May '47, HUAC members settled into Los Angeles' Biltmore Hotel for a showdown with the movie industry. The first to appear before the Committee were "friendly" witnesses, including actors Robert Taylor, Richard Arlen, and Adolphe Menjou who willingly gave names. Among others who named names were Lee J. Cobb, Clifford Odets, David Raskin, Robert Rossen, Elia Kazan, and Budd Schulberg. Studio head Jack Warner went so far as to identifying studio personnel he suspected of being subversives.

In September '47, HUAC served subpoenas to forty-three film-industry personnel. On November 25th, ten witnesses appeared at the hearings and refused to name any others. They became known as "The Hollywood Ten" and included: Alvah Bessie, screenwriter who served in the Abraham Lincoln Brigade during the Spanish civil war; Herbert Biberman, director of *Salt of the Earth* (1954); Lester Cole, screenwriter for *If I Had a Million* (1932); Edward Dmytryk, director of *The Caine Mutiny* (1954); Ring Lardner, Jr., director of *Woman of the Year* (1942); John Howard Lawson, screenwriter for *Counter Attack* (1945); Albert Maltz, director of the documentary *The House I Live In*, won an Academy Award (1945); Samuel Ornitz, organizer for Screen Actors Guild; Adrian Scott, producer of *Crossfire* (1947), who won four Academy Awards; and Trumbo, screenwriter, who won two Academy Awards while on the blacklist. They were convicted and went to federal prison. Hollywood's principal craft unions—the Screen Actors Guild (SAG), the Screen Writers Guild (SWG), and the Screen Directors Guild, (SDG)—put up little opposition to the blacklist.[551]

While the LA scare targeted the film industry, the New York scare spread across multiple spheres of the cultural industry, including Broadway theatre, local radio, newspaper reporting, live performances, and independent movies. The FBI took special interest in the Four Continent Bookstore at 822 Broadway that carried Soviet publications and Marxist literature. According to Victor Navasky, it "had a permanent motion-picture crew stationed across the street from the store," recording Four Continents Bookstore in New York. Perhaps most insidious, the scare led to a purge of innumerable college and grade-school educators due to their alleged "un-American" affiliations.[552]

Broadway did not impose a blacklist, resisting the Red Scare more humanely than the other entertainment arts. This intellectual openness enabled leading playwrights to fiercely debate Communism and the alleged Soviet threat. Maxwell Anderson, Sidney Kingsley, Henry Denker, and Ralph Berkey were staunchly anticommunist; while Miller, Lillian Hellman, James Thurber, and William Saroyan rejected the Soviet Union but warned that the anticommunist hysteria was a threat to democracy, specifically First and Fifth Amendment rights.[553] These conflicting sentiments were expressed in a dozen or so Broadway productions of the period. The theatre historian Albert Wertheim details how the debate played out in a dozen or so productions, including anticommunist plays like Arthur Koestler's *Darkness at Noon* (1951) and Maxwell Anderson's *Barefoot in Athens* (1951) as well as more critical works by James Thurber and Elliott Nugent, *The Male Animal* (1952), Lillian Hellman's restaged *The Children's Hour* (1952), Miller's *Crucible* (1953), Robert Anderson's *Tea & Sympathy* (1953), Robert Andrey's *Sing Me No Lullaby* (1954), Jerome Lawrence and Robert Lee's, *Inherent the Wind* (1955), and Henry Denker and Ralph Berkey's *Time Limit!* (1956). In the '50s, ideas still mattered on Broadway.

Nevertheless, Broadway talent was blacklisted by other groups. *Red Channels*, a scurrilous anticommunist publication, listed 151 actors, radio commentators, musicians, and theatre personalities with alleged Communist affiliations.[554] It became a hiring-hall roster. Fay and Michael Kanin, who long supported the left-wing Group Theater and other progressive causes, were among the first to be targeted; they later collaborated on the Doris Day comedy, *Teacher's Pet* (1957). Zero Mostel, famous for *The Producers*, refused to name names at a '55 HUAC hearing and was blacklisted. Herschel Bernardi, a legendary performer in the Yiddish theater and a regularly on Broadway (including performances as Zorba the Greek and

Tevyes in *Fiddler on the Roof*), was blacklisted. Uta Hagen, actress and cofounder with her husband, Herbert Berghof, of HB Studios, the acting school on Bank Street in the Village, was also blacklisted. Musicians like the legendary folksingers Pete Seeger and Ronnie Gilbert of the Weavers, along with harmonica virtuoso Larry Adler and the great lyricist E. Y. (Yip) Harburg (of *The Wizard of Oz*) were assailed, and Leonard Bernstein, Lena Horne, Josephine Baker, and Artie Shaw were all identified as subversives. "Professor" Irwin Corey, a popular stand-up comic, along with Barney Josephson, the proprietor of the Café Society, Greenwich Village's integrated night-club, were also blacklisted.[555]

The blacklist affected other New Yorkers in the public eye, most notably journalists and on-air radio and TV personalities. The *New York Times* fired four reporters who refused to comply with the Senate Internal Security Subcommittee (SISS) and register as possible subversives. Four other reporters, including three from the *Times*, were convicted of contempt of Congress and faced fines and prison terms.[556] In March 1946, the *Times* ran an advertisement critical of HUAC with the headline, "You can't talk . . . It's Un-American," and sponsored by the "Citizens to Abolish the Wood-Rankin Committee." The ad resulted in a personal visit to the paper by the committee's soon-to-be-chairman, J. Parnell Thomas (R-NJ). The paper's radio station, WQXR, had long featured commentators from a wide variety of political perspectives, including the Committee for the Defense of Leon Trotsky, the American Friends of Spanish Democracy, the Foreign Policy Association, the American Legion, and individuals such as socialist presidential candidate Norman Thomas and Zionist leader Rabbi Stephen Wise. Two weeks after Thomas's visit, the station's editorial policy changed and numerous on-air commentators were dropped.

HUAC began going after on-air radio talent following the formal end of WWII. In response, NBC and CBS imposed loyalty oaths, requiring employees to sign or lose their jobs; ABC, the smallest network, did not investigate alleged subversives. HUAC targeted seven radio commentators: Cecil Brown, William S. Gailmore, Hans Jacob, Johannes Steel, Raymond Gram Swing, J. Raymond

Walsh, and Sidney Walton; three lost their jobs and two had their airtime cut. By 1947, according to one report, twelve of the leading fourteen liberals broadcasting in the New York area were dropped while twenty-four of twenty-five conservatives remained on air.[557]

Lisa Sergio, a now all-but-forgotten '40s radio personality, is an illuminating blacklist victim. She immigrated to the United States in 1938, a repentant antifascist who began her career as Italy's first female radio announcer and Benito Mussolini's English-language interpreter. Between '39 and '46, she was featured on WQXR's "Lisa Sergio's Column of the Air"; during the war, she was NBC radio's "woman announcer" and filled in for Walter Winchell on his ABC radio show. However, in the '40s, she was listed on the FBI's Custodial Detention Index (CDI), a list of subversives who were to be considered for arrest in case of war. In 1950, Louis Budenz, a former *Daily Worker* editor and subsequent celebrity anticommunist spokesperson, named her as one of the four hundred "concealed communists" that he claimed to know. She was also one of the radio commentators HUAC targeted in '45 and, in 1950, *Red Channels* listed her among 151 actors, radio commentators, musicians, and other broadcast-industry personalities in its "Report of Communist Influence in Radio and Television."[558] Dropped by the *Times* radio station, her professional carrier as a broadcast personality and public speakers was over; in 1953, the State Department refused to renew her passport. She retreated to Vermont to allegedly take care of her ailing mother and, only after her mother died and the Red Scare ended, did she move to Washington, DC, and resume a public life.

The anticommunist blacklist took its toll on thousands of Americans throughout the country. Victims of the blacklist worked in numerous occupations, from factories, the waterfront, public school classrooms, and the nation's leading research centers to the Broadway stage and radio announcers. The blacklist was formally established as the Attorney General's List of Subversive Organizations (AGLOSO), revealed in March 1947 under President Harry Truman's Executive Order 9835. The Order required all federal employees be screened for "loyalty" and created the Loyalty Review Board to undertake the screening. However, the list had a long pre- and post-history as a form of censorship.

Faced with WWI, Congress passed the Espionage Act in 1917 and followed up with the Sedition Act in '18. The '17 Act prohibited false statements that interfered with the nation's military or promoted the efforts of an enemy; the '18 Act forbade any expression of disrespect toward the US government, the Constitution, the flag, or the military. In 1919, the Supreme Court decided unanimously, in *Schenck v. U.S.*, that Charles Schenck, general secretary of the American Socialist Party, violated the laws by mailing 15,000 anti-draft circulars to men scheduled to enter the military. Justice Oliver Wendell Holmes wrote the Court's opinion, arguing that the US government could limit freedom of speech when the nation faced a national-security threat, a "clear and present danger."

In 1939, the FBI established the Custodial Detention Index (CDI)—a.k.a. the Custodial Detention Security List, the Custodial Detention Program, and the Alien Enemy Control—to track subversives. These were people—citizens and immigrants—who were to be considered for arrest in case of war or a national-security crisis. FBI Director Hoover claimed that the CDI originated as part of the FBI's General Intelligence Division. "This division has now compiled extensive indices of individuals, groups, and organizations engaged in subversive activities," he said. The CDI list was prepared without holding Congressional hearings or without an opportunity for those identified to challenge the designation.

In 1940, as fears mounted about the coming war, the US government began to secretly screen federal employees for "loyalty" using a questionable AGLOSO-like program. The government's apparent legal basis was the 1939 Hatch Act that banned from government employment any person who held "membership in any political party or organization that advocated the overthrow of our constitutional form of government in the United States." During the war, forty-seven organizations were on this informal subversives list, most notably the CP and the pro-Nazi German American Bund. All told, there were "12 Communist or Communist 'front' organizations; 2 American Fascist organizations; 8 Nazi organizations; 4 Italian fascist organizations; and 21 Japanese organizations."[559]

But who was disloyal? And who determined loyalty? The order claimed the designation was based on whether "reasonable grounds exist for belief that the person involved is disloyal" or has "membership in, affiliation with or sympathetic association" on the Attorney General's list of "totalitarian, Fascist, Communist or subversive" organizations or groups advocating the overthrow of the US government or "to alter the form of Government of the United States by unconstitutional means." Subversion was determined by "belief"; but whose?

In September 1942, in an illegal but effective action, HUAC chairman Martin Dies leaked the list to the *Congressional Record*. The list, entitled "Communist Front Organizations," was known as Appendix IX and was officially published in 1944. It consisted of seven volumes totaling about two thousand pages and identified approximately 250 groups as Communist front organizations; the seventh volume included an index of twenty-two thousand suspected individuals. In the face of strong opposition, the full committee ordered all copies removed from the Library of Congress and destroyed.

Nevertheless, the list was quickly adopted by a wide variety of public and private groups to deny employment to or discriminate against those listed. Those adopting—and modifying—the list included the Treasury Department (e.g., tax-exemption determinations), the State Department (e.g., passport and deportation decisions), and the US military (e.g., command structure) as well as state and local governments. In addition, a growing number of civilian business sectors—e.g., federal contractors, hotel businesses, and the entertainment industries—denied employment to or discriminated against those listed. By December '46, 449 organizations had an AGLOSO designation. In 1951, HUAC came up with its own list of subversives that included many CP-front groups like the National Council of American-Soviet Friendship, the Joint Anti-Fascist Refugee Committee, the American Committee for the Protection of the Foreign Born, the American Committee for Yugoslav Relief, the Civil Rights Congress (CRC), and the American Relief for Greek Democracy. Also making the list was the Peace Information Center, an anti–Cold War group headed by W. E. B DuBois. He and four

other officials were arrested and indicted in 1950 for failing to register under the Smith Act. Most remarkable, a federal judge, James
McQuire, acquitted the five defendants.[560]

Lists of alleged subversives spread throughout American society.
In November 1956, the *Elks Magazine* featured an article, "What the
Attorney General's List Means," that began, "There are few Americans who have not heard of 'the Attorney General's subversive list.'"
It concluded, "There is no excuse for any American citizen becoming
affiliated with a group on the Attorney General's list today." More
disturbing, in 1934, the Legion of Decency established a blacklist
and, in 1947, the American Legion began making lists of people and
organizations they considered advocating radical politics. Between
1943 and '54, the FBI contracted with 60,000 legionnaires to serve as
informants—and did so without Congressional approval.[561]

The list achieved its most pronounced national status in February 1950 when Senator McCarthy announced in Wheeling, West
Virginia, "I have in my hand a list of 205 cases of individuals who
appear to be either card-carrying members or certainly loyal to the
Communist Party." McCarthy's list was never formally made public
and he kept changing the number of alleged communist suspects
depending on the audience he was addressing. The list appears to
have been based on one originally prepared some years earlier by
FBI agent Robert Lee and known as the "Lee List."

Liberal intellectuals and publication felt especially threatened by the
blacklist, fearful of being smeared by the same anticommunist brush.
As Navasky found, "the majority of center liberals lived in the penum-
bra of the degradation ceremony [of naming names] and reinforced it
by playing its game." The *New York Post* and *New Republic* refused ads
with transcripts from the Rosenberg trials and "the *New York Times*, for
example, chose not to write about what everybody knew." He singled
out *Dissent*, arguing that while it found "Stalinism was an unqualified
social evil, domestic Communists were entitled to the same rights and
presumptions as the set of our citizens." Some leading liberals, including Carey McWilliams, of *The Nation*, along with anti-Stalinist scholars like Michael Harrington, Irving Howe, Paul Goodman, C. Wright
Mills, and Erich Fromm, opposed HUAC and McCarthyism.[562]

Censorship

In February 1947, the city's Board of Education's (BOE) Committee on Instructional Affairs voted to remove Howard Fast's popular historical novel, *Citizen Tom Paine*, from all secondary-school libraries due to allegedly vulgar language. The novel was originally published in 1943 and between 1944 and 1946 was distributed to both US servicemen stationed abroad and made available oversees through the OWI.[563] By '47, it had sold over a million copies.

Dr. Frederic Ernst, the BOE's associate superintendent for high schools, never read the book yet assailed it as "vulgar" and "unfit" to be read by children. Singled out as an example of vulgar expression was one revealing section:

> Her blood is royal, and as for her mind, already she speaks enough of the King's tongue to make herself understood. Her breasts are like two Concord grapes, her behind like the succulent hams of a suckling pig. I start the bidding at fifty pounds. . . . Hennisy ripped off the blanket to reveal her nakedness when the bidding reached eighty pounds. The girl was "frightened and shivering."[564]

The banning of *Citizen Tom Paine* drew significant protest from the publishing industry and progressive groups. Representatives from eleven leading publishing houses, including Doubleday, Random House, Scribner's, Little Brown, and Farrar, Straus, issued an appeal urging the Board to reverse its decision. The ACLU, the Teachers Union (CIO), and the Association of Teachers of Social Studies, among others, joined the publishers in urging the Board to reverse its action.

A week later, at a special BOE meeting, the Board voted 6 to 1 to ban Fast's book. The lone dissenter, Brooklyn's Maximilian Moss, argued, "the lascivious and objectionable passages are quickly forgotten in the over-all effect of the book."* The public meeting was

---

* Moss's insight, to see the work as a whole, anticipated by a quarter century the Supreme Court's momentous *Miller v. California* decision (1973).

packed with two hundred spectators and the decision was assailed by representatives from eleven organizations, many close to the CP, including the CRC and Congress of American Women, as well as two city councilmen, Benjamin Davis and Peter Cacchione, both CP members; A. J. Liebling, representing the Progressive Citizens of America; the playwrights Arthur Miller and Marc Connelly; and Paul O'Dwyer of the National Lawyers Guild (and brother of the mayor, William O'Dwyer). As the *Times* reported, "No one appeared . . . to defend the removal of the book."[565]

Many wondered why the BOE had singled out Fast's popular novel for censorship, surely for something more than a few suggestive passages. (Fast was willing to prepare a specially edited textbook version of the novel, but the Board rejected the offer.) Many suspected that the blacklist was taking one more victim. In '46, HUAC subpoenaed Fast to testify regarding JAFRC's financial supporters and he refused to name names; he eventually served a three-month prison sentence at the Mill Point, West Virginia, federal penitentiary in 1950 for contempt of Congress. Following the BOE's action, a number of publishers, including Macmillan and Harcourt and Brace, removed Fast's works from its school readers. In October '47, the CP organized a rally, "The Books Are Burning," at the Manhattan Center to protest the blacklisting of Fast's work. In December, Fast gave the keynote address at a special meeting of the Young Progressive Citizens of America at NYU that 1,300 students and faculty attended.[566]

The Red Scare intensified in the late '40s, most emphatically expressed at the Peekskill riots of 1949 in which Fast was at the center. Peekskill, New York, is a small town located about fifty miles north of New York City along the Hudson River, easily reached by car, bus, or train. In the '40s, it was a popular vacation spot for working-class families, including many union workers and CP members, offering affordable rentals, kids summer camps, recreational sites, and access to the river. During the postwar period, it hosted many summer concerts, promoted by the CP and CP-front groups that featured popular entertainers, most notably Paul Robeson.*

---

* For more on Robeson, see "Freedom Fighter."

A special concert was scheduled for the night of August 27, 1949, sponsored by the CRC. Fast was to serve as master of ceremonies with Robeson and Pete Seeger among the entertainers. A day before the event, Peekskill's local newspaper, the *Evening Star*, ran a front-page headline, "Robeson Concert Here Aid 'Subversive Unit,'" noting that the CRC was on the attorney general's list. It encouraged veterans, notably men affiliated with the American Legion, Veterans of Foreign Wars, and Jewish and Catholic veterans, to show up and demonstrate their patriotism. Fast arrived early and joined a few hundred others, many women and children, setting up for the concert.

However, before the event began and the majority of the concert-goers arrived, those setting up the gathering were attacked by what Fast described as "a mob of hoodlums, joined by local police and Governor Thomas Dewey's state troopers." Fast and other concert attendees linked arms and sang "We Shall Not Be Moved." Seeger recalled, "We heard about 150 people standing around the gate shout things like 'Go back to Russia! Kikes! Nigger-lovers!' It was a typical KKK crowd, without bedsheets." Fast was particularly struck, not by a punch, but a new slogan; "They called us 'white niggers.' And that cry went on and on all through the night." Looking back, Fast reflected, "At one point I knew I would die in that terrible fight in Peekskill." Milton Flynt, head of the Peekskill American Legion, had a different experience, "Our objective was to prevent the Paul Robeson concert, and I think our objective was reached."[567]

Back in the city, progressives and liberals of every political persuasion railed against the Peekskill attack, noting that many women and children had been assaulted. A follow-up concert was quickly organized, set for a week later, September 4th. Fearful of another bloody confrontation, three thousand trade unionists along with Spanish Civil War and WWII veterans provided security and an estimated fifteen thousand people attended the event. Robeson sang, along with Seeger and the Weavers, to the crowd's enjoyment. However, as Fast observed, a "trap was set to destroy us." The police, "found plenty of drunks and hoodlums, and together they collected piles of stones on these [roadway] overpasses. . . . Every car going out of that picnic ground had to run through this gauntlet of shattered glass and smashed metal." He reflects, "It was like nothing I had ever seen."[568]

Anticommunist pressures only intensified during the early '50s as Korean War tensions increased. In '52, Fast ran for Congress in the East Bronx on the American Labor Party ticket and garnered little support. In '53, Senator McCarthy targeted his anticommunist crusade at lefty intellectuals. Operating through the Senate's Permanent Subcommittee on Investigations, he undertook hearings into the worldwide US Information Libraries system and the allegedly subversive works it distributed; simultaneously, the State Department ordered the removal of all books by suspected Communists from the shelves of US foreign libraries. Hundreds of books were removed, some reportedly burned. On McCarthy's list of library books were those by Fast as well as works by Dashiell Hammett, Helen Kay (a.k.a. Helen Colodny Goldfrank), Jerre Mangione, and Langston Hughes.[*]

On March 24, 1953, Hammett, Kay, Mangione, and Hughes appeared before McCarthy's hearings in Washington, DC. Kay was a children's book author of such works as *Insects* (1939) and *Apple Pie for Lewis* (1951); Mangione was a *Time* writer and author of *Mount Allegro* (1943); and Hughes, a leading Harlem Renaissance poet, was the author of *The Weary Blues* (1926), wrote for the *New Masses*, and was editor of *The Poetry of the Negro, 1746–1949* (1949). Hammett was a popular author of hardboiled noir detective novels, including *Red Harvest* (1929), *The Maltese Falcon* (1930), and *The Thin Man* (1934). He was a prominent CP member, having joined the party in 1937 and taught at its Jefferson School. In the early '50s, he served as president of CRC and posted bail for a group of Communists on trial for violation of the 1938 Foreign Agents Registration Act (a.k.a. the Smith Act). When the defendants jumped bail, Hammett refused to name those who provided the bail money; he was convicted of contempt and, in '51, served five months in a federal prison.[569]

---

[*] Among other African Americans singled out for their alleged Communist backgrounds were Canada Lee, Josh White, Lena Horne, and Harry Belafonte; see Victor Navasky, *Naming Names*, pp. 186–94.

A month earlier, on February 18th, Fast was subpoenaed to testify before Senator McCarthy's Government Operations Committee hearings regarding his work during the war with the Voice of America. In this showdown, Fast confronted McCarthy and its aggressive chief counsel, Roy Cohn. The opening exchange between McCarthy, Cohn, and Fast set the hearing's tone:

COHN:	When did you write *Citizen Tom Paine*, Mr. Fast?
FAST:	When did I write it? Or when was it published?
COHN:	I am sorry. When was it published? That is the date I want.
FAST:	It was published, I believe, in April of 1943.
COHN:	And at the time it was published, were you a member of the Communist party?
FAST:	I must refuse to answer that question also on the basis of the rights guaranteed to me by the First and Fifth Amendments to the Constitution.
COHN:	During the period of time you were writing the book, while you were preparing the material and writing the book, were you a member of the Communist party?
FAST:	I refuse to answer that question, for the same reasons I stated before.
McCARTHY:	Just so the record will be clear and that all the members and the staff understand, it should appear that the section of the Constitution to which the witness refers is the section which gives him the right to refuse to answer if he feels his answer may incriminate him.

Like a dog with a bone, Cohn repeatedly red-baited Fast, this time over his publications:

COHN:	Mr. Fast. I would like to ask you the same question addressed to each one of these books which you have mentioned. At the time you wrote each one of these books, were you a member of the Communist party?

FAST:	I would refuse to answer that question on the same grounds that I stated before.
COHN:	Would you refuse to answer that as to each and every one of those books enumerated, as well as to any other book you have written?
FAST:	Let me make my position plain. I will claim this privilege guaranteed to me under the Fifth and the First Amendments to the Constitution of the United States. In terms of any question which makes reference to the Communist party or organizations or periodicals cited in, let us say, the House Committee on Un-American Activities' list of so-called subversive organizations.

McCarthy queried Fast as to whether his books were published by different federal agencies, including Armed Service Books Project and the State Department, and his work for the Signal Corps. He also questioned Fast about his relations with Mrs. Roosevelt:

MCCARTHY:	Were you a social acquaintance of Eleanor Roosevelt?
FAST:	I wouldn't say that, no. That would be unfair. I met her only once, I believe.
MCCARTHY:	You met her only once?
FAST:	I believe so.
MCCARTHY:	Roughly when was that?
FAST:	I believe I met her in 1940.
. . .	
MCCARTHY:	What was the occasion of your meeting with Mrs. Roosevelt?
FAST:	I was along with a number of other people invited to the White House for lunch in late 1944.
MCCARTHY:	Who were the other people?
FAST:	Oh, I don't remember. There were a great many people there.

The day's hearing ended with a pointed exchange between the principals, including Fast's attorney, Benedict Wolf, over the committee's inept method of serving Fast with a subpoena. As Fast stated, a mysterious man showed up at his front door around 10:00 a.m., saying he had something for him "from Al." The committee's agent failed to identify himself and Fast slammed the door; later in the afternoon, another person who refused to identify himself or acknowledge that he was delivering a subpoena, knocked on Fast's door and he refused to answer; around 1:00 a.m, when Fast was asleep in bed, the agent again knocked on his door, saying he was from committee and demanded to speak to him and Fast again refused to open the door. Finally, as Fast testified, "At about 1:30 there was a pounding on the door and a ranging of the bell, which woke my children and terrified them in the time honored Gestapo methods, and I came down there, and here was this offensive character again, and this time for the first time he stated that he had a subpoena with him." The agent was accompanied by a policeman and Fast opened the door and accepted the order.[570]

Academic Freedom

On November 10, 1956, Billie Holiday gave two sold-out concerts at Carnegie Hall, singing some of her favorite songs, including "Lady Sings the Blues," "Ain't Nobody's Business If I Do," and "My Man." On stage, she was warmly celebrated by some of her generation's jazz giants, including Kenny Burrell, Roy Eldridge, and Coleman Hawkins. Also appearing on stage was Gilbert Millstein, the *New York Times*' jazz critic, who read excerpts from her recently published autobiography, *Lady Sings the Blues* (written with William Duffy). The concert marked her triumphant New York comeback and is memorialized in a celebrated album, *The Essential Billie Holiday: Carnegie Hall Concert Recorded Live.*[571]

Billie Holiday is an iconic New York outsider, celebrated for the white gardenia she wore in her hair and her unforgettable rendition of "Strange Fruit," a lamentation on the horrors of lynching. In 1999, *Time* magazine named "Strange Fruit" the "song of the century." The Library of Congress put it in the National Recording Registry. Its full power can only be truly appreciated listening—and seeing—Holiday's performance. A half century ago, "Strange Fruit" confronted a very different moral order. According to legend, a man approached Holiday at a local club and handed her a poem, "Bitter Fruit." She worked with pianist Sonny White to adapt the poem into the lyrics of a song. It was released in July 1939 and reached No. 16 on the music chart. Among those that denounced the song was *Time*, calling it a "prime piece of musical propaganda."

The man who approached Holiday was Abel Meeropol, a Dewitt Clinton (Bronx) high school English teacher and CP member. He wrote the poem in '37 after seeing a photograph of two men— Thomas Shipp and Abram Smith—being lynched; he published it under the name, "Lewis Allan." In 1940, he was called to testify before the Rapp-Coudert Committee investigating Communism in public schools. One of the issues it pressed him on was if he was paid by the party to write the song. He vehemently denied the suggestion. In 1953, following the execution of Ethel and Julius Rosenberg, the Meeropols—Abel and Anne—adopted the Rosenbergs' children, Robert and Michael, ages six and ten, respectively.

The state's Rapp-Coudert Committee was, officially, the Joint Legislative Committee to Investigate the Educational System of the State of New York. It operated between 1940 and 1942, investigating "communist infiltration" in the state public school system. Over one thousand teachers were investigated and many were dismissed, resigned, or forced to take early retirement.[572] The city reinforced state provisions with its very onerous section 903 of the City Charter. It stated that the BoE could fire anyone for "insubordination" or for refusing to answer questions pertaining to one's political beliefs, thus prohibiting employees from seeking protection against self-incrimination. Many simply resigned to avoid the humiliation of a very public red-baiting campaign.

Robert Meeropol, the natural son of the Rosenbergs and social son of the Meeropols, recalls his father's experience testifying before the committee in 1940. "This hunt for witches caused dozens to lose their jobs and Abel Meeropol, who during that time taught high school English, could have been one of them," he noted. Going further, he admitted: "Abel Meeropol did not refuse to testify. Instead he lied and evaded. He denied being a member of the Communist Party, but he was. I remember him telling me in the 1970s that he 'developed a very bad memory.'" Reflecting on the significance of his father's testimony, the younger Meeropol noted: "I suppose he could have faced a perjury charge, but he got away with it. No one ostracized Abel Meeropol because he testified. While some tactics were admired more than the course Abel took, the prevailing attitude was that as long as you did not finger others, you had acted honorably."[573]

Loyalty oaths have a long and disquieting history in the United States. The legal historian Marjorie Heins finds that oaths "kept resurfacing, especially in times of political uncertainty." Such "uncertainty" marked the Civil War, WWI, and the Depression, periods during which both federal and state/local officials used oaths to buttress the call for patriotism. Educators at both the grade school and college levels were targeted. Following WWI, the United States witnessed the first Red Scare, one marked by the Palmer Raids and the deportation of nearly 300 "aliens," including Emma Goldman and Alexander Berkman. In the wake of WWII and the rise of the Cold War, the demand for loyalty reached unprecedented levels. In 1947, the Taft-Hartley law was adopted, requiring federal employees and members of labor unions covered by the National Labor Relations Act (NLRA) sign a loyalty oath. The oath required union members to swear allegiance to the US government and declare they were not members of a group on the AGLOSO. Failure to do so could lead to the union's decertification and the union member's dismissal. By 1956, forty-two states and two thousand county and city governments, including New York state and city, adopted similar provisions and neither First nor Fifth Amendment protections were afforded those accused of being Communists.

In 1949, New York state legislators adopted the Feinberg Law to block "subversive propaganda" from being "disseminated among children in their tender years." It required all local boards of education to dismiss any teacher having committed "treasonable or seditious acts or utterances" or for belonging to an organization advocating the overthrow of the government by "force, violence or any unlawful means."

In a 1952 Supreme Court decision, *Wieman v. Updergraff*, Justice Felix Frankfurter wrote that teachers were "the priests of our democracy" because their task is "to foster those habits of open-mindedness and critical inquiry which alone make for responsible citizens." In a secular world, the classroom is one of the most scared venues of free expression. Few other social institutions encourage careful reading, rigorous discussion and having a defensible point of view. Unstated but implicit, the classroom is one of the few social institutions that encourages the explicit challenge to established authority, the student's "right" to question the teacher. The workplace, the church, the theater, and the mall are institutions that encourage conformity. On June 17, 1957, a day some labeled "Red Monday," the Court ruled against loyalty oaths in four cases. These decisions marked the turning point in the anticommunist hysteria gripping the nation. As Justice Earl Warren wrote, "To impose any straight jacket upon the intellectual leaders in our colleges and universities would imperil the future of our nation."

UNDERWORLD

FRANK COSTELLO, 1891–1973

Crime in the City

New York gangsters are not what they used to be. For four centuries, the city has cultivated an underworld of illegal and illicit activities that helped spawn notorious gangsters. Herbert Asbury's *The Gangs of New York* and Luc Sante's *Low Life*, vividly evoke nineteenth-century Gotham with tales of gangs named Bowery Boys, Plug Uglies, Short Tails, Slaughter Houses, Swamp Angels, and Whyos as well as such characters as the Five Points' Rosanna Peers, Cow-legged Sam McCarthy, Slobbery Jim, and Patsy the Barber. These characters fashioned, in turn, the underworld culture of the twentieth-century city, a culture of celebrity gangsters like Arnold Rothstein, Owney Madden, Dutch Shultz, and Meyer Lansky as well as *mafiosi* like Al Capone, Lucky Luciano, and Frank Costello.[574] These outlaws were often involved in bloody internecine turf battles with assorted rivals and cat-and-mouse confrontations with the police. Outlaw confrontations still captivate the media and the public.

Times change and so does the city's underworld. In February 2014, the *Wall Street Journal* ran a revealing story, "Mafia Is Down—but Not Out . . . Crime Families Adapt to Survive, Lowering Profile and Using Need-to-Know Tactics." Richard Frankel, special agent in charge of the FBI's New York Criminal Division, acknowledged, "I don't know that I'd say La Cosa Nostra was what it was in its heyday but I wouldn't say by any means it's gone away."[575] Perhaps today's mobsters are getting smarter having watched movies like *The Godfather* and *Goodfellas* as well as innumerable TV dramas, from *Dragnet* to *Law & Order*, *The Sopranos*, and *Boardwalk Empire*. Their persona has become a social cliché; they even sport their own reality-TV show, *Mob Wives*, and any number of video games like *Mafia 3* and *Mafia: The City of Lost Heaven*.

The *Journal* reported, "today's mafia has reverted to its roots and tried to become as invisible as possible, officials and experts say." It's still involved in old-mob rackets like loan-sharking, extortion, gambling, construction, and murder, but has begun to apply new management techniques to its business operations. One old-time syndicate, the Genovese family, "uses a rotating panel of leaders to run day-to-day affairs to avoid any one boss from being targeted by prosecutors." Gangs also use the "street boss" model where low-level toughs stand in for imprisoned dons. However, these old-school mobsters are not twenty-first-century tech savvy, with apparently little presence in Wall Street pump-and-dump scams, offshore Internet gambling and online rip-offs (e.g., fake Viagra).[576]

The flashy days of John Gotti are over; old-school gangsters are no longer among the city's chief concerns. The traditional mob is—demographically speaking—changing. The nineteenth- and twentieth-century Irish, Italian, Jewish, and "Negro" gangsters are giving way to twenty-first-century immigrants, including Russian, Balkan, Caribbean, Latin American, Chinese, and African. Globalization has undercut the city's old-world control over the illicit drug trade from Latin American and Asia. Equally critical, federal and city attention has shifted from crime to counterterrorism. The city—and nation—still resonates from the 9/11 trauma, an attack that launched the "war on terror" and the rise of the national security state with local enforcement consequences. Making matters tougher, increasing segments of what used to be illegal or illicit operations—like pornography, sex toy boutiques, homosexual encounters, gentlemen's clubs, and adult commercial sex—have become part of a mainstream, $50 billion adult sex industry.[*577]

More than a half century ago, in March 1951, a US Senate sub-committee held hearings in the federal courthouse in Foley Square on organized crime in the city, particularly its involvement with elected officials. The hearings, chaired by a young and media-savvy politician, Estes Kefauver (D-TN), helped fashion an era of political spectacle. Television was the new, breakthrough medium and live Congressional hearings on compelling issues were enormously popular. These hearings replaced FDR's folksy fireside chats as the voice of the new, postwar America.

Crimesters

In the postwar era, concern about organized crime became a national security issue. In 1949, the American Municipal Association, representing 10,000-plus cities across the country, called upon the US government to take action against what was euphemistically called "the Mob," the criminal underworld. Federal action was demanded because crime was national and operated throughout the country. It was a syndicate of illicit and illegal—but very profitable—commercial exchanges. It was ubiquitous, involving gangsters, law enforcement (i.e., police, courts, prisons), politicians (both parties), and consumers (all classes). The underworld set the limits to free-market capitalism.

Kefauver, a first-term senator, took up the challenge to determine the scale and influence of organized crime in the United States. Based on his proposal, the Senate, in May 1950, established the Special Committee on Organized Crime in Interstate Commerce. During its relatively short, fifteen-month investigative period, the committee held twenty-seven public hearings and executive sessions in fourteen cities, including Los Angeles, San Francisco, Saint Louis,

---

[*] Nonconsensual sex in all its forms—rape, sex trafficking, pedophilia and lust murder—is both immoral and illegal.

Kansas City, Detroit, and Washington, DC. In March '51, Kefauver brought his crime road show to New York and it generated national media frenzy.

Kefauver, a publicity-savvy politician, saw TV's potential and permitted live coverage of his hearings on organized crime. The first hearings were in New Orleans, accompanied by the first simultaneous radio and TV airing; it was followed by hearings in Detroit, Saint Louis, and Los Angeles (ABC's affiliate, KECA, ran sixteen hours of coverage over two days). With each market, viewership built, and when the hearings reached San Francisco, two of the city's three stations (KGO and KPIX) ran them live. The New York hearings shifted urban crime from a local issue to a national concern. On March 12th, Kefauver opened public sessions at the federal courthouse in Foley Square and six channels covered the proceedings live; WPIX carried forty-four hours of hearings and DuMont's affiliate, WADO, ran the entire proceedings, gavel to gavel.

The committee called fifty witnesses including federal and local law enforcement officials, academics, politicians, religious representatives, and—the big media draw—reputed mobsters. The most notably "underworld" figure to appear was Frank Costello (a.k.a. Francisco Castaglia), the reputed head of the "Lucky" Luciano crime family (later dubbed the Genovese family). He reputedly bankrolled the Copacabana, the city's swankest nightclub at 10 East 60th Street, and was considered the "Prime Minister of the Underworld," ostensible boss-of-bosses of the city's organized crime syndicate, the "Five Families."[578]

Costello initially refused to appear at the public hearing, insisting he was an honest businessman and would not be subject to the glare of TV cameras. The committee agreed to limit TV coverage to only Costello's hands. Costello's lawyer, George Wolf, likely negotiated the agreement and seems to have been naïve with regard to the changing media landscape. While restricting the TV camera depiction, he did not prohibit photographers or newsreel 16mm filming for later TV broadcast from courtroom coverage. He also seems to have failed to appreciate the hearings' popular appeal and the power of the visual image. Live TV viewers did not see Costello, looking like a movie star, hair slicked back and handsomely attired in an expensive suit, seated respectfully next to his attorney. TV cameras focused on his big, meaty hands as they toyed with his eyeglasses, picked up a water glass, and dabbed a handkerchief to his unseen face. As David Halberstam points out, "those hands relentlessly reflected Costello's tension and guilt." The very absence of his face and attire as well as interchanges with his attorney, elements that may have humanized him, made him appear a sinister character.[579]

Unknown to those watching the live hearings, Costello had already testified before the committee's closed sessions, once on February 13 (two hours) and again on February 15th (six hours). The public hearings were originally scheduled to take place in a relatively small courtroom on the twenty-eighth floor (room 2803) and Costello first appeared there on March 13th, testifying from 10:00 am to 5:30 p.m. However, given the enormous media turnout and popular interest, the proceedings were moved to a larger third-floor courtroom (room 318) where Costello testified on the March 14, from 10:00 a.m. to 1:00 p.m. The hearings were a true media circus. "During the entire proceeding of the witness," Wolf protested, "powerful, blinding klieg lights were focused on the witness and counsel." He then pointed out, "numerous cameras were audibly grinding, hordes of photographers were constantly roving about the room, standing on chairs, and other elevated portions of the room, as they are just at this moment, placing themselves directly in front of the witness, as they are at this moment, dashing about the room, brushing by the witness, taking close-up pictures by flashlights, at various angles: numerous reporters crowded into the room, in such close proximity to the witness, that they actually frequently brushed against him; the room was intensely hot, and without proper ventilation." It was an all-American media spectacle.[580]

The episode ended in a showdown between the two ill-matched combatants, Kefauver and Costello. The first was portrayed as the all-American Southern Jimmy Stewart starring in *Mr. Smith Goes to Washington*; his adversary was the foreigner, the "wop," the gangster, someone under suspicion. Their interchange was a televised championship boxing match that galvanized the nation:

KEFAUVER:	Now, Mr. Costello, would you state whether or not you are familiar with the testimony given yesterday by Mr. Francis McLaughlin?
COSTELLO:	I refuse to answer the question. When the proper time comes I will have plenty to say.
KEFAUVER:	Well, the chairman directs you to answer the question, Mr. Costello.
COSTELLO:	At this particular moment I will not.
KEFAUVER:	Do you refuse to follow the direction of the Chair?
COSTELLO.	Absolutely.
KEFAUVER:	The Chair directs you to answer the question and to answer such other questions as will be asked this afternoon.
COSTELLO.	I still refuse.[581]

Costello had less of a problem discussing his activities in private than shaming himself in public. Refusing to answer the Senate committee's questions, the "Prime Minister" walked out of the hearings.[582]

Virginia Hill (Hauser) followed Costello to the witness table and stole the show. Hill, nicknamed "Flamingo" by the gangster Benjamin "Bugsy" Siegel, was an attractive red head who pranced into the hearings fashionably late and, like a movie star, was adorned in a mink cape, silk gloves, and a wide-brimmed hat. She was the mob's moll, intimately—in every sense—involved with those at the highest level of the American underworld. She was Siegel's lover and a confidant to Costello, Frank Nitti, Joe Adonis, and Meyer Lansky, among many others. The highpoint of the hearing came when she reputedly asserted, "I'm the best goddamned lay in the world."[583]

Born in Lipscomb, Alabama, in 1916, Hill migrated to Chicago, lured by the 1933 World's Fair and Depression-era poverty. Rumors circulated that she plied her trade as a hooker and/or dancer, but was finally discovered waitressing at the San Carlo Italian Village, a Fair hangout for the Capone gang. There she met Joseph Epstein (a.k.a. Joey Epp), a gay accountant and associate to boss Jake "Greasy Thumb" Guzik. She worked for Epstein for many years, reputedly serving as a mob courier of money and drugs, living the good life and travelling throughout the country as well as to Mexico and Europe.

While living in New York in the late '30s and working with Adonis, a Capone ally, she met Siegel (married with two children) in a Brooklyn bar and began an affair. In '39, Hill reconnected with Siegel at a Hollywood party thrown by George Raft, a rising star; raised in Hell's Kitchen, Raft had been a muscle in the Prohibition-era Madden gang. Hill accompanied Siegel to Las Vegas where he built the legendary Flamingo Hotel, a venture backed by Lansky and company. However, the venture was plagued by mismanagement and enormous cost overruns; its grand opening was a disaster. Siegel was accused of skimming some $2 million and assassinated at Hill's Beverly Hills home in June '47.[584]

Hill walked out on Siegel before the Flamingo opened after learning he was hosting two of his other lovers, Wendy Barrie and Countess DiFrasso, at the hotel. Hill was in Paris when Siegel was murder and returned to the United States in late '47 when she hooked up with (Norman) Hans Hauser, a famous downhill skier and Sun Valley skiing instructor; in 1942, he was jailed in the United States as a Nazi spy. They married in '50 and had a son, Peter. In '51, she appeared before the Senate subcommittee. Entranced by her grand performance, Walter Winchell, America's leading gossip commentator, opined, "When the chic Virginia Hill unfolded her amazing life story, many a young girl must have wondered: who really knows best? Mother or Virginia Hill? After doing all the things called wrong, there she was on top of the world, with a beautiful home in Miami Beach and a handsome husband and baby!"[585]

For a couple of hours on March 16, both Kefauver and the committee's chief counsel, Rudolph Halley, contested like gladiators of old with the former waitress, parrying over her finances and relations with reputed mobsters. This exchange captures her spirit and that of the times.

HALLEY:	And did you ever get any money from any other person whom we might call a gangster, other than Siegel?
HILL (HAUSER):	No.
HALLEY:	Did you ever get any money from Costello?

HILL:	No.
HALLEY:	Did you ever get any money from Meyer Lansky?
HILL:	I never got money from any of those fellows.
HALLEY:	From none of those fellows?
HILL:	From none of those fellows, none of those that I've been reading about, or none that I knew. They never gave me anything.

Things got testy when Halley and Kefauver pressed Hill on her relationship with Siegel:

HALLEY:	Now, you left the United States shortly before Siegel was killed. Would you tell the circumstances that led to your leaving the United States?
HILL:	I was planning to leave the United States long before that. . . . Ben . . . got the letter and read it and saw all these things I planned to see in Europe, and these people, and he didn't like this boy that I knew in France. So then he told me I couldn't go. So then, later on, I had a big fight with him because I hit a girl in the Flamingo and he told me I wasn't a lady. We got in a big fight. I had been drinking, and I left, and I went to Paris when I was mad.
HALLEY:	Before you left, had you heard any rumors that Siegel was having trouble with any of his gangster friends?
HILL:	I never heard any kind—that he was having any trouble. And all I know, he was worried about the hotel. I hated the place, and I told him why didn't he leave it and get away from it because it was making him a nervous wreck.

Halley kept digging into Hill's personal finances and she, like a matador, raised her cape and the questions gracefully passed by:

HALLEY:	Just one thing. Mrs. Houser, you have testified now about a lot of details of your own finances and your

	own business. But are you really not in any position to give this committee any of the details you must have heard about the business of Siegel, or Adonis?
HILL:	But I never knew anything about their business. They didn't tell me about their business. Why would they tell me? I don't care anything about business in the first place. I don't even understand it.
	. . .
HALLEY:	You never heard [politics] discussed by [Adonis] or Costello?
HILL:	I never discussed politics with anybody. I don't know the first thing about politics.
HALLEY:	Did you ever sit at a table and hear anybody else discuss politics?
HILL:	I never heard him discuss anything, outside of laughing and making jokes, and like I said—in case he ever talked to anybody, or anybody he ever knew, I found other things to interest myself, I never wanted to hear about anything.
HALLEY:	You just didn't want to know anything?
HILL:	No, sir. I didn't want to know anything about anybody.[586]

Finally, after hours of a grueling cat-and-mouse exchange, Hill tried to make her way out of the Courthouse chamber only to be confronted by a throng of media folk. Pushing and shoving, she reportedly slapped a female reporter in the face and cursed out a photographer, "I hope the atom bomb falls on every one of you."

While Costello and Hill might have been the main attractions of the Senate subcommittee's first week in New York, Kefauver was the big winner. He was invited to appear as the "mystery guest" on CBS's popular Sunday night, prime-time program, *What's My Line?* It prompted commentators to humorlessly retitle the Senate hearings, "What's My Crime?" As was customary, the mystery guest signed in and the panelists, including Hal Block, Bennett Cerf, and Arlene Francis, wore blindfolds. Kefauver's presence drew what one commentator called "sustained, fervent applause." After the Senator's identity was guessed, the panelists joking with him. Block asked, "are you sure you want to be shown on television—or just your hands?" which drew laughs from the audience, and Francis gushed, "We'd love to have your ratings!"[587]

Kefauver leveraged his media celebrity into a March '51 *Time* magazine cover shot and a well received—if ghostwritten—four-part series, "What I Found in the Underworld," in an April '51 *Saturday Evening Post*. He even got a bit part in a 1951 Humphrey Bogart movie, *The Enforcer*. Based on his newfound visibility, Kefauver sought the Democratic Party's 1952 presidential nomination, even beating the incumbent, Harry Truman, in the New Hampshire primary, contributing to the president's decision not to seek the nomination. He won all but three of the party primaries, but lost the nomination to Adlai Stevenson who, in turn, lost the general election to Dwight Eisenhower. In '56, Kefauver ran as Stevenson's vice-presidential candidate and they lost to President Eisenhower and Vice President Richard Nixon.

On Monday, March 19th, the committee hearings resumed and the principal witness was William O'Dwyer, the city's former mayor (1946–'50) and the then US ambassador to Mexico. Three of O'Dwyer's former associates, Frank Bale, James Moran, and John Murtagh, also testified. The committee was interested in O'Dwyer's relations with the city's organized crime syndicate, particularly Costello. It was a relation that dated from the early '40s when O'Dwyer was the Brooklyn district attorney (1940–'42). As DA, he prosecuting the notorious Murder, Inc., gang, but failed to follow-up on the killing of its gunman, Abe (Kid Twist) Reles. The "Kid" was to testify against mob boss Albert Anastasia, but was murdered, so the purported mobster was never prosecuted. Senator Charles Tobey (R-NH) directly challenged O'Dwyer over this failure and the ambassador, playing to the TV audience, repeatedly rebuffed his accuser.

On March 20th, committee counsel Halley took up the battle with O'Dwyer, accusing him of giving cushy city jobs to gangsters or their associates. Again, the former mayor rebuffed all efforts to besmirch his reputation. However, on March 21st the hearings climaxed when John Crane, head of the Uniformed Firefighters Association, testified that in '49 he gave $10,000 in cash to O'Dwyer on the Gracie Mansion porch as a campaign contribution; at the time of the hearing, Crane was being investigated by a grand jury over the disappearance of $135,000 from the union treasury. When O'Dwyer was recalled, he raged, "I will flatly deny that." Under a growing cloud of suspicion and Eisenhower's '52 electoral victory, O'Dwyer resigned as ambassador on December 6, 1952. To avoid possible prosecution, the ambassador did not return to New York from Mexico for a decade.[588]

The Senate subcommittee issued a final report on August 31st linking crime to subversion. "The public now knows that the tentacles of organized crime reach into virtually every community throughout the country," it reported. Going further, it noted: "These criminal gangs have such power that they constitute a government within a government in this country." Looking deeper, it warned, "This secret government of crimesters is a serious menace which could, if not curbed, become the basis for a subversive movement which could wreck the very foundation of this country."[589]

Mob City

Club 82 opened in 1953 at 82 East 4th Street and became the nation's premier showcase for female—and some male—impersonators; it operated until '78. One accessed the 82 by climbing down a long, steep stairway and entering a large space featuring a central bar with tables and booths and decked out with lots of fake palm trees and other decorations. As could happen only in New York, the nation's leading transvestite performance club was located across the street from the Hell's Angel's headquarters.

The 82 was a Mafia-run joint, operated by the Genovese crime family. The ostensible owner was reported to be Mathew Jacobson and the original manager was Steve Franse. Anna Heck Genovese, Vito Genovese's second wife, supposedly operated it while the mob boss was hiding out in Italy to avoid an arrest for murder. When

Heck divorced Genovese, she squealed about the mob's operations, including its role in numerous gay clubs.*590

In the '50s—not unlike the early twenty-first century—there were many dimensions to organized crime. The Kefauver hearings played to the headline-grabbing aspects, the *spectacle* of crime. Costello, Hill and O'Dwyer represented its grand presence, its celebrity status; they suggested just how extensive crime was in the city and throughout the country. So pervasive, it was even polluting the political system. There was, however, a secondary dimension to crime that the hearings failed to address, one best understood as the *quotidian* of crime. This is the everydayness of illicit and/or illegal activities; it is the innumerable ways criminal law breaking takes place. In the '50s, such underworld transactions included cost-of-doing-business shakedowns ("strong-arm" extortion) and poor people's loans (loan-sharking) as well as neighborhood gambling (bookmaking), narcotics (illegal drugs), criminal receiving (stolen goods), labor racketeering, tax evasion (alcohol, cigarettes), vending machine scams, counterfeiting (forgeries), pornography, commercial sex, and homosexual hookups. In the '50s, New York was a city on the take, one with a thriving underworld economy with its own bankers, judges, and enforcers.

During the Roaring '20s, the line between the acceptable and the unacceptable was vigorously contested. While the Eighteenth Amendment imposed Prohibition, a growing number of Americans throughout the country rejected it. New Yorkers, from the most respected Brahman to the lowest ghetto resident, broke temperance laws with equal impunity. Yet, like illegal drug enforcement policies today, the poor and ethnic minorities of the '20s tended to be arrested and convicted far more often than the socially respectable, white, Protestant gentry. Nearly everyone along NY Route 9—what was euphemistically called the "Rum Trail" or "Whiskey Road" that ran from the Canadian border south to the Big Apple—was on the take. Federal customs agents, local law-enforcement officers, farmers, distributors, barkeeps, politicians, and beat cops all had their hands out for a buck or a bottle.

---

* See "Illicit Performance."

And they got it! Not surprising, in the city, the leading institutions of social authority—the government, courts, and police—were as corrupt as the gangsters they were sworn to suppress.

Gangsters underwrote the Roaring '20s popular nightlife and the speakeasy scene, becoming national celebrities. They were overseers of all things illegal and illicit. Chicago's Al "Scarface" Capone was the era's most celebrated crime boss, achieving legendary status as the subject of endless newspaper and newsreel stories and, in time, dozens of books, movies, and TV shows. Gotham's gangsters were less mythic figures, rather transformative characters bridging the old-world ethnic gang to the new-world crime syndicate. Costello, Siegel, Arnold Rothstein, John "Legs" Diamond, Larry Fay, Barron Wilkins, Arthur "Dutch Schultz" Flegenheimer, Frankie Uale (or Yale), Johnny Torrio, Charles "Lucky" Luciano, Owney Madden, and Lansky got their starts during the '20s and called Gotham home.

Corruption in New York was institutionalized through Tammany Hall, the city's Democratic political machine. In the decades following the Civil War, Tammany achieved its legendary status, establishing the model of political influence and corruption that would define Gotham politics until the 1930s. It secured it first major municipal powerbase in the mid-nineteenth century through control of the city's newly established police force. This served as the template of patronage, influence peddling, extortion, kickback, and shakedown rackets that defined Tammany—and city politics—for the next three-quarters of a century. Under the leadership of William March "Boss" Tweed from 1854 to 1871, Tammany gained control of the city government's growing budget and bureaucracy. One of Tweed's cronies, George Washington Plunkitt, a longtime state senator who became wealthy through Tammany politics, practiced what he called "honest graft." As Plunkett once famously stated, "The politician who steals is worse than a thief. He is a fool. With the grand opportunities all around for the man with a political pull there's no excuse for stealing a cent. . . . As for me, I see my opportunities and I take them. Honest graft."[591]

"Honest" corruption reached its zenith during the administration of New York's good-time mayor, James J. Walker. "Beau James" was elected mayor in 1926, during the highpoint of the bubble decade. He was a charismatic politician who embodied Roaring '20s wild, fictitious exuberance. Looking more like a movie star than politician, he was often featured in page one newspaper headlines accompanied by a sexy young starlet at the latest Broadway opening, political fundraiser, or one of Texas Guinan's *speaks*. Married and a Catholic, he antagonized the Church and respectable society with his very public affair with the actress Betty Compton. Often called "New York's Night Time Mayor," Walker joked quite seriously that his trusted assistant was the daytime mayor.[592]

Franklin Roosevelt, a wealthy upstate Democrat, took office as New York's governor in January '29 and had no ties to the Tammany machine. In opposition to the previous governor, Al Smith, who owed his position to the machine, FDR saw Tammany as a potential liability to his greater ambition of first securing the 1932 Democratic party nomination and then winning the presidency. In an effort to represent himself as a "clean government" progressive, Roosevelt backed Judge Samuel Seabury's investigations into New York municipal corruption. Seabury's hearings lead to revelations about the enormous corruptions deforming city government and business. Most shocking were the staggering amount of under-the-table payoffs that found their way into the pockets of politicians, city officials, and Tammany bosses, often one and the same. In the face of Seabury's revelations and mounting pressure from Governor Roosevelt, Walker resigned from office and took a slow boat to Europe with Compton.

The Waterfront

"You don't understand. I coulda had class. I coulda been a contender," laments Terry Malloy, immortally realized by Marlon Brando in a climactic scene of the 1954 movie *On the Waterfront*. He then sorrowfully admits, "I coulda been somebody, instead of a bum, which is what I am, let's face it." In addition to Brando, the movie's star-studded cast includes Lee J. Cobb (Johnny Friendly), Rod

Steiger (Charley "the Gent"), Karl Malden (Father Barry), and Eva Marie Saint (Edie Doyle). Elia Kazan directed the film; Budd Schulberg wrote the script; and Leonard Bernstein composed the music. It scooped the Academy Awards, taking Oscars for best production, screenplay, direction, actor, supporting actress, art direction, black and white photography, and editing.[593]

On the Waterfront is a morality tale, a personal saga of one man's transformation from a corrupt sinner to a virtuous citizen. Set in the New York docks of the '50s, it depicts one aspect of a city—and world—recovering from the trauma of world war. The film brought Americans a revealing, if stylized, glimpse into a world that was foreign but, over the preceding few years, had garnered much public attention. Wildcat strikes by New York and other East Coast longshoremen in 1945, '49, and '51 helped precipitate a series of US Congressional and New York State hearings on waterfront crime. They garnered front-page stories that captivated the nation. Terry Malloy became the American everyman seeking to fulfill the American Dream, the promise to be redeemed for the sacrifices endured during the Depression and war. Gangsters and a corrupt union blocked his dream of fulfillment. A decent job was the cornerstone to the new, postwar masculine identity and the achievement of the American Dream. Sadly, employment—for Malloy and everyone else—came with compromises, cutting corners and the necessary, existential, choices made in order to survive.

The film's drama revolves around Malloy's moral struggle over testifying before a crime commission investigating waterfront corruption. According to media historian Kenneth Hey, Arthur Miller hatched the original idea for a movie about the docks and crime in 1949. He had long been interested in the story of Petro Panto, a Red Hook, Brooklyn, radical dockworker who tried to organize fellow longshoremen and was murdered in July 1939. In '49, Miller was then at the top of his game; two of his plays—*All My Sons* (1947) and *Death of a Salesman* (1949)—were Broadway successes; Kazan directed *All My Sons*. In '51, Miller sent the script—*The Bottom of the River* (also titled *The Hook*)—to Kazan and proposed they work together on the movie.[594]

Miller and Kazan were very different men, both artistically and politically. Hollywood gossip has it that both had affairs with Marilyn Monroe before she married Miller. According to Hey, "Miller's clearly defined goods and evils, so evident in *All My Sons*, did not blend well with Kazan's admixture of optimism and moral ambivalence." Miller's original screenplay was more political; he framed the struggle an alliance between rank-and-file African American and Italian American dockworkers against a corrupt union. The Kazin-Shulberg story focused of an individual's moral dilemma.

In April 1952, Kazan was called to testify before HUAC and named names. He admitted being in the Communist Party (CP) for about a year-and-a-half, between 1934 and 1936, and named eight party members, including playwright Clifford Odets. (Schulberg testified before HUAC and also named names.) Four years later, in '56, Miller was subpoenaed to testify before HUAC. This followed the success of his 1953 play, *The Crucible*, a not-so-veiled creative use of the Salem witch trials of 1692 to represent the '50s HUAC, McCarthy, and Kefauver hearings. Miller appears never to have been a CP member, yet agreed with much of its analysis of American domestic and foreign policies and supported many of its causes. When called, he refused to name names and was sentenced to a $500 fine or thirty days in jail and his passport was revoked, so he missed the play's London opening in 1954. A US Circuit Court of Appeals ultimately overturned the conviction.[595]

The Shulberg-Kazan story of waterfront corruption is based on a series of investigative pieces by a reporter for the *New York Sun,* Malcolm Johnson. The twenty-four-part series, "Crime on the Waterfront," was published in November and December 1948 and won the Pulitzer Prize; in 1950, the series was published as a book, *Crime on the Labor Front.* The series ran on page one under headlines like "Mobsters Linked to Vast International Crime Syndicate" and "Rule New York Piers by Terror and Harvest Millions." The central protagonist in Johnson's anticorruption saga was a Catholic priest, John "Pete" Corridan, a Jesuit who served as associate director of the Xavier Institute of Industrial Relations at St. Francis Xavier Parish on West 16th Street in the Village. Many longshoremen who worked on the nearby Chelsea piers attended his labor classes and were church parishioners.

In the immediate postwar period, the United States was racked by pent-up labor unrest. A Depression and world war had suppressed worker demands for more than a decade. Now with peace, a nation-wide strike wave broke out in 1945–'46 that involved all sectors of the workforce. Strikers included auto workers, steel workers, lumber workers, machinists, meatpackers, flat glass workers, textile workers, oil workers, and coal miners along with truck drivers, utility, trans-portation, and communications workers as well as a teachers and municipal workers. New York and other East Coast longshoremen walked off for nineteen days. According to US Bureau of Labor Statistics, it was "the most concentrated period of labor-management strife in the country's history." Labor historian Joel Seidman finds that by the end of 1946, 4.6 million workers had been involved in strikes.[596]

A threatened railroad strike brought federal intervention. Starting in October 1945, President Harry Truman moved to quash the growing nonviolent insurrection. He first ordered the seizure of the nation's refineries, breaking the oil workers' strike; he then seized the packinghouses on the dubious ground that the strike was harming the war effort even though the war was officially over; he then seized the railroads and threatened to have the Army run the trains to prevent a possible strike; and he seized the coal mines but the miners continued their strike. Reflecting on the strike wave, Truman later mused, "We used the weapons that we had at hand in order to fight a rebel lion against the government."[597]

Prime Minister

The Kefauver hearing made Frank Costello a celebrity who faced increased scrutiny from the federal government. Because he refused to answer Senate questions, he was charged with contempt and tried twice before being convicted; he served an eighteen-month sentence that ran from August 1952 to October 1953. While in prison, the IRS initiated an investigation into his tax records and, in April '54, put him on trial for tax evasion; he was found guilty, sentenced to five years in prison and fined $30,000. Most remarkable, in '56, Costello hired Edward Bennett Williams, a prominent attorney, who secured his release due to the government's use of illegal wiretaps in its prosecution.[598]

The federal government did not give up its efforts to get Costello. The Immigration and Naturalization Service sought to "denaturalize" Costello and send him back to Italy, his birth country. The presiding judge in the trial, Edward Palmieri, dismissed the government's case and federal litigators appealed to the Second Circuit, which reversed the decision. Williams appealed Costello's prosecution to the Supreme Court and, in *United States v. Frank Costello* (1957), it "dismissed without prejudice its action for the denaturalization of defendant." The Court ruled "the government's case is permeated with the fruit of illegal wire taps." Costello once remarked, "I've had 40 lawyers, but Ed's the champ."[599] (Williams also represented HUAC witnesses and Senator McCarthy.)

While Costello was contesting with the federal government, rivals within the New York underworld began to move against the prime minister, boss of bosses. Shortly after the Court ruling, Genovese orchestrated a failed assassination attempt by Vincent "The Chin" Gigante who, allegedly, shouted, "This is for you Frank." The failed assassination attempt and the killings of Albert Anastasia and Frank Scalise contributed to Costello's decision to "retire" from the underworld after more than fifty years. He died of natural causes in 1973, at the age of eighty-two, residing in the Waldorf Astoria's penthouse.

Costello was born Francesco Castiglia in Lauropoli, Calabria, Italy, in 1891 and immigrated to the States in 1900 with his mother and brother; his father had come earlier and ran a small grocery store. Costello was drawn into neighborhood gang activities and, as a teenager, was busted repeatedly for committing petty crimes. In 1918, he married Lauretta Giegerman, a Jewish girl and neighborhood friend, and was again busted; he got ten months for carrying a gun. When released, he jumped back into the rackets, getting involved in gambling and loansharking. Prohibition brought him into association with the leading figures of the city's underworld, including Luciano, Genovese, Lanksy, Siegel, Madden, Dutch Schultz, and Rothstein, and the diversification of their operations. For example, Costello backed Sherman Billingsly's very upscale Stork Club.[600]

In the late '30s, with Genovese facing indictment and fleeing to Italy to avoid prosecution, Costello assumed de facto leadership of the Luciano crime organization. Surely one of the most bizarre episodes of WWII was the US Office of Naval Intelligence's Operation Underworld. In the wake of Pearl Harbor and an increasing number of German U-boat attacks on East Coast shipping, often targeted at the New York port, the Navy contacted Lanksy for assistance. He suggested the Luciano could organize the dockworkers for the war effort. Assisted by Costello and through the liaison of Cardinal Spellman, the armed forces vicar, with President Roosevelt, Luciano's sentence was reduced and he was transferred from the rougher Dannemora to the more comfortable Clinton penitentiary; in 1946, he was released from prison and deported to Italy.

In the wake of the American Municipal Association's 1949 warning about the growing influence of organized crime, New York's governor, Thomas Dewey, established a crime commission to investigate working conditions, union corruption, and theft on the waterfront. President Eisenhower formalized the investigation by creating the Waterfront Commission of New York Harbor in 1953. The commission, according to J. F. Cooper, involved the "collaboration of New York and New Jersey law enforcement agencies, district attorneys, federal agencies such as the FBI, Customs, and the Coast Guard, the Commission's targets have been primarily low-level union officials." It had, as he points out, "the power of life and death over every man and agency that worked on the waterfront, for in order to work or operate a company on the docks it was necessary to hold a license from the Commission."[601]

Organized crime employed a variety of schemes to squeeze the waterfront and its workers. According to a 1953 *Daily News* report, the Mickey Bowers boys controlled the Hudson River docks between 42nd and 57th Streets through control of International Longshoremen's Association (ILA) Local 824, dubbed "the pistol local."

Michelle Demeri, assistant counsel at the Waterfront Commission, identified a host of racketeering schemes used by the mob to corrupt the waterfront. They included control of ILA officials and stevedore companies; loansharking and gambling; misuse of a union or employee benefit plans; employing "no-show" workers; and cargo theft. Spruille Braden, the commission's chairman, declared, "organized crime along the waterfront costs at least $350 million a year in hidden taxes." Surprisingly missing from these reports is reference to the flesh trade or other illicit vices.[602]

Sin, Sex & the Mob

Steve Franse, the manager of Club 82, was murdered on June 18, 1953. Franse was apparently killed following a falling out with his boss, Vito Genovese, the reputed head of the Luciano crime family and who controlled the club. He was offed due to his apparent inability to manage not the 82 but Genovese's second wife, Anna Heck Genovese. She was not only a bisexual lesbian and involved in marital infidelity, but successfully sued for divorce, revealing Genovese's business interests, and testified before the state liquor authority.

Earlier in his career, Franse ran the Howdy Club, located at 47 West 3rd Street, between Mercer St. and LaGuardia Place, one of the most popular gay and gay-friendly joints in the city during the 1930s and '40s. The club was a popular lesbian hangout featuring performers like "Blackie Dennis," a male impersonator who strutted in a black tuxedo with slicked-back hair, and Red Tova Halem, a Jewish "burlesque striptease artist." (In an article commemorating her eightieth birthday, the *Jewish Weekly* described a photo of her at the club smoking a cigarette as "Bob Hope is sitting next to her and Jackie Gleason is signing an autograph nearby.") During the war, the club was popular with gay soldiers and sailors passing through the city. According to Anna Genovese, Franse had an earlier interest in the apparently mob-backed Savannah Club, a Village hotspot at 66 West 3rd Street. It was a popular "negro nightclub" offering all-black burlesque reviews; Joseph Schiavone was an owner. Prior to

Club 82, Franse ran Club 181 at 181 Second Avenue that featured female impersonators and, after the police shut it down, morphed into the 82.[603]

Three months before Franse's murder, in March '53, the city's district attorney seized the books and records of the 82 Club, Savannah Club, Club Caravan, and the Moroccan Club, all allegedly mob run. On March 25, Anna Genovese, accompanied by her attorney, H. David Frackman, testified before the liquor authority and, under oath, insisted her husband did not have interests in either Club 82 or the Moroccan Club. On June 18th, Franse's fate was played out.

There's some debate as to exactly where and how Franse was killed. According to one account, he was murdered at Joe Valachi's restaurant, La Verdi, on East 137th Street in the Bronx.[*] Valachi reported that on June 18 two gangsters—Pat Pagano and Fiore Siano—grabbed Franse in the kitchen, one holding him in an armlock while the other started punching him. Valachi noted, "He gives it to him good. It's what we call 'buckwheats,' meaning spite-work." Moving in for the kill, one of the enforcers put a heavy chain around Franse's neck and, as he struggled to free himself, the chain was tightened while the other thug kicked Franse until he stopped moving.[604]

According to another account, the killing took place in Manhattan and Franse's body was found in a car outside of 164 East 37th Street. The *New York Times* reported, "His body, badly beaten, was discovered at 9:45 a.m face down on the rear floor of his automobile, which was parked in front of 164 East Thirty-seventh Street." The *Times* added, "Detectives said a sapphire and diamond ring, a gold watch and approximately $200 in case were missing. . . . The police said that Mr. Franse . . . had left the Club 82 at 82 East Fourth Street at 4:30 a.m planning to go to a restaurant at Fifty-ninth Street and

---

[*] In October 1963, Valachi, a member of the Genovese crime family, testified before Senator John McClellan's committee and was the first major underworld figure to publicly acknowledge, under oath and on television, that the Mafia existed.

Madison Avenue." Wherever and however Franse was killed, he was one dead man.[605]

Numerous Greenwich Village nightspots were reputed to be mob-run operations. Tony Pastor's Downtown, at 130 West 3rd Street, decorated with red-painted walls, was a popular lesbian hangout that flourished during the 1930s and '40s. During the postwar period, the Moroccan Village, at 23 West 8th Street, featured drag performers and reputedly came under FBI scrutiny. The San Remo, at 93 Mac-Dougal Street, was another gay-friendly hangout also popular with Beat writers like Jack Kerouac and Allen Ginsberg.

Still other reputed mob-run gay hangouts included: the Purple Onion, at 135 West 3rd Street; the Washington Square controlled by the Gallo family; and the Bon Soir, at 40 West 8th Street, where Barbra Streisand got her start. Julius, on 159 West 10th Street, off Waverly Place, dated from 1864; it witnessed one of the earliest gay-rights sit-ins when, on April 26, 1966, four "homophile activists" staged a "sip in" challenging the state liquor authority's regulation prohibiting bars and restaurants from serving homosexuals. Still other gay-friendly clubs included the Snake Pit, the Sewer, the Checkerboard, the Tele-Star, and the Tenth of Always where only their names and reputations persist. In the early hours of June 28, 1969, the tension between the mob, New York police, and gay club patrons exploded at the Stonewall bar at 51–53 Christopher Street.[606]

The New York mob reached its pinnacle of power during the late '50s; it was, as C. Alexander Hortis writes, "fat, prosperous, and growing." It had a grip on important businesses, influenced union officials and politicians, and controlled the illegal drug trade. This success led to intense conflict not only between families, but among individual family "bosses" for greater control of the cash-rich operations. The war between Costello and Genovese for control of the Luciano family came to a head on May 2, 1957, when a gunman shot (but only wounded) Costello in the lobby of his luxurious Central Park West apartment building. A series of other mob killings captured media attention, including that of Frank Scalise in the Bronx on June 17 and Albert (Umberto) Anastasia—famously depicted in the *Godfather*—in the barbershop of the Park Sheraton hotel at 870 Seventh Ave. on October 25.[607]

Senator Kefauver's hearings on organized crime in America made Costello and other mob bosses media celebrities. Seven years later, in June to July '58, Senator McClellan again held hearings into organized crime and this time Genovese was subpoenaed to testify. Joining John McClellan was the young, handsome and ambitious Senator from Massachusetts, John F. Kennedy. The exchange between the new gladiators, Kennedy and Genovese, suggested the mob's future in the United States:

KENNEDY: She [Anna Genovese] also testified on page 4 that in addition to the Italian lottery, he [Vito Genovese] has racetracks, gambling interests, dog interests, piers . . . . Would you tell us about that?

GENOVESE: I respectfully decline to answer on the ground my answer may tend to incriminate me.

. . .

KENNEDY: Then she made some interesting statements also about the operation of some nightclubs in New York.

GENOVESE: I respectfully decline to answer on the ground my answer may tend to incriminate me.

KENNEDY: I will read you some of those. This is just a list. Here, for instance, was a question: "Do you have a piece or a part of the Club Caravan?" And the answer: "I did not; that was part of the syndicate. That belonged to his brother Mike, and all of those nightclubs." What is the syndicate she was referring to?

GENOVESE: I respectfully decline to answer on the ground that my answer may tend to incriminate me.

In two short years, Kennedy would be elected president of the United States.

CONCLUSION

SIN, THE NEW NORMAL

New Normal

New York is a different city in 2015 than it was in the 1950s. Then, it was the capital of the twentieth century, the locus of American life, and hub of the great postwar capitalist recovery. Today, it retains preeminence in financial services, media, and glamour, but its relative standing has been eclipsed both domestically and internationally. The growth of strong regional metropolises like Miami, Dallas, Chicago, Los Angeles, San Francisco, Seattle, and Washington, DC, has eroded its national hegemony. The restructuring of the global economic order has left the Big Apple a stepping-stone to Shanghai, the likely capital of the twenty-first century.

In the '50s, the city was home to 135 of the nation's largest industrial companies as well as having the world's biggest port, accounting for more than 40 percent of the nation's shipping. Today, US industrial production has been outsourced to China and other developing countries and the nation's busiest container port is Los Angeles, which is ranked nineteenth in the world, way below #1 Shanghai. The city remains the world media capital, home to the leading print, online, and TV companies as well as ad agencies; Wall Street and the City of London battle over which is the world's financial center.

Nevertheless, New York's skyline—from the Empire State Building to the post-9/11 One World Trade Center's Freedom Tower and the Statue of Liberty—remains the iconic image of global power.[608]

Six decades ago, the city's population stood at 7.9 million; in 2010, 8.2 million people called New York home. While not a major change in total population (4 percent), the city's demographic composition fundamentally changed. A half century ago, nine out of ten (7.1 million) New Yorkers were white, but drawn from different nationalities, ethnic backgrounds, and religious affiliations. In those days, such distinctions mattered; neighborhoods were Balkanized into ghettos for Germans, Irish, Italians, and Jews. And white people knew their differences.

In the twenty-first century, race matters. In 2010, whites made up either 44 percent (all whites) or 33 percent (non-Hispanic whites) of the population. In 1950, "Negros" were the second-largest population segment, accounting for less than 10 percent, about 750,000 people; in 2010, there were 2.1 million black people in the city, a quarter (26 percent) of the city's population. A half century ago, Puerto Ricans were not differentiated but included in the "white and Negro Totals" category and totaled just less than 250,000 people; in 2010, Hispanic/Latinos accounted for 2.3 million New Yorkers (28 percent). And in '50, there were only 21,400 Asians reported living in the city; in 2010, the Asian population totaled one million (12 percent).[609]

For all the city's apparent economic prowess of the '50s, it was suffering. Suburbanization was taking its toll on urban centers throughout the country and in New York it hit hard in Times Square and Harlem. The city witnessed mass "white flight," propelled by the GI Bill and Robert Moses's mad reconstruction of the New York's transport infrastructure and parks. Whereas Paris, during its postwar reconstruction, pushed the poor to the city's periphery, postwar America lured white, middle-class city dwellers to the Levittown suburbs sprawling across the country. Social life was being re-centered, shifting from the city to the 'burbs. Private homes, cars, TVs, and malls became the new American reality. Slowly, as many warned, people began to suffocate under the Leave it to Beaver ideology defining the good life, and inner cities—including New York's—were left to rot.

In the last half century, the American social landscape changed. Today, the suburbs are so *yesterday*. Postmodern, twenty-first-century life is once again lived in the city, whether San Francisco or Ashville, Seattle or Austin, but especially in New York and, in particular, Brooklyn; the hippest part of Paris is the once-gritty suburb of Pantin, now known as *Brooklyn*. One can only wonder whether, amid the current wave of the "suburbanization of poverty," the pushing of the poor out of the inner city to stagnant in peripheral towns, will whites repopulate New York by, say, 2025?[610]

A Steak

On Tuesday night, October 16, 1951, Josephine Baker, an African American entertainer and actress celebrated in Paris, was dining at the Stork Club's exclusive Cub Room. She'd come to the club, accompanied by three friends, following her sold-out performance at the Roxy Theatre. According to the *Daily News*, "They ordered drinks, which arrived. They ordered steaks, which an hour later had not."[611]

John Sherman Billingsley, know to all as "Sherm," opened the Stork Club in 1929 at 132 West 58th Street and, for over a quarter century, ran it as one of the city's grandest saloons. Sherm loved the limelight and, although married, was a notorious stage door Romeo. His original two partners, pals from his early Oklahoma gin-running days, sold their interest to a mysterious investor, one Thomas Healy. He wanted to be a silent partner, holding only a 30 percent stake in the venture and no questions asked. Shortly thereafter, Sherm found that his silent partner represented none other than the notorious Madden gang, led by Owney "The Killer" Madden. When Billingsley attempted to break the deal, one of the gangsters informed him: "We didn't pay $10,000 for an interest in the business. We paid ten for a 30 percent interest in everything you do for the rest of your life."[612] So much for a silent partner.

Sherm and the club were Broadway icons until it closed in 1965. Early on, he regularly visited Texan Guinan's speakeasies and, when he had trouble filling the house during its difficult early days, Tex sent the young gossip columnist Walter Winchell over to do a story on the city's newest, hottest nightspot. The story put the Stork Club on the map. Like other *speaks*, however, Prohibition agents repeatedly closed it down. After one raid, Sherm moved the club to, first, 51 1/2 East 51st Street, and then, in 1934, to 3 East 53rd Street where it remained a fixture of café society for decades.

The Cub Room—disparaged as the "snub" room by those excluded—was the club's most exclusive section, its inner sanctum, located just inside the front door, was separated off by an allegedly solid gold chain. Only Sherm's best customers got in and, of course, they included anybody with fame, fortune, or a gun in their pocket. Over the years, the Stork offered fine food that emphasized French cuisine. Its most famous contribution to popular dining was the chicken hamburger that combined boned and ground chicken mixed with salt, pepper, nutmeg, butter, heavy cream, and breadcrumbs. It was served with tomato sauce, french-fried sweet potatoes and buttered green peas. It became a late-night delicacy.[613]

Fatefully, that October 1951 night, after drinks, the waiter served Baker's companions but did not deliver her meal, a steak and crab salad. Baker took umbrage when her white dinner companions— Mr. and Mrs. Roger Rico from Paris (Rico, a bass singer, had recently replaced Ezio Pinza in South Pacific)—received their meals before her and her friend, Bessie Buchanan, an African American woman, former Broadway dancer, and political activist.* Baker took the incident as a racial insult, something that would not happen in Paris. Angered, the two black women walked out in protest. Over the next few days, word of the incident spread, taken up by the NAACP, local papers, and the gossip columnist Ed Sullivan.

Baker was no ordinary entertainer, an accommodating black celebrity. Growing up in Saint Louis, she fled the city following the 1917 race riot and relocated to New York as a song-and-dance performer, even appearing on Broadway in blackface.[614] She fled to

---

* Bessie Buchanan, a prominent Harlem socialite and former chorus-line dancer who performed in *Shuffle Along* and at the Cotton Club, was elected to the state Assembly in 1954, the first African American woman to hold the position.

Paris, ultimately staring in a number called "Danse Sauvage" that was set in an African jungle and appeared in the legendary Folies Bergère. Biography Phyllis Rose argues that Baker reconceptualized the image of the female black entertainers. "With her sophistication and couture wardrobe, her act now in every way called attention to her artifice, the triumph of art over nature," she notes.[615]

In the wake of Germany's invasion of France, Baker worked for the Resistance and, using her performance tours as a cover, carried coded messages written in invisible ink to underground members throughout Europe. She finally fled France, returning to the United States but to a far less welcoming environment. Legal historian Mary Dudziak notes, "She [Baker] and her white husband, Jo Bouillon, were refused service by thirty-six New York hotels." She was a strong advocate for racial justice, supporting the family of Willie McGee, an African American executed for allegedly raping a white woman, by paying for his funeral; she appeared at the trial of the Trenton Six in support of the African American men accused of murdering a white shop owner; and she also attempted to integrate a Washington, DC, whites-only soda fountain at the Hecht department store. In recognition of her effort, the NAACP held a "Josephine Baker Day" on May 20, 1951.[616]

Winchell was one of the nation's leading twentieth-century "pundits," a gossip columnist. Burt Lancaster, as J. J. Hunsecker, immortalizes him in the 1957 movie *Sweet Smell of Success*. He began his career reporting for the *New York Graphic* and, in '29, was hired by Hearst's *Daily Mirror*. For the next half century, he held court at the Stork Club's Table 50. At his peak, Winchell reportedly reached fifty million people—a third of the nation's population—through his daily column, "On-Broadway," syndicated to two thousand newspapers. His Sunday nationwide radio program famously began, "Mr. and Mrs. North and South America and all ships at sea . . . Let's go to press!"

In the late '30s, Winchell became a close associate of FBI director J. Edgar Hoover. According to Curt Gentry, "Unquestionably each used the other. It was Winchell, more than any other journalist, who sold the G-man image to America." In the '50s, Winchell was a fervent anticommunist, a staunch supporter of Senator Joe McCarthy and a social friend of Roy Cohn, McCarthy's assistant. During the Army-McCarthy hearings, Cohn apparently provided Winchell with supposedly secret documents that Winchell, in turn, alluded to in his newspaper columns. Following the hearings, he was subpoenaed to testify before a Senate panel, the Watkins Committee, which censured McCarthy in '54.[617] It marked the nadir of Winchell's career.

Baker's apparent racial insult became the talk of the town and Winchell was torn. He was at the Stork that night and greeted Baker when she arrived; when he left, he passed her and Rico making calls on the club's pay phone. Winchell initially denied his presence at the club and, after being caught, argued that he knew little of what actually happened. He casually knew Baker and was considered a liberal on the race issue, sympathetic to her concern. But he was deeply in debt to Sherm and the Stork for his career and ongoing access to celebrities. He attempted to square the circle, defending the club, wondering if Baker was too racially sensitive. Faced with strong reaction to his sentiment, he went on the offensive. He contacted Hoover, requesting substantiation of Baker's relations with the CP. The FBI provided him with long-forgotten Baker quotes from before the war praising Mussolini and even had Sugar Ray Robinson defend him. Baker sued Winchell, but the suit was dismissed. Adding insult to injury, Rico was fired from "South Pacific."

The Stork Club incident became a national litmus test when it was picked up by *Confidential*, a rightwing Los Angeles gossip tabloid published by Robert Harrison. In its coverage, Baker was described as a "phoney" and "outright liar" who was motivated "for her own cynical ends." According to one review, Harrison "suggested [she] was a Communist."[618] Still others picked up the story, including Lyle Stuart, a legendary Gotham independent publisher who had earlier worked with both Samuel Roth and Bill Gaines. In 1951, Stuart launched *Exposé*, a monthly political newsletter that repeatedly covered the episode. He distributed the newsletter featuring the Baker story at Times Square newsstands and it ultimately sold 91,000 copies. Roth offered him $1,000 to expand the articles into a book that became *The Secret Life of Walter Winchell*, published in 1953. Winchell used his national media pulpit to attack Stuart who, in term, sued him for libel. In '55, Stuart won a tax-free $40,000 libel award against Winchell.[619]

Winchell also attacked Samuel Roth, calling him "scummy" and the "King of Pornography."[620] Winchell retained Howard Rushmore to investigate Roth and his wife and son, Peggy and Richard, and Rushmore sent Winchell a *Confidential* article, "America on Guard! Sam Roth the Louse of Lewisburg," which he may have written. One of Rushmore's reports illuminates the tenor of the period: "That ex-convict publisher, who publishes trash (by an ex-convict extortionist) also published a book by Hitler's exhelper, George Sylvester Viereck. His name is Samuel Roth of New York and Lewisburg Federal Penitentiary. This louse (in 1948) was quoted as saying that Alger Hiss was telling the truth. (I have the proof, Chump.)" Rushmore was particularly disturbed by Roth's support for Hiss.[621]

Analysis

During the '50s, the city was the epicenter of two "wars"—a "cold war" waged against subversion and a "hot war" against sin. Now, the Soviet Union has been discarded to the dustbin of history and radical culture has been integrated into the marketplace. During the battles of the '50s, many paid dearly, some with their lives. Looking back, one has to ask why?

This book assesses these twin wars as, metaphorically, two sides of the same historical experience. It focuses on three interlinked threads—sin, sex, and subversion. Many other threads are not explored, like infrastructure (e.g., roadways), business (e.g., banking), and government (e.g., elections). Each thread includes a series of separate strands that illuminate aspects of New York life during the critical 1950s, each that challenging the dominant moral order. The individual outsiders who anchor each chapter were, not surprisingly, often overwhelmed by the challenges they confronted. With few exceptions, those profiled did not personally know any of the others profiled. New York was a big city.

Can one make a connection between the 1950s and 2015? At best, it would be less a line, however uneven, than a foreshadowing, or a historical anticipation of what would—unknowable at the time—come. The profiles presented occurred essentially historically simultaneously, yet were mostly separate and distinct. The book's three analytic threads include a series of strands that, individually, explore a social issue that has shaped the United States since WWII. These strands, and the individuals who anchor the analysis, are summarized as follows:

Sin:

- Gender—Christine Jorgensen: if science could alter one's biological sex, what was fixed, unalterable? Today, Chelsea Manning and Caitlyn Jenner are just two of a growing number of Americans (including children) undergoing gender reassignment.
- Moral corruption—William Gaines: if comic books could inspire teens to crime and illicit sex, what was innocent? In 2014, New York's Comic Con drew 151,000 attendees.
- Obscene images—Irving Klaw: if Bettie Page and others in the porn racket were hounded, sometimes busted, how did "pornography" gain ever-greater popularity? Today, porn is a $12-plus billion business.
- Prurient words—Samuel Roth: if publishing or saying "dirty" words could get one a federal prison sentence, why did writers continue to write and publishes continue to publish? And readers continue to avidly read obscene works? The phenomenal success of E. L. James's *Fifty Shades of Grey* books and movie knockoff shows how porn has gone mainstream.

Sex:

- Prostitution—Polly Adler: if people can sell their labor power for wages, why can't they sell themselves for sex? While illegal throughout the country, prostitution is estimated to be an $18 billion business.
- Homosexuality—Liberace: the June 2015 Supreme Court decision legalizing gay marriage ends the all-too-long characterization of homosexuality as a sin, perversion, or pathology.

- Performance—Club 82 female impersonators: if gender reassignment is accepted, cross-dressing seems so '50s. Live sex shows, especially in drag have become just another Vegas spectacles, a form of showmanship, no longer illicit, illegal, or perverse.
- Identity—Milton Berle: if traditional conventions are challenged, how are masculinity and femininity defined?; a new value system has taken hold, one reminiscent of Kinsey's seven-point scale of human sexual identity.
- Sexuality—Wilhelm Reich: if nature is in crisis, why not human nature, the living, erotic body? Yet, with greater freedom of sexual expression, practice has been increasingly disciplined, like a circus animal performance.
- Birth control—Margaret Sanger: for millennia, the moral order subordinated sex to the demands of procreation, seeing sex for pleasure a sin. Contraceptives are one example of the human ability to regulate nature.

Subversion:

- Culture—Times Square: '50s street culture of seedy, immoral indulgences gave illicit pleasure its edge. What happens when the unacceptable goes mainstream and is integrated into the marketplace?
- Loyalty—Julius and Ethel Rosenberg: who is a national-security threat? Today, one wonders who is a real enemy and who is being used by those in power as a pseudo-enemy?
- Race—Paul Robeson: why do "police lynchings," the killing of unarmed men of color, persist? Will the race question be superseded by the inequality issue?
- Criticism—Howard Fast: what can be said? What are the limits of free speech in a democracy? Who sets the limit to free expression on an individual's ability to nonviolently challenge established authority?
- Crime—Frank Costello: if someone can make money from what is unacceptable, why does it remain so? Attempts to police morality have repeated failed as the wars on crime, on drugs, on commercial sex—and other vices—continue to fail.

The dozen or so individuals profiled in this book suggest a range of experiences—personal, social, and political—faced by those who challenged convention during the tumultuous '50s. A few—Milton Berle's comedy and Margaret Sanger's pill—found success during their lifetime with American society adopting their unacceptable as normal. Other outsiders profiled suffered—and often lost—in their battles challenging the accepted moral order. Julius and Ethel Rosenberg were executed; Samuel Roth, Howard Fast, and Wilhelm Reich went to federal prison; William Gaines, Paul Robeson, and Frank Costello were forced to testify before federal investigations. Still others faced endless persecution but survived. Christine Jorgensen faced insurmountable odds and became a media celebrity; today, there are an estimated 700,000 trans people live in the United States. While Liberace could not accept his "gay" being, homosexuality is now an all-American identity. And Polly Adler's commercial sex is acceptable as long as its "consensual" and age appropriate.

Outsiders

New York is a city of "outsiders," of people who don't quite fit in and who, through the force of personality and belief, promote changes of the moral order. Since its founding in 1608, Gotham has celebrated—and scorned—outsiders as mavericks and rule-breakers, deviants and bohemians, activists, rebels, and radicals, gangsters, wackos, nonconformists, perverts, undesirables, outliers, and outlaws. Those with power, whether moral, financial, or political, have long sought to determine what was acceptable and restrict those who questioned their rule, often forcefully suppressing those who challenged their authority. Yet, over time, the establishment's power was undermined and the moral order profoundly shifted.

All-too-many conventional portraits of the Big Apple focus on the city's legendary gentry. This is the grand American aristocracy, the old money of Astor, Carnegie, the Rockefellers, and the Vanderbilts as well as the new *nouveau riche* like Bloomberg and Koch. They embody wealth and power; their names denote some of the city's grandest institutions, including libraries, concert halls, and university buildings. However, there are other people, *outsiders*, often forgotten, who've left their own—if less visible, no less important—imprint on city life.

In the '50s, the nation was at war with itself. The media presented the Ozzie & Harriet suburban world of peace, prosperity, and conformity as the social norm. It represented the moral order, signifying the fulfillment of progress, the American Dream. Amid this cultural fiction, proponents of the old moral order, with roots reaching back to the Puritans, were resurgent, driven by the twin fears of Communism and immorality. For them, such moral corruption undermined all aspects of American life, from geopolitics to family relations to personal sex. The campaign against these threats involved the US Congress and law enforcement throughout the country as well as pundits, preachers, school officials, and ordinary citizens. This moral revenge culminated in the execution of two American citizens, Julius and Ethel Rosenberg, for refusing to name names.

New York outsiders of the '50s challenged the accepted moral order, whether involving sin, sex, or subversion. They included publishers, musicians, performers, writers, club owners, labor organizers, scholars, shopkeepers, school teachers, photographers and filmmakers, scientists, inventors, strippers, pansies, politicians, revolutionaries, hookers, drag queens, hustlers, and, most importantly, ordinary adults seeking an unconventional good time or expressing unacceptable thoughts, aesthetically or politically. Many were single WWII veterans, others were married couples, homosexuals, and innumerable other deviants and dissidents. Some were communists, denounced as Soviet sympathizers; others were accused of corrupting the nation's youth; many were arrested, convicted, and imprisoned for violating decency and espionage laws. Many lost their jobs and went to jail; a few were successful, many long forgotten, others immortal. Some outsiders embraced their subversive role, fully cognizant of their place in the social crisis remaking the nation; others insisted they were merely expressing their rights to free expression and a free market. Nevertheless, their efforts incubated the unacceptable.

A story from old claims that Henry Hudson served gin to a party of Lenape Indians in 1608 on what is today's Manhattan Island.

According to this legend, "the Indians passed out, to a man." The often-forgotten part of the story is that the Lenape named the place "Manahachtanienk"—*the island where we all became intoxicated.* New York outsiders have been pushing the limits ever since.

Resistance to the status quo, to the established moral and political order, began to bubble up in the 1960s. On Easter Sunday, March 28, 1967, ten thousand instrument playing, joyously singing, wildly dancing, and marijuana smoking people, all sporting brightly colored outfits, jammed the Central Park Sheep Meadow for one of the nation's earliest Be-Ins. As the *Village Voice* reported, "Bonfires burned on the hills, their smoke mixing with bright balloons among the barren trees and high, high above kites wafted in the air. Rhythms and music and mantras from all corners of the meadow echoed in exquisite harmony, and thousands of lovers vibrated into the night. It was miraculous." Two weeks later, on April 15, between one hundred and four hundred thousand protesters (depending on source), including the Reverend Martin Luther King, Jr., Harry Belafonte, and Dr. Benjamin Spock, gathered in the park for one of the first mass anti-Vietnam War demonstrations. Something was happening in New York and throughout the nation.[622]

The Central Park Be-In was part of the '67 Summer of Love, a counterculture movement championing a new, sensuous, and ethical notion of pleasure. It proclaimed a sexual revolution, one that challenged traditional sexual customs and legal standards. Amid the more widespread revelry, including the seventy-five thousand people who gathered for San Francisco's Be-In in Golden Gate Park, a heretofore underground culture celebrating sexual pleasure went public. It included hippies, homos, nudists, swingers, and free lovers of every stripe. It was a sexual-freedom movement infused with the passion of civil-rights protesters, antiwar activists, feminist militants, and the emerging gay-rights movements. It vibrated with the excesses of drugs—from marijuana to peyote to LSD—and rock & roll. Often overlooked, in June 1967, the Supreme Court overturned, in *Loving v. Virginia,* a state statute barring interracial marriage as a violation of the Fourteenth Amendment.[623]

Behind this naïve, utopian optimism, a deeper crisis was brewing. The Vietnam War was faltering, exposed as a military disaster and a political nightmare. In March 1968, the US military committed one of the most egregious war crimes of the post-WWII era, the My Lai massacre. Economically, the war was a disaster. The postwar American Dream sank as the war's vast costs, in body count and endless expenses, mounted. Later in '68, Chicago hosted the Democratic National Convention that drew thousands of Vietnam War protesters who battled city police live on primetime, nationwide TV. It was followed by the infamous trial of the Chicago 8 (less one): David Dellinger, National Mobilization Committee; Rennie Davis and Thomas Hayden, Students for a Democratic Society; Abbie Hoffman and Jerry Rubin, Yippies (i.e., Youth International Party); and activists Lee Weiner and John Froines; Bobby Seale, leader of the Black Panther Party, was forcefully suppressed during the trial.

The Chicago trial played out against a deepening conservative backlash, one that would be formally articulated by Patrick Buchanan, a top advisor to President Richard Nixon, as the "Southern strategy." It was a devil's bargain struck by conservative and racist politicians with white voters to protect traditional "white skin privilege" through the ballet. It harnessed the deeply felt—and threatened—beliefs in racism, patriarchy, and homophobia into a powerful political movement that, four decades later, continues to wield considerable influence in the Republican Party. It's worked for decades and will likely be a key part in the Republican's 2016 campaign playbook.

Culture Wars & Outsiders

During the last century, the United States has suffered through three bitter culture wars. This book focuses on the second war that took place during the post-WWII era and the '50s, and that involved conflicts waged by conservatives against the threats of sin, sex, and subversion. The Christian right's effort faltered in the face of the failing Vietnam War and mounting social unrest, from inner-city uprisings, the counterculture, and a militant antiwar movement.

That second modern culture war was followed by today's third culture war, a powerful Christian conservative reaction to the 1973

Roe decision legalizing a woman's right to an abortion. This war is now in decline, as evidenced by changing public attitudes toward homosexuality, teen sex education, pornography, (adult) "consensual" commercial sex, and expanded free speech. However, bitter antiabortion moralists continue to oppose women's reproductive rights, especially at the state level. Parallel to this campaign, a vindictive Obama administration is out to get alleged "national security threats," whether whistleblower or "jihadists," while the threat from white-nationalist "terrorists" increases.

Transitional, "pre-modern" cultural wars took place between the end of Civil War era and the end of WWI. It was an era marked by rapid industrialization, vast immigration, and the rise of the Robber Barons. Vigorous antisex, antialcohol, and antiobscenity campaigns took place. Congress adopted the punitive Comstock obscenity laws in 1873, the 1910 Mann Act and, in 1919 and 1920, respectively, the Eighteenth Amendment prohibiting the sale of alcoholic beverages and the Nineteenth Amendment granting women the vote. The period saw thirty thousand alleged prostitutes rounded up during WWI as national security threats as possible syphilis carriers and antiwar activists arrested and hundreds of suspect aliens deported.[624] The failure of Prohibition and an ever-deepening Depression ended the first modern culture war of the late nineteenth and early twentieth centuries.

In the 1950s, New York was the epicenter of the second culture war, this one consisting of two "fronts"—a "cold war" waged against subversion and a "hot war" against sin. Each was a separate and distinct terrain of struggle; each marked by defining issues and staunch proponents. But they often overlapped, one reinforcing the other. Many in authority, whether elected official, preacher or pundit, equated illicit sex (e.g., homosexuality) with subversion (i.e., Communism). It was a period in which numerous people—outsiders, celebrated and anonymous—crisscrossed one another yet lived relatively separate lives, often with little or no knowledge of the others.

Could the '50s happen again? Could an African American celebrity like Josephine Baker be refused service in New York's finest establishment? Was the killing of a black Staten Island resident a "police lynching" and a direct result of the institutional racism embodied in Baker's steak? Can a new culture war—this one against an allegedly "national security threat," an immoral sinner, or a targeted minority—be waged again?

Sin, Sex & Subversion poses these questions, but does not offer answers. Rather, the book is a warning as to what once happened and could occur yet again. If it did it would affect many aspects of social life, involving celebrities and anonymous people alike. Politics is more than voting, more than who's in office; politics reverberates throughout cultural and personal life.

A critical reconsideration of the '50s makes clear that history is more than linear, more than a series of "tipping points." Events take place in tandem, simultaneous with other developments, serving as both causes and consequences. This process forges a momentum embodying often-contradictory forces, functioning like an historical glacier or tectonic plate that, over time, pushes society in an unplanned, unanticipated direction. New York during the '50s was witness to such a process, one defined by overlapping and contradictory struggles. No one of the '50s could have anticipated city life in the twenty-first century. It marked the beginning—and end—of the American Century.

The Bush-era culture wars are ebbing. Homosexuality is legal, teen sex-education has led to a decline in teen pregnancies, and adult "consensual" sex is a multibillion dollar enterprise; the notable exception remains a woman's right to terminate her pregnancy. Subversion is limited to the threats posed by jihadists, whistleblowers, radical environmentalists, white nationalists, and outright spies. The political system is beginning to fragment, with the far-right Republicans contesting progressive Democrats for ideological influence. This ideological contestation defines the new normal.

The outsiders of the '50s were mostly defeated, their threats temporarily suppressed. Some went to prison, others lost their livelihood, many were shamed, denounced as traitors; two were executed. Yet, like a smoldering wildfire, their spirit caught a forceful gust of wind from the growing civil-rights, counterculture, women's, gay-rights, and free-speech movements. It ignited a blaze that remade America. Collectively, they had a significant influence on city life, defining the twenty-first-century moral order. We live in their shadows.

BIBLIOGRAPHY

The bibliography is organized as follows:

Government Publications
Legal Cases
Books
Articles & Chapters
Newspapers
Online Publications
Websites
Manuscripts & Other Sources

Government Publications

Martha Alschuler, *The Origins of the Law of Obscenity*, Technical Report of the Commission on Obscenity and Pornography (Washington, DC: U.S. Government Printing Office, 1971).

Amara Bachu, U.S. Census Bureau, "Trends in Premarital Childbearing: 1930–1994," October 1999.

Central Intelligence Agency, "An Idiot System for Intelligence," September 22, 1993.

———— "Origins of the Congress for Cultural Freedom, 1949–50, Cultural Cold War." Executive Order 10450: Security requirements for Government employment (1953).

Federal Bureau of Investigation, FBI, "The Atomic Spy Case."

———— "Violent Crimes Against Children: Innocence Lost (June 2013).

———— "FBI Records: The Vault, "Custodial Detention Security Index."

Kristin Finklea, Adrienne L. Fernandes-Alcantara and Alison Siskin, "Sex Trafficking of Children in the United States: Overview and Issues for Congress Specialist in Immigration Policy," Congressional Research Service, January 28, 2015.

National Institutes of Health, "Crude birth rates, fertility rates, and birth rates, by age, race, and Hispanic origin of mother: United States, selected years 1950–2012."

National Security Act of 1947 (50 U.S.C. 401). Franklin D. Roosevelt, "Presidential Directive Of September 6, 1939."

Mitra Toossi, "A century of change: the U.S. labor force, 1950–2050," U.S. Bureau of Labor Statistics, Monthly Labor Review May 2002.

Siskin, Alison and Liana Sun Wyler, "Trafficking in Persons: U.S. Policy and Issues for Congress," Congressional Research Service, February 19, 2013.

U.S. Census Bureau, "Estimated Median Age at First Marriage: 1890 to present," Annual Social and Economic Supplements, 2014.

U.S. Department of Justice, "National Anti-Slavery and Human Trafficking Awareness Month Press Conference," January 15, 2013.

U.S. House of Representatives, Committee on Un-American Activities (HUAC) Hearing Regarding Espionage in the U.S. Government, 80th Congress (2nd Session), 1948.

—— HUAC, "The American Negro in the Communist Party" (1954).

—— HUAC, "Annual report for the year 1953."

—— HUAC, "Communist Activities Among Puerto Ricans in New York City and Puerto Rico" (1959).

—— HUAC, Alger Hiss, testimony (August 5,1948).

—— HUAC, John Howard Lawson, testimony, October 27, 1947.

—— HUAC, "Report on Civil Rights Congress as a communist front organization" (1947).

U.S. Senate, Hearings Before the Subcommittee to Investigate Juvenile Delinquency of the Judiciary, April 21, 22, and June 4, 1954.

—— Final Report, August 31, 1951.

—— Internal Security Subcommittee (SISS) Subversive Influence in the Educational Process (September 8, 1952 - September 15, 1953).

—— Motion pictures and juvenile delinquency: A part of the investigation of juvenile delinquency in the United States. (Report No. 2055) (Washington, DC: U.S. Government Printing Office, 1956).

—— Permanent Subcommittee on Investigations of the Committee on Government Operations (McCarthy Hearings 1953–54), vol. 1.

—— Special Committee on Organized Crime in Interstate Commerce (1950).

U.S. Department of Treasury, "History of 'In God We Trust.'" Elizabeth Waldman, "Labor force statistics perspective from a family perspective," Bureau of Labor Statistics (1983).

Richard H. Walker, "Testimony Concerning The Involvement of Organized Crime on Wall Street," House Subcommittee on Finance and Hazardous Materials, Committee on Commerce, September 13, 2000.

The White House, "The Obama Administration's Record on Human Trafficking Issues," April 9, 2013.

—— "Progress Report: The Obama Administration's Efforts to Combat Human Trafficking at Home and Abroad,"

Erin Wittkon, "President Proclaims National Slavery and Human Trafficking Prevention Month, Department of Defense, DoDLive, January 3, 2013.

Legal Cases

Adams Theatre Co. v. Keenan, 17 N.J. 267, 96 A.2d 519 (1953).

Brown v. Board of Education of Topeka, 347 U.S. 483 (1954).

Burstyn v. Wilson, 342 U.S. 495 (1952).

Byrne v. Karalexis [I Am Curious (yellow)], 396 U.S. 976 (1969) and 401 U.S. 216 (1971).

Chase Manhattan Bank v. New York World's Fair 1964–1965 Corporation et al., Defendants, 51 Misc.2d 673 (1966).

City of Renton v. Playtime Theatres, 475 U.S. 41 (1986).

Communist Party of the United States v. Subversive Activities Control Board, 351 U.S. 115 (1956).

Communist Party of the United States v. Subversive Activities Control Board, 367 U.S. 1 (1961).

Federal Communications Commission v. Pacifica Foundation, 438 U.S. 726 (1978).

Jacobellis v. Ohio 378 U.S. 184 (1964).

Kent v. Dulles, 357 U.S. 116 (1958).

Loving v. Virginia, 388 U.S. 1 (1967).

MANual Enterprises v. Day, 370 U.S. 478 (1962).

Miller v. California, 413 U.S. 15 (1973).

Mutual Film Corporation v. Industrial Commission of Ohio, 236 U.S. 230 (1915).

New York v. Feliciano, 10 Misc.2d 836 (1958).

New York v. Ferber, 458 U.S. 747 (1982).

People v Doyle, 304 N.Y. 120 (1952).

People v. Maggio, 11 N.Y.2d 1064 (1962).

Reno v. American Civil Liberties Union, 521 U.S. 844 (1997).

Roth v. U.S, 354 U.S. 476, 77 S.Ct. 1304 (1957).

BIBLIOGRAPHY

Schenck v. U.S., 249 U.S. 47 (1919).

State of Indiana v. Bei Bei Shuai, No. 49A02–1106-CR-486 (2012).

United States v. One Book Entitled Ulysses by James Joyce, 72 F.2d 705, 706 (1934).

United States v. Frank Costello, 350 U.S. 359 (1957).

United States v. One Package of Japanese Pessaries, 86 F.2d 737 (1936).

Wieman v. Updegraff, 344 U.S. 183 (1952).

Young v. American Mini Theatres, 427 U.S. 50 (1976).

Books

Polly Adler, *A House Is Not a Home* (New York: Popular Library, 1953).

Mariah Adlin, *The Brooklyn Thrill-Kill Gang and the Great Comic Book Scare of the 1950s* (New York: Praeger, 2014).

Robert C. Allen, *Horrible Prettiness: Burlesque and American Culture* (Chapel Hill: University of North Carolina Press, 1992).

Herbert Asbury, *The Gangs of New York: An Informal History of the Underworld* (New York: Free Press, 2001).

Beth Bailey, *Sex in the Heartland* (Cambridge, MA: Harvard University Press, 1999).

Michelle Baldwin, *Burlesque and the New Bump-n-Grind* (Sydney, Australia: Speck Press, 2004).

Harry Benjamin and Robert Edward Lee Masters, *Prostitution and Morality: A Definitive Report on the Prostitute in Contemporary Society and an Analysis of the Causes and Effects of the Suppression of Prostitution* (New York: Julian Press, 1964).

Milton Berle (with Haskel Frankel), *An Autobiography with Fifty Years of Photos* (NewYork: Delacorte Press, 1974).

William Berle and Brad Lewis, *My Father, Uncle Miltie* (New York: Barricade Books, 1999).

Iwan Block, *The Sexual Extremities of the World* (New York: Book Awards, 1964).

Ken Bloom, *Broadway: An Encyclopedic Guide to the History, People and Place of Times Square* (New York: Facts on File, 1991).

Ralph Blumenthal, *The Stork Club: America's Most Famous Nightspot and the Lost World of Café Society* (New York: Little, Brown & Company, 2000).

Norman O. Brown, *Life Against Death: The Psychoanalytic Meaning of History* (Middletown, CT: Wesleyan University Press, 1985).

Vern Bullough, *Science in the Bedroom: A History of Sex Research* (New York: Basic Books, 1994).

Edwin G. Burrows and Mike Wallace, *Gotham: A History of New York City to 1898* (New York: Oxford University Press, 1999).

David Carter, *Stonewall: The Riots That Sparked the Gay Revolution* (New York: Macmillan, 2010).

David Caute, *The Great Fear: The Anti-Communist Purge Under Truman and Eisenhower* (New York: Simon and Schuster, 1978).

Jerome Charyn, *Gangsters and Gold Diggers: Old New York, the Jazz Age, and the Birth of Broadway* (New York: Thunder Mouth Press, 2005).

George Chauncey, *Gay New York: Gender, Urban Culture, and the Making of the Gay Male World, 1890–1940* (New York: Basic Books, 1994).

Ellen Chesler, *Woman of Valor: Margaret Sanger and the Birth of the Birth Control Movement in America* (New York: Simon & Schuster, 1992).

Kim Christy, *The Complete Reprint of Exotique: The First 36 Issues, 1951–1957* (New York: Taschen America, 1998).

Ward Churchill and Jim Vander Wall, *The COINTELPRO Papers: Documents from the FBI's Secret Wars Against Dissent in the United States* (Boston: South End Press, 1990).

John Cooney, *The American Pope: The Life and Times of Francis Cardinal Spellman* (New York: Times Books, 1984).

Richard J. Corber, *Homosexuality in the Cold War: Resistance and the Crisis of Masculinity* (Durham, NC: Duke University Press, 1997).

Paul Cressey, *Taxi-Dance Hall: A Sociological Study in Commercialized Recreation and City Life* (Chicago: University of Chicago Press, 1932).

BIBLIOGRAPHY

Simone de Beauvoir, *The Second Sex* (New York: Vintage, 1953).

Phillip Deery, *Red Apple: Communism and McCarthyism in Cold War New York* (New York: Fordham University Press, 2014).

Kelly Dennis, *Art/Porn: The History of Seeing and Touching* (London: Berg Publishers, 2009).

John D'Emilio, *Sexual Politics, Sexual Communities* (Chicago: University of Chicago Press, 1983).

John D'Emilio and Estelle B. Freedman, *Intimate Matters: A History of Sexuality in America* (New York: Harper & Row, 1988).

Samuel R. Delany, *Times Square Red, Times Square Blue* (New York: New York University Press, 1999).

Nelson A. Denis, *War Against All Puerto Ricans: Revolution and Terror in America's Colony* (New York: Nation Books, 2015).

Richard F. Docter, *Becoming a Woman: A Biography of Christine Jorgensen* (New York: Hawthorn Press/ Routledge, 2008).

Ann Douglas, *Terrible Honesty: Mongrel Manhattan in the 1920s* (New York: Farrar, Straus and Giroux, 1995).

Martin Duberman, *Paul Robeson: A Biography* (New York: Ballantine Books, 1989).

——— *Stonewall (*New York: Penguin, 1993).

Jonathan Eig, *The Birth of the Pill: How Four Crusaders Reinvented Sex and Launched a Revolution* (New York: Norton, 2014).

Jack El-Hai, *The Laboromist: A Maverick Medical Genius and His Tragic Quest to Rid the World of Mental Illness* (New York: John Wiley, 2005).

Marc Eliot, *Down 42nd Street: Sex, Money, Culture, and Politics at the Crossroads of the World* (New York: Warner Books, 1991).

Lewis A. Erenberg, *Steppin' Out: New York Nightlife and the Transformation of American Culture* (Chicago: University of Chicago Press, 1984).

Lillian Faderman, *Odd Girls and Twilight Lovers: A History of Lesbian Life in Twentieth-Century America* (New York: Columbia University Press, 1991).

Howard Fast, *Citizen Tom Paine* (New York: Duell, Sloan & Pearce, 1943).

Richard Foster, *The Real Bettie Page: The Truth About the Queen of the Pinups* (New York: Citadel Press, 2005).

Betty Friedan, *The Feminine Mystique* (New York: Norton, 1963).

Monroe Fry, *Sex, Vice, and Business* (New York: Ballantine, 1959).

Jonathan Gathorne-Hardy, *Alfred C. Kinsey: Sex the Measure of All Things, A Biography (*London: Pimlicio, 1999).

Curt Gentry, *J. Edgar Hoover: The Man and the Secrets* (New York: Norton, 1991).

Jay A. Gertzman, *Bookleggers and Smuthounds: The Trade in Erotica, 1920–1940* (Philadelphia: University of Pennsylvania Press, 1999).

Timothy Gilfoyle, *City of Eros: New York City, Prostitution, and the Commercialization of Sex, 1790–1920* (New York: Norton, 1992).

——— *A Pickpocket's Tale: The Underworld of Nineteenth-Century New York* (New York: W. W. Norton, 2007).

Dorothy Butler Gillman, *Paul Robeson: All-American* (Washington, DC: New Republic Books, 1978).

Barbara Gordon, *Woman's Body, Woman's Rights: A Social History of Birth Control in America* (New York: Grossman, 1976).

David Hajdu, *The Ten-Cent Plague: The Great Comic-Book Scare and How It Changed America* (New York: Farrar, Straus and Giroux, 2008).

David Halberstam, *The Fifties* (New York: Fawcett Books, 1993).

John Heidenry, *What Wild Ecstasy: The Rise and Fall of the Sexual Revolution* (New York: Simon & Schuster, 1997).

Marjorie Heins, *Priests of Our Democracy: The Supreme Court, Academic Freedom,and the Anti-Communist Purge* (New York: New York University Press, 2013).

Harald Hellmannzsh, *The Best of American Girlie Magazines* (Cologne, Germany: Taschen, 1997).

Daniel Horowitz, *Betty Friedan and the Making of* The Feminine Mystique: *The American Left, the Cold War, and Modern Feminism* (Amherst: University of Massachusetts Press, 1998).

BIBLIOGRAPHY

C. Alexander Hortis, *The Mob and the City: The Hidden History of How the Mafia Captured New York* (Amherst, NY: Prometheus Books, 2014).

Diana Emery Hulick, *Diane Arbus and Her Imagery* (Princeton, 1984).

Janice M. Irvine, *Disorders of Desire: Sex and Gender in Modern American Sexology* (Philadelphia: Temple University Press, 1990).

Kenneth T. Jackson, ed., *The Encyclopedia of New York City* (New Haven: Yale University Press, 1995).

Russell Jacoby, *Social Amnesia: A Critique of Contemporary Psychology from Adler to Laing* (Boston: Beacon Press, 1975).

James H. Jones, *Alfred C. Kinsey: A Public/Private Life* (New York: W. W. Norton, 1997).

Charles Kaiser, *The Gay Metropolis: 1940–1996* (Boston: Houghton Mifflin, 1997).

Elizabeth Lapovsky Kennedy and Madeline Davis, *Boots of Leather, Slippers of Gold: The History of a Lesbian Community* (New York: Penguin, 1993).

Jack Kerouac, *On the Road* (New York: Viking, 1957).

Ronald Kessler, *The Bureau: The Secret History of the FBI* (New York: St. Martin's, 2002).

Alfred Kinsey, Wardell B. Pomeroy, and Clyde E. Martin, *Sexual Behavior in the Human Male* (Philadelphia: W. B. Saunders Company, 1948).

Alfred C. Kinsey, Wardell B. Pomeroy, Clyde E. Martin, and Paul H. Gebhard, *Sexual Behavior in the Human Female* (Philadelphia: W. B. Saunders Company, 1953).

Eric Kroll, *The Complete Reprint of John Willie's Bizarre* (2 Volumes) (Los Angeles: Taschen, 1996).

Richard Kuh, *Foolish Figleaves?: Pornography in and out of Court* (New York: Macmillan, 1967).

A. H. Lawrence, *Duke Ellington and His World: A Biography* (New York: Routledge, 2001).

Craig Loftin, *Masked Voices: Gay Men and Lesbians in Cold War America* (Albany: State University of New York Press, 2012).

Kat Long, *The Forbidden Apple: A Century of Sex & Sin in New York City* (New York: Ig Publishing, 2009).

John Loughery, *The Other Side of Silence—Men's Lives and Gay Identities: A Twentieth-Century History* (New York: Henry Holt, 1998).

Steven Luber, *Infoculture: The Smithsonian Book of Information Age Inventions* (Boston: Houston Mifflin, 1993).

Herbert Marcuse, *Eros & Civilization: A Philosophic Inquiry into Freud.* (New York: Vintage Books, 1962).

Neil Miller, *Sex-crime Panic: A Journey to the Paranoid Heart of the 1950s* (Los Angeles: Alyson Books, 2002).

Herbert Mitgang, *Once Upon a Time in New York: Jimmy Walker, Franklin Roosevelt, and the Last Great Battle of the Jazz Age* (New York: Simon & Schuster, 2000).

Bill Morgan, *The Beat Generation in New York: A Walking Tour of Jack Kerouac's City* (San Francisco: City Lights Books, 1997).

Lloyd Morris, *Incredible New York: High Life and Low Life from 1850 to 1950* (Syracuse, NY: Syracuse University Press, 1996).

Eddie Muller and Daniel Faris, *Grindhouse: The Forbidden World of "Adults Only" Cinema* (Gordonsville, VA: St. Martin's Press, 1996).

David Nasaw, *Going Out: The Rise and Fall of Public Amusements* (New York: Basic Books, 1993).

Victor Navasky, *Naming Names* (New York: Penguin Books, 1981).

William E. Nelson, *The Legalist Reformation: Law, Politics, and Ideology in New York, 1920–1980* (Chapel Hill: University of North Carolina, 2011).

Amy K. Nyberg, *Seal of Approval: The History of the Comics Code* (Jackson, MS: University Press of Mississippi, 1998).

Richard O'Connor, *Hell's Kitchen: The Riotous Days of New York's West Side* (New York: Lippincott, 1958).

Gilbert Osofsky, *Harlem: The Making of a Ghetto, Negro New York, 1890–1930* (New York: Harper & Row, 1971).

Laurence O'Toole, *Pornocopia: Porn, Sex, Technology and Desire* (London: Serpent's Tail, 1998).

James Petersen, *The Century of Sex: Playboy's History of the Sexual Revolution* (New York: Grove Press, 1999).

Kathy Peiss, *Zoot Suit: The Enigmatic Career of an Extreme Style* (Philadelphia: University of Pennsylvania Press, 2011).

BIBLIOGRAPHY

Burton W. Peretti, *Nightclub City: Politics and Amusement in Manhattan* (Philadelphia: University of Pennsylvania Press, 2007).

Darden Asbury Pyron, *Liberace: An American Boy* (Chicago: University of Chicago Press, 2000).

Leslie Reagan, *When Abortion Was a Crime: Women, Medicine, and Law in the United States, 1867–1973* (Berkeley, CA: University of California Press, 1996).

Ilse Ollendorff Reich, *Wilhelm Reich: A Personal Biography* (New York: St. Martin's Press, 1969).

Wilhelm Reich, *The Bioelectrical Investigation of Sexuality and Anxiety* (New York: Farrar, Straus, and Giroux, 1982).

David Riesman, with Nathan Glazer and Reuel Denney, *The Lonely Crowd* (New Haven, CT: Yale University Press, 1950).

Paul Robeson, *Here I Stand* (Boston: Beacon Press, 1958).

Paul Robinson, *The Modernization of Sex* (New York: Harper & Row, 1976).

David Rosen, *Sex Scandals America: Politics & The Ritual of Public Shaming* (Toronto: Key Publishing, 2009).

Ruth Rosen, *The Lost Sisterhood: Prostitution in America, 1900–1918* (Baltimore: Johns Hopkins University Press, 1982).

Samuel Roth, *Jews Must Live* (New York: Golden Hind Press, 1934).

Luc Sante, *Low Life: Lures and Snares of Old New York* (New York: Farrar, Straus, and Giroux, 1991).

Eric C. Schneider, *Vampires, Dragons, and Egyptian Kings: Youth Gangs in Postwar New York* (Princeton, NJ: Princeton University Press, 1999).

Walter Schneir, *Final Verdict: What Really Happened in the Rosenberg Case* (New York: Melville House, 2010).

Hal Sears, *The Sex Radicals: Free Love in High Victorian America* (Lawrence: The Regents Press of Kansas, 1977).

Joel Seidman, *American Labor from Defense to Reconversion* (Chicago: University of Chicago Press, 1953).

Myron Sharaf, *Fury on Earth: A Biography of Wilhelm Reich* (New York: Da Capo Press, 1983).

Arnold Shaw, *52nd Street: The Street of Jazz* (New York: Da Capo Press, 1977).

Rachel Shteir, *Striptease: The Untold History of the Girlie Show* (New York: Oxford University Press, 2004).

Susan Smulyan, *Popular Ideologies: Mass Culture at Mid-Century* (Philadelphia: University of Pennsylvania Press, 2007).

Justin Spring, *Secret Historian: The Life and Times of Samuel Steward, Professor, Tattoo Artist and Sexual Renegade* (Farrar, Strauss, and Giroux, 2010).

Claudia Springer, *Electronic Eros: Bodies and Desire in the Postindustrial Age* (Austin, TX: University of Texas Press, 1996).

John C. Spurlock, *Free Love: Marriage and Middle-Class Radicalism in America, 1825–1860* (New York: New York University Press, 1988).

Jess Stearn, *Sisters of the Night: The Startling Story of Prostitution in New York City* (New York: Julian Messner, Inc., 1956).

——— *The Grapevine: A Report on the Secret World of the Lesbian* (Garden City, NY: Doubleday & Co., 1964).

A. W. Stencell, *Girl Show: Into the Canvas World of Bump and Grind* (Toronto: ECW Press, 1999).

Robert Stoller, *Porn: Myths for the Twentieth Century* (New Haven, CT: Yale University Press, 1991).

Whitney Strub, *Obscenity Rules: Roth v. United States and the Long Struggle over Sexual Expression* (Lawrence, KS: University Press of Kansas, 2013).

Anthony Summers, *Official and Confidential: The Secret Life of J. Edgar Hoover* (New York: Putnam's Sons, 1993).

Reay Tannahill, *Sex in History* (New York: Scarborough House, 1992).

Gay Talese, *Thy Neighbor's Wife* (New York: Random House, 1981).

Jennifer Terry, *An American Obsession: Science, Medicine, and Homosexuality in Modern Society* (Chicago: University of Chicago Press, 1999).

Andrea Tone, *Devices and Desires: A History of Contraceptives in America* (New York: Hill & Wang, 2001).

James Traub, *The Devil's Playground: A Century of Pleasure and Profit in Times Square* (New York: Random House, 2004).

BIBLIOGRAPHY

Randolph Trumbach, *Sex and the Gender Revolution, Vol. 1: Heterosexuality and the Third Gender of Enlightenment London* (Chicago: University of Chicago Press, 1998).

Harry S. Truman, *Memoirs*, vol. 1 (Garden City: Doubleday, 1955).

Christopher Turner, *Orgasmatron: Wilhelm Reich and the Invention of Sex* (New York: Farrar, Straus, and Giroux, 2011).

Stanley Walker, *The Night Club Era* (Baltimore, MD: Johns Hopkins University Press, 1999; originally published in 1933).

Elizabeth Siegel Watkins, *On the Pill: A Social History of Oral Contraceptives, 1950–1970* (Baltimore: John Hopkins University Press, 1998).

Nathan Ward, *Dark Harbor: The War for the New York Waterfront* (New York: Farrar, Straus, and Giroux, 2010).

E. B. White, *Here Is New York* (New York: Little Bookroom, 1999).

Linda Williams, *Hard Core: Power, Pleasure, and the Frenzy of the Visible* (Berkeley, CA: University of California Press, 1989).

James Wilson, *Bulldaggers, Pansies, and Chocolate Babies: Performance, Race, and Sexuality in the Harlem Renaissance* (Ann Arbor, MI: University of Michigan Press, 2010).

Charles Winick and Paul Kinzie, *The Lively Commerce: Prostitution in the United States* (New York: New American, 1972).

Richard Zacks, *Island of Vice: Theodore Roosevelt's Doomed Quest to Clean Up Sin-Loving* (New York: Doubleday, 2012).

Eli Zaretsky, *Secrets of the Soul: A Social and Cultural History of Psychoanalysis* (New York: Vintage, 2005).

Articles & Chapters

Karen Abbot, "The House that Polly Adler Built," *Smithsonian*, April 12, 2012.

Amy L. Baker, "Gentlemen's Clubs and Casinos in Las Vegas," *UNLV Gaming Research & Review Journal*, 14, no. 1 (2010).

Jason Barnosky, "The Violent Years: Responses to Juvenile Crime in the 1950s," *Polity*, 38, no. 3 (July 2006).

R. F. Baumeister and Jennifer L. Butler, "Sexual Masochism: Deviance Without Pathology," in *Sexual Deviance: Theory, Assessment, and Treatment*, eds. D. R. Laws and W. O'Donohue (New York: Guilford Press, 1997).

Barbara J. Beeching, "Paul Robeson and the Black Press: The 1950 Passport Controversy," *The Journal of African American History*, 87 (Summer, 2002).

Walter Benjamin, "Paris, Capital of the Nineteenth Century," in *Illuminations: Essays & Reflections*, ed. Hannah Arendt (New York: Houghton Mifflin Harcourt, 1968).

––––– "The Work of Art in the Age of Mechanical Reproduction," in *Illuminations*, ed. Hannah Arendt (New York: Shocken Books, 1969).

Ernest Borneman, "United States versus Hollywood: The Case of an Antitrust Suit," in *The American Film Industry*, ed. Tino Balio (Madison, WI: University of Wisconsin Press, 1985).

Joanne Boucher, "Betty Friedan and the Radical Past of Liberal Feminism," *New Politics*, 9, no 3. (Summer 2003).

Helen Gurley Brown, "Women Alone, Oh Come Now!," *Sex and the Single Girl*, excerpt, in *Sexual Revolution*, ed. Jeffery Escoffier (New York: Thunder Mouth Press, 2003).

Christina Catalano, "Shaping the American Woman: Feminism and Advertising in the 1950s," *Constructing the Past*: 3, no. 1 (2002).

Leo Cherne, "How to Spot a Communist," *Look*, March 4, 1947.

Janie Chuang, "Rescuing Trafficking from Ideological Capture: Prostitution Reform and Anti-Trafficking Law and Policy," *University of Pennsylvania Law Review*, 158, no. 6 (May 2010).

J. F. Cooper, "The New York Waterfront Commission: A Command Center for Organized Crime"; *EIR* 9, no. 28 (July 27, 1982).

Jonathan Coopersmith, "Pornography, Technology, and Progress," *ICON* 4 (1998).

Allison P. Davis, "Most of You Are Sexting During Work," *New York*, August 6, 2014.

BIBLIOGRAPHY

Michelle J. Demeri, "The 'Watchdog' Agency: Fighting Organized Crime on the Waterfront in New York and New Jersey," *Offer of Proof*, 38, no. 1 (Winter 2012); *Criminal and Civil Confinement*, vol. 38.

Reuel Denny, "The Dark Fantastic," *The New Republic*, May 3, 1954.

Pierre Desrochers and Christine Hoffbauer, "The Post War Intellectual Roots of the Population Bomb," *The Electronic Journal of Sustainable Development*, 1, no. 3 (Summer 2009).

Robert L. Dickinson, "The End of 'Hush and Pretend,'" in *About the Kinsey Report: Observations by 11 Experts on "Sexual Behavior of the Human Male,"* eds. Donald Porter Geddes and Enid Curie (New York: Signet Books, 1948).

Mary L. Dudziak, "Josephine Baker, Racial Protest, and the Cold War," *Journal of American History*, 81, no. 2 (September 1994).

Freeman Dyson, "Scientist, Spy, Genius: Who Was Bruno Pontecorvo?," *New York Review of Books*, March 5, 2015.

Nicholas Eberstadt, "World Population Crisis," *Philanthropy*, December 1998.

William N. Eskridge, "Privacy Jurisprudence and the Apartheid of the Closet, 1946–1961," *Florida State University Law Review*, 1997.

Howard Fast, "Remembering Peekskill, USA, 1949," *Pennsylvania History*, 66, no. 1 (Winter 1999).

Paul Friedman, "Sexual Deviations," in *American Handbook of Psychiatry*, vol. 1, ed. Silvano Arieti (New York: Basic Books, 1959).

Richard W. Gable "The Politics and Economics of the 1957–1958 Recession," *The Western Political Quarterly*, 12, no. 2 (June 1959).

Dan Georgakas, "The Hollywood Blacklist," in *Encyclopedia of the American Left*, eds. Mari Jo Buhle, Paul Buhle, and Dan Georgakas (Urbana and Chicago: University of Illinois Press, 1992).

Wolcott Gibbs, "Books," *New Yorker*, May 8, 1954.

Marvin E. Gettleman, "'No Varsity Teams': New York's Jefferson School of Social Science, 1943–1956," *Science & Society*, 66, no. 3 (Fall 2002).

Robert Justin Goldstein, "Prelude to McCarthyism: The Making of a Blacklist," *National Archives*, 38, no. 3 (Fall 2006).

Stephen Jay Gould, "Carrie Buck's Daughter," *Natural History*, July 1984.

Leslie M. Harris, "From Abolitionist Amalgamators to 'Rulers of Five Points': The Discourse of Interracial Sex and Reform in Antebellum New York City," in *Sex, Love, Race: Crossing the Boundaries in North American History*, ed. Martha Hodes (New York: New York University Press, 1999).

Gordon Hendricks, "The History of the Kinetoscope," in *The American Film Industry*, ed. T. Balio (Madison, WI: University of Wisconsin Press, 1985).

Kenneth Hey, "Ambivalence as a Theme in 'On the Waterfront' (1954): An Interdisciplinary Approach to Film Study," *American Quarterly*, 31, no. 5 (Winter 1979).

John Holliday, "A History of Modern Pornographic Film and Video," in *Porn 101: Eroticism, Pornography, and the First Amendment*, eds. J. Elias, V. D. Elias, V. Bullough, G. Brewer, J. Douglas, and W. Jarvis (Amherst, NY: Prometheus Books, 1999).

Marilyn Irvin Holt, "Children as Topic No. 1 White House Conferences Focused on Youths and Societal Changes in Postwar America," *Prologue Magazine*, Summer 2010.

J. Edgar Hoover, "How Safe is Your Daughter?," *American Magazine*, July 1947.

D. K. "How has organised crime adapted to globalisation?," *The Economist*, August 15, 2013.

Diana Emery Hulick, "Diane Arbus's Women and Transvestites: Separate Selves," *History of Photography*, 16 (1992).

J. H. Humbach, "'Sexting' and the First Amendment," *Hastings Constitutional Law Quarterly*, 37 (2010).

Lynn Hunt, "Introduction: Obscenity and the Origins of Modernity, 1500–1800," in *The Invention of Pornography, 1500–1800: Obscenity and the Origins of Modernity*, ed. Lynn Hunt (Cambridge, MA: MIT Press, 1993).

Casey Ichniowski and Anne Preston, "The Persistence of Organized Crime in New York City Construction: An Economic Perspective," *Industrial and Labor Relations* Review, 42, no. 4 (July 1989).

Ken Jordan, "Barney Rosset, The Art of Publishing No. 2," *Paris Review*, no. 145 (Winter 1997).

Mark Kelley, "The Golden Age of Comic Books: Representations of American Culture from the Great Depression to the Cold War," Marquette University, April 1, 2009.

BIBLIOGRAPHY

Natasha Kraus, "Desire Work, Performativity, and the Structuring of a Community: Butch/Fem Relations of the 1940s and 1950s," *Frontiers: A Journal of Women Studies*, 17, no. 1 (1996).

Vanessa Martins Lamb, "The 1950's and the 1960's and the American Woman: The Transition from the 'Housewife' to the Feminist," *History* (2011).

Tamara Rice Lave, "Only Yesterday: The Rise and Fall of Twentieth Century Sexual Psychopath Laws," *Louisiana Law Review*, 69, no. 3 (Spring 2009).

Gershon Legman, "Minority Report on Kinsey," in *The Sexual Conduct of Men and Women: A Minority Report*, ed. Norman Lockridge (New York: Hogarth House, 1948).

Jill Lepore, "The Last Amazon," *New Yorker*, September 22, 2014.

Thom Magister, One Among Many: The Seduction and Training of a Leatherman in *Leatherfolk: Radical Sex, People, Politics and Practice,* ed. Mark Thompson (Boston: Alyson Publications, 1991).

"Manners & Morals: It's Back," *Time*, March 8, 1948.

Dwight MacDonald, "Profiles: A Caste, A Culture, A Market – II," *The New Yorker*, November 29, 1958.

Louis Menand, "A Friend of the Devil," review of *Patriotic Betrayal: The Inside Story of the CIA's Secret Campaign to Enroll American Students in the Crusade Against Communism*, by Karen Paget, *New Yorker*, March 23, 2015.

Jeremiah Moss, "Sisters of the Night," *The Partisan Review*, August 3, 2012.

Glenn Myers, "Freud's Influence on Psychiatry in America," *Psychoanalytic Quarterly*, 9 (1940).

Tony Ortega, "The 1967 Central Park Be-In: A 'Medieval Pageant," *The Village Voice*, February 5, 2010.

David Park, "The Kefauver Comic Book Hearings as Show Trial: Decency, Authority, and the Dominated Expert," *Cultural Studies*, 16, no. 2 (2002).

Tony Perucci, "The Red Mask of Sanity: Paul Robeson, HUAC, and the Sound of Cold War Performance," *TDR* 53, no. 4 (Winter, 2009).

Julia Pine, "In Bizarre Fashion: The Double-Voiced Discourse of John Willie's Fetish Fantasia," *Journal of the History of Sexuality*, 22, no. 1 (2013).

Richard Randall, "Censorship: From *The Miracle* to *Deep Throat*," in *The American Film Industry*, ed. T. Balio (Madison: University of Wisconsin Press, 1985).

Leo Rosten, "Taxi-Dance," *The New Yorker,* December 31, 1938.

Gayle Rubin, "The Catacombs: A Temple to the Butthole," in *Deviations: A Gayle Rubin Reader* (Durham, NC: Duke University Press, 2011).

Stephen W. Salant, Athan Theoharis and David Levin, reply by Allen Weinstein, "The Hiss Case: An Exchange," *The New York Review of Books,* May 27, 1976.

Eric Schaefer, "The Obscene Seen: Spectacle and Transgression in Postwar Burlesque Films," *Cinema Journal*, 36, no. 2 (Winter 1997).

Elizabeth Schulte, "The trial of Ethel and Julius Rosenberg," *International Socialist Review,* issue 29 (May/June 2003).

Lydia Shrier, Mei-Chiung Shih, and Laura Hacker, "Improved Affect Following Coitus: A Functional Perspective on Adolescent Sexual Behavior," *Journal of Adolescent Health*, 36, no. 2 (2005).

Robert Simonson and Andrew Gans, "Uta Hagen, Legendary Stage Actress and Teacher, Dead at 84," *Playbill*, January 15, 2004.

Joseph Slade, "Eroticism and Technological Regression: The Stag Film," *History and Technology*, 22, no. 1 (March 2006).

Susan Sontag, "The Pornographic Imagination," in *Styles of Radical Will* (New York: Anchor Books, 1969).

Stacy Spaulding, "Off the Blacklist, But Still a Target: The Anti-Communist Attacks on Lisa Sergio," *Journalism Studies*, 10, no. 6 (2009).

Emily Stanton, "Study: At Least 100,000 Children Being Used in U.S. Sex Trade," *U.S. News*, July 8, 2013.

William J. Stern, "The Unexpected Lessons of Times Square's Comeback," *City Journal*, Autumn 1999.

Edwin Sutherland, "The Diffusion of Sexual Psychopath Laws," *American Journal of Sociology*, issue 56 (1950).

Clarence Taylor, "Race, Class, and Police Brutality in New York City: the Role of the Communist Party in the Early Cold War Years," *Journal of African American History*, 98 (Spring 2013).

Verta Taylor, "Social Movement Continuity: The Women's Movement in Abeyance," *American Sociological Review*, 54, no. 5 (October 1989).

"Theatre: New Plays in Manhattan," *Time,* July 18, 1927.

Rick Valelly, "The Conflicted Gay Pioneer," *The American Prospect*, October 8, 2013.

Sudhir Venkatesh, "How Tech Tools Transformed New York's Sex Trade," *Wired*, January 31, 2011.

Ronald Weitzer, "Sex Trafficking and the Sex Industry: The Need for Evidence-Based Theory and Legislation," *Journal of Criminal Law and Criminology*, 101, no. 4 (Fall 2011).

Albert Wertheim, "The McCarthy Era and the American Theatre," *Theatre Journal*, 34, no. 2 (May 1982).

Jamie L. Williams, "Teens, Sexts, & Cyberspace: The Constitutional Implications of Current Sexting & Cyberbullying Laws," *William & Mary Bill of Rights Journal*, 20, no. 3 (2012).

David Wittels, "What Can We Do About Sex Crimes," *Saturday Evening Post*, December 11, 1948.

Newspapers

The Austin Chronicle
The Daily Mail
The Guardian
The Independent
The Los Angeles Times
Manchester Guardian
New York Daily News
New York Herald Tribune
The New York Times
Reading Eagle
Staten Island Advance
Sun Sentinel
UPI
The Wall Street Journal
The Washington Post
Variety
The Windy City Times

Online Publications

"Abortion Bills," GovTrack.us.

ACLU, "State of Indiana v. Bei Bei Shuai," March 31, 2011.

———"The Smith Act and the Supreme Court, An American Civil Liberties Union Analysis, Opinion and Statement of Policy" (1952).

American National Biography Online: "Frederic Wertham."

Wayne Anderson, "Hidden History: Tobi Marsh & Club 82," *Huffington Post*, June 14, 2012.

Megan Annitto, "Emerging State Safe Harbor Responses to Sex Trafficking andProstitution of Minors," Juvenile Justice Information Exchange, September 19, 2012.

Sebastian Anthony, "Just how big are porn sites?," *Extremetech*, April 4, 2012.

"An Assessment of the Adult Entertainment Industry in Texas," Bureau of Business Research, IC2 Institute, and the Institute on Domestic Violence and Sexual Assault of the University of Texas at Austin, March 2009.

"Beauty Lies in the Eyes of the Beholder: Virginia Hill," Glamour Girls of the Silver Screen.

"The Birth of a Nation and Black Protest," Roy Rosenzweig Center for History and New Media, George Mason University.

Ralph Blumenthal, "Look Who Dropped in at the Stork," *New York Times*, July 1, 1996.

Dan Bryan, "Lesbian Pulp Fiction—the 1950s Phenomenon," *American History USA*, January 10, 2013.

Jacqueline A. Carleton, "Isle Ollendorff, Mother of Peter Reich Interviewed," September 20, 1977, Part I.

"Children of the Blacklist: Robert Meeropol," *Dreamers & Fighters:* The NYC Teacher Purges.

Steve Courtney, "The Robeson riots of 1949," *The Reporter Dispatch*, September 5, 1982.

St. Sukie de la Croix, *Chicago Whispers: A History of LGBT Chicago before Stonewall*.

Cora Currier, "Charting Obama's Crackdown on National Security Leaks," ProPublica.

Roger Ebert, "Russ Meyer Busts Sleazy Stereotype," *Roger Ebert Interviews*, November 15, 1985.

BIBLIOGRAPHY

Lisa E. Davis, "The Bagatelle," *Lost Womyn's Space*, September 7, 2011.

"The Deuce," CityRealty.com.

"Divorce and Divorce Rates, Alabama and the United States, 1950–2010," Alabama Department of Public Health, 2010.

Dwight D. Eisenhower, "Remarks at the Dartmouth College Commencement Exercises, Hanover, NJ, June 14, 1953, The American Presidency Project.

William Eskridge, "Privacy Jurisprudence and the Apartheid of the Closet, 1946–1961." Florida State University.

"FAQ: Assassination Attempt on President Truman's Life," Harry S. Truman Library and Museum.

"Fetal Homicide Laws," National Conference of State Legislators, March 2015.

Russ Fisher, "John Landis Gathering Funds for Biopic About Mad Magazine Publisher Bill Gaines," *Slash Film*, May 16, 2010.

Will Forbis, "Interesting Motherfuckers: Doris Wishman," *Acid Logic*.

"Four Teens Caught in Sexting Sandal in Norridge," CBS, March 17, 2015

Elizabeth Gurley Flynn, "Statement at the Smith Act Trial," April 24 1952, American Rhetoric: Top 100 Speeches.

Kelly Flynn, "Danni's Hard Drive to Adult Content Success," CNN, October 21, 2000.

Gary J. Gates, "How Many People are Lesbian, Gay, Bisexual and Transgender?," Williams Institute, April 2011.

Gay Marriage," Pew Research, February 23, 2014.

Tony Ge, "Going Deep Inside the Adult Entertainment Industry," *Arbitrage Magazine*.

Josh Gerstein, "James Risen subpoena faces new review," Politico, October 10, 2014.

Jessica Glasscock, "Striptease," *Love to Know*.

Emma Goldman, "There Is No Communism in Russia" (1935), The Anarchist Library.

Paul Goodman, "The Politics of Being Queer," 1969.

"Grand Jury Resistance: One Size Does Not Fit All," Rosenberg Fund for Children.

"The Gruesome Tale of Jacqueline Smith," *Real Choice*.

Guttmacher Institute, "Facts on American Teens' Sexual and Reproductive Health," August 2011.

—— "In just the last 4 years, states have enacted 231 abortion restrictions" (2011–2014).

Jay Gertzman, "Arrests and Prosecutions of Samuel Roth." Authors Guild.

—— "1950s Sleaze and the Larger Literary Scene: The Case of Times Square Porn King Eddie Mishkin." Authors Guild.

"Virginia Hill; the statement could not be found in her official testimony," Hotties of History.

"A History of Federal Funding for Abstinence-Only-Until-Marriage Programs," Sexuality Information and Education Council of the United States (SIECUS).

"History of Theatres in New York City," Made in NYC, Mayor Office of Film, Theatre & Broadcasting.

"How Cosmo Changed the World," *Cosmopolitan*, May 3, 2007.

"Hubert's Museum," *Show History*.

"Interview: About Irving Klaw—Interview with Paula Klaw" (1980), *American Suburb X*, May 29, 2013.

"An Interview with William M. Gaines, Part One of Three," *The Comics Journal*, October 12, 2010.

Christopher J. Jarmick, "Doris Wishman," *Great Directors*, October 2002.

Robert Jensen, "Just a Prude? Feminism, Pornography, and Men's Responsibility," *Free Inquiry*, 4 (1997).

"Bruce Jenner: The Interview," ABC, April 24, 2105.

Rich Juzwiak and Aleksander Chan, "Unarmed People of Color Killed by Police, 1999–2014," *Gawker*, December 8, 2014.

Elizabeth Kneebone and Emily Garr, "The Suburbanization of Poverty: Trends in Metropolitan America, 2000 to 2008," Brookings Institute, January 2010.

Gilbert King, "The Senator and the Gangsters," Smithsonian.com, April 18, 2012.

Lisa Kogen, "Ethel Rosenberg, 1915–1953," Jewish Women's Archives.

Samantha Lachman, "Flood Of Abortion-Restricting Bills Filed In State Legislatures Following GOP Sweep," *Huffington Post*, February 12, 2015.

Elaine Laporte, "Ex-Broadway showgirl marks 80 with Petaluma bat mitzvah," J-Weekly.com, March 14, 1997.

Legal Information Institute, Cornel University, "Advocating Overthrow of Government," (18 U.S. Code § 2385).

Reed Lee, "United States v. Michael Williams," Free Speech Coalition Analysis.

Douglas O. Linder, "The *Confidential* Magazine Trial: An Account" (2010).

—— "Lenny Bruce" (2003).

Jim Linderman, "Lost Films of Sleaze Artist William Mishkin and Lili Dawn."

"Live from Carnegie Hall: Paul Robeson," Carnegie Hall, May 9, 1958.

Jamie Lovett, "New York Comic Con Was Attended By 151,000 People, Surpasses San Diego," Comicbook. com, October 13, 2014.

Henry R. Luce, "The American Century," Information Clearing House (originally published in *Life* magazine February 17, 1941).

Raoul MacFarlane, *Man to Man Yearbook*, Spring 1972.

"Marriages and Divorces, 1900–2009," Infoplease.

Jim Martin, "Who Killed Wilhelm Reich," Feral House (May 2005).

Wendy McElroy, "A Feminist Defense of Pornography," *Free Inquiry*, 17, no. 4 (1997).

Nell Minow, "New York Comic-Con 2014: 3D Printing and DIY," *Huffington Post*, October 14, 2014.

"Moondog Alan Freed, 1951–1965," *The Pop History Dig*.

Chris Morris, "Things Are Looking Up in America's Porn Industry," NBC, January 20, 2015.

Mostly About Organized Crime," *Friends of Ours*, December 7, 2014.

Ms. Bob, "Tabloids & Men's Soft Core, part 4," *Transgender Forum*, July 23, 2012.

National Colloquium 2012 Final Report, "An Inventory and Evaluation of the Current Shelter and Services Response to Domestic Minor Sex Trafficking," May 2013.

National Conference of State Legislatures (NCSL), "2012 Legislation Related to 'Sexting.'"

New York City Bar Association, "Report on the NYPD's Stop-and-Frisk Policy."

New York City Government population (1967).

—— Demographic History.

"New York Crime Rates, 1960–2013," Disaster Center.

New York Police Department, "Police Commissioner Kelly Announces 'Demand Side' Focus in Increased Arrests for Soliciting and Human Trafficking," June 19, 2012.

Alexandra Nikolchev, "A brief history of the birth control pill," PBS Need to Know, May 7, 2010.

"Nuyoricans," *What-When-How*.

"On This Day: Puerto Rican Nationalists Launch Assault on US Congress," *Finding Dulcinea Staff*, March 1, 2001;

Kenneth O'Reilly, "Hoover and the Un-Americans," Writing, University of Pennsylvania.

Richard Perez, "Traveling Backwards in Fethistory," May 10, 2014.

—— "Oh Those Kinky, Kinky Boots!... Circa 1950," June 7, 2014.

Planned Parenthood, "A History of Birth Control Methods," January 2012.

Frances Fox Piven and Richard Cloward, "The unemployed workers' movement," Libcom.

David M. Powers, "Banned Books Weeks and an Incident in Boston," October 13, 2012, *History of Christianity*.

"Rapp-Coudert Committee," The Struggle for Free Speech at CCNY, 1931–42.

"Red Channels: The Report of Communist Influence in Radio and Television (1950), *Authentic History*.

Wilhelm Reich's Course Descriptions and Bio Reprinted from the 1940 and 1941; New School for Social Research [course] Bulletin.

David Rosen, "Genital Casualties: Military Failure & the Crisis in Masculinity," *CounterPunch*, April 12–14, 2013.

—— "Ways of Seeing: Movies on Mobile Devices," *FilmInFocus*, November 19, 2008.

—— "Sex Crime Charade: Why Have Prostitution Arrests Dropped by 50 Percent?," *CounterPunch*, August 2–4, 2013.

—— "A Tale of Two Pols: Carlos Danger v. Beau James," *CounterPunch*, July 26–28, 2013.

—— "We Are All Sexters Now: America's Favorite Amateur Porn," *Salon*, August 16, 2014;

—— "Weiner Roast: The Politics of Narcissism," *CounterPunch*, June 15, 2011.

——— "Weiner Redux: Political Rehabilitation & the End of the Culture Wars," *CounterPunch*, May 23, 2013.

"The Rosenberg Trial," History of Federal Judiciary.

Renato M. E. Sabbatini, *The History of Shock Therapy in Psychiatry* (2004).

Dena Sacco, Rebecca Argudin, James Maguire, and Kelly Tallong, "Sexting: Youth Practices and Legal Implications," Berkman Center for Internet & Society, Research Publication No. 2010–8, June 22, 2010.

Frank Schick, "Paperback Publishing" (1958).

Carl Schreck, "Russian Gangs Of New York," Radio Free Europe, November 11, 2014.

Tobias Seamon, "A View From the Crow's Wood," *Morning News*, June 21, 2005.

Joe Sergi, "The Incredible True Story of Joe Shuster's NIGHTS OF HORROR," *Comic Book Legal Defense Fund*, October 3, 2012.

"Snowden 'aiding our enemies,' former CIA chief of staff says time," RT.com, June 14, 2013

"Spooky Business: A New Report on Corporate Espionage Against Non-Profits," Center for Corporate Policy, November 20, 2013.

"Strip Club Statistics," *Statistic Brain*, October 14, 2014,

"Strip Street," *Jeremiah's Vanishing New York*, January 26, 2011.

"Stop-and-Frisk Data," New York Civil Liberties Union.

Cheryl Sullenger, "73 Abortion Facilities Shut Down in 2014, 75% of Abortion Clinics Closed Since 1991," *LifeNews.com*, December 29, 2014.

Laureen Trainer, "The Missing Photographs: An Examination of Diane Arbus's Images of Transvestites and Homosexuals from 1957 to 1965," *American Suburb X*, October 2, 2009.

"The Trial of Eros Magazine," *The Realist*, no. 44 (October 1963).

John Tuohy, "We Only Kill Each Other: The Mob at War," We Only Kill Each Other.

Tuskegee Institute Archives, "Lynchings: By Year and Race (1882–1968)."

"The Village Barn," Jeremiah's Vanishing New York, April 2, 2013.

Daniel Wallis, "Los Angeles porn actors must wear condoms, appeals court rules," Reuters, December 15, 2014.

Rebecca Williams, "The Rockefeller Foundation, the Population Council, and Indian Population Control," Rockefeller Archives.

Janis Wolak, David Finkelhor and Kimberly J. Mitchell, "Trends in Arrests for Child Pornography Production: The Third National Juvenile Online Victimization Study (NJOV-3)," April 13, 2012.

"You Are the Un-Americans, and You Ought to be Ashamed of Yourselves": Paul Robeson Appears Before HUAC" *History Matters*, June 12, 1956.

Websites

42nd Street
   http://www.nysonglines.com/42st.htm
Apple
   http://support.apple.com/specs/
"Behind the Candelabra" (Steven Soderbergh)
   http://www.hbo.com/movies/behind-the-candelabra#/
Milton Berle
   http://www.imdb.com/name/nm0000926/
   https://archive.org/details/theMiltonBerleShow-3April1956w/Elvis & ester Williams on US ship
Ty Bennett
   http://www.blakstone.com/Dragstravaganza%20Site/bennett.html
Box Office Mojo: 2013 Domestic Grosses;
   http://boxofficemojo.com/yearly/chart/?yr=2013
Bertolt Brecht, Appearance Before the HUAC, October 30, 1947
   http://hcc.humanities.uci.edu/humcore/Student/archives/HUACBrecht.htm
Lenny Bruce
   https://www.youtube.com/watch?v=1edm2x5gx9Q

http://www.lennybruceofficial.com/chronology-the-50's/
Christine Jorgensen
   http://www.christinejorgensen.org
Comic-Con International
   http://www.comic-con.org/about#sthash.BIhWZdTN.dpuf
Comichron: The Comic Chronicles
   http://www.comichron.com/monthlycomicssales/2013.html
—— "Comic Book Sales By Year"
   http://www.comichron.com/yearlycomicssales.html;
Frank Costello
   http://www.allposters.com/-sp/Frank-Costello-s-Hands-on-TV-During-Kefauver-Hearings-
      Posters_i9361553_.htm
Dull Tool Dim Bulb
   http://dulltooldimbulb.blogspot.com/2011/06/weegee-bettie-page-and-fbi-last.html#.VCltn0smUds
Bob Dylan, "Lenny Bruce"
   http://www.bobdylan.com/us/songs/lenny-bruce
Folsom Street Fair
   http://www.folsomstreetevents.org/
Bill Gaines
   http://www.samuelsdesign.com/comics/pages/crime-horror/crime_suspenstories22.htm
   http://www.madmagazine.com/tags/william-m-gaines
   http://cbldf.org/resources/history-of-comics-censorship/history-of-comics-censorship-part-1/
Allen Ginsberg, *Howl*
   http://www.poetryfoundation.org/poem/179381
Ralph Ginzburg, *Eros Unbound* (1999);
   http://www.evesmag.com/ginzburg.htm
Wiliam Heise, *The Kiss* (1896)
   http://www.youtube.com/watch?v=mTHzr8_wfK0
Virginia Hill
   http://www.youtube.com/watch?v=zqSnKj4K274
   http://archive.org/stream/investigationofo07unit/investigationofo07unit_djvu.thttps://www.
      youtube.com/watch?v=C5YkC17N12M
Billie Holiday, 1954 sessions
   http://www.billieholidaysongs.com/recording-sessions/1954-sessions/
Billie Holiday, "Strange Fruit"
   https://www.youtube.com/watch?v=h4ZyuULy9zs
Billie Holiday, "Strange Fruit" (lyrics), 10 Protest Songs;
   https://10protestsongs.wikispaces.com/Billie+Holiday+-+Strange+Fruit
HUAC
   http://hidvl.nyu.edu/video/000031640.html
Hubert Humphrey
   http://www.senate.gov/artandhistory/history/common/generic/VP_Hubert_Humphrey.htm
Inflation calculator
   http://www.usinflationcalculator.com
Julius', One of the Oldest Gay Bars in New York
   http://www.juliusbarny.com/Gay-Bar-About-New-York-NY.html
Irving Klaw movies
   http://archive.org/search.php?query=creator%3A%22Irving%20Klaw%22
Estes Kefauver
   http://www.youtube.com/watch?v=-p7q7vgadHA
Liberace
   https://www.youtube.com/watch?v=9tUrMuqS2uQ
The Liberace Foundation

www.Liberace.org

"Milton Luros - Summary Bibliography," ISFBD;
   http://www.isfdb.org/cgi-bin/ea.cgi?27518

Arthur Miller
   https://www.youtube.com/watch?v=4gjf_8hxXx0

Russ Myer
   https://www.youtube.com/watch?v=ICXyXarWjrc

Paul O'Dwyer
   https://www.youtube.com/watch?v=hpjYaQzxShY
   http://www.nyc.gov/html/nyc100/html/classroom/hist_info/mayors.html#o'dwyer

Grietje Reyniers
   http://d1xkzao2ij.site.aplus.net/genealogy/docs/d_reyniers_grietje_1602_bio.pdf

Paul Robeson, "Joe Hill"
   http://www.youtube.com/watch?v=n8Kxq9uFDes
   https://www.youtube.com/watch?v=KN9dPSRtyLQ
   http://www.rdio.com/artist/Paul_Robeson/album/Words_Like_Freedom/track/Huac_Hearing_
      (June_12,_1956)/

Rosenbergs
   AtomicArchive.com
   National Committee to Reopen the Rosenberg Case (NCRRC)
   http://ncrrc.org

Stonewall and Beyond
   http://www.columbia.edu/cu/lweb/eresources/exhibitions/sw25/case1.html

United Nations (map)
   https://www.google.com/maps/@40.748876,-73.968009,17z

The Unlimited Strip Club List
   https://www.tuscl.net/r.php?RID=7;

Doris Wishman
   https://www.youtube.com/watch?v=h8QcOe8I-kI and

Manuscripts & Other Sources

"Sanford 'Les' E. Aday," Henry Madden Library, California State University, Fresno, Special Collections
   Library.

Jane Addams, *The Spirit of Youth and the City Streets* (New York: McMillian, 1909).

Frank Campenni, "Citizen Howard Fast: A Critical Biography," PhD diss., University of Wisconsin—
   Madison, 1971.

Elizabeth Alice Clement, "Trick or Treat: Prostitution and Working-Class Women's Sexuality in New York
   City, 1900–1932," PhD diss., University of Pennsylvania, 1998.

Karen Glynn, "Early Comic Strips 1898–1916," Duke University Libraries.

James D. McCabe, *Lights and Shadows of New York Life* (Philadelphia, PA: National Publishing Company,
   1872).

"Paul Robeson collection, 1925–1956," New York Public Library, Archives.

John Roach Straton, "*The Menace of Immorality in Church and State* (New York: George H. Doran Co.,
   1920).

NOTES

Notes to Introduction

1 Adam Liptak, "Supreme Court Ruling Makes Same-Sex Marriage a Right Nationwide," *The New York Times*, June 26, 2015.
2 Saba Mehedy, "'Fifty Shades of Grey' sinks 73% in 2nd weekend, still tops box office," Alison Flood, "Fifty Shades of Grey trilogy has sold 100m copies worldwide."
3 Christine Jorgensen website; "Donald Trump spars with transgender Beauty Queen," *The Daily Mail*, April 3, 2012; Laura Pullman, "If she did want to check if I'm a man she'd be impressed"; see also "The Quest for Transgender Equality," *New York Times*, editorial, May 4, 2015.
4 David Rosen, "Genital Casualties: Military Failure & the Crisis in Masculinity."
5 Christine Jorgensen website.
6 Ibid., *Time*, April 20, 1953.
7 E. B. White, *Here Is New York*, p. 55.
8 Marc Eliot, *Down 42nd Street*, p. 37.
9 "Moondog Alan Freed, 1951–1965," The Pop History Dig.
10 Richard W. Gable "The Politics and Economics of the 1957–1958 Recession," pp. 557–59.
11 David Halberstam, *The Fifties*, pp. 132–139; Kenneth T. Jackson, ed., *The Encyclopedia of New York City*, p. 241.
12 Martha Alschuler, *The Origins of the Law of Obscenity*, pp. 77–81.
13 "Children of the Blacklist"
14 The *U.S. v. One Book Entitled Ulysses by James Joyce* (1934); *Burstyn v. Wilson*, (1952); *Roth v. U.S.* (1957).
15 Dwight D. Eisenhower, "Remarks at the Dartmouth College Commencement Exercises."
16 U.S. Department of Treasury, "History of 'In God We Trust.'"
17 Dan Bryan, "Lesbian Pulp Fiction—the 1950s Phenomenon"; Whitney Strub, *Obscenity Rules*, pp. 115, 29–30; Frank Schick, "Paperback Publishing," p. 97.
18 Billie Holiday, 1954 sessions.
19 Arnold Shaw, *52nd Street*, p. 197.
20 Billie Holiday, "Strange Fruit" (video).
21 Billie Holiday, "Strange Fruit" (lyrics).
22 "Children of the Blacklist."
23 John Cello Holmes, "This Is the Beat Generation"; Halbersham, *op. cit.*, p. 301.
24 Paul Friedman, "Sexual Deviations," pp. 592–93.
25 Emylia N. Terry, "Christine Jorgensen and the Media: Identity Politics in the Early 1950s" (University of Nevada, Las Vegas, 2012), pp. 4–5, 18.
26 Richard F. Docter, *Becoming a Woman: A Biography of Christine Jorgensen* (New York: Hawthorn Press/Routledge, 2008).
27 "Bars Marriage Permit: Clerk Rejects Proof of Sex from Christine Jorgensen," *The New York Times*, April 4, 1959.
28 Docker, *op. cit.*, p. 226.
29 Gary J. Gates, "How Many People are Lesbian, Gay, Bisexual and Transgender?," Williams Institute.
30 "Bruce Jenner: The Interview," ABC, April 24, 2105.

NOTES

31 "125 Seized iin Times Square In a Drive on Undersireables," *New York Times*, July 31, 1954; "23 More Undersireables Are Seized in Times Square as Round-Up Spreads," *New York Times*, August 1, 1954.

32 "Times Sq. a Midway Zone Backers Say," *New York Times*, April 19, 1952; "Busines Group Asks Times Square 'Purge,'" *New York Times*, November 25, 1952.

33 "Hubert's Museum," *Show History*.

34 "'Honky-Tonk's Hit as Times Sq. Blot," *New York Times*, January 13, 1953.

35 "3 Candidates Urge Times Sq. Clean-Up, *New York Times*, October 20, 1953.

36 United Nations (map).

37 Marc Eliot, *Down 42nd Street*, p. 39.

38 Jack Kerouac, *On the Road* (New York: Viking, 1957), p. 106.

39 Eliot, op. cit., p. 71.

40 "The Deuce," CityRealty.com.

41 James Traub, *The Devil's Playground*, pp. 113–14.

42 Bill Morgan, *The Beat Generation in New York*, p. 22.

43 Allen Ginzberg, "Howl."

44 Eliot, op. cit., p. 37.

45 Arnold Shaw, *52nd Street*, pp. 326–33, 322–23.

46 Shaw, op. cit., p. 325.

47 "Written on the Screen," *New York Times*, February 28, 1915.

48 "The Birth of a Nation and Black Protest," Roy Rosenzweig Center for History and New Media, George Mason University.

49 Ken Bloom, *Broadway: An Encyclopedic Guide to the History, People and Place of Times Square*, p. 338.

50 "History of Theatres in New York City," Made in NYC, Mayor Office of Film, Theatre & Broadcasting.

51 Ibid., p. 96.

52 Ibid., pp. 269–70.

53 Eliot, op. cit., p. 36; Adler, *A House is Not a Home*, p. 263.

54 Brooks Atkinson, "At the Theatre," *New York Times*, June 29, 1950.

55 Milton Bracker, "Life on W. 42d Street: A Study in Decay," *New York Times*, May 14, 1960.

56 *Chase Manhattan Bank v. New York World's Fair 1964–1965 Corporation et al., Defendants.*

57 "President Turns Earth to Start Lincoln Center," *The New York Times*, May 15, 1959.

58 Samuel R. Delany, *Times Square Red, Times Square Blue*, p. 127.

59 William J. Stern, "The Unexpected Lessons of Times Square's Comeback," *City Journal*, Autumn 1999.

Notes to Comic-Book Corruption

60 Lovett, "New York Comic Con."

61 Comic-Con International.

62 Comichron, "The Comic Chronicles."

63 Chomihom, "Comic Book Sales By Year"; Box Office Mojo: 2013 Domestic Grosses;

64 Patersen, *The Century of Sex,* pp. 217, 219; Barnosky, "The Violent Years"; Park, "The Kefauver Comic Book Hearings as Show Trial," pp. 259–88.

65 "An Interview with William M. Gaines, Part One of Three."

66 Gaines comics (web).

67 Karen Glynn, "Early Comic Strips 1898–1916."

68 David Hajdu, *The Ten-Cent Plague*, pp. 21–22.

69 Mark Kelley, "The Golden Age of Comic Books," p. 2.

70 Hajda, op. cit., pp. 35, 193.

71 Amy K. Nyberg, *Seal of Approval*, p. 15.

72 US Senate, "Hearings Before the Subcommittee to Investigate Juvenile Delinquency," April 21, 22 and June 4, 1954.

73 Hajdu, op. cit., p. 272.

74 U.S. Senate, op. cit.

75 Ibid.

76 Ibid., pp. 329.

77 David M. Powers, "Banned Books Weeks and an Incident in Boston."

78 J. Edgar Hoover, "Youth Running Wild"; Hajdu, op. cit., p. 86.

79 Kathy Peiss, *Zoot Suit*.

80 Barnosky, op. cit., p. 327.

81 Barnosky, op. cit., p. 323.

82 Hadja, op. cit., pp.104–08, 144–45, 293–94.

83   Ibid., p. 312.
84   Ibid., pp. 95–96.
85   Ibid., pp. 311–12.
86   Joe Sergi, "The Incredible True Story of Joe Shuster's NIGHTS OF HORROR."
87   Joe Sergi, "1948: The Year Comics Met Their Match."
88   Dwight MacDonald, "Profiles," p. 76.
89   Russ Fisher, "John Landis Gathering Funds for Biopic About Mad Magazine Publisher Bill Gaines."

Notes to Obscene Image
89   David Rosen, "Weiner Roast"; David Rosen, "Weiner Redux"; David Rosen, "A Tale of Two Pols: Carlos Danger v. Beau James."
91   Janis Wolak, David Finkelhor and Kimberly J. Mitchell, "How Often Are Teens Arrested for Sexting?," p. 2; Dena Sacco, Rebecca Argudin, James Maguire and Kelly Tallong, "Sexting," pp. 21–24; and Reed Lee, "United States v. Michael Williams."
92   Caitlin Dewey, "A guide to safe sexting: How to send nude photos without ruining your life, career and reputation," *The Washington Post*, July 11, 2014.
93   "Senators Start Morals Hearings," *New York Times*, May 25, 1955; "Smut Held Cause of Delinquency," *New York Times*, June 1, 1955.
94   John D'Emilio and Estelle B. Freedman, *Intimate Matters*, p. 283; see also U.S. Senate, "Juvenile Delinquency."
95   US Senate, op. cit.; $2.00 in the 1950s is equal to about $17.50 in 2013 dollars.
96   John Heidenry, *What Wild Ecstasy*, p. 376; Eric Kroll, *The Complete Reprint of John Willie's Bizarre*, p. 13.
97   Richard Foster, *The Real Bettie Page*, p. 84.
98   Rick Kalw, "The Notorious Irving Klaw," *The Austin Chronicle*, March 10, 2006.
99   Foster, op. cit., pp. 57–58; James Petersen, *The Century of Sex*, p. 249.
100   Walter Benjamin, "The Work of Art in the Age of Mechanical Reproduction," pp. 218–19.
101   Steven Luber, *Infoculture*, p. 51.
102   J. W. Slade, "Eroticism and Technology Regression," p. 28.
103   Williams, op. cit., p. 34.
104   Ibid., p 25.
105   David Nasaw, *Going Out*, p. 154.
106   Jane Addams, *The Spirit of Youth and the City Streets*, p. 86.
107   Wiliam Heise, *The Kiss* (1896).
108   Williams, op. cit., pp. 286–87 n 10.
109   Ibid., 26; Slade, op. cit., pp. 13–14.
110   Ibid., p. 74.
111   Slade, op. cit., p. 30.
112   "Monarch of Pin-Up Business," *New York Times*, November 16, 1947.
113   Foster, op. cit., p. 55.
114   "Pin-Up Man," *New York Herald Tribune*, June 25, 1944; "Monarch of the Pin-Up Business," *New York Times*, November 16, 1947.
115   Foster, op. cit., p. 60.
116   Jim Linderman, "Lost Films of Sleaze Artist William Mishkin and Lili Dawn,"
117   Foster, op. cit., pp. 57–58; Petersen, op. cit., p. 249.
118   Foster, op. cit., pp. 40–50; see also Bettie Page (web).
119   Dull Tool Dim Bulb.
120   Petersen, op. cit., p. 249; Foster, op. cit., p. 63.
121   Richard Perez, "Oh Those Kinky, Kinky Boots! . . . Circa 1950"; see also, Foster, op. cit., p. 59.
122   Foster, op. cit., p. 59.
123   "Interview: About Irving Klaw," American Suburb X.
124   Foster, op. cit., pp. 57–58; Petersen, op. cit., p. 49.
125   Eric Schaefer, "The Obscene Seen," pp. 41–66.
126   Foster, op. cit., p. 79.
127   US Senate, "Juvenile Delinquency," op. cit.; Klaw movies (web).
128   Foster, op. cit., p. 81; US Senate, "Juvenile Delinquency," op. cit.
129   Heidenry, op. cit., p. 377; Foster, op. cit., pp. 82–83.
130   "Arraign 33 in Smut Drive," *New York Herald Tribune*, May 30, 1956.

131 Finn Vigeland, "Movie Star News' pin-up collection to be auctioned off as famed store closes," *New York Daily News*, July 30, 2012; "Deaths" (Klaw), *New York Times*, September 9, 1966.
132 Linda Williams, *Hard Core*, p. 74.
133 Joseph Slade, "Eroticism and Technological Regression," p. 30.
134 Kelly Dennis, *Art/Porn*, pp. 100–20.
135 Kat Long, *The Forbidden Apple*, pp. 131–33; Laurence O'Toole, *Pornocopia*, p. 103.
136 Williams, op. cit., p. 99.
137 Richard Randall, "Censorship," p. 522,
138 Christopher J. Jarmick, "Doris Wishman," Great Directors; see also YouTube.
139 Roger Ebert, "Russ Meyer Busts Sleazy Stereotype"; Justin Kroll, "Michael Winterbottom Eyed to Direct Will Ferrell's 'Russ & Roger Go Beyond' (EXCLUSIVE)"; see also YouTube.
140 "Nude Pose Considered," *Reading Eagle*, June 17, 1955.
141 Eddie Muller and Daniel Faris, *Grindhouse*, p. 62.
142 Ibid., p. 63.
143 Will Forbis, "Interesting Motherfuckers: Doris Wishman," *Acid Logic*.
144 Ernest Borneman, "United States versus Hollywood," p. 459.
145 Richard Randall, *"Censorship,"* p. 511.
146 Coopersmith, op. cit., pp. 106–07.
147 Heindenry, op. cit., pp. 263–64.
148 John Holliday, "A History of Modern Pornographic Film and Video," pp. 341–51; Coopersmith, op. cit., 107.
149 Joan Mower, "Firm Agrees to Pay $50,000 Fine in 'Dial-a-Porn' Case," Associated Press.
150 Claudia Springer, *Electronic Eros*, pp. 53–54; see also Kelly Flynn, "Danni's Hard Drive to Adult Content Success," CNN.
151 Wendy McElroy, "A Feminist Defense of Pornography," *Free Inquiry*; Robert Jensen, "Just a Prude," *Free Inquiry*.
152 Richard Verrier, "On Location: Porn production plummets in Los Angeles," *Los Angeles Times*, August 6, 2014.
153 Chris Morris, "Things Are Looking Up in America's Porn Industry," NBC.
154 Sexuality Information and Education Council of the United States (SIECUS), "A History of Federal Funding for Abstinence-Only-Until-Marriage Programs," no date.
155 Guttmacher Institute, "Facts on American Teens' Sexual and Reproductive Health"; Lydia Shrier, Mei-Chiung Shih and Laura Hacker, "Improved Affect Following Coitus," *Journal of Adolescent Health*.
156 Apple; David Rosen, "Ways of Seeing," Films-in-Focus; "U.S. Smartphone Use in 2015," Pew Research, May 2015.
157 Mitchell, op. cit.; Wolak, op cit.
158 UPI, "Teen Sexting Arrests Often Involve Adults," National Conference of State Legislatures (NCSL), "2012 Legislation Related to 'Sexting'"; Jamie L. Williams, "Teens, Sexts, & Cyberspace: The Constitutional Implications of Current Sexting & Cyberbullying Laws," *William & Mary Bill of Rights Journal*, pp. 1017–50.
159 *New York v. Ferber*.

Notes to Prurient Word

160 *Roth v. U.S.* (1957).
161 Daniel Kreps, "Nipple Ripples: 10 Years of Fallout From Janet Jackson's Halftime Show."
162 *FCC v. Pacifica Foundation* (1978).
163 Jay A. Gertzman, *Bookleggers and Smuthounds*, p. 230.
164 Ibid., p. 23.
165 Samuel Roth, *Jews Must Live*.
166 Gertzman, op. cit., p. 222.
167 Richard Perez, "Traveling Backwards in Fethistory"; *Roth v. United States* (1957).
168 Gertzman, op. cit., pp. 276–82; Richard Kuh, *Foolish Figleaves?*, p. 24; U.S. Attorney General, pp. 307–08.
169 John Heidenry, *What Wild Ecstasy*, pp. 60–64; Petersen, pp. 205–60.
170 Allen Ginsberg, *Howl*.
171 Perez, op. cit.
172 Dan Bryan, "Lesbian Pulp Fiction."
173 Margalit Fox, "Tereska Torrès, 92, Writer of Lesbian Fiction, Dies," *New York Times*, September 24, 2012.

174 Sarah Toce, "Interview with lesbian pulp novelist Marijane Meaker," *Windy City Times*, June 27, 2012.
175 Gwertzman, op. cit., pp. 276–80; Straub, op. cit., pp. 180–81.
176 Jay Gwertzman, "Arrests and Prosecutions of Samuel Roth."
177 H Harald Hellman. *The Best of American Girlie Magazines*, Preface.
178 Ibid.
179 Eric Kroll, *The Complete Reprint of John Willie's Bizarre*, p. 7; see also Julia Pine, "In Bizarre Fashion: The Double-Voiced Discourse of John Willie's Fetish Fantasia," pp. 1–33.
180 Kim Christy, *The Complete Reprint of* Exotique, pp. 7–8.
181 *Exotique*, No. 21 (1957), pp. 3–4.
182 William Eskridge, "Privacy Jurisprudence and the Apartheid of the Closet, 1946–1961," no page, footnotes 342, 341 and 343.
183 Ibid., William N. Eskridge, "Privacy Jurisprudence and the Apartheid of the Closet, 1946–1961," p. 339.
184 Kuh, op. cit., p. 28.
185 Ibid., pp. 101–02.
186 Ibid., pp. 145, 150.
187 Ibid., p. 55.
188 Ralph Ginzburg, *Eros Unbound* (1999); "The Trial of Eros Magazine," *The Realist*.
189 Ken Jordan, "Barney Rosset"; *Byrne v. Karalexis* [I Am Curious (yellow)] (1969) and (1971).

Notes to Illicit Performance
190 "United States Strip Clubs," The Unlimited Strip Club List; "Strip Club Statistics," Statistic Brain.
191 "An Assessment of the Adult Entertainment Industry in Texas," Bureau of Business Research.
192 Amy L. Baker, "Gentlemen's Clubs and Casinos in Las Vegas," 2010.
193 "United States Strip Clubs," op. cit.
194 Raoul MacFarlane, *Man to Man Yearbook*; see also St. Sukie de la Croix, *Chicago Whispers*, p. 239.
195 "Mostly About Organized Crime," *Friends of Ours*, December 7, 2014.
196 Inflation calculator.
197 Ms. Bob, "Tabloids & Men's Soft Core, part 4," Transgender Forum; "Ty Bennett"; Wayne Anderson, "Hidden History: *Huffington Post*; Stephen Holden, "Life and death at the edge,' *New York Times*, September 3, 1993.
198 Laureen Trainer, "The Missing Photographs," *American Suburb X*; see also Diana Emery Hulick. "Diane Arbus's Women and Transvestites," pp. 32–39; and *Diane Arbus and Her Imagery* (Princeton, 1984).
199 Randolph Trumbach, *Sex and the Gender Revolution*, pp. 197, 136 and 157–59.
200 Iwan Block, *Sexual Life in England: Past and Present*, p. 327; see also Trumbach, op. cit., pp. 107, 157–59
201 Allen *Horrible Prettiness*, 271.
202 Lloyd Morris, *Incredible New York*, p. 259.
203 Iwan Block, *The Sexual Extremities of the World*, p. 63.
204 Rachel Shteir, *Striptease*, pp. 11–13.
205 Lewis A. Erenberg, *Steppin' Out*, p. 213.
206 Robert C. Allen, *Horrible Prettiness*, p. 12; *New York Times* quote in Allen, p. 14; see also Michelle Baldwin, *Burlesque and the New Bump-n-Grind*, p. 1.
207 Allen, op. cit., p. 271.
208 Stanley Walker, *The Night Club Era*, p. 178; John Roach Straton, *The Menace of Immorality in Church and State*, p. 59.
209 Shteir, op. cit., pp. 247, 270.
210 *Adams Theatre Co. v. Keenan*.
211 Elizabeth Alice Clement, "Trick or Treat," pp. 179–90.
212 Paul Cressey, *Taxi-Dance Hall*, pp. 47–49, 242–43, 250–51, 263–64 and 276 fn.
213 Clement, op. cit., p. 190; Leo Rosten, "Taxi-Dance," *The New Yorker*.
214 A. W. Stencell, *Girl Show*, p. 65.
215 Ibid., p. 81.
216 Ibid., p. 82.
217 Ibid., p. 84.
218 Ibid., pp. 67, 74–75.
219 Ibid., pp. 89–90.
220 Ibid., pp. 92–95.

221 "McCaffrey Rule Burlesque Means Strip, Despite Webster," *New York Herald Tribune*, April 21, 1955; Walter Arm, "Burlesque Revival is Set, But Strip Acts Are Barred," *New York Herald Tribune*, May 20, 1955; Shteir, op. cit., p. 295.

222 "Manners & Morals: Its Back," *Time*.

223 Arnold Shaw, *52nd Street*, pp. 318, 334–39; Shteir, op. cit., p. 250; see also Jessica Glasscock, "Striptease," Love to Know."

224 Johnny Mercer, "'Top Banana': Burlesque's Not Dead Yet: The Minsky Dynasty Reborn in Musica," *New York Herald Tribune*, October 28, 1951.

225 Jess Stearn, *Sisters of the Night*, p. 53; Jeremiah Moss, "Sisters of the Night," *The Partisan Review*.

226 "Strip Street," Jeremiah's Vanishing New York.

227 Doug Lindner (2003), "Lenny Bruce"

228 Bob Dylan, "Lenny Bruce."

Notes to Flesh Trade

229 Dean Balsamini, "Now that it's moved off the street, prostitution is off the radar in Staten Island," *Staten Island Advance*, June 9, 2013.

230 New York Police Department, "Police Commissioner Kelly Announces "Demand Side" Focus in Increased Arrests for Soliciting and Human Trafficking"; Joe Kemp, "NYPD sting charges 156 johns in second massive prostitution bust in metropolitan area this week," *New York Daily News*, June 6, 2013.

231 Sudhir Venkatesh, "How Tech Tools Transformed New York's Sex Trade, *Wired*.

232 Joseph Berger, "Prostitution Investigation at Day Spas Results in 19 Arrests," *New York Times*, July 11, 2013.

233 Polly Adler, *A House Is Not a Home*, p. 223.

234 Ibid., pp. 113 and 273.

235 Ibid., p. 34.

236 A. H. Lawrence, *Duke Ellington and His World*, pp. 72, 135.

237 Adler, op. cit., p. 18; see also, Karen Abbot, "The House that Polly Adler Built," *Smithsonian*; Mara Bovsun, "Justice Story: Polly Adler's 17 arrests put modern madams to shame," *New York Daily News*, March 18, 2012.

238 Adler, op. cit., p. 57.

239 Ibid., pp. 177–78.

240 Ibid., pp. 263, 264–65.

241 Monroe Fry, *Sex, Vice, and Business*, p. 36.

242 Ibid., pp. 38–39.

243 Charles Winick and Paul Kinzie, *The Lively Commerce*, p. 207.

244 Alfred Kinsey, *Sexual Behavior in the Human Male*, p. 607.

245 Winick and Kinzie, op. cit., pp. 208–09.

246 Ibid., pp. 91–92.

247 Ibid., p. 297.

248 Ibid., p. 320.

249 Harry Benjamin and R. E. L. Masters, *Prostitution and Morality*, p. 150.

250 Winick and Kinzie, op. cit., p. 31.

251 Benjamin and Masters, op. cit., p. 155.

252 Edwin G. Burrows and Mike Wallace, *Gotham*, p. 34.

253 Ibid., pp. 31–33.

254 Tobias Seamon, "A View From the Crow's Wood," *Morning News*; Burrows and Wallace, op. cit., pp. 34–35; Grietje Reyniers.

255 James D. McCabe, *Lights and Shadows of New York Life*, p. 490; Richard O'Connor, *Hell's Kitchen*, pp. 92–94.

256 Ruth Rosen, *The Lost Sisterhood*, p. xvii.

257 John D'Emilio and Estelle B. Freedman, *Intimate Matters*, pp. 50–51; see also Winick and Kinsie, *op. cit.*, p. 41; Jess Stearn, *Sisters of the Night*, p. 41; Benjamin and Masters, op. cit., p. 311.

258 Winick and Kinzie, op. cit., p. 263.

259 Ibid., pp. 158–59, 176, 226, 263–65.

260 Ibid., pp. 53, 131–84; see also Benjamin and Masters, op. cit., pp. 91, 119–91.

261 Stearn, op. cit., pp. 197–82; Wolsey, op. cit., p. 231.

262 Fry, op. cit., p. 146.

263 Ibid., p. 144.

264 Adler, op. cit., pp. 129–30.
265 "Police Corruption: A Look at History," *New York Times*, September 24, 1986.
266 Adler, op. cit., p. 130.
267 Ibid., p. 173; see also Herbert Mitgang, *Once Upon a Time in New York*, pp. 119–20; Rachel Shteir, *Striptease*, p. 142.
268 Ibid., pp. 175–76.
269 *New York Times*, March 20, 1935 and May 13, 1935; Adler, ibid., pp. 265–67.
270 *New York Times*, March 6, 1935.
271 Adler, op. cit., p. 197.
272 Ibid., pp. 200–14.
273 Ibid., p. 257.
274 Gay Talese, *Thy Neighbor's Wife*, p. 314.
275 Ibid., pp. 309–10.
276 Ibid., p. 303.
277 Ibid., p. 305.
278 Ibid., pp. 307–08, 311–14.

Notes to Lavender Peril

279 Adam Liptak, "Supreme Court Ruling Makes Same-Sex Marriage a Right Nationwide," *New York Times*, June 26, 2015.
280 "Gay Marriage," Pew Research; Support for same-sex marriage hits new high; half say Constitution guarantees right," *Washington Post*, March 5, 2014.
281 Liberace (video).
282 The Liberace Foundation; see also Darden Asbury Pyron, *Liberace*, pp. 79–129.
283 Pyron, op.cit., pp. 194–97 and 223–33.
284 Charles Kaiser, *The Gay Metropolis*, p. 96.
285 John Cooney, *The American Pope*, p. 109.
286 Anthony Summers, *Official and Confidential:* pp. 254–55.
287 David Rosen, *Sex Scandals America*, pp. 113–14.
288 Ronald Kessler, *The Bureau*, pp. 107–11.
289 Anthony Summer, "The Man Who Collected Dirt," *The Independent*.
290 Paul Friedman, "Sexual Deviations," pp. 1107, 1117.
291 *New York v. Feliciano* (1958).
292 Craig Loftin, *Masked Voices*, p. 206.
293 William Eskridge, "Privacy Jurisprudence and the Apartheid of the Closet," no page (footnote 244).
294 William E. Nelson, *The Legalist Reformation*, p. 19.
295 John Loughery, *The Other Side of Silence*, p. 168; see also Friedman, op. cit.
296 James Petersen, *The Century of Sex*, p. 217.
297 Jennifer Terry, *An American Obsession*, pp. 329–33.
298 Lillian Faderman, *Odd Girls and Twilight Lovers*, p. 140.
299 Terry, op. cit., p. 336.
300 Ibid., p. 338.
301 John D'Emilio, *Sexual Politics, Sexual Communities*, p. 228.
302 Executive Order 10450; see also Terry, op. cit., pp. 242–44, Petersen, op. cit., p. 214.
303 Terry, op. cit., p. 347.
304 D'Emilio, op. cit., p. 52.
305 Terry, op. cit., p. 356.
306 Elizabeth Lapovsky Kennedy and Madeline Davis, *Boots of Leather, Slippers of Gold*, p. 113.
307 Ibid., p. 11.
308 Ibid., p. 374.
309 Ibid., pp. 191, 205.
310 Ibid., p. 93.
311 Ibid., pp. 198–200, 207.
312 Jess Stearn, *The Grapevine*, pp. 10, 3, 8, 15, 43, 73, 91, 155, 127, 215, and 189–93.
313 Julius', One of the Oldest Gay Bars in New York.
314 Lisa E. Davis, "The Bagatelle," Lost Womyn's Space, September 7, 2011.
315 Loughery, op. cit., p. 215.
316 Ibid.
317 Benjamin and Masters, op. cit., p. 328.

318   Gayle Rubin, "The Catacombs," p. 225; Justin Spring, *Secret Historian*, p. 83.
319   Loughery, op. cit., pp. 214–15.
320   Thom Magister, "One among many," p. 102.
321   Rubin, op. cit., p. 224.
322   Linda Beltan, "Return of the Wild Ones," *Wall Street Journal*, July 23, 1997.
323   Alan Ginsberg, "Howl."
324   Liberace website.
325   Darden Asbury Pyron, *Liberace*, pp. 223–29, 233–34.
326   Ibid., pp. 97–99.
327   Ibid., p. 319.
328   Ibid., pp. 370–77; Steven Soderbergh, "Behind the Candelabra" (movie).
329   George Chauncey, *Gay New York*, pp. 337–59; see also "Stonewall and Beyond."
330   Duberman, op. cit., p. 183.
331   Kaiser, op. cit., p. 197.
332   R.F Baumeister and Jennifer L. Butler, "Sexual Masochism," pp. 225–39.
333   Folsom Street Fair.

Notes to Identity Crisis

334   Henry R. Luce, "The American Century," Information Clearing House (originally published in *Life* magazine February 17, 1941).
335   National Institutes of Health, "Crude birth rates, fertility rates, and birth rates, by age, race, and Hispanic origin of mother"; "Marriages and Divorces, 1900–2009," Infoplease; Divorce and Divorce Rates, Alabama and the United States, 1950–2010," Alabama Department of Public Health.
336   Jose A. DelReal, "Voter turnout in 2014 was the lowest since WWII," *Washington Post*, November 10, 2014.
337   William Berle and Brad Lewis, *My Father, Uncle Miltie*, pp. 64, 171, 186,
338   David Halberstam, *The Fifties*, pp. 527–28.
339   Ibid., p. 15.
340   Milton Berle (with Haskel Frankel), *An Autobiography*, pp. 47–50, 145–47, 182; Milton Berle (video).
341   M. Berle, ibid., pp. 270–72; John J. O'Conner, "Review/Television: Milton Berle—Mr. Television; A Zillion Gags (Not Counting Repeats)," The *New York Times*, March 15, 1994.
342   M. Berle, op. cit., pp. 283, 293, 168.
343   Ibid., pp. 164, 202, 184.
344   John Loughery, *The Other Side of Silence*, pp. 161–62.
345   "Censored: Allegedly Outed Bi Celebs"; Charles Kaiser, *The Gay Metropolis*, pp. 95–96.
346   Charles Kaiser, ibid., pp. 89–94.
347   Rick Valelly, "The Conflicted Gay Pioneer, *The American Prospect*.
348   Paul Goodman, "The Politics of Being Queer."
349   Susan Smulyan, *Popular Ideologies*, p. 117.
350   *Look*, May 1, 1956, pp. 104–06; *Life*, April 9, 1956, pp. 111–14.
351   David Riesman, *The Lonely Crowd*.
352   Richard J. Corber, *Homosexuality in the Cold War*, pp. 23–36.
353   Halberstam, op. cit., p. 278; Robert L. Dickinson, "The End of 'Hush and Pretend," p. 163.
354   Alfred Kinsey, et al, *Sexual Behavior in the Human Male*, pp. 193–296, 583–678; Alfred Kinsey, et al., *Sexual Behavior in the Human Female*, p. 503; Reay Tannahill, *Sex in History*, p. 404; Janice M. Irvine, *Disorders of Desire*, pp. 31–66.
355   Kinsey, Male, op. cit., pp. 263–65.
356   Ibid., pp. 373–74, 571–82
357   Ibid., pp. 610, 623, 639.
358   Halberstam, op. cit., p. 280.
359   Gershon Legman, "Minority Report on Kinsey," pp. 13–32; Jennifer Terry, *An American Obsession*, pp. 305–06, 307–14; and James H. Jones, *Alfred C. Kinsey*, pp. 577–80.
360   Kinsey, Female, op. cit., pp. 101–31.
361   Ibid., p. 163.
362   Ibid., p. 164.
363   Ibid., pp. 346, 352.
364   Ibid., pp. 416–17.
365   Ibid., p. 453.
366   Ibid., p. 472.

367   Jonathan Gathorne-Hardy, *Alfred C. Kinsey*, pp. 188, 407.
368   Tony Perucci, "The Red Mask of Sanity, p. 23.
369   Perucci, op. cit., p. 24; see also Leo Cherne, "How to Spot a Communist," *Look*.
370   Perucci, op. cit., pp. 24, 27.
371   Eli Zaretsky, *Secrets of the Soul*, pp. 276–306; Glenn Myers, "Freud's Influence on Psychiatry in America," *Psychoanalytic Quarterly*, pp. 229–35.
372   Zaretsky, op. cit., pp. 288, 277.
373   Paul Friedman, "Sexual Deviations," pp. 592–93.
374   Russell Jacoby, *Social Amnesia*, p. 46–72; see also Paul Robinson, *The Modernization of Sex*.
375   Jack El-Hai, *The Laboromist*.
376   Renato M. E. Sabbatini, *The History of Shock Therapy in Psychiatry*.
377   Wilhelm Reich, *The Bioelectrical Investigation of Sexuality and Anxiety*; Myron Sharaf, *Fury on Earth*, pp. 360–82.
378   Herbert Marcuse, *Eros & Civilization*; see also Norman O. Brown, *Life Against Death*.

Notes to Sex Panic
379   Erin Wittkon, "President Proclaims National Slavery and Human Trafficking Prevention Month," Department of Defense.
380   The White House, "The Obama Administration's Record on Human Trafficking Issues"; see also The White House, "Progress Report."
381   Alison Siskin and Liana Sun Wyler, "Trafficking in Persons."
382   Ronald Weitzer, "The Social Construction of Sex Trafficking."
383   Kristin Finklea, Adrienne L. Fernandes-Alcantara and Alison Siskin, "Sex Trafficking of Children in the United States:" Congressional Research Service.
384   Federal Bureau of Investigation (FBI), "Violent Crimes Against Children: Innocence Lost"; see also Department of Justice, "National Anti-Slavery and Human Trafficking Awareness Month Press Conference,"
385   National Colloquium 2012 Final Report, "An Inventory and Evaluation of the Current Shelter and Services Response to Domestic Minor Sex Trafficking,"
386   Megan Annitto, "Emerging State Safe Harbor Responses to Sex Trafficking and Prostitution of Minors," Juvenile Justice Information Exchange; David Rosen, "Sex Crime Charade."
387   Ilse Ollendorff Reich, *Wilhelm Reich*, p. xxi.
388   Myron Sharaf, *Fury On Earth*, p. 477.
389   J. Edgar Hoover, "How Safe is Your Daughter?," *American Magazine*, pp. 32–33.
390   David Wittels, "What Can We Do About Sex Crimes," *Saturday Evening Post*, p. 30.
391   Tamara Rice Lave, "Only Yesterday," *Louisiana Law Review*.; see also Edwin Sutherland, "The Diffusion of Sexual Psychopath Laws," *American Journal of Sociology*, pp. 142–48.
392   J. Paul De River, *The Sexual Criminal*, pp. xli–xliii, 428–38.
393   Mariah Adlin, *The Brooklyn Thrill-Kill Gang and the Great Comic Book Scare of the 1950s* (Praeger, 2014); Joe Sergi, "The Incredible True Story of Joe Shuster's NIGHTS OF HORROR."
394   Eric C. Schneider, *Vampires, Dragons, and Egyptian Kings*, pp. 5–26.
395   John Loughery, *The Other Side of Silence*, pp. 241–44; Jennifer Terry, *An American Obsession*, p. 349.
396   William E. Nelson, *The Legalist Reformation*, pp. 17–18, 20 and 73; see also Neil Miller, *Sex-crime Panic*.
397   Beth Bailey, *Sex in the Heartland*, pp. 45–46
398   Harry Benjamin and Robert Edward Lee Masters, *Prostitution and Morality*, pp. 29–30, 379.
399   Loughery, op. cit., 159.
400   Lillian Faderman, *Old Girls and Twilight Lovers*, p. 140.
401   Christopher Turner, *Orgasmatron*, p. 205.
402   Turner, ibid., p. 39; Wilhelm Reich's Course Descriptions, New School.
403   Ollendorff, op. cit., p. 53.
404   Ollendorff,, ibid., p. 54; Jacqueline A. Carleton, "Isle Ollendorff, Mother of Peter Reich Interviewed."
405   Sharaf, op. cit., p. 277.
406   Ibid., pp. 298 and 306 (italicization in original).
407   Ibid., p. 303.
408   Ibid., p. 333.
409   Jim Martin, "Who Killed Wilhelm Reich."
410   Ollendorff Reich, op. cit., p. 83.
411   Turner, op. cit., p. 281.

412 Ibid., p. 364.
413 Ibid., pp. 284–85.
414 Marcuse, op. cit., p. 239.

Notes to The Pill
415 Ed Pilkington, "Indiana woman charged with feticide after unborn child's death," *Guardian*, August 26, 2014.
416 ACLU, "State of Indiana v. Bei Bei Shuai."
417 "Fetal Homicide Laws," National Conference of State Legislators.
418 Emily Bazelon, "Purvi Patel Could Be Just the Beginning," *New York Times*, April 1, 2015.
419 Martha Alschuler, *The Origins of the Law of Obscenity.*
420 "Abortion Bills," GovTrack.us.
421 "In just the last 4 years, states have enacted 231 abortion restrictions," Guttmacher Institute; Samantha Lachman, "Flood of Abortion-Restricting Bills Filed in State Legislatures Following GOP Sweep," *Huffington Post*; Cheryl Sullenger, "73 Abortion Facilities Shut Down in 2014," LifeNews.com.
422 Vern Bullough, *Science in the Bedroom*, p. 192; Tone, op. cit., p. 211; Eig, op. cit., p. 6.
423 Tone, op. cit., p. 107.
424 David Halberstam, *The Fifties*, p. 283.
425 Ann Douglas, *Terrible Honesty.*
426 Ellen Chesler, *Woman of Valor*, pp. 65–66.
427 Chesler, op. cit., p. 200.
428 Ibid., p. 349.
429 "Two Men Accused in Fatal Abortion," *New York Times*, January 13, 1956; see also "The Gruesome Tale of Jacqueline Smith," *Real Choice.*
430 "7 Arrested in Raid on 'Abortion Mill,'" *New York Times*, April 4, 1951; "7 Arraigned Here in Abortion Plot," *New York Times*, April 5, 1951; "Indictments Name 8 in an Abortion 'Mill,'" *New York Times*; and "Ex-Interne Sentenced," *New York Times*, Feb 28, 1952; Leslie Reagan, *When Abortion Was a Crime*, p. 171.
431 4 Admit Abortion Charges," *New York Times*, April 22, 1955; "Bronx Indicts 11 in Abortion Raid," *New York Times* June 18, 1954.
432 "8 Arrested in Raid on Abortion Ring," *New York Times*, July 24, 1954; "3 Doctors Seized as Abortion Ring," *New York Times*, December 5, 1959.
433 Reagan, op. cit., pp. 196–98, 194.
434 Jonathan Eig, *The Birth of the Pill*, p. 114.
435 "A History of Birth Control Methods," Planned Parenthood; "Education Urged in Birth Control," *New York Times*; "New Kinsey Study Cites Pregnancy," *New York Times*, February 25, 1958
436 Reagan, op. cit., p. 205.
437 Ibid., pp. 206–07; "Grand Jury to Scan Brooklyn Abortions," *New York Times*, December 11, 1953.
438 "Dilemma is Seen in Abortion Law," *New York Times*, July 28, 1959.
439 Reagan, op. cit., p. 214.
440 Eig, op. cit., pp. 73–77.
441 Ibid., pp. 103–04, and 105.
442 Tone, op. cit., pp. 220–24.
443 Chesler, op. cit., p. 216.
444 "Mrs. Sanger Urges U.S. Sterility Plan," *New York Times*, October 26, 1950.
445 Eig, op. cit., pp. 149–50.
446 Ibid., p. 148; Stephen Jay Gould, "Carrie Buck's Daughter."
447 Barbara Gordon, *Woman's Body, Woman's Rights*, p. 393.
448 Elizabeth Siegel Watkins, *On the Pill*, pp. 17–19.
449 Rebecca Williams, "The Rockefeller Foundation, the Population Council, and Indian Population Control," p. 3.
450 Nicholas Eberstadt, "World Population Crisis," *Philanthropy*; Gordon, op. cit., pp. 396, 397.
451 Eberstadt, ibid.
452 Betty Friedan, *The Feminine Mystique*, p. 15.
453 Halberstam, op. cit., pp. 592–96.
454 Verta Taylor, "Social Movement Continuity, pp. 761–75.
455 Gordon, op. cit., p. 360; for a nuanced assessment of '50s representation of women in magazine advertisements, see Christina Catalano, "Shaping the American Woman: Feminism and Advertising in the 1950s," pp. 45–55.

456   Taylor, op. cit., p. 765; see also U.S. Census Bureau, "Estimated Median Age at First Marriage: 1890 to present"; Amara Bachu, U.S. Census Bureau, "Trends in Premarital Childbearing: 1930–1994"; Mitra Toossi, "A century of change," U.S. Bureau of Labor Statistics; Elizabeth Waldman, "Labor force statistics perspective from a family perspective," Bureau of Labor Statistics.

457   Simon De Beauvoir, *The Second Sex*, p. 301.

458   Vanessa Martins Lamb, "The 1950's and the 1960's and the American Woman," pp. 44, 32, 39; see also Gordon, op. cit., p. 361.

459   Taylor, op. cit., p. 772.

460   Ibid., p. 764.

461   Gordon, op. cit., p. 369; Watkins, op. cit., p. 53; Alexandra Nikolchev, "A brief history of the birth control pill," PBS Need to Know.

462   Eig, op. cit., p. 306.

463   Helen Gurley Brown, "Women Alone, Oh Come Now!," p. 73; "How Cosmo Changed the World," *Cosmopolitan*.

464   Watkins, op. cit., p. 59; Gordon, op. cit., p. 410.

Notes to Red Scare

465   Glenn Greenwald, "NSA collecting phone records of millions of Verizon customers daily," *The Guardian*, June 6, 2013.

466   "Snowden 'aiding our enemies,' former CIA chief of staff says time," RT.com.

467   Barton Gellman and Greg Miler, "'Black budget' summary details U.S. spy network's successes, failures and objectives," *Washington Post*, August 29, 2013.

468   "Chronology of a Spy Case," *New York Times*, June 20, 1953.

469   "Rosenbergs Bar 'Deal' They Say U.S. Offered," *New York Herald Tribune*.

470   "Pair Silent to End," *New York Times*, June 20, 1953; "Rosenberg Dies First; Both Silent," *New York Herald Tribune*, June 20, 1953.

471   "The Rosenberg Story: Their Crime and Trial," *New York Herald Tribune*, June 20, 1953.

472   "Kaufman Rejects 11th-Hour Appeal, *New York Times*, June 20, 1953.

473   "The Rosenberg Story: The Crime and the Trial," *New York Herald Tribune*, June 20, 1953.

474   "Execution of the Rosenbergs," *Guardian*, June 20, 1953.

475   "Caskets of Rosenbergs Kept Open All Night at Brooklyn Mortuary," *New York Herald Tribune*, June 21, 1953.

476   Sam Roberts, "Figure in Rosenberg Case Admits to Soviet Spying," *New York Times,* September 11, 2008.

477   Victor Navasky, *Naming Names*, pp. 113–15.

478   "Rosenberg Judge Guarded," *New York Herald Tribune*, June 14, 1963; "The Rosenberg Trial," History of Federal Judiciary.

479   Elizabeth Schulte, "The Trial of Ethel and Julius Rosenberg," *International Socialist Review,* issue 29, May/June 2003.

480   "Rosenbergs Died As Paupers," *New York Herald Tribune*, June 26, 1953.

481   "Reds Spur Protests on Rosenbergs, *New York Herald Tribune*, June 17, 1953.

482   David Caute, *The Great Fear*, pp. 61–62.

483   "7,000 in Capital March for Spies," *New York Times*, June 15, 1953; "Eisenhower is Denounced to 5,000 in Union Sq. Rally," *New York Times*, June 20, 1953; see also National Committee to Reopen the Rosenberg Case.

484   "Caskets of Rosenbergs Kept Open All Night at Brooklyn Mortuary," *New York Herald Tribune*, June 21, 1953; "Rosenbergs Eulogized As Martyrs at Funeral," *New York Herald Tribune*, June 22, 1953; "Funeral of Spies this Afternoon," *New York Times*, June 21, 1953.

485   B. J. Cutler, "Rosenbergs Eulogized As Martyrs at Funeral," *New York Herald Tribune*, June 22, 1953.

486   U.S. House of Representatives, Committee on Un-American Activities Hearing Regarding Espionage in the U.S. Government, 80th Congress (2nd Session), 1948.

487   Alger Hiss HUAC Testimony; "The Hiss Case," Stephen W. Salant, et al., *New York Review of Books*, May 27, 1976; see also, Navasky, op. cit., 4–5.

488   Franklin D. Roosevelt, "Presidential Directive Of September 6, 1939."

489   Story of the 1947–1949 Freedom Train; National Security Act of 1947.

490   *Communist Party v. Subversive Activities Control Board* (1956); *Communist Party v. Subversive Activities Control Board* (1961).

491   Marjorie Heins, *Priests of Our Democracy,* pp. 131–51; see also U.S. Senate Internal Security Subcommittee (SISS) *Subversive Influence in the Educational Process*; and Senator Hubert Humphrey.

492   Kenneth O'Reilly, "Hoover and the Un-Americans."

493 Lisa Kogen, "Ethel Rosenberg, 1915–1953," Jewish Women's Archives; "Rosenbergs," AtomicArchive.com.
494 FBI, "The Atomic Spy Case."
495 Frances Fox Piven and Richard Cloward, "The unemployed workers' movement."
496 Legal Information Institute, "Advocating Overthrow of Government."
497 Caute, op. cit., pp. 178–79; "The Smith Act and the Supreme Court," ACLU; Elizabeth Gurley Flynn, "Statement at the Smith Act Trial," American Rhetoric.
498 Heins, op. cit., p. 32.
499 Marvin E. Gettleman, "'No Varsity Teams,'" pp. 342, 343/n, 348–52.
500 Spencer Ackerman, "US cited controversial law in decision to kill American citizen by drone," The Guardian, June 23, 2014.

Notes to Freedom Fighter
501 Rich Juzwiak and Aleksander Chan, "Unarmed People of Color Killed by Police."
502 "New York Crime Rates, 1960–2013," Disaster Center.
503 "Report on the NYPD's Stop-and-Frisk Policy," New York City Bar Association; "Stop-and-Frisk Data," New York Civil Liberties Union.
504 "Live from Carnegie Hall: Paul Robeson," Carnegie Hall; Paul Robeson, "Joe Hill" (video).
505 Martin Duberman, Paul Robeson, p. 462.
506 David Caute, The Great Fear, 248.
507 Duberman, op. cit., pp. 438–39.
508 CIA, "Origins of the Congress for Cultural Freedom, 1949–50, Cultural Cold War."
509 Duberman, op. cit., pp. 342–44; see also Barbara J. Beeching, "Paul Robeson and the Black Press," The Journal of African American History, pp. 339–354.
510 Duberman, op. cit., pp. 357–58.
511 Ibid., pp. 359–60; Dorothy Butler Gillman, Paul Robeson, pp. 140–42.
512 Duberman, op. cit., p. 384.
513 Clarence Taylor, "Race, Class, and Police Brutality in New York City," Journal of African American History, p. 205–06.
514 Ibid., p. 207.
515 Ibid., p. 206.
516 Paul Robeson, Here I Stand, pp. 6–8.
517 Duberman, op. cit., pp. 19–21, 36–39, 53–54.
518 Lewis, op. cit., pp, 104–05.
519 Duberman, op. cit., pp. 113–15; Gillman, op. cit., p. 55; Robeson letter, The Manchester Guardian, October 23, 1929.
520 Emma Goldman, "There Is No Communism in Russia" (1935), The Anarchist Library.
521 Duberman, op. cit., pp. 184–85; Gillman, op. cit., pp. 75–77, 83.
522 Duberman, ibid., p. 185; Gillman, ibid., p. 78.
523 Duberman, ibid., pp. 215–17, 220.
524 Gillman, op. cit., p. 99.
525 Duberman, op. cit., p. 284.
526 Ibid., pp. 400, 411, 425.
527 New York City Government population.
528 Ward Churchill and Jim Vander Wall, The COINTELPRO Papers, pp. 64–67; see also Nelson A. Denis, War Against All Puerto Ricans, pp. 191–202, 209–21.
529 "FAQ," Harry S. Truman Library and Museum.
530 "On This Day: Puerto Rican Nationalists Launch Assault on US Congress," Finding Dulcinea Staff.
531 Caute, op. cit., pp. 121–22, 435.
532 Churchill and Vander Wall, op. cit., pp. 69, 74; FBI Records, The Vault, "COINTELPRO."
533 Churchill and Vander Wall, op. cit., p. 36; see also Robeson video.
534 Caute, op. cit., pp. 185–86; Gerald Meyer, Vito Marcantonio, p. 80–84.
535 Duberman, op. cit., pp 247–48.
536 Duberman, ibid., p. 297; Gillman, op. cit., p. 113.
537 HUAC, "Report on Civil Rights Congress as a communist front organization."
538 "You Are the Un-Americans, and You Ought to be Ashamed of Yourselves," History Matters; see also Robeson (radio).
539 "Paul Robeson collection, 1925–1956," New York Public Library, Archives.
540 Caute, op. cit., p. 178.

NOTES

Notes to Radical Voices
541 Cora Currier, "Charting Obama's Crackdown on National Security Leaks," ProPublica.
542 David Caute, The Great Fear.
543 Harry Schwartz, "Reds Renounced by Howard Fast," New York Times, February 1, 1957.
544 Frank Campenni, "Citizen Howard Fast."
545 David Caute, op. cit., pp. 185–86.
546 Phillip Deery, Red Apple, p. 39.
547 Ibid., pp. 47–49.
548 Ibid., pp. 64–65.
549 Ibid., pp. 70–72
550 Caute. op. cit., p. 536.
551 HUAC, John Howard Lawson testimony.
552 CIA, "An Idiot System for Intelligence."
553 Albert Wertheim, "The McCarthy Era and the American Theatre," p. 222.
554 Stacy Spaulding, "Off the Blacklist, But Still a Target," p. 792.
555 Robert Simonson and Andrew Gans, "Uta Hagen, Legendary Stage Actress and Teacher, Dead at 84," Playbill.
556 Spaulding, op. cit., p. 790.
557 Ibid., pp. 794–95.
558 Ibid., p. 792; see also "Red Channels," Authentic History.
559 Robert Justin Goldstein, "Prelude to McCarthyism," National Archives; FBI Records: The Vault, "Custodial Detention Security Index."
560 Spaulding, op. cit., p. 797; FBI, ibid; Caute, op. cit., p. 176.
561 Spaulding, ibid., p. 796.
562 Victor Navasky, Naming Names, pp. 334, 415, 323–24.
563 "School Board Committee Backs Ban on Book 'Citizen Tom Paine,'" New York Times, February 27, 1947; Deery, op. cit., pp. 40–41.
564 Howard Fast, Citizen Tom Paine, pp. 22–23.
565 NYT/Feb 26/'47, Feb 27/'47
566 Deery, op. cit., p. 42.
567 Howard Fast, "Remembering Peekskill, USA, 1949," Pennsylvania History, p. 66; Steve Courtney, "The Robeson riots of 1949," The Reporter Dispatch.
568 Fast, op. cit., p. 67.
569 Caute, op. cit., pp. 178–80; see also Dan Georgakas, "The Hollywood Blacklist."
570 U.S. Senate Permanent Subcommittee on Investigations of the Committee on Government Operations, pp. 484–98;
571 Billie Holiday, "Strange Fruit" (sessions).
572 "NYC schools' 1950s anti-Communist probe target of court fight as woman seeks records on her parent," Associated Press, New York Daily News, April 26, 2012.
573 "Grand Jury Resistance: One Size Does Not Fit All," Rosenberg Fund for Children.

Notes to Underworld
574 Herbert Asbury, The Gangs of New York and Luc Sante, Low Life.
575 Sean Gardiner and Pervaiz Shallwani, "Mafia Is Down—but Not Out Crime Families Adapt to Survive, Lowering Profile and Using Need-to-Know Tactics," Wall Street Journal, February 18, 2014.
576 Casey Ichniowski and Anne Preston, "The Persistence of Organized Crime in New York City Construction," Industrial and Labor Relations Review, pp. 549–65; Richard H. Walker, "Testimony Concerning The Involvement of Organized Crime on Wall Street," House Subcommittee on Finance and Hazardous Materials, Committee on Commerce.
577 "How has organised crime adapted to globalisation?," Economist; Carl Schreck, "Russian Gangs Of New York," Radio Free Europe, November 11, 2014.
578 "O'Dwyer-Costello Meeting on War Frauds Admitted, New York Times, February 16, 1951; "Hearings on Crime to Open March 12," New York Times, February 27, 1951.
579 Doherty, op. cit., p. 366; Halberstam, op cit., p. 192.
580 US Senate, Special Committee on Organized Crime in Interstate Commerce.
581 US Senate, "Investigation of organized crime in interstate commerce," pp. 877–1021, 1170–79, 1258–62, 1489–93, 1585–1601, 1625–59 and 1661–76.
582 "Slain 'Bugsy' Siegel 'Girl Friday' Steals Senate crime Inquiry Show," New York Times, March 16, 1951; Virginia Hill (video).

583 Virginia Hill; Hotties Of History; the statement could not be found in the official transcript.

584 "Beauty Lies in the Eyes of the Beholder: Virginia Hill."

585 Gilbert King, "The Senator and the Gangsters," Smithsonian.com.

586 U.S. Senate, "Investigation of organized crime in interstate commerce."

587 Doherty, op. cit., p. 113; What's My Line Senator Estes Kefauver, March 18, 1951, video (web).

588 Jay Maeder, "Federal Men Kefavuver and O'Dwyer, March 1951," New York Daily News, November 5, 2000. "William O'Dwyer: 100th Mayor, 1946–1950"; see also O'Dwyer video (web); US Senate, "Investigation of organized crime in interstate commerce," pp. 1326–1401, 1491–1580.

589 US Senate Special Committee to Investigate Organized Crime in Interstate Commerce, Final Report.

590 C. Alexander Hortis, The Mob and the City, p. 170.

591 Herbert Mitgang, Once Upon a Time in New York, pp. 40–42.

592 Ibid.

593 Kenneth Hey, "Ambivalence as a Theme in 'On the Waterfront' (1954), p. 692.

594 Ibid., p. 669.

595 Nathan Ward, Dark Harbor; New York Times, September 24, 2010; see also Arthur Miller video (web).

596 Joel Seidman, American Labor from Defense to Reconversion, pp. 235.

597 Harry S. Truman, Memoirs, p. 504.

598 Howard Abadinsky, Organized Crime, pp. 114–16.

599 Joseph Hearst, "Costello Wins Round in Citizenship Battle," Chicago Tribune, April 8, 1957; United States v. Frank Costello (1957).

600 Jerome Charyn, Gangsters and Gold Diggers, pp. 135–36.

601 J. F. Cooper, "The New York Waterfront Commission," pp. 59–60.

602 Jay Maeder, "Nest of Pirates," New York Daily News, November 22, 2000; "'Watchdog' Agency," pp. 257–79.

603 Hortis, op. cit., pp. 168–69; Elaine Laporte, "Ex-Broadway showgirl marks 80 with Petaluma bat mitzvah," J-Weekly.com; "The Village Barn," Jeremiah's Vanishing New York.

604 Hortis, ibid., p. 70; John Tuohy, "We Only Kill Each Other: The Mob at War," We Only Kill Each Other.

605 "Brutal Mugging Fatal: Body of Night Club Ex-Owner Is Found in His Car," New York Times, June 20, 1953.

606 David Carter, Stonewall, pp. 48–50, 123, 143; Martin Duberman, Stonewall, pp. 115–16, 183, 212, 218, 297n, 304n,

607 Duberman, ibid., pp. 225–31, 235–47.

Notes to Conclusion

608 World Shipping Council, "Top 50 Container Ports."

609 NYC Demographic History.

610 "The Brooklyn effect: Cities around the world eager to be crowned the newest hipster paradise," New York Daily News, November 12, 2014; Elizabeth Kneebone and Emily Garr, "The Suburbanization of Poverty: Trends in Metropolitan America, 2000 to 2008," Brookings Institute, January 2010.

611 David Hinckley, "Firestorm Incident at the Stork Club, 1951," New York Daily News, November 9, 2004.

612 Ralph Blumenthal, "Look Who Dropped in at the Stork."

613 Ralph Blumenthal, The Stork Club, p. 301.

614 Mary L. Dudziak, "Josephine Baker, Racial Protest, and the Cold War," p. 554.

615 Dudziak, op. cit., p. 554q.

616 Ibid., pp. 548, 550.

617 Curt Gentry, J. Edgar Hoover, p. 218; see also US Senate, Select Committee to Study Censure Charges.

618 Douglas Linder, "The Confidential Magazine Trial: An Account," 2010.

619 Jay Gertzman, Bookleggers and Smuthounds, p. 251.

620 Whitney Strub, Obscenity Rules, p. 117.

621 Jay Gertzman, op. cit., p. 253.

622 Tony Ortega, "The 1967 Central Park Be-In: A 'Medieval Pageant," The Village Voice, February 2010.

623 Loving v. Virginia (1967).

624 Richard Zacks, Island Of Vice.

INDEX

INDEX

INDEX

INDEX